Solutions Manual

RPG IV Programming on the AS/400®

Stanley E. Myers

PRENTICE HALL, Upper Saddle River, NJ 07458

Acquisitions Editor: Laura Steele
Editorial Assistant: Kate Kaibni
Special Projects Manager: Barbara A. Murray
Production Editor: Jonathan Boylan
Supplement Cover Manager: Paul Gourhan
Supplement Cover Designer: PM Workshop Inc.
Manufacturing Buyer: Pat Brown

Printed in the United States of America

10 9 8 7 6 5 4 3 2 1

ISBN 0-13-671736-5

Prentice-Hall International (UK) Limited, London
Prentice-Hall of Australia Pty. Limited, Sydney
Prentice-Hall Canada, Inc., Toronto
Prentice-Hall Hispanoamericana, S.A., Mexico
Prentice-Hall of India Private Limited, New Delhi
Prentice-Hall (Singapore) Pte. Ltd.,
Prentice-Hall of Japan, Inc., Tokyo
Editora Prentice-Hall do Brazil, Ltda., Rio de Janeiro

TABLE OF CONTENTS

CHAPTER 1
QUESTION ANSWERS

1. Control Language, Data Management, Work Management, Programmer Services, System Operator Services, Communication Support, and Security.

2. "Object" is a generic term for the various types of data structures managed by OS/400. Objects include programs, files, queues, job descriptions, and libraries.

3. **DSPUSRPRF** (*Display User Profile*).

4. Passwords are encrypted and stored for use by the system. No one, not even the system Security Officer, can display a password.

5. A system value contains data specific to the individual AS/400 system's environment.

6. Password expiration interval
   Assistance level
   Display sign-on information
   Limit device sessions
   Keyboard buffering
   Language identifier
   Country identifier
   Coded character set identifier

7. ***SAVSYS** allows the programmer to save, restore, and free storage for all objects on the system. ***JOBCTL** allows the programmer to hold, release, cancel, clear, or change any job on the system. It also allows them to IPL the system, start writers, and stop active subsystems.

8. A current library is the default library for storing objects created by the user.

9. The priority limit is the highest job scheduling and output scheduling priorities which can be assigned to a user's jobs. Priorities range from 0 to 9, with 0 being the highest priority and 9 being the lowest.

10. **DSPMSG** (Display Messages).

11. The library list is a list of libraries which can be searched to find any object requested. The list is composed of four parts: the System Library List, the Product Library, the Current Library, and the User Library List. When an object referenced (without specification of a particular library) each library in the list is searched (in the order in which they appear on the list) until a match is found on object name type.

12. **EDTLIBL** (*Edit Library List*) command - controls the addition, removal, and repositioning of libraries in a library list.

    The **ADDLIBLE** (*Add Library List Entry*) command - controls the addition of a library to a library list without reviewing the list.

    The **CRTLIB** (*Create Library*) command - creates a new library.

    The **DSPLIBL** (*Display Library List*) command - displays a library list.

13. These entries may not be higher than the entry for the highest scheduling priority parameter on the user's profile.

14. The joblog is a listing of the messages generated by a job.

15. When debugging a command language program (CLP) a programmer might change this parameter to ***YES** in order to record the CL statements as they execute in a joblog.

16. The routing data entry "**QCMDB**".

17. **WRKSBMJOB** (*Work with Submitted Jobs*).

18. **WRKSPLF** (*Work with Spooled Files*).

19. **WRKOUTQ** (*Work with Output Queue*).

20. Source files store the source code for physical, display, logical, printer, RPG IV program, and CL programs. The programmer may elect to use the default source files that are supplied by the AS/400 software or create his or her own.

21. The four default source files are **QDDSSRC**, **QRPGLESRC**, **QRPGSRC**, and **QCLSRC**. To avoid confusion, physical, display, logical, and printer file source should be stored in **QDDSSRC**; RPG IV source programs in **QRPGLESRC**; RPG II or III programs in **QRPGSRC**, and CL programs in **QCLSRC**.

22. **QGPL** (*General Purpose Library*)

23. **QRPGLESRC**

24. **CRTSRCPF** (*Create Source Physical File*)

25. Only the source code generated by SEU is stored in **QRPGLESRC**.

PROGRAMMING ASSIGNMENTS

Notes to the Instructor:

1. This exercise is designed to familiarize the student with his/her programming environment. What the student will be

allowed to view, and the way in which it is presented, will depend upon how the system's Security Officer has defined that environment. For example, students assigned an assistance level of *BASIC in their user profile will be presented with simpler list displays when performing this exercise than students granted an assistance level of *INTERMED. Display presentation may also vary based upon the release level of the AS/400 operating system (OS/400).

2. The PRINT key may be used to record the display screens viewed by the student.

Programming Assignment 1-1: EXPLORE PROGRAMMER'S ENVIRONMENT

Steps 1 & 2: The DSPUSRPRF command

```
                        Display User Profile - Basic

User profile . . . . . . . . . . . . . . :  SMYERS
Previous sign-on . . . . . . . . . . . . :  07/08/97  09:15:41
Sign-on attempts not valid . . . . . . . :  0
Status . . . . . . . . . . . . . . . . . :  *ENABLED
Date password last changed . . . . . . . :  06/07/94
Password expiration interval . . . . . . :  *SYSVAL
   Date password expires  . . . . . . . .      08/06/97
Set password to expired  . . . . . . . . :  *NO
User class . . . . . . . . . . . . . . . :  *PGMR
Special authority  . . . . . . . . . . . :  *JOBCTL
                                            *SAVSYS
Group profile  . . . . . . . . . . . . . :  QPGMR
Owner  . . . . . . . . . . . . . . . . . :  *GRPPRF
Group authority  . . . . . . . . . . . . :  *NONE
Assistance level . . . . . . . . . . . . :  *SYSVAL
Current library  . . . . . . . . . . . . :  SMYERS
                                                                 More...

Press Enter to continue



F3=Exit   F12=Cancel
(C) COPYRIGHT IBM CORP. 1980, 1992.
```

```
                        Display User Profile - Basic

User profile . . . . . . . . . . . . . . :  SMYERS
Initial menu . . . . . . . . . . . . . . :  MAIN
Library  . . . . . . . . . . . . . . . . :  *LIBL
Initial program  . . . . . . . . . . . . :  INLPGM
   Library . . . . . . . . . . . . . . . :    SMYERS
Limit capabilities . . . . . . . . . . . :  *NO
Text . . . . . . . . . . . . . . . . . . :  STANLEY MYERS
Display sign-on information . . . . . . . :  *SYSVAL
Limit device sessions  . . . . . . . . . :  *SYSVAL
Keyboard buffering . . . . . . . . . . . :  *SYSVAL
Maximum storage allowed  . . . . . . . . :  *NOMAX
   Storage used . . . . . . . . . . . . . :    2843
Highest scheduling priority  . . . . . . :  5
Job description  . . . . . . . . . . . . :  SMYERS
Library  . . . . . . . . . . . . . . . . :  SMYERS
                                                                 More...

Press Enter to continue.

F3=Exit   F12=Cancel
```

```
                        Display User Profile - Basic

     User profile . . . . . . . . . . . . . . . :    SMYERS
     Accounting code  . . . . . . . . . . . . :      DP
     Message queue  . . . . . . . . . . . . . :      SMYERS
       Library  . . . . . . . . . . . . . . . :        QUSRSYS
     Message queue delivery . . . . . . . . . :      *NOTIFY
     Message queue severity . . . . . . . . . :      00
     Output queue . . . . . . . . . . . . . . :      SMYERS
       Library  . . . . . . . . . . . . . . . :        QGPL
     Printer device . . . . . . . . . . . . . :      *WRKSTN
     Special environment  . . . . . . . . . . :      *SYSVAL
     Attention program  . . . . . . . . . . . :      QCMD
       Library  . . . . . . . . . . . . . . . :        QSYS
     Language identifier  . . . . . . . . . . :      *SYSVAL
     Country identifier . . . . . . . . . . . :      *SYSVAL
     Coded character set identifier . . . . . :      *SYSVAL
     User options . . . . . . . . . . . . . . :      *NONE
                                                                    Bottom
     Press Enter to continue.

     F3=Exit    F12=Cancel
```

Step 3: Submit DSPJOBD to run in batch mode

Display Job Description (DSPJOBD) Listing

```
                                 Job Description Information                        Page 1
         5738SS1 V2R2M0  920925                              BLUESYS   7/08/94 09:24:35

         Job description:  SMYERS        Library:   SMYERS

         User profile . . . . . . . . . . . . . . . . . :   *RQD
         CL syntax check  . . . . . . . . . . . . . . . :   *NOCHK
         Hold on job queue  . . . . . . . . . . . . . . :   *NO
         End severity . . . . . . . . . . . . . . . . . :   30
         Job date . . . . . . . . . . . . . . . . . . . :   *SYSVAL
         Job switches . . . . . . . . . . . . . . . . . :   00000000
         Inquiry message reply  . . . . . . . . . . . . :   *RQD
         Job priority (on job queue)  . . . . . . . . . :   5
         Job queue  . . . . . . . . . . . . . . . . . . :   QBATCH
           Library  . . . . . . . . . . . . . . . . . . :     QGPL
         Output priority (on output queue)  . . . . . . :   5
         Printer device . . . . . . . . . . . . . . . . :   *USRPRF
         Output queue . . . . . . . . . . . . . . . . . :   SMYERS
           Library  . . . . . . . . . . . . . . . . . . :     QGPL
         Message logging:
           Level  . . . . . . . . . . . . . . . . . . . :   4
           Severity . . . . . . . . . . . . . . . . . . :   0
           Text . . . . . . . . . . . . . . . . . . . . :   *SECLVL
         Log CL program commands  . . . . . . . . . . . :   *NO
         Accounting code  . . . . . . . . . . . . . . . :   *USRPRF
         Print text . . . . . . . . . . . . . . . . . . :   *SYSVAL
         Routing data . . . . . . . . . . . . . . . . . :   QCMDB
         Request data . . . . . . . . . . . . . . . . . :   *NONE
         Device recovery action . . . . . . . . . . . . :   *SYSVAL
         Time slice end pool  . . . . . . . . . . . . . :   *SYSVAL
         Text . . . . . . . . . . . . . . . . . . . . . :   stan myers
         Initial library list:
           PROGRAMS
           QGPL
           QTEMP

                         * * * * *  E N D  O F  L I S T I N G  * * * *
```

Step 4 - The WRKSBMJOB command

Note that student is required to read and interpret the

Chapter 1 - The AS/400 Environment

display in order to determine what OUTQ contains the spooled file created in step 3.

```
                        Work with Submitted Jobs              BLUESYS
                                                       07/08/94  09:24:49
    Submitted from . . . . . . . . :     *USER

    Type options, press Enter.
      2=Change   3=Hold   4=End    5=Work with   6=Release    7=Display message
      8=Work with spooled files

    Opt   Job         User         Type     -----Status----- Function
     8    SMYERS      SMYERS       BATCH     OUTQ


                                                                 Bottom
    Parameters or command
    ===>
    F3=Exit   F4=Prompt   F5=Refresh   F9=Retrieve   F11=Display schedule data
    F12=Cancel
```

```
                       Work with Job Spooled Files

    Job:   SMYERS          User:   SMYERS        Number:    216538

    Type options, press Enter.
      1=Send   2=Change   3=Hold   4=Delete   5=Display   6=Release   7=Messages
      8=Attributes         9=Work with printing status

                       Device or                    Total   Current
    Opt   File         Queue        User Data  Status Pages    Page   Copies
     _    QPRTJOBD     SMYERS       DSPJOBD    RDY    1                1
     _    QPJOBLOG     JOBLOGS      SMYERS     RDY    1                1




                                                                 Bottom
    Parameters for options 1, 2, 3 or command
    ===>
    F3=Exit   F10=View 3   F11=View 2   F12=Cancel   F22=Printers   F24=More keys
```

Step 5: The WRKOUTQ command

Students should note that the output queue library and the type of output parameters contain default values. The student is instructed to request printed output.

The Work with OUTQ (WRKOUTQ) Command Prompt

```
                       Work with Output Queue (WRKOUTQ)

    Type choices, press Enter.

    Output queue . . . . . . . . . . > SMYERS        Name, *ALL
       Library  . . . . . . . . . .      *LIBL       Name, *LIBL, *CURLIB
    Output . . . . . . . . . . . .      *PRINT      *, *PRINT
```

```
                                                                    Bottom
    F3=Exit   F4=Prompt   F5=Refresh   F12=Cancel   F13=How to use this display
    F24=More keys
```

The Work with OUTQ (WRKOUTQ) Listing

```
5738SS1  V2R2M0  920925      Work With Output Queue      SMYERS      in QGPL    7/08/94  9:27:23   Page 1

File       User   User Data Status Pages Copies Form Type Pty File Number Job      Number Date     Time
QPRTJOBD  SMYERS DSPJOBD    RDY      1      1    *STD       5        1      SMYERS   224198 07/08/94 13:06:17
QPRTSPLQ  SMYERS            RDY      1      1    *STD       5        1      PROGRMR  223593 07/08/94 13:06:29

         * * * * *  E N D   O F   L I S T I N G  * * * * *
```

Step 6: The WRKSPLF command

Basic Assistance Level Display

```
                          Work with Printer Output
                                                     System:   BLUESYS
    User . . . . . .    SMYERS       Name, *ALL, F4 for list

    Type options below, then press Enter.  To work with printers, press F22.
      2=Change   3=Hold   4=Delete    5=Display          6=Release    7=Message
      9=Work with printing status   10=Start printing    11=Restart printing

          Printer/
    Opt   Output      Status
    __    DSPJOBD     Not assigned to printer (use Opt 10)
    __    QPRTSPLQ    Not assigned to printer (use Opt 10)



                                                                    Bottom
    F1=Help   F3=Exit       F5=Refresh    F6=Completed printer output
    F11=Dates/pages/forms   F20=Include system output    F24=More keys
```

Intermediate Assistance Level Display

```
                          Work with All Spooled Files
    Type options, press Enter.
      1=Send   2=Change   3=Hold   4=Delete   5=Display   6=Release   7=Messages
      8=Attributes         9=Work with printing status
                                Device or                  Total    Cur
    Opt  File       User       Queue        User Data  Sts Pages  Page  Copy
    __   QPJOBLOG   SMYERS     JOBLOGS      SMYERS     RDY   1            1
    __   QPRTJOBD   SMYERS     SMYERS       DSPJOBD    RDY   1            1
    __   QPRTSPLQ   SMYERS     SMYERS                  RDY   1            1



                                                                    Bottom

    Parameters for options 1, 2, 3 or command
    ===>_____
    F3=Exit    F10=View 3    F11=View 2    F12=Cancel    F22=Printers    F24=More keys
```

Step 7: Printing spooled output

```
                        Change Printer Output

        User . . . . . . . . :  SMYERS       Date . . . . . . . . :  07/08/94
        Printer output . . . :  DSPJOBD      Time . . . . . . . . :  09:24:35
        Pages . . . . . . . :  1
        Status . . . . . . . :  Not assigned to printer

        Type choices below, then press Enter.

        Printer to use . . . . . .   prt01____     Name, F4 for list

        Copies and pages:
          Number of copies . . . .   1_           1-255
          First page to print  . .   1_           Number
          Last page to print . . .   *LAST        Number, *LAST

        Type of forms  . . . . . .   *STD____     Form type, *STD

        Print this output next . .   N            Y=Yes, N=No

        Save printer output  . . .   N            Y=Yes, N=No

        F1=Help   F3=Exit   F5=Refresh   F12=Cancel
```

Programming Assignment 1-2: WORKING WITH LIBRARIES

Step 1:

To create a library, enter the **CRTLIB** command on a command line and press **F4**. After following screen displays, a student must respond to the prompts.

```
                        Create Library (CRTLIB)
        Type choices, press Enter.
        Library  . . . . . . . . . . . .    MYERS_____    Name
        Library type . . . . . . . . .      *PROD_____    *PROD, *TEST
        Text 'description' . . . . . . .    *BLANK_____
        _____

                                                                         Bottom
        F3=Exit   F4=Prompt   F5=Refresh   F10=Additional parameters   F12=Cancel
        F13=How to use this display        F24=More keys
```

Step 2:

To add the library created in Step 1 to your library list, enter the **ADDLIBLE** command on a command line and press **F4**. After the following screen displays, the student must respond to the prompts. Note that the **EDTLIBL** command may also be used to add a library to a library list.

```
                        Add Library List Entry (ADDLIBLE)
        Type choices, press Enter.
        Library  . . . . . . . . . . . .    MYERS_____    Name
        Library list position:
          List position  . . . . . . .      *FIRST_       *FIRST, *LAST, *AFTER...
          Reference library  . . . . . .    _____     Name

                                                                         Bottom
        F3=Exit   F4=Prompt   F5=Refresh   F12=Cancel   F13=How to use this display
        F24=More keys
```

Chapter 1 - The AS/400 Environment

Step 3:

To display a library list, enter the **DSPLIBL** command on a comman line and press **F4**. The a screen similiar to the following wil display:

```
5763SS1 V3R1M0  940909                      Library List

     Library      Type        Text Description

     QSYS         SYS         System Library
     QSYS2        SYS         System Library for CPI's
     QHLPSYS      SYS
     QUSRSYS      SYS         System Library For Users
     MYERS        CUR         Myers Development Library
     FILELIB      USR         Production File Library
     PGMLIB       USR         Production Software Library
     QGPL         USR         General Purpose Library
     QTEMP        USR
```

Step 4:

To reposition a library in your library list, enter the EDTLIB command on a command line and press **F4**. Type in the new sequence number and press **F3** to exit.

```
                         Edit Library List

Type new/changed information, press Enter.
  To add a library, type name and desired sequence number.
  To remove a library, space over library name.
  To change position of a library, type new sequence number.

Sequence                    Sequence                 Sequence
Number      Library         Number     Library        Number     Library
 010        QSYS             120       _____         230       _____
 020        QSYS2            130       _____         240       _____
 030        QHLPSYS          140       _____         250       _____
 040        QUSRSYS          150       _____
 010        MYERS            160       _____
 060        FILELIB          170       _____
 070        PGMLIB           180       _____
 080        QGPL             190       _____
 090        QTEMP            200       _____
 100        _____          210       _____
 110        _____          220       _____

F3=Exit          F5=Refresh              F12=Cancel
```
└ type in new sequence number

Step 5:

To remove a library from a library list, enter the **EDTLIBL** command o a command line and press **F4**. Space over the library name to b removed from the list and press **F3** to exit.

```
                         Edit Library List

Type new/changed information, press Enter.
  To add a library, type name and desired sequence number.
  To remove a library, space over library name.
  To change position of a library, type new sequence number.
```

```
Sequence                      Sequence                      Sequence
Number    Library             Number    Library             Number    Library
 010      QSYS                 120      _____              230      _____
 020      QSYS2                130      _____              240      _____
 030      QHLPSYS              140      _____              250      _____
 040      QUSRSYS              150      _____
 050      ┌──────              160      _____
 060      │ FILELIB            170      _____
 070      │ PGMLIB             180      _____
 080      │ QGPL               190      _____
 090      │ QTEMP              200      _____
 100      │ _____             210      _____
 110      │ _____             220      _____


F3=Exit          F5=Refresh              F12=Cancel
```
└ library name blanked out

Programming Assignment 1-3: WORKING WITH SOURCE FILES

Step 1:

Display the **QGPL** library to find the system-supplied source files
Note that the user may have copied the default source files to
other libraries and/or created his or her own source files.

Step 2:

```
                    Create Source Physical File (CRTSRCPF)

Type choices, press Enter.
File . . . . . . . . . . . . . > MYERS        Name
  Library . . . . . . . . . .     *CURLIB     Name, *CURLIB
Record length . . . . . . . .     92          Number
Member, if desired . . . . . .    *NONE       Name, *NONE, *FILE
Text 'description' . . . . . .    *BLANK

_____

                                                                Bottom
F3=Exit   F4=Prompt   F5=Refresh   F10=Additional parameters   F12=Cancel
F13=How to use this display       F24=More keys
```

Take the ***NONE** default in the previous figure for the type of members
that may be stored in the source file.

Step 3:

Type the **DLTF** command on a command line and press **F4**. The following
display will appear. Enter the source file name to be deleted and
press **F3** to exit.

```
                       Delete File (DLTF)

Type choices, press Enter.

File . . . . . . . . . . . .     MYERS        Name, generic*
  Library . . . . . . . . . .     *CURLIB     Name, *LIBL, *CURLIB...

                                                                Bottom
F3=Exit   F4=Prompt   F5=Refresh   F10=Additional parameters   F12=Cancel
F13=How to use this display       F24=More keys
```

CHAPTER 2
QUESTION ANSWERS

1. Relational Data Base

2. <u>Generic Database</u>   <u>DB2/400 Database</u>

   tables   files
   view   logical file
   columns   fields
   rows   records

3. A physical file stores the data; whereas, a logical file creates an access path to process the related physical file(s) in some other order (different view).

4. *Keyed* and *nonkeyed*.

5. A *keyed* physical file is processed in a default ascending key value order. A *nonkeyed* physical file is processed in arrival sequence (the order in which the records are stored in the file).

6. An *externally described* physical file has its record and field attributes stored <u>outside</u> of an RPG IV program in a DDS format.

   A *program described* physical file does not have a DDS format. The record and field attributes must be defined in the RPG IV program with *Input Specification* instructions.

7. A *composite* key is one that includes more than one field in the related physical file. Keys are defined in the physical file by including a **K** in column 17 of the DDS format after the fields are defined. If a *composite key* is specified, additional fields with the letter **K** must be listed. Any key field specified must be a field previously defined in the record format.

8. By one or more *logical files*.

9. a) Determine the fields that are to included in the file's record format; b) enter record and field names and attributes on DDS form (this step may be omitted for by an experienced programmer); c) enter source statements via SEU; d) exit SEU and save the source; e) compile, debug, and store the error-free object in a library.

10. *Data Description Specifications* (**DDS**).

    The logical levels of coding for an *nonkeyed* physical file are *record* and *field*.

    The logical levels of coding for a *keyed* physical file are *file*, *record*, *field*, and *key*. If the file is to support duplicate key values and does not reference another file, the *file* level may be omitted.

11. ONE.

12. A *non-keyed* physical file.

13.

Line#	Field	Entry	Explanation
1	T	R	Defines the entry as a record.
	Name+++++	Q212PFR	Defines the record format name.
2-4	Name+++++	DEPTNUMBER-DESCRIPTION	Name of character fields
	Len++	3, 6, 20	Specifies the field size.
	Dp		A blank in the three fields defines them as character
5-6	Name++++++	QTYONHAND-UNIT_COST	Specifies the field names
	Len++	5, 6	Specifies the field sizes
	T		The letter P or blank defines the numeric fields as packed
	Dp	0	Defines the QTYONHAND as an integer.
	Dp	4	Defines UNIT_COST with four "decimal positions.

If the **T** and **Dp** entries were omitted, the fields would default as character.

14. The letter **P** in the **T** field defines the numeric field as *packed decimal format*. The **Len++** entry specifies the *unpacked size*. Note that a blank in the **T** field will also define a numeric field as packed.

15. The **UNIQUE** keyword must be entered in the *Functions* field at the *file* level (above the *record* level).

To define the file with a *composite* key, the letter **K** must be entered on line 7 and 8 in the **T** field before the DEPTNUMBER and PARTNUMBER field names. No other field entries are permitted in the definition of key fields.

16. COLHDG - *Field level* keyword that assigns a different name to the field for prompting in SDA or DFU.

DESCEND - *Key level* keyword that stores the keys in the index (table of keys and the record addresses) in a descending key value order.

EDTCDE - *Field level* keyword used to edit a numeric field value with an RPG IV type edit code. When specified in a physical file, it is only functional for *display* or *printer files*.

EDTWRD - *Field level* keyword used for editing functions not supported by any of the **EDTCDE** keywords. Only functional for *display* and *printer files*.

LIFO - *File level* keyword that processes records that have the same key value in a last-in-first-out order instead of the default first-in-first-out order.

REF — *File level* keyword that references another physical file for its record and field attributes.

REFFLD — *Field level* keyword that accesses another physical file for a related field attribute.

TEXT — *Record or field level* keyword to supply a detailed description of the record or field.

UNIQUE — *File level* keyword that specifies that the physical file is not to support records with the same key value.

17. Number **8** for the *Option* prompt; a file name for the *Parm* prompt; and **PF** for the *Type* prompt (*Parm 2* is not used). *Source file name* through *Job Description* entries are usually accessed from the *user's profile*.

18. *Source Entry Utility* (**SEU**). A prompt line displays the field names included in the related DDS form type. To access the prompt for a new statement, **IP** is entered in the statement number area and the Enter key pressed. After the syntax is entered and the Enter key pressed, the instruction is moved to its consecutive location in the source program. A new prompt line will display for an additional entry.

19. **F3** is pressed which displays the **EXIT** screen. If the physical file's source is to be saved, the defaults on this display may be taken and the code saved by pressing the Enter key (not **F3**) The source will be stored in the library specified.

20. TWO, a *Source* listing and *Expanded Source* listing. The *Source* listing includes header information (see Figure 2-11 in text and the source code as entered. The Expanded Source listing includes **COLHDGS** for each field (even if not specified in the source code) and **TEXT** keywords. In addition, the *Field Length* *Buffer Positions Out and In* are also included.

21. CRTPF (*Create Physical File*).

22. If a physical file is to be defined without a DDS format and/c if any of the default attributes are to be changed.

23. DSPFD (*Display File Description*). DSPFFD (*Display File Field Description*).

24. CHGPF — Provides for limited changes to an existing physical file.

CLRPFM — Clears the physical file of all data.

CPYF — Copies all or some of the records in a physical file t an output device. Output may be specified in ***CHAR** c ***HEX** format.

> **DSPPFM** - Displays the records in a physical file in a character or hexidecimal format and in a side-by-side or over-and-under format.
>
> **RMVM** - Removes a member from a physical file.
>
> **DLTF** - Deletes a physical file.

25. The file, record, and field attributes are defined in the first member of the physical file created with DDS syntax which may or may not contain data. Members, built with the attributes of the first member, store the data.

26. ONE. The physical file must be created explicitly with the CRTPF command and the *Maximum number of members* paramater changed to support the number of members required.

27. **ADDPFM** - Controls the addition of a member to the physical file after it is created and loaded with data.

> **RNMM** - Changes the name of an existing member.
>
> **RMVM** - Removes a member and it's data.
>
> **CHGPFM** - Supports limited changes to a member including the expiration date, whether the member may be shared, and text description.

28. With a Control Language program. The first member.

29. A physical file may be loaded with data by: the Data File Utility (**DFU**), output from a batch or interactive RPG IV program, output of a sort program, output from a tape-stored file, output from the **CPYF** utility, output from a **Query** program, and by a vendor-suppllied utility.

30. Packed size = $\dfrac{9}{2}$ = 4.5 or 5

    Under-and-over format: 00046
                                   2135F (F indicates a positive value)

31. Unpacked size: 5 x 2 - 1 = 9

    Unpacked value: 003178964

32. Letter **F** indicates a positive numeric value. D indicates a negative numeric value.

PROGRAMMING ASSIGNMENTS

Notes to the Instructor:

> 1. A complete listing generated from compiling the source is included for Assignment 2-1. Each part of the listing should be explained to the students. Note that assignments

2-2 and 2-3 include only the source listing segment.

2. The solutions for all of the assignments in this chapter include a CPYF file listing in either *HEX or *CHAR format. Students should be taught to read the *HEX format.

3. For some assignments, students should be required to enter the data for their files. This will require them to learn DFU and understand the significance of accurate data.

Programming Assignment 2-1: ACTIVE EMPLOYEE FILE

```
5763SS1 V3R1M0  940909              Data Description              STAN/P21PSM          7/23/97 20:09:37
File name . . . . . . . . . . . . . . . . . . :   P21PSM
  Library name  . . . . . . . . . . . . . . . :   STAN
File attribute  . . . . . . . . . . . . . . . :   Physical
Source file containing DDS  . . . . . . . . . :   QDDSSRC
  Library name  . . . . . . . . . . . . . . . :   STAN
Source member containing DDS  . . . . . . . . :   P21PSM
Source member last changed  . . . . . . . . . :   07/23/97  20:07:42
Source listing options  . . . . . . . . . . . :   *SOURCE     *LIST       *NOSECLVL
DDS generation severity level . . . . . . . . :   20          **
DDS flagging severity level . . . . . . . . . :   00
File type . . . . . . . . . . . . . . . . . . :   *DATA
Authority . . . . . . . . . . . . . . . . . . :   *LIBCRTAUT
Replace file  . . . . . . . . . . . . . . . . :   *NO
Text  . . . . . . . . . . . . . . . . . . . . :   Programming Assignment 2-1 - PF
Compiler  . . . . . . . . . . . . . . . . . . :   IBM AS/400 Data Description Processor
                                 Data Description Source
SEQNBR  *...+....1....+....2....+....3....+....4....+....5....+....6....+....7....+....8  Date
  100       * PROGRAMMING ASSIGNMENT 2-1                                                 07/22/97
  200       A        R P21PSMR                                                           07/22/97
  300       A          EMPNUMBER      4         COLHDG('EMPLOYEE NUMBER')                 07/22/97
  400       A          LAST_NAME     16         COLHDG('EMPLOYEE LAST NAME')             07/22/97
  500       A          FIRSTINIT      1         COLHDG('FIRST INITIAL')                   07/22/97
  600       A          SECNDINIT      1         COLHDG('SECOND INITIAL')                  07/22/97
  700       A          SSNUMBER      9P 0       COLHDG('SOCIAL SECURITY NO')              07/22/97
  800       A        K EMPNUMBER                                                          07/22/97
              * * * * *  E N D   O F   S O U R C E  * * * * *
5763SS1 V3R1M0  940909              Data Description              STAN/P21PSM          7/23/97 20:09:37
                                 Expanded Source
                                                                        Field    Buffer position
SEQNBR  *...+....1....+....2....+....3....+....4....+....5....+....6....+....7....+....8 length    Out     I
  200              R P21PSMR
  300                EMPNUMBER      4A  B   COLHDG('EMPLOYEE NUMBER')        4        1       1
                                            TEXT('EMPLOYEE NUMBER')
  400                LAST_NAME     16A  B   COLHDG('EMPLOYEE LAST NAME')    16        5       5
                                            TEXT('EMPLOYEE LAST NAME')
  500                FIRSTINIT      1A  B   COLHDG('FIRST INITIAL')          1       21      21
                                            TEXT('FIRST INITIAL')
  600                SECNDINIT      1A  B   COLHDG('SECOND INITIAL')         1       22      22
                                            TEXT('SECOND INITIAL')
  700                SSNUMBER      9P 0B    COLHDG('SOCIAL SECURITY NO')     5       23      23
                                            TEXT('SOCIAL SECURITY NO')
  800              K EMPNUMBER
              * * * * *  E N D   O F   E X P A N D E D   S O U R C E  * * * * *
5763SS1 V3R1M0  940909              Data Description              STAN/P21PSM          7/23/97 20:09:37
                                 Message Summary
  Total        Informational      Warning       Error        Severe
                   (0-9)          (10-19)      (20-29)       (30-99)
    0              0                0             0             0
* CPC7301      00              Message . . . . :  File P21PSM created in library STAN.
              * * * * *  E N D   O F   C O M P I L A T I O N  * * * * *
```

CPYF listing in *HEX format:

14

```
RCDNBR   *...+... 1 ...+... 2 ...+..
    1    0001WASHINGTON      GG + '-
         FFFFECECCDCEDD444444CC07279
         0001612895736500000771319F
    2    0016LINCOLN         AT +jf¦
         FFFFDCDCDDD444444444CE08984
         0016395363500000000131016F
    3    0018GRANT           US b h¼
         FFFFCDCDE4444444444EE08285
         0018791530000000000421218F
    4    0032ROOSEVELT       FD h m¼
         FFFFDDDECECDE4444444CC08295
         0032966255533000000641814F
    5    0033TRUMAN          HS h_p
         FFFFEDEDCD444444444CE08493
         0033394415000000000821817F
    6    0034EISENHOWER      DD i p
         FFFFCCECDCDECD444444CC08091
         0034592558665900000441917F
    7    0039CARTER          J prq
         FFFFCCDECD4444444444D409791
         0039319359000000000101718F
    8    0040REAGAN          R  q-
         FFFFDCCCCD4444444444D400199
         0040951715000000000902118F
```

Programming Assignment 2-2: EASTERN STATES FILE

```
SEQNBR  *...+....1....+....2....+....3....+....4....+....5....+....6....+....7
  100     A          R P22PSMR                  TEXT('CUSTOMER RECORD')
  200     A            STATE        20          TEXT('STATE NAME')
  300     A            CAPITL       25          TEXT('STATE CAPITAL')
  400     A            SCODE         2          TEXT('STATE CODE')
  500     A            CITY         25          TEXT('LARGEST CITY')
```

CPYF listing in *CHAR format:

```
RCDNBR   *...+... 1 ...+... 2 ...+... 3 ...+... 4 ...+... 5 ...+... 6 ...+... 7 .

    1  MAINE              AUGUSTA                MEPORTLAND
       DCCDC4444444444444444CECEEEC44444444444444444DCDDDEDCDC444444444444444444
       4195500000000000000001474231000000000000000000004576933154000000000000000

    2  NEW HAMPSHIRE      CONCORD                NHMANCHESTER
       DCE4CCDDECCDC4444444CDDCDDC44444444444444444DCDCDCCCEECD444444444444444444
       5560814728995000000036536940000000000000000005841538523590000000000000000

    3  VERMONT            MONTPELIER             VTBURLINGTON
       ECDDDDE444444444444444DDDEDCDCCD44444444444444EECEDDCDCEDD444444444444444444
       559465300000000000000046537539590000000000000005324939573650000000000000000

    4  MASSACHUSETTS      BOSTON                 MABOSTON
       DCEECCCEECEEE4444444CDEEDD44444444444444444444DCCDEEDD444444444444444444444
       412213842533200000002623650000000000000000000041262365000000000000000000000

    5  CONNECTICUT        HARTFORD               CTBRIDGEPORT
       CDDDCCECCCEE4444444CCDECDDC44444444444444444CECDCCCCDDDE444444444444444444
       365553393430000000008193669400000000000000000003329947576930000000000000000

    6  RHODE ISLAND       PROVIDENCE             RIPROVIDENCE
       DCDCC4CEDCDC4444444DDDECCCDCC44444444444444444DCDDDECCCDCC444444444444444444
       986450923154000000007965945535000000000000000009979659455350000000000000000

    7  NEW YORK           ALBANY                 NYNEW YORK
       DCE4EDDD4444444444444CDCCDE44444444444444444444DEDCE4EDDD444444444444444444
       5560869200000000000001321580000000000000000000005855608692000000000000000000

    8  PENNSYLVANIA       HARRISBURG             PAPHILADELPHIA
       DCDDEEDECDCDCC4444444444CCDDCECEDC44444444444444444DCDCCDCCCDDCCC444444444444
```

```
          75552835159100000000081999224970000000000000007178931453789100000000000000

  9  NEW JERSEY          TRENTON            NJNEWARK
     DCE4DCDECE4444444444EDCDEDD4444444444444444444DDDCECDD4444444444444444444
     5560159258000000000039553650000000000000000005155619200000000000000000000

 10  DELAWARE            DOVER              DEWILMINGTON
     CCDCECDC444444444444CDECD4444444444444444444444CCECDDCDCEDD4444444444444444
     4531619500000000000046559000000000000000000000004569349573650000000000000000

 11  MARYLAND            ANNAPOLIS          MDBALTIMORE
     DCDEDCDC444444444444CDDCDDDCE4444444444444444444DCCCDECDDDC4444444444444444
     4198315400000000000015517639200000000000000000004421339469500000000000000000

 12  VIRGINIA            RICHMOND           VANORFOLK
     ECDCCDCC444444444444DCCCDDDC4444444444444444444ECDDDCDDD4444444444444444444
     5997959100000000000099384654000000000000000000005156966320000000000000000000

 13  WEST VIRGINIA       CHARLESTON         WVHUNTINGTON
     ECEE4ECDCCDCC4444444CCCDDCEEDD4444444444444444EECEDECDCDCEDD4444444444444444
     65230599795910000000381935236500000000000000000658453957365000000000000000000

 14  NORTH CAROLINA      RALEIGH            NCCHARLOTTE
     DDDEC4CCDDDCDC4444444DCDCCCC4444444444444444444DCCCCDDDEEC4444444444444444444
     5693803196395100000091359780000000000000000000005338193633350000000000000000

 15  SOUTH CAROLINA      COLUMBIA           SCCOLUMBIA
     EDEEC4CCDDDCDC4444444CDDEDCCC4444444444444444444ECCDDEDCCC4444444444444444444
     2643803196395100000036344291000000000000000000002336344291000000000000000000
                                                        •2
 16  GEORGIA             ATLANTA            GAATLANTA
     CCDDCCC444444444444444CEDCDEC44444444444444444444CCCEDCDEC4444444444444444444
     756979100000000000000133153100000000000000000007113315310000000000000000000

 17  FLORIDA             TALLAHASSEE        FLJACKSONVILLE
     CDDDCCC444444444444444ECDDCCCEECC44444444444444444CDDCCDEDDECDDC4444444444444
     63699410000000000000031331812255000000000000000006311322655933500000000000000
```

Programming Assignment 2-3: CUSTOMER MAILING FILE

```
|SEQNBR  *...+....1....+....2....+....3....+....4....+....5....+....6....+....7
|  100     A         R P23PSMR                    TEXT('CUSTOMER RECORD')
|  200     A           NAME          15           COLHDG('CUSTOMER NAME')
|  300     A           STREET        14           COLHDG('STREET ADDRESS')
|  400     A           CITY          10           COLHDG('CUSTOMER CITY')
|  500     A           STATE          2           COLHDG('STATE CODE')
|  600     A           ZIP           5P 0         COLHDG('ZIP CODE')
```

CPYF listing in *HEX format:

```
|RCDNBR  *...+... 1 ...+... 2 ...+... 3 ...+... 4 ...+... 5

   1  ANDREW GUMP     1 SUN AVENUE  MIAMI     FL h
      CDCDCE4CEDD4444F4EED4CECDEC44CCDC44444CD081
      1549560744700001024501555450049149000006388F

   2  DICK TRACY      CELL 8        ALCATRAZ  CA +
      CCCD4EDCCE44444CCDD4F4444444CDCCEDCE44CC070
      49320391380000035330800000000013313919003177F

   3  BEETLE BAILEY  "A" COMPANY   FORT DIX  NJ |?
      CCCEDC4CCCDCE447C74CDDDCDE444CDDE4CCE44DD066
      255335021935800F1F0364715800069930497005166F

   4  CHARLIE BROWN  8 DOGHOUSE ST.ANYWHERE  US
      CCCDDCC4CDDED44F4CDCCDDEEC4EE4CDEECCDC44EE000
      38193950296653080467864250238158685950004200F

   5  MOON MULLINS    16 TIDE ROAD  LAKEVILLE CT ñ"
      DDDD4DEDDCDE444FF4ECCC4DCCC44DCDCECDDC4CE047
      46650443395200016039450961400312559335033669F
```

16

```
  6  LI'L ABNER      80 PATCH LANE DOG PATCH SCrr⌐
     DC7D4CCDCD44444FF4DCECC4DCDC4CDC4DCECC4EC999
     39D30125590000080071338031550467071338023 99F

  7  STANLEY MYERS  18 SMITH DRIVENORWALK    CT e¦
     EECDDCE4DECDE44FF4EDCEC4CDCECDDDECDD444CE084
     231535804859200180249380499555569613200033 65F
```

•3

CHAPTER 3
QUESTION ANSWERS

1. Based on the program specifications, the instructions are written on the pre-printed coding forms. The experienced programmer usually skips the procedure and enters the code directly with **SEU**.

   Completed specification forms (if used) are referenced for entering the source instructions with **SEU**.

   The program is compiled by the **CRTBNDRPG** command, or by option 3 on the Programmer Menu, or by option 14 in the Programmer Development Manager.

   If any terminal errors (type 20 and above) occur, **SEU** must be used to correct the source code and the program recompiled. This procedure must be continued until the program is free of terminal errors.

   When the source is free of terminal errors, an object is created in the designated library.

2. **SEU** (*Source Entry Utility*). The *Prompt* and *Format* methods.

3. *Control, File Description, Definition, Input, Calculations,* and *Output.*

4. *Control* - Provides entries for changes in the default date and/or time formats and editing, forms alignment control, decimal editing, and change in the default currency symbol character. If none of the defaults are to be changed, the programmer does not have to include this specification in the RPG IV program.

   File Description - Instructions define the attributes of all file types processed by the program.

   Definition - Instructions define arrays, tables, data structures, data areas, named constants, and work fields.

   Input - Instructions define the fields in a program described file. Seldom used in RPG IV programs.

   Calculations - Instructions define arithmetic statements, formulas, and decision making. Controls array and table processing, physical file maintenance, and display, logical, and printer file processing.

   Output - Include instructions to define a program described printer file. Page and line spacing, constants, variable field values, and editing are controlled in this specification type. If an externally described printer file is included in the RPG IV program, the instructions for this specification are not

18

required.

5. The specification types must be included in an RPG IV program in an **H, F, D, I, C, O** compilation order. Note that the **H** (Control) Specifications is automatically supplied by the compiler, and unless special functions are to be specified, it may be omitted from the source program. The minimum specification types that must be included in a stand alone RPG IV program are **F** and **O**. A terminal error will be generated if instructions are not in the required compilation order.

6. **CRTBNDRPG** (*Create Bound RPG Program*) and **CRTRPGMOD** (*Create RPG Module*). The **CRTRPGMOD** command must be used when the RPG IV program is to be "bound" with other program into a executable module (discussed in Chapter 19).

7. Information (**00**), Warning (**10**), Error (**20**), and Severe Error (**30+**). Errors identified as **20** and above prevent compilation of an RPG IV program.

8. Page 1, general information and parameter values. Page 2, the Source Listing. Page 3, a Cross Reference. Page 4, the Message Summary. Page 5 the Final Summary.

9. The minimum entries in the *File Description Specifications* to process an externally described file include:

   a) Letter **F** in colmun 6.
   b) Filename left-justified in columns 7-16.
   c) An **I** in column 17.
   d) **F** column 18.
   e) An **E** in column 22.
   f) If the physical file is keyed and it is to be processed in the default key value order, a **K** must be entered in position 34. However, if the file is not keyed, or if the keyed file is to be processed in arrival sequence, this entry is omitted.
   g) The device name DISK must be entered left-justified in positions 36-42.

10. The minimum entries in the *File Description Specifications* to process a program described physical file include:

   a) Answers for a, b, c, d, and g are the same as question 9.
   b) An **F** must be specified in column 22.
   c) Record length in positions 23-27.
   c) No entry is made in column 34.

11. The minimum entries in the *File Description Specifications* to process a externally described physical file with traditional RPG include:

   a) Answers for a, b, c, e, f, and g are the same as question 9.
   b) Letter **P** must be specified in position 18 instead of an **F**.

12. a) **F** missing in position 17 for GLACTS.
    b) DISC must be spelled DISK.
    c) Because the PRINTER file is program described (**F** in position 22), a record length entry must be specified in the **Rlen+** field.

13. *File Description, Calculations and Output Specifications*. Note if the RPG Logic Cycle is used to process the file, only *File Description* and *Output Specifications* are required.

14. Same answer as question 13.

15. *File Description* and *Output Specifications*.

16. Required to define the field attributes in a program described physical file. Also used to load run time arrays (discussed in Chapter 10).

17. Name the record type(s) in a program described file. Indicators **01** through **99** are used for this purpose.

    They function as switches in the program. When a record type is read, the specified indicator will be turned on which is used to condition subsequent calculations and/or output.

    The indicators are specified in column 21-22 of the *Input Specifications*.

    They are <u>set on</u> when the related record type is read.

    They are <u>set off</u> after the last output instruction in the program is executed and/or when end-of-file is tested.

18. When an indicator is entered in one of the indicator positions of a calculation or output instruction, it conditions the instruction so that it is executed only when the indicator is "on".

19. Line 1 - **Filename++** entry missing. Must include the name of the physical file.
    Ri entry missing. Must include a **01** to **99** *Record Identifying Indicator*.
    Line 2 - Cust-no must be specified as Cust_no. Hyphens are not permitted in a field (or file name).
    Line 3 - 1Custnam cannot begin with a digit. **From+** field entry is missing.
    Line 4 - Cust Type cannot include an imbedded blank.
    Line 5 - $Cust_Amt is missing the **To+++** field entry.

20. When the end of the input file is read in an RPG IV or RPG program.

21. To read records from the input file, control printing, and determine an end of file condition to end the program.

22. **READ** operation - Reads one record from a physical file.

    DOW operation - Controls iterative processing (looping) with a relational test.

    EXCEPT operation - Controls output from calculations.

    ENDDO operation - Ends a **DOW** (or **DO** or **DOU**) group.

23. The **READ** instruction must include an indicator in positions 75-76 to test for an end-of-file condition.

    The **DOW** instruction must include a relational test with an **EVAL** statement in positions 36-80 (*extended Factor 2* field).

    The **EXCEPT** instruction must include an output record (exception) name in *Factor 2* (positions 36-49).

    Another **READ** instruction must be included within the **DOW** group to read more than one record from the Glacts file.

24. When end-of-file is read. Any **LR** (last record) processing may be specified.

25. *Record Description* area (positions 7-39) includes the name of the output file, record type (**H**, **D**, **E**, or **T**), skipping and spacing control, and when output will execute based on the indicator(s) specified or the exception name.

    Field Description area (positions 21-45) specifies the fields and/or constants that will be output and editing.

26. The system printer. **QPRINT** may also be used. For externally described PRINTER files, the related file name must be specified.

27. Defines an exception output record.

28. A programmer-supplied name defined in *Factor 2* of an **EXCEPT** instruction. It is referenced on a *Record Description* output record in the Excnam++++ field (positions 30-39).

29. The low-order (last) position of a field or constant.

30. Line 1 - Output file name missing in the *Filename++* field.
    E, not **F**, must be specified in the *D* field (position 17).
    Space before (*++B* field) or Space after (*++A* field) and/or Skip before (*Sb+* field) or Skip after (*Sa+* field) entry or entries missing.
    Line 3 - ActName has the same end position as ACTNUM.
    Line 4 - ACT-TYPE contains an invalid hyphen.
    Line 5 - O in the *Y* (edit code) field is not a valid edit code.
    End++ (end position) field entry is missing.

31. Edit codes control the editing of numeric field values (zero suppression, insertion of commas, insertion of decimal point, minus sign or CR for negative values, and date editing.

PROGRAMMING ASSIGNMENTS

Notes to the Instructor:

1. The related physical file from a Chapter 2 programming assignment must have been created and loaded with data before any of the assignments in this chapter are started.

2. The student must use the field names specified in the related physical file.

Programming Assignment 3-1: ACTIVE EMPLOYEE LISTING

Note that a partial compile listing is included for this assignment. Other assignmments will only include the source listing section.

```
Line   <--------------------- Source Specifications ---------------------------><---- Comments ----> Do
Number ....1....+....2....+....3....+....4....+....5....+....6....+....7....+....8....+....9....+...10 Num
                          S o u r c e   L i s t i n g
   1 * Progamming Assignment 3-1 - ACTIVE EMPLOYEE LISTING....
   2 FP21PSM    IF   E        K DISK
     *--------------------------------------------------------------------------------*
     *                                   RPG name          External name              *
     * File name. . . . . . . . :        P21PSM            STAN/P21PSM                 *
     * Record format(s) . . . . . :      P21PSMR           P21PSMR                     *
     *--------------------------------------------------------------------------------*
   3 FQSYSPRT   O   F  132        PRINTER
   4
*RNF2318 00     3 000300  Overflow indicator OA is assigned to PRINTER file QSYSPRT.
   5=IP21PSMR
     *--------------------------------------------------------------------------------*
     * RPG record format . . . . : P21PSMR                                            *
     * External format . . . . . : P21PSMR : STAN/P21PSM                              *
     *--------------------------------------------------------------------------------*
   6=I                          A    1    4  EMPNUMBER            EMPLOYEE NUMBER
   7=I                          A    5   20  LAST_NAME            EMPLOYEE LAST NAME
   8=I                          A   21   21  FIRSTINIT            FIRST INITIAL
   9=I                          A   22   22  SECNDINIT            SECOND INITIAL
  10=I                          P   23   27  OSSNUMBER            SOCIAL SECURITY NO
  11 C            READ      P21psm                     ----LR    read first record
  12 C            DOW       *INLR = *OFF                          dow LR ind is off   B01
  13 C            EXCEPT    Detailine                             print a line        01
  14 C            READ      P21psm                     ----LR    read next record     01
  15 C            ENDDO                                           end dow group       E01
  16
  17 OQsysprt  E           Detailine      2
  18 O                         EmpNumber            13
  19 O                         FirstInit            20
  20 O                         SecndInit            22
  21 O                         Last_Name            40
  22 O                         SSNumber             58
     * * * * *  E N D   O F   S O U R C E  * * * * *

                    M e s s a g e   S u m m a r y
 Msg id  Sv Number Message text
*RNF2318 00      1 No overflow indicator is specified; indicator assigned and
                   automatic skip to 06 generated.
*RNF7066 00      1 Record-format name of Externally-Described file is not used.
```

```
*RNF7086 00      1 RPG handles blocking for the file. INFDS is updated only when
                   blocks of data are transferred.
         * * * *  E N D   O F   M E S S A G E   S U M M A R Y  * * * *
5763RG1 V3R1M0  940909 RN      IBM ILE RPG/400        STAN/P31RSM
                         F i n a l   S u m m a r y
  Message Totals:
    Information  (00) . . . . . . . :        3
    Warning     (10) . . . . . . . :        0
    Error       (20) . . . . . . . :        0
    Severe Error (30+) . . . . . . :        0
    -------------------------------   -------
    Total . . . . . . . . . . . . :         3
  Source Totals:
    Records . . . . . . . . . . . :         22
    Specifications . . . . . . . . :        19
    Data records . . . . . . . . . :         0
    Comments  . . . . . . . . . . :          1
         * * * *  E N D   O F   F I N A L   S U M M A R Y  * * * *
Program P31RSM placed in library STAN. 00 highest severity. Created on 97/07/23 at 20:20:48.
         * * * *  E N D   O F   C O M P I L A T I O N * * * *
```

Note: The ellipsis indicate that supplemental information in this compile listing have been deleted for brevity. Informational errors for this program are automatically supplied by the compiler and are unavoidable.

Printed Report: **

0001	G G	WASHINGTON	017321799
0016	A T	LINCOLN	018091864
0018	U S	GRANT	018221885
0032	F D	ROOSEVELT	018821945
0033	H S	TRUMAN	018841973
0034	D D	EISENHOWER	018901971
0039	J	CARTER	019771981
0040	R	REAGAN	020111989

Programming Assignment 3-2: EASTERN STATE REPORT LISTING

```
Line   <--------------------- Source Specifications --------------------------><---- Comments ----> Do
Number ....1....+....2....+....3....+....4....+....5....+....6....+....7....+....8....+....9....+...10 Num
                     S o u r c e   L i s t i n g
    1  * Programming Assignment 3-2 - EASTERN STATE REPORT LISTING....
    2 FP22psm    IF  E           DISK
      *--------------------------------------------------------------------------------------*
      *                                 RPG name          External name                      *
      * File name. . . . . . . . :      P22PSM            STAN/P22PSM                         *
      * Record format(s) . . . . :      P22PSMR           P22PSMR                             *
      *--------------------------------------------------------------------------------------*
    3 FQsysprt   O   F  132          PRINTER
    4
  RNF2318 00     3 000300  Overflow indicator OA is assigned to PRINTER file QSYSPRT.
    5=IP22PSMR
      *--------------------------------------------------------------------------------------*
      * RPG record format  . . . . :    P22PSMR                                              *
      * External format  . . . . . :    P22PSMR : STAN/P22PSM                                *
      *--------------------------------------------------------------------------------------*
    6=I                           A    1   20  STATENAME
    7=I                           A   21   45  CAPITAL
    8=I                           A   46   47  STATECODE
    9=I                           A   48   72  LARGECITY
   10 C              READ     P22psm                          ----LR   read first record
   11 C              DOW      *INLR = *OFF                             dow LR ind. is off   B01
   12 C              EXCEPT   Detailine                                print record          01
```

```
   13 C                     READ      P22psm                              ----LR    read next record      01
   14 C                     ENDDO                                                   end dow group         E01
   15
   16 OQsysprt   E                    Detailine     2
   17 O                              StateCode             7
   18 O                              StateName            35
   19 O                              Capital              70
   20 O                              LargeCity           105
      * * * *  E N D   O F   S O U R C E  * * * *
```

└ Informational error identified because a page overflow indicator was not specified in this prorgram.
This error will be included in the compile listings of all RPG IV programs that specify printer output
and do not include a page overflow indicator.

Printed Report:

ME	MAINE	AUGUSTA	PORTLAND
NH	NEW HAMPSHIRE	CONCORD	MANCHESTER
VT	VERMONT	MONTPELIER	BURLINGTON
MA	MASSACHUSETTS	BOSTON	BOSTON
CT	CONNECTICUT	HARTFORD	BRIDGEPORT
RI	RHODE ISLAND	PROVIDENCE'	PROVIDENCE
NY	NEW YORK	ALBANY	NEW YORK
PA	PENNSYLVANIA	HARRISBURG	PHILADELPHIA
NJ	NEW JERSEY	TRENTON	NEWARK
DE	DELAWARE	DOVER	WILMINGTON
MD	MARYLAND	ANNAPOLIS	BALTIMORE
VA	VIRGINIA	RICHMOND	NORFOLK
WV	WEST VIRGINIA	CHARLESTON	HUNTINGTON
NC	NORTH CAROLINA	RALEIGH	CHARLOTTE
SC	SOUTH CAROLINA	COLUMBIA	COLUMBIA
GA	GEORGIA	ATLANTA	ATLANTA
FL	FLORIDA	TALLAHASSEE	JACKSONVILLE

Programming Assignment 3-3: CUSTOMER MAILING LIST

```
Line    <--------------------- Source Specifications --------------------------><---- Comments ----> Do
Number  ....1....+....2....+....3....+....4....+....5....+....6....+....7....+....8....+....9....+...10 Num
                        S o u r c e   L i s t i n g
    1 * Programming Assignment 3-3 - CUSTOMER MAILING LIST....
    2 FP23psm   IF   E            DISK
      *--------------------------------------------------------------------------------------------*
      *                              RPG name          External name                               *
      * File name. . . . . . . . . : P23PSM            STAN/P23PSM                                  *
      * Record format(s) . . . . . : P23PSMR           P23PSMR                                      *
      *--------------------------------------------------------------------------------------------*
    3 FQsysprt  O    F  132        PRINTER                           -
    4
 *RNF2318 00    3 000300  Overflow indicator OA is assigned to PRINTER file QSYSPRT.
    5=IP23PSMR
      *--------------------------------------------------------------------------------------------*
      * RPG record format  . . . . : P23PSMR                                                        *
      * External format  . . . . . : P23PSMR : STAN/P23PSM                                          *
      *--------------------------------------------------------------------------------------------*
    6=I                           A    1   15  CUSTNAME              CUSTOMER NAME
    7=I                           A   16   29  STREET                CUSTOMER STREET
```

24

```
  8=I                          A   30   39 CITY             CUSTOMER CITY
  9=I                          A   40   41 STATE            CUSTOMER STATE
 10=I                          P   42   44 OZIP_CODE        CUSTOMER ZIP CODE
 11 C           READ     P23psm                    ----LR   read first record
 12 C           DOW      *INLR = *OFF              ----LR   dow LR ind. is off    B01
 13 C           EXCEPT   Detailine                          print record          01
 14 C           READ     P23psm                    ----LR   read first record     01
 15 C           ENDDO                                       end dow grop          E01
 16
 17 OQsysprt  E          Detailine      1
 18 O                    CustName             24
 19 O         E          Detailine      1
 20 O                    Street               23
 21 O         E          Detailine      3
 22 O                    City                 19
 23 O                    State                26
 24 O                    Zip_Code             34
    * * * *  E N D   O F   S O U R C E   * * * *
```

Printed Report:

```
┌─────────────────────────────────────┐
│   ANDREW GUMP                        │
│   1 SUN AVENUE                       │
│   MIAMI           FL   08881         │
│                                      │
│   DICK TRACY      *)                 │
│   CELL 8                             │
│   ALCATRAZ        CA   07770         │
│                                      │
│   BEETLE BAILEY                      │
│   "A" COMPANY                        │
│   FORT DIX        NJ   06666         │
│                                      │
│   CHARLIE BROWN                      │
│   8 DOGHOUSE ST.                     │
│   ANYWHERE        US   00000         │
│                                      │
│   MOON MULLIN                        │
│   16 TIDE ROAD                       │
│   LAKEVILLE       CT   06497         │
│                                      │
│   LI'L ABNER                         │
│   80 PATCH LANE                      │
│   DIG PATCH       SC   99999         │
│                                      │
│   STANLEY MYERS                      │
│   18 SMITH PLACE                     │
│   NORWALK         CT   06854         │
└─────────────────────────────────────┘
```

Programming Assignment 3-4: PROGRAM DESCRIBED PHYSICAL FILE PROCESSING

Notes to the Instructor:

1. The example program shown is a modification of Programming Assignment 3-1.

2. Explain the changes in the *File Description* -instruction to process a program described file (F instead of E, record size specified, and deletion of the K entry).

3. Explain the instructions needed in the *Input Specifications* to support program described file processing. Indicate that the field names do not have to be the same as those in the physical file (providing it has a DDS format). However, the *From*

and *To* field locations must be exact.

```
Line    <-------------------- Source Specifications --------------------------><---- Comments ----> Do
Number  ....1....+....2....+....3....+....4....+....5....+....6....+....7....+....8....+....9....+...10 Num
                          S o u r c e   L i s t i n g
      1 * Progamming Assignment 3-4 - PROGRAM DESCRIBED PF PROCESSING....
      2 FP21PSM    IF  F   27        DISK
      3 FQSYSPRT   O   F  132        PRINTER
      4
*RNF2318 00      3 000300  Overflow indicator OA is assigned to PRINTER file QSYSPRT.
      5 IP21PSM    SM
      6 I                                1    4   EmpNumber
      7 I                                5   20   Last_Name
      8 I                               21   21   FirstInit
      9 I                               22   22   SecndInit
     10 I                           P   23   27   OSSNumber
    ·11
     12 C                  READ    P21psm                      ----LR      read first record
     13 C                  DOW     *INLR = *OFF                            dow LR ind is off       B01
     14 C                  EXCEPT  Detailine                               print a line           01
     15 C                  READ    P21psm                      ----LR      read next record       01
     16 C                  ENDDO                                           end dow group          E01
     17
     18 OQsysprt   E              Detailine      2
     19 O                         EmpNumber           13
     20 O                         FirstInit           20       **
     21 O                         SecndInit           22
     22 O                         Last_Name           40
     23 O                         SSNumber            58
        * * * *   E N D   O F   S O U R C E   * * * *
```

Printed Report: Is identical to that shown on page 23.

Programming Assignment 3-5: TRADITIONAL RPG SYNTAX

Notes to the Instructor:

1. This program uses the RPG LOGIC cycle which automatically opens and closes the files, reads records from the input file, and tests for the end of file condition. Consequently, for this example, no *Calculation Specification* instructions are required.

2. Because exception output is not specified, the RPG LOGIC CYCLE automatically processes output after a record is read. The output record is defined at detail time (**D** in position 17) and conditioned with a N1P indicator that prevents a blank line from being printed at 1P (First Page) time.

```
Line    <-------------------- Source Specifications --------------------------><---- Comments ----> Do
Number  ....1....+....2....+....3....+....4....+....5....+....6....+....7....+....8....+....9....+...10 Num
                          S o u r c e   L i s t i n g
      1 * Progamming Assignment 3-5 - TRADITIONAL RPG SYNTAX....
      2 FP21PSM    IP  E        K DISK
        *-------------------------------------------------------------------------------------------*
        *                                RPG name          External name                            *
        * File name. . . . . . . . . : P21PSM           STAN/P21PSM                                 *
        * Record format(s) . . . . . : P21PSMR          P21PSMR                                     *
        *-------------------------------------------------------------------------------------------*
      3 FQSYSPRT   O   F  132        PRINTER
      4
*RNF2318 00      3 000300  Overflow indicator OA is assigned to PRINTER file QSYSPRT.
```

```
    5=IP21PSMR
      *-------------------------------------------------------------------*
      * RPG record format  . . . . :  P21PSMR                             *
      * External format  . . . . . :  P21PSMR : STAN/P21PSM               *
      *-------------------------------------------------------------------*
    6=I                         A    1    4  EMPNUMBER          EMPLOYEE NUMBER
    7=I                         A    5   20  LAST_NAME          EMPLOYEE LAST NAME
    8=I                         A   21   21  FIRSTINIT          FIRST INITIAL
    9=I                         A   22   22  SECNDINIT          SECOND INITIAL
   10=I                         P   23   27  0SSNUMBER          SOCIAL SECURITY NO
   11 OQsysprt    D    N1P                 2
   12 O                     EmpNumber           13
   13 O                     FirstInit           20
   14 O                     SecndInit           22
   15 O                     Last_Name           40
   16 O                     SSNumber            58
      * * * *   E N D   O F   S O U R C E   * * * *
```

Printed Report: Is identical to that shown on page 23.

9

27

CHAPTER 4
QUESTION ANSWERS

1. On *Output Specification* instructions.

2. End position entries will depend on where constants are
    located on the printer spacing chart.

```
3 ...+... 4 ...+... 5 ...+... 6 ...+... 7 ...+... 8
Field++++++++++YB.End++PConstant/editword/DTformat++
                  50 'SALARIED EMPLOYEE PAYROLL'
                  76 'INFORMATION'
```

3. *Skip Before* entry in positions 46-48 (*Sb* field) of the output
    form advances the paper in the printer to the specified line
    on the same or following page <u>before</u> printing the line. A
    Skip After entry in positions 49-51 (*Sa* field) advances the
    paper to the specified line on the same or following page
    after printing.

4. **NO.** If *Skip Before* or *After* was specified for every line
    type, one line would be printed per page.

5. **FORMLEN** keyword must be specified in the keyword field of the
    File Description instruction for the PRINTER file.

6. When the designated overflow line is sensed, the line is
    printed and program control advances the paper to the
    specified *Skip Before* or *After* entry for the next page.
    A default overflow line for stock paper is assigned when
    the computer system is initially configured, but may be
    changed in an RPG IV program with a **FORMLEN** keyword specified
    in the *Keyword* field (positions 44-80) of the *File Description*
    Specification instruction for the PRINTER file.

7. **OA-OG and OV.** An *Overflow Indicator* is defined in the *File*
    Specifications in the *Keywords* field with the **FORMOFL** keyword
    for the PRINTER file. In RPG IV programs that do not use the
    logic cycle, the page overflow is intentionally set on to
    print the first page of a report on a new page. Subsequent
    page overflow will occur automatically when the overflow line
    is detected.

8. **UDATE,** default format is MMDDYY or ***DATE,** default is MMDDYYYY.

9. **UMONTH, UDAY,** and **UYEAR.**

10. Include the **DATFMT** keyword in the Header Specifications.
    Four, options of the eight, include ***MDY**, ***YMD**, ***DMY**, and
    *JUL. Other formats are ***USA**, ***EUR**, and ***JIS**. The default
    format for the **DATFMT** keyword is ***ISO** which accesses the
    session (or system) date in an **yyyymmdd** format.

DATFMT option	Format Accessed
*MDY	mmddyy
*YMD	yymmdd
*DMY	ddmmyy
*JUL	yyddd
*USA	mmddyyyy
*EUR	ddmmyyyy
*JIS	yyyymmdd

See Figure 4-5 (page 65) for valid separator characters.

11. The special word **PAGE** provides for page numbering beginning with 0001 is automatically incrementing by 1 for each sub-sequent page. **PAGE1** through **PAGE 7** are other special RPG IV words that provide for different page numbering and/or when more than one PRINTER file is included in program.

12. The **UDATE** instruction is missing an edit code entry in the Y field (position 44). Because **UDATE** will be accessed in a default **mmddyy** format, the **4** entry for the *End++* field is too small (must be at least **8** with editing).

    The '**GENERAL LEDGER ACCOUNT** constant is missing the closing single quote and an *End++* field entry.

    The **BALANCES'** entry is missing a beginning single quote.

    The special word **PAGE** (or any *Field+++++++++* entry) cannot be on the same instruction line with a constant.

13. In the *Definition, Input,* or *Calculation Secification* instructions of an RPG IV program.

14. **30. 30** decimal positions. The number of decimal positions specified cannot be greater than the size of the field.

15. A *decimal data error* will occur that will halt processing giving the operator the option to generate a program dump, end the job, or ignore the error.

16. Decimal characters are not included in the storage of numeric data. The location of the decimal point is *implied* in memory by its *Data Description* (for physical files) or in an RPG IV program by a *Definition, Input,* or *Calculation Specification* instruction.

17. *Explicit* decimals consume a storage position and are usually specified only in the editing of numeric values and in literals that are printed or displayed.

18. Only numeric fields.

19. *Editing* is the process of suppressing leading zeros, in-

    sertion of a decimal point in non-integer numeric values, insertion of commas, inclusion of dollar signs, and the insertion of special character in the body of a numeric field value.

20.   With Edit Codes and Edit Words.

21.   With Edit Codes 1, 2, 3, 4, 5-9 (user-defined), A, B, C, D, J, K, L, M, N, O, P, Q, X, Y, and Z.

22.

Value	Edited Result
081198	8/11/98
0811	8/11
08	8
000000	
12311998	12/31/1998

23.   With the **CHGJOB** (*Change Job*) command from the command line of any AS/400 display that has a command line.

24.   The default job (system) date is installed when the AS/400 system is initially configured. It is defined (accessed) in an RPG IV program with a **DATE** or ***DATE** special word.

25.   .00; spaces; 123,456; 10000.00; .99; 2,000,001CR; 2,000.00; 1000; 124,590- (Note edit code **Z** will not provide a decimal)

    Note: 6 indicates -1 and } -0

26.

Edited Result	Required Edit Word	Comment
012-22-3456	'0bbb-bb-bbbb'	Leading zero required
1/02/90	'0b/bb/bb'	
****10.00	'bbbb,bb*.bb'	Only 1 asterisks needed
$99.44	'bbbb,b$0.bb'	zero required after $
(203) 333 4444	'0(bbb)&bbb&bbbb'	Leading zero required
$ 5,000.00	'$bbb,bb0.bb'	Fixed dollar sign
18.75 CR	'bb,bb0.bb&CR'	CR will only print when -
$ 2,135,001-	'$bb,bbb,b0b-'	- will only print when -
150.00 DEBIT	'bb,bb0.bb&DEBIT'	DEBIT will always print

    b indicates a blank value

27.   No. The format of an *edit word* may be larger than the related field, but not smaller.

28.   With an **edit code**, a fixed $ is specified on a separate coding line with its own end position reference. A floating $ is entered on the same coding line as the field and **edit code**.

    With an **edit word**, a *fixed $* is entered in the high-order byte followed by space. A floating $ is included in an **edit word** by immediately following it with a 0. To provide for the $, an **edit word** must be at least one byte larger than the field edited.

29. 66 lines when the printer is set at 6 lines per inch. Usually on line 54, when 6 lines are provided at the top and bottom of a page.

30. The *File Description Specifications* in the **Keyword** field with a **FORMLEN** keyword in definition of the PRINTER file. The entry to change the form length to 8 would be **FORMLEN(8)**.

31. Line, laser, ink jet, and dot matrix.

PROGRAMMING ASSIGNMENTS

Programming Assignment 4-1: SALARIED EMPLOYEE REPORT

```
Line   <--------------------- Source Specifications ---------------------><---- Comments ----> Do
Number ....1....+....2....+....3....+....4....+....5...₊+....6....+....7....+....8....+....9....+...10 Num
                        S o u r c e   L i s t i n g
   1 * PA 4-1: Salaried Employee Report....
   2 FP41PSM    IF   E              DISK
     *----------------------------------------------------------------------------------*
     *                              RPG name         External name                      *
     * File name. . . . . . . . :   P41PSM           STAN/P41PSM                         *
     * Record format(s) . . . . :   P41PSMR          P41PSMR                             *
     *----------------------------------------------------------------------------------*
   3 FQsysprt   O   F 132          PRINTER
   4
*RNF2318 00     3 000300  Overflow indicator OA is assigned to PRINTER file QSYSPRT.
   5=IP41PSMR
     *----------------------------------------------------------------------------------*
     * RPG record format . . . . :   P41PSMR                                            *
     * External format . . . . . :   P41PSMR : STAN/P41PSM                              *
     *----------------------------------------------------------------------------------*
   6=I                          A    1    4  EMP_NUMBER
   7=I                          A    5   20  LAST_NAME
   8=I                          A   21   21  FIRST_INIT
   9=I                          A   22   22  SECND_INIT
  10=I                          P   23   27  OSSNUMBER
  11=I                          P   28   31  2WEK_SALARY
  12=I                          P   32   36  2YTD_SALARY
  13 C            EXCEPT    Heading                             print heading lines
  14 C            READ      P41psm                    ----LR    read first record
  15 C            DOW       *INLR = *OFF                        dow LR is off          B01
  16 C            EXCEPT    Detailine                           print a record          01
  17 C            READ      P41psm                    ----LR    read first record       01
  18 C            ENDDO                                         end dow group          E01
  19
  20 OQsysprt  E           Heading        3 01
  21 O                     UDATE          Y    12
  22 O                                        51 'SALARIED EMPLOYEE LISTING'
  23 O                                        81 'PAGE'
  24 O                     PAGE                86
  25 O         E           Heading        2
  26 O                                        14 'EMP NO'
  27 O                                        36 'EMPLOYEE NAME'
  28 O                                        57 'SS NO'
  29 O                                        69 'SALARY'
  30 O                                        82 'YTD SALARY'
  31 O         E           Detailine      2
  32 O                     Emp_Number          13
  33 O                     First_Init          20
  34 O                     Secnd_Init          22
  35 O                     Last_Name           40
  36 O                     SSNumber            60 '0  -  -   '
```

31

```
37 O                        Wek_Salary    1    70
38 O                        Ytd_Salary    1    82
   * * * *  E N D  O F  S O U R C E  * * * *
```

Printed Report:

```
7/05/98              SALARIED EMPLOYEE LISTING                    PAGE    1


     EMP NO          EMPLOYEE NAME              SS NO      SALARY   YTD SALARY

      0001      G G  WASHINGTON            010-73-1799    800.00    16,000.00

      0016      A T  LINCOLN               018-09-1864  1,100.00    44,000.00

      0018      U S  GRANT                 018-22-1885    515.99       519.99

      0032      F D  ROOSEVELT             018-82-1945    950.00     9,500.00

      0033      H S  TRUMAN                018-84-1973    999.99    29,999.70

      0034      D D  EISENHOWER            018-90-1971  1,400.00    29,400.00

      0039      J    CARTER          *1    019-77-1981    230.00     9,200.00

      0040      R    REAGAN                020-11-1989  2,000.00    20,000.00
```

Programming Assignment 4-2: DATA PERSONNEL SALARY LISTING

```
Line    <--------------------- Source Specifications ------------------------><---- Comments ----> Do
Number  ....1....+....2....+....3....+....4....+....5....+....6....+....7....+....8....+....9....+...10 Num
                        S o u r c e   L i s t i n g
    1 * PA 4-2: Data Processing Salary Listing....
    2 FP42PSM   IF  E           DISK
      *------------------------------------------------------------------------------------------*
      *                        RPG name            External name                                 *
      * File name. . . . . . . . . :  P42PSM        STAN/P42PSM                                   *
      * Record format(s) . . . . . :  P42PSMR       P42PSMR                                       *
      *------------------------------------------------------------------------------------------*
    3 FQsysprt  O   F  132       PRINTER
    4
*RNF2318 00     3 000300  Overflow indicator OA is assigned to PRINTER file QSYSPRT.
    5=IP42PSMR
      *------------------------------------------------------------------------------------------*
      * RPG record format  . . . . :  P42PSMR                                                     *
      * External format  . . . . . :  P42PSMR : STAN/P42PSM                                       *
      *------------------------------------------------------------------------------------------*
    6=I                         A    1   25  JOB_TITLE
    7=I                         P   26   28 2AVG_SALARY
    8=I                         P   29   30 0EMPLOYEES
    9 C              EXCEPT     Heading                                 print heading lines
   10 C              READ       P42psm                        ----LR    read first record
   11 C              DOW        *INLR = *OFF                            dow LR is off          B01
   12 C              EXCEPT     Detailine                               print a record          01
   13 C              READ       P42psm                        ----LR    read first record       01
   14 C              ENDDO                                              end dow group          E01
   15
   16 OQsysprt   E              Heading       2 01
   17 O                         UDATE      Y     8                  -
   18 O                                          51 'PAGE'
   19 O                         PAGE            56
   20 O          E              Heading       3
   21 O                                          26 'AVERAGE WEEKLY SALARY OF'
   22 O                                          52 'DATA PROCESSING PERSONNEL'
   23 O          E              Heading       1
   24 O                                           9 'NUMBER OF'
   25 O                                          28 'JOB TITLE'
   26 O                                          49 'AVERAGE'
```

```
27 O        E        Heading      2
28 O                              9 'EMPLOYEES'
29 O                             52 'WEEKLY SALARY'
30 O        E        Detailine    2
31 O                 Employees          6
32 O                 Job_Title         36
33 O                 Avg_Salary   1    49
     * * * * *  E N D   O F   S O U R C E  * * * * *
```

Printed Report:

```
5/05/98                                          PAGE    1

        AVERAGE WEEKLY SALARY OF DATA PROCESSING PERSONNEL


NUMBER OF              JOB TITLE                  AVERAGE
EMPLOYEES                                     WEEKLY SALARY

    10          APPLICATION PROGRAMMERS       $ 500.00

     3          SYSTEMS PROGRAMMERS           $ 650.00

     8          COMPUTER OPERATORS            $ 275.00

     4          SYSTEMS ANALYST    *)         $ 750.00

    10          DATA ENTRY CLERKS             $ 250.00

     3          PROGRAMMER TRAINEES           $ 300.00

     2          RECORDS CLERKS                $ 225.00

     1          DATA PROCESSING MANAGER       $ 825.00

     2          OPERATOR SUPERVISORS          $ 450.00
```

Programming Assignment 4-3: AVERAGE ITEMIZED DEDUCTION REPORT

```
Line   <-------------------- Source Specifications -------------------------><---- Comments ----> Do
Number ....1....+....2....+....3....+....4....+....5....+....6....+....7....+....8....+....9....+...10 Num
                       S o u r c e   L i s t i n g
   1 * PA 4-3: Average Itemized Deductions For Federal Income Taxes....
   2 FP43PSM    IF  E            DISK
    *--------------------------------------------------------------------------*
    *                          RPG name        External name                  *
    * File name. . . . . . . . : P43PSM        STAN/P43PSM                     *
    * Record format(s) . . . . : P43PSMR       P43PSMR                         *
    *--------------------------------------------------------------------------*
   3 FQsysprt   O   F  132       PRINTER
   4
*RNF2318 00     3 000300  Overflow indicator OA is assigned to PRINTER file QSYSPRT.
   5=IP43PSMR
    *--------------------------------------------------------------------------*
    * RPG record format  . . . . : P43PSMR                                     *
    * External format  . . . . . : P43PSMR : STAN/P43PSM                       *
    *--------------------------------------------------------------------------*
   6=I                          A   1   12 DEDUCTION
   7=I                          P  13   15 01R25_30
   8=I                          P  16   18 01R31_40
   9=I                          P  19   21 01R41_50
  10=I                          P  22   24 01R51_75
  11=I                          P  25   27 01R76_100
  12=I                          P  28   30 01R101_200
  13 C          EXCEPT  Heading                         print heading lines
  14 C          READ    P43psm                ----LR    read first record
  15 C          DOW     *INLR = *OFF                     dow LR is off        B01
  16 C          EXCEPT  Detailine                        print a record        01
  17 C          READ    P43psm                ----LR    read first record      01
  18 C          ENDDO                                    end dow group        E01
```

```
19
20 OQsysprt    E           Heading     3 01
21 O                                          54 'AVERAGE ITEMIZED DEDUCTON'
22 O                                          63 'SCHEDULE'
23 O                       UDATE       Y 92
24 O           E           Heading     1
25 O                                          10 'ITEMIZED'
26 O                                          25 '$25,000-'
27 O                                          38 '$30,000-'
28 O                                          51 '$40,000-'
29 O                                          64 '$50,000-'
30 O                                          78 '$ 75,000-'
31 O                                          92 '$100,000-'
32 O           E           Heading     2
33 O                                          11 'DEDUCTION'
34 O                                          24 '30,000'
35 O                                          37 '40,000'
36 O                                          50 '50,000'
37 O                                          63 '75,000'
38 O                                          77 '100,000'
39 O                                          91 '200,000'
40 O           E           Heading     0
41 O                                          17 '$'
42 O                                          31 '$'
43 O                                          44 '$'
44 O                                          57 '$'
45 O                                          70 '$'
46 O                                          84 '$'
47 O           E           Detailine   2
48 O                       Deduction      12
49 O                       IR25_30     1  23
50 O                       IR31_40     1  37
51 O                       IR41_50     1  50
52 O                       IR51_75     1  63
53 O                       IR76_100    1  77
54 O                       IR101_200   1  91
     * * * * *  E N D   O F   S O U R C E  * * * * *
```

Printed Report:

		AVERAGE ITEMIZED DEDUCTION SCHEDULE				
ITEMIZED DEDUCTION	$25,000- 30,000	$30,000- 40,000	$40,000- 50,000	$50,000- 75,000	$ 75,000- 100,000	$100,000- 200,000
MEDICAL	$ 3,306	$ 3,137	$ 3,612	$ 4,002	$ 6,003	$ 12,087
INTEREST	4,662	5,011	5,667	6,595	8,847	13,324
TAXES	2,069	2,477	3,015	4,049	5,888	9,359
CONTRIBUTION	1,129	1,213	1,315	1,665	2,112	3,442

Programming Assignment 4-4: STUDENT ENROLLMENT REPORT

```
Line   <--------------------- Source Specifications ----------------------><---- Comments ----> Do
Number ....1....+....2....+....3....+....4....+....5....+....6....+....7....+....8....+....9....+...10 Num
                    S o u r c e   L i s t i n g
   1 * PA 4-4: Student Enrollment Report....
   2 FP44PSM   IF  E           DISK
       *-------------------------------------------------------------------------------*
       *                        RPG name           External name                       *
       * File name. . . . . . . . :  P44PSM        STAN/P44PSM                          *
       * Record format(s) . . . . :  P44PSMR       P44PSMR                              *
       *-------------------------------------------------------------------------------*
   3 FQsysprt  O   F 132       PRINTER
   4
*RNF2318 00    3 000300  Overflow indicator OA is assigned to PRINTER file QSYSPRT.
   5=IP44PSMR
       *-------------------------------------------------------------------------------*
       * RPG record format  . . . . :  P44PSMR                                         *
```

Chapter 4 - Report Headings and Editing

```
          * External format . . . . . :  P44PSMR : STAN/P44PSM                        *
      *-----------------------------------------------------------------------------*
    6=I                          P    1    5 OSS_NUMBER
    7=I                          A    6    6 SEX
    8=I                          A    7   36 STU_NAME
    9=I                          P   37   42 OTELEPHONE
   10=I                          A   43   57 TECHNOLOGY
   11=I                          P   58   59 OTEST_MARK
   12 C            EXCEPT     Heading                        print heading lines
   13 C            READ       P44psm               ----LR    read first record
   14 C            DOW        *INLR = *OFF                   dow LR is off          B01
   15 C            EXCEPT     Detailine                      print a record         01
   16 C            READ       P44psm               ----LR    read first record      01
   17 C            ENDDO                                     end dow group         E01
   18
   19 OQsysprt  E         Heading       3 01
   20 O                   UDATE         Y     8
   21 O                                      36 'ENTERING STUDENT'
   22 O                                      59 'ENROLLMENT INFORMATION'
   23 O                                      75 'PAGE'
   24 O                   PAGE                80
   25 O         E         Detailine     1
   26 O                                      28 'STUDENT NUMBER:'
   27 O                   SS_Number           40 '0   -   -    '
   28 O         E         Detailine     1
   29 O                                      26 'STUDENT NAME:'
   30 O                   Stu_Name            59 '*'
   31 O         E         Detailine     1
   32 O                                      23 'TELEPHONE:'
   33 O                   Telephone           38 '0(   )-   -    '
   34 O         E         Detailine     1
   35 O                                      24 'TECHNOLOGY:'
   36 O                   Technology          40
   37 O         E         Detailine     3
   38 O                                      17 'SEX:'
   39 O                   Sex                 19
   40 O                                      62 'ENTRANCE TEST MARK:'
   41 O                   Test_Mark     Z     67
        * * * *  E N D   O F   S O U R C E  * * * *
```

Printed Report:

```
   5/05/98              ENTERING STUDENT ENROLLMENT INFORMATION          PAGE    1


                 STUDENT NUMBER: 011-22-3333
                 STUDENT NAME:   LAMONT CRANSTON
                 TELEPHONE: (203)-777-8888
                 TECHNOLOGY: DATA
                 SEX: M                          ENTRANCE TEST MARK:   90


                 STUDENT NUMBER: 066-44-5432
                 STUDENT NAME:   LOIS LANE
                 TELEPHONE: (212)-999-4322
                 TECHNOLOGY: CHEMISTRY
                 SEX: F                          ENTRANCE TEST MARK:   85


                 STUDENT NUMBER: 124-11-1235
                 STUDENT NAME:   FRANK N STEIN
                 TELEPHONE: (914)-266-8413
                 TECHNOLOGY: ARCHITECTURAL
                 SEX: M                          ENTRANCE TEST MARK:   78


                 STUDENT NUMBER: 077-88-9999
                 STUDENT NAME:   D R ACULA
                 TELEPHONE: (913)-444-5555
                 TECHNOLOGY: PREP PROGRAM
                 SEX: M                          ENTRANCE TEST MARK:   60
```

```
STUDENT NUMBER: 124-11-1235
STUDENT NAME:   REDDI WATT
TELEPHONE: (203)-377-7865
TECHNOLOGY: MECHANICAL
SEX: F                          ENTRANCE TEST MARK:   100
```

CHAPTER 5
QUESTION ANSWERS

1. Provides for free-format numeric, logical, relational, and character expressions.

2. Addition +; Subtraction -; Multiplicaton *; Division /; and Exponentiation **.

3. First: Exponentiation **; second: division /; third: addition +; fourth: subtraction -.

4. In FLDA. The field to the left of the equal sign.

5. Half rounds the value stored in FLDA.

6. In the physical file, logical file or *Definition, Input,* or *Calculation Specification* instructions of an RPG IV program.

7. First: addition + (within the parentheses); second: the FLDB * 1.5 function; tird: division /; fourth: the last multiplication * function.

8. In FLDX. The field to the left of the equal sign.

9. Numeric literal. Numeric entries: 30 with a maximum of 30 decimal positions. Character entries: 256.

10. In FLDD. The field to the left of the equal sign.

11. FLDF

12. FDLE

13. In FLDM. The field to the left of the equal sign.

14. Either FLDN or FLDO.

15. Either FLDN or FLDO.

16. In FLDH. The field to the left of the equal sign.

17. FLDJ

18. FLDI

19. In FLDQ. The field to the left of the equal sign.

20. Either FLDR or FLDS.

21. **MVR** (*Move Remainder*) and **SQRT** (*Square Root*).

22. Because the remainder of the division is to be saved, the EVAL expression cannot be used. Instead, the traditional RPG solution is specified.

```
*.. 1 ...+... 2 ...+... 3 ...+... 4 ...+... 5 ...+... 6 ...+... 7 ...+... 8
CLON01Factor1+++++++Opcode&ExtFactor2+++++++Result+++++++Len++D+HiLoEq....
C    FLDL        DIV      FLDM       FLDN
C                MVR                 FLDO
```

23.

```
*.. 1 ...+... 2 ...+... 3 ...+... 4 ...+... 5 ...+... 6 ...+... 7 ...+... 8
CLON01Factor1+++++++Opcode&ExtFactor2+++++++Result+++++++Len++D+HiLoEq....
C                SQRT     FLDG       FLDJ
```

24. Figurative
    <u>Constant</u>   <u>Function</u>

   *BLANK/*BLANKS   Value of blanks. May only be used with character fields.

   *ZERO/*ZEROS   Value of zeros. May be used with any field type.

   *HIVAL   Value of 9s for numeric fields and hexidecimal FFs for character fields.

   *LOVAL   Value of negative 9s for numeric fields and hexidecimal zeros for character fields.

   *ALL'X...'   Value in the X string is repeated and stored in the Result field item.

   *ON   Indicates that the item contains all 1s.

   *OFF   Indicates that the item contains all 0s.

   *NULL   Null value used with pointers.

25. (1) 45.29;   (2) 100.00;   (3) .46

26.

```
*.. 1 ...+... 2 ...+... 3 ...+... 4 ...+... 5 ...+... 6 ...+... 7 ...+... 8
CLON01Factor1+++++++Opcode&ExtFactor2+++++++Result+++++++Len++D+HiLoEq....
C                EVAL        *INLR = *ON
```

27.

```
*.. 1 ...+... 2 ...+... 3 ...+... 4 ...+... 5 ...+... 6 ...+... 7 ...+... 8
CLON01Factor1+++++++Opcode&ExtFactor2+++++++Result+++++++Len++D+HiLoEq....
C                EVAL        AmtPaid = *ALL'*'
```

28.

```
*.. 1 ...+... 2 ...+... 3 ...+... 4 ...+... 5 ...+... 6 ...+...-7 ...+... 8
CLON01Factor1+++++++Opcode&ExtFactor2+++++++Result+++++++Len++D+HiLoEq....
C                EVAL        CompTotal = *ZEROS
```

29.

```
*.. 1 ...+... 2 ...+... 3 ...+... 4 ...+... 5 ...+... 6 ...+... 7 ...+... 8
CLON01Factor1+++++++Opcode&ExtFactor2+++++++Result+++++++Len++D+HiLoEq....
C                EVAL        ProcessMode = *BLANKS
```

30. ***IN** initializes a predefined **99** element - one position array elements to zeros.

31. Array element **90** is initialized to blank.

32. Indicator **LR** is turned on.

33. With an **EVAL**, **MOVE**, **MOVEL**, or **Z-ADD** instruction. Note that fields specified in *Definition Specification* instructions may be initialized to a value with the **INZ** keyword.

34. With an **EVAL**, **MOVE**, or **MOVEL** instruction. Note that fields specified in Definition Specification instructions may be initialized to va value with the **INZ** keyword.

35. **ADD, SUB, MULT, DIV, MVR,** and **SQRT.** Entered in SEU with the C format.

36. The function of the **SETON** operation is to turn on one, two, or three indicators for some program function specified in the *HiLoEq* fields of a calculation instruction.

    The function of the **SETOF** operation is to turn off one, two, or three indicators specified in the HiLoEq fields of a calculation instruction. This operation is often used as a housekeeping function to turn off indicators that are not automatically turned off when the next record is processed. One, two, or three indicators may be turned on by one **SETON** operation or off by one **SETOF** operation.

37. After **MOVE** instruction is executed:
FLDA	FLDB
12345	0012345

38. After **MOVE** instruction is executed:
FLDC	FLDD
ABCDEF	DEF

39. After **MOVEL** instruction is executed:
FLDP	FLDQ
ABCDEF	ABC

40. After **MOVEL** instruction is executed:
FLDR	FLDS
1234	0001234

41. YES. YES.

42. NO.

PROGRAMMING ASSIGNMENTS

Notes to the instructor:

1. Emphasize that the student must determine the *Result*

Field sizes for the calculation statements required in these assignments.

2. Stress that mathematical proof (bench testing) is necessary to determine if the report generated by the student's program is correct.

Programming Assignment 5-1: COMPUTATION OF SIMPLE INTEREST

```
Line   <--------------------- Source Specifications ------------------------><---- Comments ----> Do
Number ....1....+....2....+....3....+....4....+....5....+....6....+....7....+....8....+....9....+...10 Nu
                         S o u r c e   L i s t i n g
    1 * PA 5-1: Computation of Simple Interest....
    2 FP51psm    IF  E           DISK
      *--------------------------------------------------------------------------------------------*
      *                                   RPG name           External name                        *
      * File name. . . . . . . . :        P51PSM             STAN/P51PSM                           *
      * Record format(s) . . . . :        P51PSMR            P51PSMR                               *
      *--------------------------------------------------------------------------------------------*
    3 FQsysprt   O   F 132        PRINTER
    4
*RNF2318 00    3 000300  Overflow indicator OA is assigned to PRINTER file QSYSPRT.
    5 DInterest        S             8 2              **
    6 DAmountDue       S             9 2
    7 DAnnum_Rate      S             5 3
    8
    9=IP51PSMR

      *--------------------------------------------------------------------------------------------*
      * RPG record format  . . . . :      P51PSMR                                                  *
      * External format  . . . . . :      P51PSMR : STAN/P51PSM                                    *
      *--------------------------------------------------------------------------------------------*

   10=I                         P   1   3 0LOAN_NO
   11=I                         P   4   8 2PRINCIPAL
   12=I                         P   9  11 5INTRATE
   13=I                         P  12  14 0LOANDATE
   14 C                EXCEPT    Headings
   15 C                READ      P51psm                          ----LR    read first record
   16 C                DOW       *INLR = *OFF                               dow LR is off         B01
   17 C                EVAL      Annum_Rate = IntRate * 100                 pct expression        01
   18 C                EVAL (H)  Interest = Principal * IntRate * LoanDate                        01
   19 C                          / 365                                      compute interest      01
   20 C                EVAL      AmountDue = Principal + Interest                                 01
   21 C                EXCEPT    Detailine                                  print detail line     01
   22 C                READ      P51psm                          ----LR    read first record     01
   23 C                ENDDO                                                end dow group         E01
   24
   25 C                EVAL      *INLR = *ON                                end program
   26 OQsysprt   E          Headings         3 01
   27 O                                               42 'SIMPLE INTEREST LOAN'
   28 O                                               58 'SCHEDULES AS OF'
   29 O                          UDATE         Y      67
   30 O          E          Headings          1
   31 O                                                7 'LOAN'
   32 O                                               38 'INTEREST RATE'
   33 O                                               49 'TIME IN'
   34 O                                               63 'INTEREST'
   35 O                                               76 'TOTAL'
   36 O          E          Headings          2
   37 O                                                8 'NUMBER'
   38 O                                               20 'PRINCIPAL'
   39 O                                               34 '/ANNUM'
   40 O                                               47 'DAYS'
   41 O                                               61 'ON LOAN'
   42 O                                               78 'AMOUNT DUE'
   43 O          E          Detailine         2
   44 O                          Loan_No             7
   45 O                                               11 '$'
   46 O                          Principal    1       21
   47 O                          Annum_Rate   1       33
   48 O                                               34 '%'
```

```
49 O              LoanDate    Z    47
50 O                               53 '$'
51 O              interest    1    62
52 O                               67 '$'
53 O              AmountDue   1    79
     * * * *  E N D  O F  S O U R C E  * * * *
```

Printed Report:

```
              SIMPLE INTEREST LOAN SCHEDULES AS OF  7/29/98


   LOAN              INTEREST RATE   TIME IN    INTEREST      TOTAL
  NUMBER  PRINCIPAL     /ANNUM        DAYS      ON LOAN    AMOUNT DUE

   10000  $120,000.00   8.500%        120      3,353.42  $  123,353.42

   10001  $  3,000.00   7.000%        185        106.44  $    3,106.44

   10002  $ 10,250.00   9.100%        730      1,865.50  $   12,115.50

   10003  $    475.00  10.250%         90         12.01  $      487.01

   10004  $  1,000.00  12.125%         60         19.93  $    1,019.93
```

Programming Assignment 5-2: GROSS PROFIT ANALYSIS REPORT

```
Line   <--------------------- Source Specifications --------------------------><---- Comments ----> Do
Number ....1....+....2....+....3....+....4....+....5....+....6....+....7....+....8....+....9....+...10 Num
                         S o u r c e   L i s t i n g
   1 * PA 5-2: Gross Profit Analysis Report....
   2 FP52psm   IF  E           DISK
     *-------------------------------------------------------------------------------------------*
     *                          RPG name         External name                                  *
     * File name. . . . . . . . : P52PSM          STAN/P52PSM                                    *
     * Record format(s) . . . . : P52PSMR         P52PSMR                                        *
     *-------------------------------------------------------------------------------------------*
   3 FQsysprt  O   F 132         PRINTER
   4
*RNF2318 00    3 000300  Overflow indicator OA is assigned to PRINTER file QSYSPRT.
   5 DHold1          S             3 2
   6 DHold2          S             3 2
   7 DHold3          S             3 2
   8 DPercent        S             5 5                          trade discount pct
   9 DNet_SP         S             6 2                          net selling price
  10 DTradeDscnt     S             6 2                          trade discount
  11 DGrossProft     S             6 2                          gross profit
  12 DGPDecimal      S             5 5                          gross profit decimal
  13 DGPPercent      S             5 3                          GP percent
  14
  15=IP52PSMR
     *-------------------------------------------------------------------------------------------*
     * RPG record format  . . . . : P52PSMR                                                      *
     * External format  . . . . . : P52PSMR : STAN/P52PSM                                        *
     *-------------------------------------------------------------------------------------------*
  16=I                       P    1    2 0ITEM_NO
  17=I                       A    3   32  DESCRPTION
  18=I                       P   33   36 2CATALOGLST
  19=I                       P   37   38 2DISCOUNT1
  20=I                       P   39   40 2DISCOUNT2
  21=I                       P   41   42 2DISCOUNT3
  22=I                       P   43   46 2ITEM_COST
  23 C           EXCEPT     Headings
  24 C           READ       P52psm                    ----LR   read first record
  25 C           DOW        *INLR = *OFF                       dow LR is off         R01
  26 C           EVAL       Hold1 = 1.00 - Discount1           pct expression         01
  27 C           EVAL       Hold2 = 1.00 - Discount2           pct expression         01
  28 C           EVAL       Hold3 = 1.00 - Discount3           pct expression         01
  29 C           EVAL       Percent = Hold1 * Hold2            compute percent        01
```

41

```
  30
  31 C                    IF         Discount3 > 0                              greater than zero?  BO:
  32 C                    EVAL       Percent = Percent * Hold3                   Hold3 > 0            0:
  33 C                    ENDIF                                                  end IF group         EO:
  34
  35 C                    EVAL(H)    Net_SP = CatalogLst * Percent               Net Selling Price    O
  36 C                    EVAL       TradeDscnt = CatalogLst - Net_SP            compute trade discnt O
  37 C                    EVAL       GrossProft = Net_SP - Item_Cost             compute net SP       O
  38 C                    EVAL (H)   GPDecimal = GrossProft / Net_SP             compute GP decimal   O
  39 C                    EVAL       GPPercent = GPDecimal * 100                 compute GP percent   O
  40 C                    EXCEPT     Detailine                                   print detail line    O
  41 C                    READ       P52psm                          ----LR      read first record    O
  42 C                    ENDDO                                                  end dow group        EO
  43
  44 C                    EVAL       *INLR = *ON                                 end program
  45 OQsysprt   E              Headings        3 01
  46 O                                                  62 'GROSS PROFIT ANALYSIS'
  47 O                                                  69 'REPORT'
  48 O                              UDATE         Y     112
  49 O          E              Headings        1
  50 O                                                  53 'CATALOG'
  51 O                                                  64 'TRADE'
  52 O                                                  81 'NET SELLING'
  53 O                                                  98 'GROSS'
  54 O                                                 110 'GROSS'
  55 O          E              Headings        2
  56 O                                                   9 'ITEM#'
  57 O                                                  31 'DESCRIPTION'
  58 O                                                  51 'LIST'
  59 O                                                  65 'DISCOUNT'
  60 O                                                  78 'PRICE'
  61 O                                                  88 'COST'
  62 O                                                  99 'PROFIT'
  63 O                                                 112 'PROFIT %'
  64 O          E              Detailine       2
  65 O                         Item_No                   7
  66 O                         Descrption               40
  67 O                         CatalogLst     1         53
  68 O                         TradeDscnt     1         65
  69 O                         Net_SP         1         79
  70 O                         Item_Cost      1         90
  71 O                         GrossProft     1        100
  72 O                         GPPercent      1        110
  73 O                                                 112 '%'
       * * * *   E N D   O F   S O U R C E   * * * *
```

Printed Report:

		CATALOG LIST	TRADE DISCOUNT	NET SELLING PRICE	COST	GROSS PROFIT	GROSS PROFIT %
	GROSS PROFIT ANALYSIS REPORT						7/29/98
ITEM#	DESCRIPTION						
720	BROTHER JR-35 PRINTER	1,400.00	562.10	837.90	610.00	227.90	27.199
776	EXP-770 SILVER REED PRINTER	1,495.00	536.33	958.67	730.00	228.67	23.853
789	JUKI 6100 PRINTER	599.00	112.46	486.54	375.00	111.54	22.925
799	P12 DIABLO SYSTEMS PRINTER	699.00	134.56	564.44	345.00	219.44	38.877
820	H-P LASERJET+ PRINTER	3,495.00	805.60	2,689.40	2,268.00	421.40	15.669

Programming Assignment 5-3: DETERMINATION OF ECONOMIC ORDER QUANTIT

```
 Line    <--------------------- Source Specifications ----------------------------><---- Comments ----> Do
 Number  ....1....+....2....+....3....+....4....+....5....+....6....+....7....+....8....+....9....+...10 Nu
                  S o u r c e   L i s t i n g
    1 * PA 5-3: Determination of Economic Order Quantity....
    2 FP53psm   IF   E            DISK
```

```
      *--------------------------------------------------------------------------*
      *                              RPG name        External name               *
      * File name. . . . . . . . . : P53PSM          STAN/P53PSM                 *
      * Record format(s) . . . . . : P53PSMR         P53PSMR                     *
      *--------------------------------------------------------------------------*
    3 FQsysprt   O   F  132       PRINTER
    4
*RNF2318 00     3 000300  Overflow indicator OA is assigned to PRINTER file QSYSPRT.
    5 DHold1              S              10 0
    6 DHold2              S               9 6
    7 DHold3              S               7 6
    8 DEoq                S               4 0
    9 DOrdPerYr           S               3 0
   10
   11=IP53PSMR

      *--------------------------------------------------------------------------*
      * RPG record format . . . . : P53PSMR                                      *
      * External format . . . . . : P53PSMR : STAN/P53PSM                        *
      *--------------------------------------------------------------------------*
   12=I                        A    1    25 ITEMNM
   13=I                        P   26    28 0USAGE
   14=I                        P   29    30 0ORDCST
   15=I                        P   31    33 2UNTCST
   16=I                        P   34    36 4CARCST
   17 C           EXCEPT    Headings
   18 C           READ      P53psm                          ----LR   read first record
   19 C           DOW       *INLR = *OFF        **                   dow LR is off         B01
   20 C          ·EVAL      Hold1 = 2 * Usage * OrdCst                numerator of equatn   01
   21 C           EVAL      Hold2 = UntCst * CarCst                   denomerator           01
   22 C           EVAL(H)   Hold3 = Hold1 / Hold2                     quotient              01
   23 C           SQRT      Hold3            Eoq                      compute eoq           01
   24 C           EVAL(H)   OrdPerYr = Usage / Eoq                    orders per year       01
   25
   26 C           EXCEPT    Detailine                                print detail line     01
   27 C           READ      P53psm                          ----LR   read first record     01
   28 C           ENDDO                                              end dow group         E01
   29
   30 C           EVAL      *INLR = *ON                              end program
   31 OQsysprt  E          Headings      2 01
   32 O                    *DATE         Y     10
   33 O                                        31 'ECONOMIC ORDER'
   34 O                                        55 'QUANTITIES OF INVENTORY'
   35 O                                        61 'ITEMS'
   36 O                                        74 'PAGE'
   37 O                    PAGE                80
   38 O         E          Headings      2
   39 O                                        18 'ITEM NAME'
   40 O                                        45 'ANNUAL USAGE'
   41 O                                        55 'EOQ'
   42 O                                        76 'ORDERS PER YEAR'
   43 O         E          Detailine     2
   44 O                    ItemNm              25
   45 O                    Usage         2     43
   46 O                    Eoq           2     55
   47 O                    OrdPerYr      2     69
      * * * * *  E N D   O F   S O U R C E  * * * * *
```

Printed Report:

7/29/1998	ECONOMIC ORDER QUANTITIES OF INVENTORY ITEMS		PAGE	1
	ITEM NAME	ANNUAL USAGE	EOQ	ORDERS PER YEAR
LEFT-HAND MONKEY WRENCH		10,000	1,264	8
MEN'S DIESEL SHAVER		20,000	632	32
ATOMIC TOOTHBRUSH		40,000	318	126
FUEL-INJECTED LAWN MOWER		200	8	25
LASER TOOTHPICKS		30,000	1,608	19

Chapter 5 - EVAL Expression and Arithmetic Functions

Programming Assignment 5-4: UNION PROPOSAL FOR HOURLY EMPLOYEES

```
Line   <--------------------- Source Specifications --------------------------><---- Comments ----> Do
Number ....1....+....2....+....3....+....4....+....5....+....6....+....7....+....8....+....9....+...10 Num
                             S o u r c e   L i s t i n g
     1 * PA 5-4: Union Proposal For Hourly Employees....
     2 FP54psm    IF   E            DISK
       *--------------------------------------------------------------------------------*
       *                                RPG name        External name                   *
       * File name. . . . . . . . . : P54PSM          STAN/P54PSM                       *
       * Record format(s) . . . . . : P55PSMR         P55PSMR                           *
       *--------------------------------------------------------------------------------*
     3 FQsysprt   O    F  132        PRINTER
     4
*RNF2318 00      3 000300  Overflow indicator OA is assigned to PRINTER file QSYSPRT.
     5 DCurrentWP         S              6 2
     6 DPropRate          S              4 2
     7 DProposedWP        S              6 2
     8 DTotProWP          S              8 2
     9 DTotCurWP          S              8 2
    10 DProIncreas        S              8 2
    11
    12=IP55PSMR
       *--------------------------------------------------------------------------------*
       * RPG record format  . . . . : P55PSMR                                           *
       * External format  . . . . . : P55PSMR : STAN/P54PSM                             *
       *--------------------------------------------------------------------------------*
    13=I                         P    1    5 OSS_NUMBER
    14=I                         A    6   25 EMPLOYEE
    15=I                         P   26   28 2HRLY_RATE
    16 C           EXCEPT    Headings                         print headings
    17 C           READ      P54psm              ----LR       read first record
    18 C           DOW       *INLR = *OFF                     dow LR is off          B01
    19 C           EVAL(H)   CurrentWP = Hrly_Rate * 35       compute current wp     01
    20 C           EVAL      TotCurWP = TotCurWP + CurrentWP  accum CurrentWP        01
    21 C           EVAL(H)   PropRate = Hrly_Rate * 1.07      Proposed Hrly Rate     01
    22 C           EVAL      ProposedWP = PropRate * 35       Total Proposed WP      01
    23 C           EVAL      TotProWP = TotProWP + ProposedWP accum CurrentWP        01
    24 C           EVAL      ProIncreas = TotProWP - TotCurWP Proposed Increase      01
    25
    26 C           EXCEPT    Detailine                        print detail line      01
    27 C           READ      P54psm              ----LR       read next record       01
    28 C           ENDDO                                      end dow group          E01
    29
    30 C           MOVE      *ALL'-'   Line        80         load line value
    31 C           EXCEPT    TotaLines                        print total lines
    32 C
    33 C           EVAL      *INLR = *ON                      end program
    34 OQsysprt   E          Headings      2 01
    35 O                     *DATE       Y    10
    36 O                                      47 'UNION PROPOSAL FOR HOURLY'
    37 O                                      57 'EMPLOYEES'
    38 O                                      75 'PAGE'
    39 O                     PAGE             80
    40 O         E          Headings      3
    41 O                                      28 'WORK WEEK: 35 HOURS'
    42 O                                      72 'PROPOSED INCREASE: 7.0%'
    43 O         E          Headings      1
    44 O                                      33 'CURRENT'
    45 O                                      48 'CURRENT'
    46 O                                      63 'PROPOSED'
    47 O                                      78 'PROPOSED'
    48 O         E          Headings      2
    49 O                                      16 'EMPLOYEE NAME'
    50 O                                      35 'HOURLY RATE'
    51 O                                      49 'WEEKLY PAY'
    52 O                                      64 'HOURLY RATE'
    53 O                                      79 'WEEKLY PAY'
    54 O         E          Detailine     2
    55 O                     Employee         20
    56 O                     Hrly_Rate     1  32
    57 O                     CurrentWP     1  48
```

44

```
58 O                    PropRate        1    62
59 O                    ProposedWP      1    78
60 O           E        TotaLines       2
61 O                    Line                 80
62 O           E        TotaLines       2
63 O                                         10 'SUMMARY:'
64 O           E        TotaLines       1
65 O                                         28 'TOTAL PROPOSED WEEKLY PAY:'
66 O                                         30 'S'
67 O                    TotProWP        1    40
68 O           E        TotaLines       2
69 O                                         27 'TOTAL CURRENT WEEKLY PAY:'
70 O                    TotCurWP        1    40
71 O           E        TotaLines       0
72 O                                         27 'PROPOSED WEEKLY INCREASE:'
73 O                                         30 'S'
74 O                    ProIncreas      1    40
     * * * * *  E N D   O F  S O U R C E  * * * * *
```

Printed Report:

```
7/30/1998          UNION PROPOSAL FOR HOURLY EMPLOYEES          PAGE   1

     WORK WEEK: 35 HOURS                  PROPOSED INCREASE: 7.0%


                        CURRENT       CURRENT       PROPOSED      PROPOSED
     EMPLOYEE NAME    HOURLY RATE    WEEKLY PAY    HOURLY RATE   WEEKLY PAY

     HENRY WADSWORTH    10.00         350.00         10.70        374.50

     JOHN BYRON         12.50         437.50         13.38        468.30

     EDGAR POE          10.25         358.75         10.97        383.95

     JAMES LONGFELLOW   15.00         525.00         16.05        561.75

     WILLIAM SHAKESPEARE 16.00        560.00         17.12        599.20

     ------------------------------------------------------------------
     SUMMARY:

     TOTAL PROPOSED WEEKLY PAY: S  2,387.70
     TOTAL CURRENT WEEKLY PAY:     2,231.25

     PROPOSED WEEKLY INCREASE: S    156.45
```

Programming Assignment 5-5: CERTIFICATES OF DEPOSIT ANALYSIS REPORT

```
Line  <---------------------- Source Specifications -----------------------><---- Comments ----> Do
Number ....1....+....2....+....3....+....4....+....5....+....6....+....7....+....8....+....9....+...10 Num
                       S o u r c e   L i s t i n g
   1 * PA 5-5: Certificates of Deposit Analysis Report....
   2 FP55psm    IF E          DISK
     *------------------------------------------------------------------------------------*
     *                         RPG name          External name                            *
     * File name. . . . . . . . : P55PSM          STAN/P55PSM                             *
     * Record format(s) . . . . . : P55PSMR        P55PSMR                                *
     *------------------------------------------------------------------------------------*
   3 FQsysprt   O   F 132       PRINTER
   4
*RNF2318 00    3 000300  Overflow indicator OA is assigned to PRINTER file QSYSPRT.
   5 DDailyRate      S           9 9
   6 DCompondAmt     S           8 2
   7 DCompondInt     S           8 2
   8 DDailyPct       S           8 8                        trade discount pct
   9 DAnnPct         S           5 3                        net selling price
  10
  11=IP55PSMR
     *------------------------------------------------------------------------------------*
     * RPG record format  . . . . : P55PSMR                                               *
     * External format  . . . . . : P55PSMR : STAN/P55PSM                                 *
     *------------------------------------------------------------------------------------*
```

45

```
12=I                          A    1    4  ACCTNO
13=I                          P    5    9 2PRINCIPAL
14=I                          P   10   12 5ANNRATE
15=I                          P   13   14 0ANNPERDS
16=I                          P   15   17 0TIMEINDAYS
17 C            EXCEPT    Headings
18 C            READ      P55psm                      ----LR   read first record
19 C            DOW       *INLR = *OFF                         dow LR is off         B01
20 C            EVAL      DailyRate = AnnRate / AnnPerds        compute daily rate    01
21 C            EVAL      CompondAmt = Principal * (1 + DailyRate) **               01
22 C                      TimeInDays                                                 01
23 C            EVAL      CompondInt = CompondAmt - Principal                        01
24 C            EVAL      DailyPct = DailyRate * 100            pct expression        01
25 C            EVAL      AnnPct = AnnRate * 100                pct expression        01
26
27 C            EXCEPT    Detailine                            print detail line     01
28 C            READ      P55psm                      ----LR   read first record     01
29 C            ENDDO                                          end dow group         E01
30
31 C            EVAL      *INLR = *ON                          end program
32 OQsysprt  E            Headings        1 01
33 O                      UDATE         Y    8
34 O                                        50 'CERTIFICATES OF DEPOSIT'
35 O                                        59 'ANALYSIS'
36 O                                        77 'PAGE'
37 O                      PAGE              83
38 O         E            Headings        3       *)
39 O                                        49 'INTEREST COMPOUNDED'
40 O                                        55 'DAILY'
41 O         E            Headings        1
42 O                                        32 'ANNUAL'
43 O                                        43 'DAILY'
44 O                                        56 'INTEREST'
45 O                                        67 'COMPOUND'
46 O                                        79 'COMPOUND'
47 O         E            Headings        2
48 O                                         8 'ACT NO'
49 O                                        20 'PRINCIPAL'
50 O                                        31 'RATE'
51 O                                        43 'RATE'
52 O                                        54 'DAYS'
53 O                                        66 'AMOUNT'
54 O                                        79 'INTEREST'
55 O         E            Detailine       2
56 O                      AcctNo               7
57 O                      Principal      1    20
58 O                      AnnPct         1    30
59 O                                        31 'X'
60 O                      DailyPct       1    43
61 O                                        44 'X'
62 O                      TimeInDays     Z    53
63 O                      CompondAmt     1    67
64 O                      CompondInt     1    79
   * * * * *   E N D   O F   S O U R C E   * * * *
```

Printed Report:

7/29/98		CERTIFICATES OF DEPOSIT ANALYSIS INTEREST COMPOUNDED DAILY				PAGE 1
ACT NO	PRINCIPAL	ANNUAL RATE	DAILY RATE	INTEREST DAYS	COMPOUND AMOUNT	COMPOUND INTEREST
1000	1,000.00	10.000%	.02739720%	365	1,105.15	105.15
2000	1,000.00	10.000%	.02739720%	180	1,050.54	50.54
3000	1,000.00	6.500%	.01780820%	365	1,067.15	67.15
4000	1,000.00	6.500%	.01780820%	180	1,032.57	32.57

CHAPTER 6
QUESTION ANSWERS

1. **IF, ELSE, DO, DOU, DOW, CAS, SELECT, WHEN, OTHER.** They reduce or eliminate the need for test and conditioning indicators.

2. The function of the **IF** operation is to test the *Factor 1* and *2* field or literal values for a one or more relational conditions. An **ELSE** statement controls the false action when the **IF** statement test is false.

3. **GT, LT, EQ, GE, LE, NE**

4. With an **AND** or **OR** operators or combinations of the two.

5. YES. NO, an **ELSE** operation must be specified with a related **IF** statement.

6. An **ENDIF** or **END** operation.   ••

7. Instructions 2, 5, and 6.

8. Instructions 3, 4, 5, and 6.

9. Indicates the end of an **IF** or **IF/ELSE** group of statements. The **ENDIF** or **END** statement is always required with an **IF** statement.

10. True and False action.

11. *Factor 1* and *2* items must be the same type (numeric/numeric or character/character.

12. Instructions on lines 3, 6, and 7.

13. Instructions on lines 4, 5, 6, and 7.

14. Instructions on lines 4. 5, 6, and 7.

15. When one or both of the test conditions specified in the **IF** statement is/are false as indicated in the answers for questions 13 and 14.

16. After the **IF** or **ELSE** group of instructions are executed.

17. Yes, in an **AND** relationship all tests must be made.

18. Instructions on lines 3, 6, and 7.

19. Instructions on lines 3, 6, and 7.

20. Instructions on lines 3, 6, and 7.

21. When one or both of the relational tests on lines 1 or 2 is false.

22. After the **IF** or **ELSE** group of instructions are executed.

23. NO. If the first test is true, the second one is not tested.

24. **DO, DOU,** and **DOW.** The **DO** operation does not require a programmer-supplied counter for loop control.

25. The *Factor 1* entry initializes the index (Times) specified in the *Result field* to 2. If a *Factor 1* entry is not made, the counter will be automatically initialized to 1.

26. The *Factor 2* entry (IntPeriods) specifies the number of times the **DO** loop is to be executed.

27. The *Result* field entry (Times) is the programmer-supplied index that at is automatically incremented by 1 for every pass through the **DO** group. Incrementation of the index may be changed by including the required numeric literal, field, array, table or data structure name in *Factor 2* of the **END** (or **ENDDO**) operation.

28. The required **END** (or **ENDDO**) operation indicates the end of the **DO** group. The *Factor 2* entry 2 increments the index by 2 for every iteration instead of default 1.

29. Exit from the **DO** group will occur when the value in the index (Times) is greater than the item in *Factor 2* (IntPeriods).

30. Only a greater than relational test.

31. Instructions 2 and 3.

32. At the **ENDDO** instruction on line 3.

33. With a programmer-supplied counter.

34. The **DOW** operation performs the relational test at the **DOW** instruction, whereas the **DOU** operation tests the condition at its related **END** (or **ENDDO**) operation.

35. Instructions 2 and 3.

36. At the **DOW** statement on line 1.

37. With a programmer-supplied counter.

38. Both must be the same type (numeric or character).

39. Specifically, the **WHEN** and **OTHER** operations. However, any RPG IV operations may be included within the **SELECT** group.

40. The **WHEN** operation.

41. Instructions on lines 3, 8, and then the instruction following line 8.

42. The **WHEN** instruction on line 4 is tested.

43. Instructions on lines 5, 8, and then the instruction following line 8.

44. Instructions on lines 6, 7, 8, and then the instruction following line 8.

45. Instructions on lines 6, 7, 8, and then the instruction following line 8.

46. **SELEC, WHxx, OTHER, IFxx, ELSE, DO, DOWxx,** and **DOUxx.** The **xx** entry must be **EQ, GT, LT, GE, LE,** or **NE.**

46. The **COMP** (*Compare*) operation.

47. The **GOTO** operation with a related **TAG** label.

48. The **CAB** (*Compare and Branch*) operation.

PROGRAMMING ASSIGNMENTS

Notes to the Instructor:

1. Inform the class that any conditioning indicators specified in calculations will <u>not</u> be acceptable. For this and subsequent chapter, all programs must use one or more of the structured operations when applicable.

Programming Assignment 6-1: SALES JOURNAL

```
|Line   <---------------------- Source Specifications --------------------------><---- Comments ----> Do |
|Number ....1....+....2....+....3....+....4....+....5....+....6....+....7....+....8....+....9....+...10 Num|
                             S o u r c e   L i s t i n g
    1 * PA 6-1: Sales Journal....
    2 FP61psm   IF  E           DISK
      *------------------------------------------------------------------------------------------------*
      *                                 RPG name        External name                                  *
      * File name. . . . . . . . . :    P61PSM          STAN/P61PSM                                     *
      * Record format(s) . . . . . :    P61PSMR         P61PSMR                                         *
      *------------------------------------------------------------------------------------------------*
    3 FQsysprt  O   F  132       PRINTER OFLIND(*INOF)
    4
    5 DSalesTax      S            6 2
    6 DGrossSale     S            8 2
    7 DTotalSales    S            8 2
    8 DTotalTax      S            7 2
    9 DTotalGross    S            9 2
   10
   11=IP61PSMR
      *------------------------------------------------------------------------------------------------*
      * RPG record format  . . . . :    P61PSMR                                                         *
      * External format  . . . . . :    P61PSMR : STAN/P61PSM                                           *
      *------------------------------------------------------------------------------------------------*
   12=I                          P   1    4 OSALEDATE
   13=I                          A   5   33  CUSTNAME
```

49

```
14=I                             P  34    37 OINVOICE#
15=I                             P  38    41 2SALEAMOUNT
16 C                EVAL       *INOF = *ON                              turn on OF indicator
17 C                READ       P61psm                        ----LR     read first record
18 C                DOW        *INLR = *OFF                             dow LR is off          B01
19
20 * Heading control....
21 C                IF         *INOF = *ON                              OF indicator on?       B02
22 C                EXCEPT     Headings                                 print heading lines    02
23 C                EVAL       *INOF = *OFF                             turn off OF indicatr   02
24 C                ENDIF                                               end IF group           E02
25
26 C                SELECT                                              begin select group     B02
27 C                WHEN       SaleAmount = *ZERO                       equal to zero?         X02
28 C                EXCEPT     ErrorLine1                               print zero msg         02
29 C                WHEN       SaleAmount < *ZERO                       less than zero?        X02
30 C                EXCEPT     Errorline2                               print negative msg     02
31 C                OTHER                                               positive SaleAmount    X02
32 C                EVAL(H)    SalesTax = SaleAmount * .075             compute SalesTax       02
33 C                EVAL       GrossSale = SaleAmount + SalesTax        compute GrossSales     02
34 C                EXCEPT     GoodLine                                 print good record      02
35 C                EVAL       TotalSales = TotalSales + SaleAmount     compute TotalSales     02
36 C                EVAL       TotalTax = TotalTax + SalesTax           compute TotalTax       02
37 C                EVAL       TotalGross = TotalGross + GrossSale      compute TotalGross     02
38 C                ENDSL                                               end SELECT group       E02
39 C                                                                                           E02
40 C                READ       P61psm                        ----LR     read next record       01
41 C                ENDDO                         *'                    end dow group          E01
42
43 C                EXCEPT     TotalLine                                print total line
44 C                EVAL       *INLR = *ON                              end job
45
46 OQsysprt  E            Headings     2    03
47 O                   UDATE        Y    9
48 O                                     56 'SALES JOURNAL'
49 O                                     94 'PAGE'
50 O                   PAGE              99
51 O         E            Headings     1
52 O                                    100 'TOTAL AMOUNT'
53 O         E            Headings     2
54 O                                      7 'DATE'
55 O                                     34 'ACCOUNT DEBITED'
56 O                                     56 'INVOICE NO.'
57 O                                     72 'AMOUNT OF SALE'
58 O                                     85 'SALES TAX'
59 O                                     97 'OF SALE'
60 O         E            GoodLine     2    03
61 O                   SaleDate     Y    9
62 O                   CustName          42
63 O                   Invoice#     Z    52
64 O                   SaleAmount   1    69
65 O                   SalesTax     1    84
66 O                   GrossSale    1    99
67 O         E            ErrorLine1   2
68 O                   SaleDate     Y    9
69 O                   CustName          42
70 O                   Invoice#     Z    52
71 O                                     82 'SALE AMOUNT ZERO ...'
72 O         E            ErrorLine2   2
73 O                   SaleDate     Y    9
74 O                   CustName          42
75 O                   Invoice#     Z    52
76 O                                     86 'SALE AMOUNT NEGATIVE ...'
77 O         E            TotalLine    1
78 O                   TotalSales   1    69
79 O                   TotalTax     1    84
80 O                   TotalGross   1    99
   * * * * *  E N D  O F  S O U R C E  * * * * *
```

Printed Report:

8/31/96	SALES JOURNAL	PAGE	1
		TOTAL AMOUNT	

DATE	ACCOUNT DEBITED	INVOICE NO.	AMOUNT OF SALE	SALES TAX	OF SALE
8/01/96	HUDSON MOTOR CAR COMPANY	40000	812.00	60.90	872.90
8/09/96	PACKARD COMPANY	40001	SALE AMOUNT ZERO ...		
8/11/96	THE HUPMOBILE COMPANY	40002	8,570.10	642.76	9,212.86
8/16/96	THE TUCKER CAR COMPANY	40003	SALE AMOUNT NEGATIVE ...		
8/21/96	AUBURN INCORPORATED	40004	45.00	3.38	48.38
8/27/96	BRICKLIN LIMITED	40005	1,068.91	80.17	1,149.08
8/30/96	THE LOCOMOBILE CAR COMPANY	40006	2,140.00	160.50	2,300.50
8/31/96	STUDEBAKER CARS INCORPORATED	40007	50.50	3.79	54.29
			12,686.51	951.50	13,638.01

Programming Assignment 6-2: SALESMAN SALARY/COMMISSION REPORT

```
Line    <--------------------- Source Specifications --------------------------><---- Comments ----> Do
Number  ....1....+....2....+....3....+....4....+....5....+..?*6....+....7....+....8....+....9....+...10 Num
                          S o u r c e   L i s t i n g
   1 * PA 6-2: Salesman Salary/Commission Report....
   2 FP62psm    IF   E           DISK
     *----------------------------------------------------------------------------------------------*
     *                                RPG name         External name                                *
     * File name. . . . . . . . :   P62PSM            STAN/P62PSM                                    *
     * Record format(s) . . . . . :  P62PSMR           P62PSMR                                       *
     *----------------------------------------------------------------------------------------------*
   3 FQsysprt    O   F  132        PRINTER OFLIND(*INOF)
   4
   5 DExtraSales     S            8 2
   6 DExtraComm      S            8 2
   7 DCommSales      S            8 2
   8 DNetSales       S            8 2
   9 DSalary         S            8 2
  10 DCommission     S            8 2
  11 DTotalSales     S            9 2
  12 DTotReturns     S            8 2
  13 DTotNetSale     S            9 2
  14 DTotalComm      S            9 2
  15
  16=IP62PSMR
     *----------------------------------------------------------------------------------------------*
     * RPG record format . . . . :   P62PSMR                                                         *
     * External format  . . . . . :  P62PSMR : STAN/P62PSM                                           *
     *----------------------------------------------------------------------------------------------*
  17=I                          A    1    5 SALEPERSN#
  18=I                          A    6   30 SALEPNAME
  19=I                          P   31   32 0YRSEMPLYED
  20=I                          P   33   37 2SALEAMOUNT
  21=I                          P   38   41 2SALERETURN
  22 C              EVAL      *INOF = *ON                    turn on OF indicator
  23 C              READ      P62psm                ----LR   read first record
  24 C              DOW       *INLR = *OFF                   dow LR is off         B01
  25
  26 * Heading control....
  27 C              IF        *INOF = *ON              -     OF indicator on?      B02
  28 C              EXCEPT    Headings                       print heading lines   02
  29 C              EVAL      *INOF = *OFF                   turn off OF indicatr  02
  30 C              ENDIF                                    end IF group          E02
  31
  32 * Housekeeping....
  33 C              EVAL      ExtraComm = *ZERO              initialize field      01
  34 C              EVAL      ExtraSales = *ZERO             initialize field      01
  35 C              EVAL      CommSales = *ZERO              initialize field      01
  36
```

```
37  * Compute Commission Sales...
38 C                    EVAL      NetSales = SaleAmount - SaleReturn      compute net sales    01
39 C                    IF        NetSales > 2000                        > 2000?              B02
40 C                    EVAL      CommSales = NetSales - 2000            compute commsales     02
41 C                    ENDIF                                            end IF group         E02
42
43  * Calculations for employees with less than 2 years employment..
44 C                    SELECT                                           begin select group   B02
45 C                    WHEN      YrsEmplyed < 2                         equal to zero?       X02
46 C                    EVAL      Salary = 600                           initialize Salary     02
47 C                    EVAL      Commission = CommSales * .12           compute Commission    02
48 C                    IF        CommSales > 25000                      > 25000?             B03
49 C                    EVAL      ExtraSales = CommSales - 25000         compute ExtraSales    03
50 C                    EVAL      ExtraComm = ExtraSales * .02           compute ExtraComm     03
51 C                    ENDIF                                            end IF group         E03
52
53  * Calculations for employees with 2 or more years employment..
54 C                    OTHER                                                                X02
55 C                    EVAL      Salary = 1000                          initialize Salary     02
56 C                    EVAL      Commission = CommSales * .20           compute Commission    02
57 C                    IF        CommSales > 30000                      > 25000?             B03
58 C                    EVAL      ExtraSales = CommSales - 30000         compute ExtraSales    03
59 C                    EVAL      ExtraComm = ExtraSales * .05           compute ExtraComm     03
60 C                    ENDIF                                            end IF group         E03
61 C                    ENDSL                                            end SELECT group     E02
62
63  * Compute salary + commissions amount....
64 C                    EVAL      Commission = Commission + Salary + ExtraComm  compute Commission  01
65
66  * Accumulate Totals....
67 C                    EVAL      TotalSales = TotalSales + SaleAmount    compute TotalSales   01
68 C                    EVAL      TotReturns = TotReturns + SaleReturn    compute TotReturns   01
69 C                    EVAL      TotNetSale = TotNetSale + NetSales      compute TotNetSale   01
70 C                    EVAL      TotalComm = TotalComm + Commission      compute TotalComm    01
71 C                    EXCEPT    DetailLine                             print DetailLine     01
72 C                                                                                          01
73 C                    READ      P62psm                        ----LR   read next record     01
74 C                    ENDDO                                            end dow group        E01
75
76 C                    EXCEPT    TotalLine                              print total line
77 C                    EVAL      *INLR = *ON                            end job
78
79 OQsysprt    E        Headings       3     01
80 O                    UDATE          Y     8
81 O                                         68 'COMMISSION REPORT'
82 O                                        106 'PAGE'
83 O                    PAGE                111
84 O           E        Headings       1
85 O                                        107 'SALARY/'
86 O           E        Headings       2
87 O                                         10 'SALESMAN #'
88 O                                         30 'SALESMAN NAME'
89 O                                         47 'EMP YRS'
90 O                                         61 'GROSS SALES'
91 O                                         73 'RETURNS'
92 O                                         90 'NET SALES'
93 O                                        108 'COMMISSION'
94 O           E        DetailLine     2
95 O                    SalePersn#           7
96 O                    SalepName           37
97 O                    YrsEmplyed     Z    44
98 O                    SaleAmount     1    60
99 O                    SaleReturn     1    73
100 O                   NetSales       1    90
101 O                   Commission     1   108
102 O          E        TotalLine      1
103 O                                        48 'TOTALS..........'
104 O                   TotalSales     1    60
105 O                   TotReturns     1    73
106 O                   TotNetSale     1    90
107 O                   TotalComm      1   108
      * * * * *  E N D   O F   S O U R C E  * * * * *
```

52

Printed Report:

8/03/98			COMMISSION REPORT			PAGE 1
SALESMAN #	SALESMAN NAME	EMP YRS	GROSS SALES	RETURNS	NET SALES	SALARY/ COMMISSION
11111	SIEGFRIED HOUNDSTOOTH	4	11,250.50	1,000.00	10,250.50	2,650.10
11112	FELIX GOODGUY	1	28,000.00	.00	28,000.00	3,740.00
22222	OTTO MUTTENJAMMER	6	100,000.00	.00	100,000.00	24,000.00
33333	HANS OFFENHAUSER	1	2,500.00	700.00	1,800.00	600.00
44444	BARNEY OLDFIELD	3	1,900.00	.00	1,900.00	1,000.00
55555	WILLIAM PETTY	2	22,000.00	.00	22,000.00	5,000.00
		TOTALS.........	165,650.50	1,700.00	163,950.50	36,990.10

Programming Assignment 6-3: PAYROLL REGISTER

```
Line   <--------------------- Source Specifications --------------------------><---- Comments ----> Do
Number ....1....+....2....+....3....+....4....+....5....+....6....+....7....+....8....+....9....+...10 Num
                         S o u r c e   L i s t i n g
   1 * PA 6-3: Payroll Register....
   2 FP63psm    IF  E           DISK
     *----------------------------------------------------------------------------------*
     *                          RPG name       External name                            *
     * File name. . . . . . . . : P63PSM        STAN/P63PSM                              *
     * Record format(s) . . . . : P63PSMR       P63PSMR                                  *
     *----------------------------------------------------------------------------------*
   3 FQsysprt   O   F 132       PRINTER OFLIND(*INOF)
   4
   5 DSS            S             5  2
   6 DFwt           S             6  2
   7 DNet           S             6  2
   8 DUnder         S             6  2
   9
  10=IP63PSMR
     *----------------------------------------------------------------------------------*
     * RPG record format  . . . . : P63PSMR                                             *
     * External format  . . . . . : P63PSMR : STAN/P63PSM                               *
     *----------------------------------------------------------------------------------*
  11=I                           P   1   5 OSSNO
  12=I                           A   6  25  EMPNAM
  13=I                           P  26  29 2YTDWAG
  14=I                           P  30  33 2YTDFWT
  15=I                           P  34  37 2YTDSS
  16=I                           P  38  41 2WEKSAL
  17 C              EVAL      *INOF = *ON                         turn on OF indicator
  18 C              READ      P63psm                    ----LR    read first record
  19 C              DOW       *INLR = *OFF                        dow LR is off       B01
  20
  21 * Heading control....
  22 C              IF        *INOF = *ON                         OF indicator on?    B02
  23 C              EXCEPT    Headings                            print heading lines  02
  24 C              EVAL      *INOF = *OFF                 -      turn off OF indicatr 02
  25 C              ENDIF                                         end IF group        E02
  26
  27 C              EVAL      SS = *ZERO                          initialize SS field  01
  28 C              EVAL      Fwt = WekSal * .20                  compute fwt          01
  29 C              EVAL      Net = WekSal - Fwt                  compute net pay      01
  30
  31 C              IF        Ytdss < 3855.60                     less than?          B02
  32 C              EVAL      Under = 3855.60 - Ytdss             compute remaining ss 02
```

```
33 C              EVAL      SS = WekSal * .0765         compute ss          02
34 C              IF        Under < SS                 under test          B03
35 C              EVAL      SS = Under                 initialize ss       03
36 C              ENDIF                                 end inner IF group  E03
37 C              EVAL      Net = Net - SS             compute net pay     02
38 C              EVAL      Ytdss = Ytdss + SS         accumulate SS       02
39 C              EVAL      YtdWag = YtdWag + WekSal   accum YtdWag        02
40 C              ENDIF                                 end outer IF group  E02
41
42 C              EVAL      YtdFwt = YtdFwt + Fwt      accumulate fwt      01
43 C              EXCEPT    DetailLine                 print record        01
44
45 C              READ      P63psm              ----LR read next record    01
46 C              ENDDO                                 end dow group       E01
47
48 C              EVAL      *INLR = *ON                end job
49
50 OQsysprt   E          Headings      3    01
51 O                     UDATE         Y    8
52 O                                       64 'PAYROLL REGISTER'
53 O                                      105 'PAGE'
54 O                     PAGE              110
55 O          E          Headings      2
56 O                                        6 'SS#'
57 O                                       29 'EMPLOYEE NAME'
58 O                                       44 'YTD WAGES'
59 O                                       56 'YTD FWT'
60 O                                       67 'YTD SS'
61 O                                       79 'WEEK PAY'
62 O                                       90 'WEEK FWT'
63 O                                      100 'WEEK SS'
64 O                                      110 'NET PAY'
65 O          E          DetailLine    2
66 O                     SSNo          12 '0  -  -    '
67 O                     EmpNam        33
68 O                     YtdWag    1   45
69 O                     YtdFwt    1   57
70 O                     YtdSS     1   68
71 O                     WekSal    1   79
72 O                     Fwt       1   90
73 O                     SS        1   99
74 O                     Net       1  110
     * * * * *  E N D   O F   S O U R C E  * * * * *
```

Printed Report:

11/23/98		PAYROLL REGISTER						PAGE 1
SS#	EMPLOYEE NAME	YTD WAGES	YTD FWT	YTD SS	WEEK PAY	WEEK FWT	WEEK SS	NET PAY
050-44-6666	BETTY BURPO	3,000.00	600.00	229.50	500.00	100.00	38.25	361.75
001-01-2345	DICK TRACY	50,400.00	10,080.00	3,855.60	750.00	150.00	57.37	542.63
100-70-9876	SHERLOCK HOLMES	60,000.00	12,200.00	3,855.60	1,000.00	200.00	.00	800.00
020-32-4321	JAMES BOND	50,800.00	10,160.00	3,855.60	800.00	160.00	30.60	609.40
020-40-0050	INSPECTOR GADGET	50,400.00	10,260.00	3,855.60	900.00	180.00	.00	720.00
110-88-9999	PERRY MASON	385.00	77.00	29.45	275.00	55.00	21.03	198.97

Programming Assignment 6-4: STOCKBROKER'S COMMISSION REPORT

```
Line    <--------------------- Source Specifications -------------------------><---- Comments ----> Do
Number  ....1....+....2....+....3....+....4....+....5....+....6....+....7....+....8....+....9....+...10 Num
                         S o u r c e   L i s t i n g
   1 * PA 6-4: Stockholder's Commission Report....
   2 FP64psm   IF   E          DISK
  *-------------------------------------------------------------------------*
  *                           RPG name         External name                *
```

```
      * File name. . . . . . . . :  P64PSM        STAN/P64PSM                              *
      * Record format(s) . . . . :  P64PSMR       P64PSMR                                  *
     *---------------------------------------------------------------------------------------*
   3 FQsysprt   O   F 132        PRINTER OFLIND(*INOF)
   4
   5 DTotalCost     S          10 2
   6 DCommission    S           9 2
   7 DTotalNY       S           4 0
   8 DTotalAM       S           4 0
   9 DTotalOV       S           4 0
  10
  11=IP64PSMR
     *---------------------------------------------------------------------------------------*
      * RPG record format  . . . . :  P64PSMR                                               *
      * External format  . . . . . :  P64PSMR : STAN/P64PSM                                 *
     *---------------------------------------------------------------------------------------*
  12=I                         A   1   5  ACTNUMBER
  13=I                         A   6  25  STOCKNAME
  14=I                         P  26  29  ONO_SHARES
  15=I                         P  30  33 3SHARECOST
  16=I                         A  34  35  EXCHANGE
  17 C              EVAL      *INOF = *ON                       turn on OF indicator
  18 C              READ      P64psm                  ----LR    read first record
  19 C              DOW       *INLR = *OFF                      dow LR is off          B01
  20
  21 * Heading control....
  22 C              IF        *INOF = *ON          *?           OF indicator on?       B02
  23 C              EXCEPT    Headings                          print heading lines    02
  24 C              EVAL      *INOF = *OFF                      turn off OF indicatr   02
  25 C              ENDIF                                       end IF group           E02
  26
  27 C              EVAL      TotalCost = No_Shares * ShareCost compute TotalCost      01
  28
  29 C              SELECT                                      begin SELECT group     B02
  30 C              WHEN      Exchange = 'NY'                   test for NY exchange   X02
  31 C              EVAL      Commission = TotalCost * .051     compute commission     02
  32 C              EVAL      TotalNY = TotalNY + 1             accum NY transactons   02
  33 C              WHEN      Exchange = 'AM'                   test for AM exchange   X02
  34 C              EVAL      Commission = TotalCost * .042     compute commission     02
  35 C              EVAL      TotalAM = TotalAM + 1             accum AM transaction   02
  36 C              OTHER                                                              X02
  37 C              EVAL      Commission = TotalCost * .035     compute commission     02
  38 C              EVAL      TotalOV = TotalOV + 1             accum AM transaction   02
  39 C              ENDSL                                       end SELECT group       E02
  40
  41 C              EXCEPT    DetailLine                        print record           01
  42
  43 C              READ      P64psm                  ----LR    read next record       01
  44 C              ENDDO                                       end dow group          E01
  45
  46 C              EXCEPT    Summarylin
  47 C              EVAL      *INLR = *ON                       end job
  48
  49 OQsysprt   E         Headings      2   01
  50 O                    UDATE         Y    8
  51 O                                      45 'STOCK BROKER'
  52 O                                      63 'COMMISSION REPORT'
  53 O                                      94 'PAGE'
  54 O                    PAGE              99
  55 O         E         Headings      1
  56 O                                      43 'SHARES'
  57 O                                      54 'PRICE/'
  58 O                                      71 'PURCHASE IN'
  59 O                                      81 'STOCK'
  60 O                                      93 'BROKER'
  61 O         E         Headings      2
  62 O                                       7 'ACT#'
  63 O                                      30 'STOCK PURCHASED'
  64 O                                      44 'PURCHASED'
  65 O                                      53 'SHARE'
  66 O                                      69 'DOLLARS'
  67 O                                      82 'EXCHANGE'
  68 O                                      95 'COMMISSION'
  69 O         E         DetailLine    2
```

```
70 O                      ActNumber      8
71 O                      StockName      32
72 O                      No_Shares   1  43
73 O                      ShareCost   1  55
74 O                      TotalCost   1  72
75 O                      Exchange       79
76 O                      Commission  1  96
77 O         E            SummaryLin 1 1
78 O                                     26 'NUMBER OF NY'
79 O                                     49 'EXCHANGE TRANSACTIONS:'
80 O                      TotalNY     1  54
81 O         E            SummaryLin     1
82 O                                     26 'NUMBER OF AM'
83 O                                     49 'EXCHANGE TRANSACTIONS:'
84 O                      TotalAM     1  54
85 O         E            SummaryLin     0
86 O                                     26 'NUMBER OF OV'
87 O                                     49 'EXCHANGE TRANSACTIONS:'
88 O                      TotalOV     1  54
   * * * *  E N D   O F   S O U R C E  * * * *
```

Printed Report:

8/04/98		STOCK BROKER COMMISSION REPORT				PAGE 1
ACT#	STOCK PURCHASED	SHARES PURCHASED	PRICE/ SHARE	PURCHASE IN DOLLARS	STOCK EXCHANGE	BROKER COMMISSION
10000	IBM CORPORATION	1,000	57.125	57,125.00	NY	2,913.37
12000	ECHLIN MFG	50	25.500	1,275.00	OV	44.62
13000	BENQUET INC	10,000	4.250	42,500.00	NY	2,167.50
14000	BIC CORPORATION	300	2.600	780.00	AM	32.76
15000	BLACK & DECKER	1,500	23.750	35,625.00	OV	1,246.87
16000	TRANS-LUX	100,000	9.125	912,500.00	AM	38,325.00
17000	ALCIDE CORPORATION	25,000	3.125	78,125.00	OV	2,734.37
18000	PEOPLE'S BANK	4,000	9.500	38,000.00	OV	1,330.00
19000	XEROX	100	51.375	5,137.50	NY	262.01
20000	DU PONT	300	88.125	26,437.50	NY	1,348.31

```
        NUMBER OF NY EXCHANGE TRANSACTIONS:   4
        NUMBER OF AM EXCHANGE TRANSACTIONS:   2
        NUMBER OF OV EXCHANGE TRANSACTIONS:   4
```

Programming Assignment 6-5: STRAIGHT-LINE DEPRECIATION SCHEDULE

```
Line  <---------------------- Source Specifications ---------------------------><---- Comments ----> Do
Number ....1....+....2....+....3....+....4....+....5....+....6....+....7....+....8....+....9....+...10 Num
            S o u r c e   L i s t i n g
   1  * PA 6-5: Straight-Line Depreciation Schedule....
   2 FP65psm    IF  E          DISK
      *---------------------------------------------------------------------------------------------*
      *                          RPG name           External name                                   *
      * File name. . . . . . . . :  P65PSM           STAN/P65PSM                                     *
      * Record format(s) . . . . . :  P65PSMR          P65PSMR                                       *
      *---------------------------------------------------------------------------------------------*
   3 FQsysprt   O   F 132       PRINTER OFLIND(*INOF)
   4
   5 DYear          S              4 0
   6 DDepAmount     S              7 0
```

56

```
   7 DAnnualDep        S              7 0
   8 DYrsCounter       S              2 0
   9 DAccumDep         S              7 0
  10 DBookValue        S              7 0
  11 DExcess           S              7 0
  12
  13=IP65PSMR
      *---------------------------------------------------------------------*
      * RPG record format  . . . . :  P65PSMR                               *
      * External format  . . . . . :  P65PSMR : STAN/P65PSM                 *
      *---------------------------------------------------------------------*
  14=I                        A    1   25  ASSETNAME
  15=I                        P   26   29  OPURCHDATE
  16=I                        P   30   34  2COST
  17=I                        P   35   36  OEUL
  18=I                        P   37   40  OSALVALUE
  19 C                EVAL      *INOF = *ON
  20 C                READ      P65psm                           ----LR   read first record
  21 C                DOW       *INLR = *OFF                               dow LR is off         B01
  22 * Heading print control....
  23 C                IF        *INOF = *ON                                OF indicator on?      B02
  24 C                EXCEPT    Headings                                   print heading lines    02
  25 C                EVAL      *INOF = *OFF                               turn off OF indicatr   02
  26 C                ENDIF                                                end IF group          E02
  27
  28 * Housekeeping....
  29 C                MOVE      PurchDate    Year                 **       move yr to year        01
  30 C                MOVEL     19           Year                          compute fwt            01
  31 C                EVAL      DepAmount = Cost - SalValue                compute deprecbl amt   01
  32 C                EVAL      AnnualDep = DepAmount / Eul                compute annual dep     01
  33
  34 * Calculate AnnualDEp, AccumDep, and BookValue for the asset's eul....
  35 C                DO        Eul          YrsCounter                    until counter > eul   B02
  36 C                EVAL      AccumDep = AccumDep + AnnualDep            accumm annualdep       02
  37 C                EVAL      BookValue = Cost - AccumDep                compute bookvalue      02
  38
  39 * Last year's depreciation computation....
  40 C                IF        YrsCounter = Eul AND BookValue > SalValue  compound test         B03
  41 C                EVAL      Excess = BookValue - SalValue              compute excess amt     03
  42 C                EVAL      AnnualDep = AnnualDep + Excess             increment AnnualDep    03
  43 C                EVAL      AccumDep = AccumDep + Excess               increment AccumDep     03
  44 C                EVAL      BookValue = SalValue                       initialize book        03
  45 C                ENDIF                                                end IF group          E03
  46
  47 C                EXCEPT    DetailLine                                 print record           02
  48 C                EVAL      Year = Year + 1                            increment year         02
  49 C                ENDDO                                                end DO group          E02
  50
  51 C                EVAL      AccumDep = *ZERO                           initialize AccumDep    01
  52 C                READ      P65psm                           ----LR   read next record       01
  53 C                EVAL      *INOF = *ON                                new asset hdg contrl   01
  54 C                ENDDO                                                end dow group         E01
  55
  56 C                EVAL      *INLR = *ON                                end job
  57
  58 OQsysprt  E           Headings    1    01
  59 O                      UDATE       Y     8
  60 O                                        38 'DEPRECIATION SCHEDULE'
  61 O                                        59 'PAGE'
  62 O                      PAGE              64
  63 O         E           Headings    3
  64 O                                        37 'STRAIGHT-LINE METHOD'
  65 O         E           Headings    2
  66 O                                        10 'ASSET:'
  67 O                      AssetName         36
  68 O                                        52 'PURCHASE DATE:'
  69 O                      PurchDate   Y     61
  70 O         E           Headings    2
  71 O                                         9 'COST:'
  72 O                      Cost        1     22
  73 O                                        32 'EUL:'
  74 O                      Eul         Z     35
  75 O                                        55 'SALVAGE VALUE:'
  76 O                      SalValue    :     62
```

```
77 O          E         Headings      1
78 O                                      25 'ANNUAL'
79 O                                      42 'ACCUMULATED'
80 O                                      52 'BOOK'
81 O          E         Headings      2
82 O                                      12 'YEAR'
83 O                                      28 'DEPRECIATION'
84 O                                      43 'DEPRECIATION'
85 O                                      53 'VALUE'
86 O          E         DetailLine    2
87 O                    Year             12
88 O                    AnnualDep     1  28
89 O                    AccumDep      1  42
90 O                    BookValue     1  55
      * * * * *  E N D   O F   S O U R C E  * * * * *
```

Printed Report:

```
1/04/98          DEPRECIATION SCHEDULE              PAGE    1
                 STRAIGHT-LINE METHOD


    ASSET: BPT MILLING MACHINE       PURCHASE DATE:  5/14/97

    COST:    15,000.00    EUL: 7     SALVAGE VALUE:  3,000
                                  ..
                    ANNUAL      ACCUMULATED     BOOK
            YEAR  DEPRECIATION  DEPRECIATION    VALUE

            1997      1,714         1,714      13,286

            1998      1,714         3,428      11,572

            1999      1,714         5,142       9,858

            2000      1,714         6,856       8,144

            2001      1,714         8,570       6,430

            2002      1,714        10,284       4,716

            2003      1,716        12,000       3,000
---------------------------------------------------------

1/04/98          DEPRECIATION SCHEDULE              PAGE    2
                 STRAIGHT-LINE METHOD


    ASSET: IBM AS/400 - MODEL E       PURCHASE DATE:  2/10/97

    COST:   375,000.00     EUL: 5     SALVAGE VALUE: 20,000

                    ANNUAL      ACCUMULATED     BOOK
            YEAR  DEPRECIATION  DEPRECIATION    VALUE

            1997     71,000        71,000      304,000

            1998     71,000       142,000      233,000

            1999     71,000       213,000      162,000

            2000     71,000       284,000       91,000

            2001     71,000       355,000       20,000
---------------------------------------------------------

1/04/98          DEPRECIATION SCHEDULE              PAGE    3
                 STRAIGHT-LINE METHOD


    ASSET: IBM MICRO - PENTIUM       PURCHASE DATE:  1/11/97

    COST:    2,800.00     EUL: 3     SALVAGE VALUE:    400
```

YEAR	ANNUAL DEPRECIATION	ACCUMULATED DEPRECIATION	BOOK VALUE
1997	800	800	2,000
1998	800	1,600	1,200
1999	800	2,400	400

1/04/98   DEPRECIATION SCHEDULE   PAGE   4
                 STRAIGHT-LINE METHOD

ASSET: OFFICE FURNITURE   PURCHASE DATE: 10/01/97
COST: 9,000.00   EUL: 10   SALVAGE VALUE: 600

YEAR	ANNUAL DEPRECIATION	ACCUMULATED DEPRECIATION	BOOK VALUE
1997	840	840	8,160
1998	840	1,680	7,320
1999	840	2,520	6,480
2000	840	3,360	5,640
2001	840	4,200	4,800
2002	840	5,040	3,960
2003	840	5,880	3,120
2004	840	6,720	2,280
2005	840	7,560	1,440
2006	840	8,400	600

1/04/98   DEPRECIATION SCHEDULE   PAGE   5
                 STRAIGHT-LINE METHOD

ASSET: FACTORY BUILDING   PURCHASE DATE: 6/15/97

COST: 1,200,000.00   EUL: 18   SALVAGE VALUE: 0

YEAR	ANNUAL DEPRECIATION	ACCUMULATED DEPRECIATION	BOOK VALUE
1997	66,666	66,666	1,133,334
1998	66,666	133,332	1,066,668
1999	66,666	199,998	1,000,002
2000	66,666	266,664	933,336
2001	66,666	333,330	866,670
2002	66,666	399,996	800,004
2003	66,666	466,662	733,338
2004	66,666	533,328	666,672
2005	66,666	599,994	600,006
2006	66,666	666,660	533,340
2007	66,666	733,326	466,674

2008	66,666	799,992	400,008
2009	66,666	866,658	333,342
2010	66,666	933,324	266,676
2011	66,666	999,990	200,010
2012	66,666	1,066,656	133,344
2013	66,666	1,133,322	66,678
2014	66,678	1,200,000	0

CHAPTER 7
QUESTION ANSWERS

1. *Internal Subroutines* are a related groups of statements in-cluded in calculations that are processed separately from the normal RPG processing cycle.

   They are included in an RPG IV program to isolate groups of statements related to a common function and in turn support structured programming.

2. **EXSR** (*Invoke Subroutine*) - An **EXSR** instruction causes program control to branch to the subroutine specified in the *Result* field.

   BEGSR (*Beginning of Subroutine*) - A **BEGSR** instruction indi-indicates the beginning of the subroutine named in *Factor 1*.

   ENDSR (*End of Subroutine*) - An **ENDSR** instruction specifies the end of the related subroutine.

3. After all detail and total time calculations. The sequence of instructions in calculations are detail, total, and then internal subroutines which begin with a **BEGSR** statement and ended with an **ENDSR** operation.

4. The related **EXSR** statement(s) in detail or total time calcula-tions.

5. After the subroutine's **ENDSR** operation is executed, control returns to the instruction following the related **EXSR** state-ment.

6. Any RPG IV operations and/or indicators.

7. The **CAS** operation includes the functions of the **COMP** and **EXSR** statements. It reduces coding (one statement instead of two) and eliminates the need for *Resulting* and *Condition-ing* indicators.

   The **xx** entry in the **CAS** operation indicates the relational tests: **GT**, **LT**, **EQ**, **GE**, **LE**, and **NE**.

8. One or more **CAS** instructions terminated by an **ENDCS** or **END** operation.

9. When the value in FieldA is equal to the value in FieldB, the **CASEQ** statement will branch control to the Subroutin1 internal subroutine.

   Program control returns to the first executable instructions following the related **ENDCS** operation.

10. If the test in the **CASEQ** statement on line 10 is false, the **CASGT** statement on line 20 is tested. If the value in FieldA is greater than the value in FieldC, a branch is made to the

Subroutin2 internal subroutine.

11. If the **CAS** tests on lines 10 and 20 are false, this **CAS** instruction will be executed and control will branch to the internal subroutine Subroutin3.

    After executing the subroutine, program control returns to the first instruction after the related **ENDCS** (or **END**) operation.

12. By the RPG IV **TIME** operation, *Definition Specification* instruction, *Input Specification* instruction, or a **CL** command.

13. **hhmmss, hhmmssmmddyy,** or **hhmmssmmddyyyy.**

14. **hhmmss**

15. **hhmmssmmddyy**

16. **hhmmssmmddyyyy**

17. The system or job time in an **hh:mm:ss** edited format.

18. Defines SystemTime as a "standalone" field.

19. Letter **T** in position 40 defines the entry as a time field.

20. Specifies the time value in an ***HMS:** edited format (i.e. **hh:mm:ss**).

21. ***ISO, *USA, *EUR,** and ***JIS**

22. Is the separator character. An ampersand (&) may also be used.

23. A *Control Field* is one that is tested for a change in value which will generate *Control Break* processing.

24. In a *Control Field* value ascending or descending order.

25. If the physical file is not in a required ascending or descending *Control Field* value order; the file may be accessed in the necessary order by a **logical file** or by **sorting.**

26. In programmer-controlled control break processing, the *Control Field* value from the physical file must be moved into a hold-holding field.

    Two *Control Field* values must be moved into holding fields.

27. State, first; county, second; and town, third.

28. Town, first; county, second; and state, third.

29. The *Control Group Total* field must be initialized to zero and the *Control Field* value from the current record must be moved into its related holding field.

30. Indicators **L1-L9**. They are defined in the *Input Specifications* and used as *conditioning* or *resulting* indicators in calculations or *conditioning* indicators for output instructions.

31. Automatically, when a change in the *Control Field* value is determined.

32. **L1** must be specified on line 20 in the *L0* field (positions 7 and 8).

    L2 must be specified on line 30 in the *L0* field (positions 7 and 8).

    L3 must be specified on line 40 in the *L0* field (positions 7 and 8).

    LR will not specified in calculations, but will be on output to support end of file processing.

33. The instruction on line 10 only.

34. The instructions on lines 10 and 20.

35. The instructions on lines 10, 20, and 30.

36. The instructions on line 10, 20, 30, and 40.

37. Control Level Indicators **L1**, **L2**, and **L3**.

    Output is printed at total time for output records conditioned by the **L1**, **L2**, **L3**, and **LR** indicators.

38. Total time output instructions conditioned with the **L1** *Control Level Indicator*.

39. Total time output instructions conditioned with the **L1** and **L2** *Control Level Indicators*.

40. Total time output instructions conditioned with the **L1**, **L2**, and **L3** *Control Level Indicators*.

41. Refer students to Appendix F - Figure F-1 (step 3).

PROGRAMMING ASSIGNMENTS

Programming Assignment 7-1: VOTER REPORT BY TOWN AND STATE TOTALS

```
iLine   <-------------------- Source Specifications --------------------><---- Comments ----> Do
iNumber ....1....+....2....+....3....+....4....+....5....+....6....+....7....+....8....+....9....+...10 Num|
                          S o u r c e   L i s t i n g
    1 * PA 7-1: Voter report by town and state totals....
    2 FP71psm    IF  E        K DISK
      *-------------------------------------------------------------------------------------*
      *                        RPG name         External name                               *
      * File name. . . . . . . . :  P71PSM        STAN/P71PSM                                *
```

```
    * Record format(s) . . . . . : P71PSMR          P71PSMR                              *
    *-----------------------------------------------------------------------------------*
 3 FQsysprt   O   F 132         PRINTER OFLIND(*INOF)
 4
 5 DTownTotal      S          7 0
 6 DStateTotal     S          9 0
 7 DTown#Hold      S          3
 8
 9=IP71PSMR
    *-----------------------------------------------------------------------------------*
    * RPG record format  . . . . : P71PSMR                                              *
    * External format  . . . . . : P71PSMR : STAN/P71PSM                                *
    *-----------------------------------------------------------------------------------*
10=I                        A    1    4  DISTRICTNO
11=I                        A    5    7  TOWNNO
12=I                        A    8    9  COUNTYNO
13=I                        P   10   13  OVOTERS
14 C           READ     P71psm                           ----LR   read first record
15 C           EXSR     HousekepSR                                exit to subroutine
16 C           DOW      *INLR = *OFF                              dow LR is off       B01
17
18  * Heading control....
19 C           IF       *INOF = *ON                               OF on?              B02
20 C           EXCEPT   Headings                                  print heading lines  02
21 C           EVAL     *INLR = *OFF                              turn off LR indicatr 02
22 C           ENDIF                                              end IF group        E02
23
24  * Test for control break (townNo change)....
25 C   TownNo  CASNE    Town#Hold     TownSR                      contol break?        01
26 C           ENDCS                                              end CAS group        01
27
28 C           EVAL     TownTotal = TownTotal + Voters            accum town total     01
29 C           EXCEPT   DetailLine                                print record         01
30 C           READ     P71psm                           ----LR   read next record     01
31 C           ENDDO                                              end DO group        E01
32
33  * Branch to end of file subroutine....
34 C           EXSR     EofSR                                     branch to subroutine
35
36 C           EVAL     *INLR = *ON                               turn on LR indicator
37
38  * Begin subroutines....
39 C   HouseKepSR BEGSR                                           begin subroutine
40 C           EVAL     Town#Hold = TownNo                        initialize hold fld
41 C           EVAL     *INOF = *ON                               turn on OF indicatr
42 C           ENDSR                                              end subroutine
43
44 C   TownSR  BEGSR                                              begin subroutine
45 C           EVAL     StateTotal = StateTotal + TownTotal       accum state total
46 C           EXCEPT   TownLine                                  print town total
47 C           EVAL     Town#Hold = TownNo                        initialize hold fld
48 C           EVAL     TownTotal = *ZERO                         initialize to zero
49 C           ENDSR                                              end subroutine
50
51 C   EofSR   BEGSR                                              begin subroutine
52 C           EXSR     TownSR                                    branch to subroutine
53 C           EXCEPT   EofLine                                   print final totals
54 C           ENDSR                                              end subroutine
55
56 OQsysprt  E          Headings      3 01
57 O                     UDATE        Y      8
58 O                                        52 'STATE OF CONFUSION'
59 O                                        80 'PAGE'
60 O                     PAGE               85
61 O         E          Headings      2
62 O                                        27 'DISTRICT'
63 O                                        37 'TOWN'
64 O                                        68 'VOTERS'
65 O         E          DetailLine    1
66 O                     DistrictNo         25
67 O                     TownNo             36
68 O                     Voters        2    69
69 O         E          TownLine     1 2
70 O                                        43 'TOTAL VOTERS FOR TOWN'
71 O                     Town#Hold          47
```

```
72 O                    TownTotal   2   69
73 O                                71  '*'
74 O          E         EofLine     0
75 O                                44 'TOTAL VOTERS FOR STATE'
76 O                    StateTotal  2   69
   * * * *   E N D   O F   S O U R C E  * * * *
```

Printed Report:

```
8/05/98                     STATE OF CONFUSION              PAGE    1


            DISTRICT    TOWN                     VOTERS

              1000      100                     215,625
              1010      100                      82,784
              1020      100                     104,716
              1030      100                      12,899
              1040      100                     267,004

            TOTAL VOTERS FOR TOWN 100           683,028 *

              2000      200                      57,800
              2010      200                      14,111
              2020      200                     118,923
              2030      200            **        73,807

            TOTAL VOTERS FOR TOWN 200           264,641 *

              3000      300                     200,749
              3010      300                     111,111

            TOTAL VOTERS FOR TOWN 300           311,860 *

              4000      400                      67,242
              4010      400                     104,338
              4020      400                      99,917
              4030      400                     178,615
              4040      400                     222,234
              4050      400                      33,845
              4060      400                     117,871
              4070      400                      64,899
              4080      400                      45,348
              4090      400                     888,888

            TOTAL VOTERS FOR TOWN 400         1,823,197 *


            TOTAL VOTERS FOR STATE           3,082,726
```

Programming Assignment 7-2: VOTER REPORT BY TOWN, COUNTY, AND STATE TOTALS

```
Line   <-------------------- Source Specifications --------------------><---- Comments ----> Do
Number ....1....+....2....+....3....+....4....+....5....+....6....+....7....+....8....+....9....+...10 Num
                    S o u r c e   L i s t i n g
  1 * PA 7-1: Voter report by town and state totals....
  2 FP71psm   IF  E        K DISK
    *---------------------------------------------------------------------------*
    *                         RPG name        External name                     *
    * File name. . . . . . . . . :  P71PSM    STAN/P71PSM                        *
    * Record format(s) . . . . . :  P71PSMR   P71PSMR                            *
    *---------------------------------------------------------------------------*
  3 FQsysprt  O   F  132      PRINTER OFLIND(*INOF)
  4
  5 DTownTotal      S        7  0
  6 DContyTotal     S        8  0
  7 DStateTotal     S        9  0
  8 DTown#Hold      S        3
```

65

```
 9 DConty#Hold      S              2
10 DTime            S              6 0
11
12=IP71PSMR
   *---------------------------------------------------------------------------*
   * RPG record format . . . . : P71PSMR                                       *
   * External format . . . . . : P71PSMR : STAN/P71PSM                         *
   *---------------------------------------------------------------------------*
13=I                           A   1    4  DISTRICTNO
14=I                           A   5    7  TOWNNO
15=I                           A   8    9  COUNTYNO
16=I                           P  10   13 0VOTERS
17 C            READ      P71psm                       ----LR   read first record
18 C            EXSR      HousekepSR                             exit to subroutine
19 C            DOW       *INLR = *OFF                           dow LR is off        B01
20
21 * Heading control....
22 C            IF        *INOF = *ON                            OF on?               B02
23 C            EXCEPT    Headings                               print heading lines    02
24 C            EVAL      *INLR = *OFF                           turn off LR indicatr   02
25 C            ENDIF                                            end IF group         E02
26
27 * Test for control breaks....
28 C            SELECT                                           begin SELECT group   B02
29 C            WHEN      Conty#Hold <> CountyNo                 county control break X02
30 C            EXSR      TownSR                                 branch to subroutine   02
31 C            EXSR      CountySR                               branch to subroutine   02
32 C            WHEN      Town#Hold <> TownNo                    town control break?  X02
33 C            EXSR      TownSR                                 branch to subroutine   02
34 C            ENDSL                                            end SELECT group     E02
35
36 C            EVAL      TownTotal = TownTotal + Voters         accum town total       01
37 C            EXCEPT    DetailLine                             print record           01
38 C            READ      P71psm                       ----LR   read next record       01
39 C            ENDDO                                            end DO group         E01
40
41 * Branch to end of file subroutine....
42 C            EXSR      EofSR                                  branch to subroutine
43
44 C            EVAL      *INLR = *ON                            turn on LR indicator
45
46 * Begin subroutines....
47 C   HouseKepSR   BEGSR                                        begin subroutine
48 C            EVAL      Town#Hold = TownNo                     initialize hold fld
49 C            EVAL      Conty#Hold = CountyNo                  initialize field
50 C            EVAL      *INOF = *ON                            turn on OF indicatr
51 C            TIME                  Time                       access system time
52 C            ENDSR                                            end subroutine
53
54 C   TownSR       BEGSR                                        begin subroutine
55 C            EVAL      ContyTotal = ContyTotal + TownTotal    accum state total
56 C            EXCEPT    TownLine                               print town total
57 C            EVAL      Town#Hold = TownNo                     initialize hold fld
58 C            EVAL      TownTotal = *ZERO                      initialize to zero
59 C            ENDSR                                            end subroutine
60
61 C   CountySR     BEGSR                                        begin subroutine
62 C            EVAL      StateTotal = StateTotal + ContyTotal   accum state total
63 C            EXCEPT    CountyLine                             print town total
64 C            EVAL      Conty#Hold = CountyNo                  initialize hold fld
65 C            EVAL      ContyTotal = *ZERO                     initialize to zero
66 C            ENDSR                                            end subroutine
67
68 C   EofSR        BEGSR                                        begin subroutine
69 C            EXSR      TownSR                                 branch to subroutine
70 C            EXSR      CountySR                               branch to SR
71 C            EXCEPT    EofLine                                print final totals
72 C            ENDSR                                            end subroutine
73
74 OQsysprt  E          Headings       1 01
75 O                    UDATE        Y       8
76 O                                        52 'STATE OF CONFUSION'
77 O                                        80 'PAGE'
78 O                    PAGE                 85
79 O        E          Headings         3
```

```
 80 O                    Time                 8 ' : : '
 81 O                                        39 'VOTERS REPORT BY'
 82 O                                        64 'DISTRICT, TOWN, & COUNTY'
 83 O          E         Headings      2
 84 O                                        27 'DISTRICT'
 85 O                                        37 'TOWN'
 86 O                                        49 'COUNTY'
 87 O                                        68 'VOTERS'
 88 O          E         DetailLine    1
 89 O                    DistrictNo         25
 90 O                    TownNo             36
 91 O                    CountyNo           46
 92 O                    Voters        2    69
 93 O          E         TownLine      1 1
 94 O                                        43 'TOTAL VOTERS FOR TOWN'
 95 O                    Town#Hold          47
 96 O                    TownTotal     2    69
 97 O                                        71 '*'
 98 O          E         CountyLine    1 2
 99 O                                        45 'TOTAL VOTERS FOR COUNTY'
100 O                    Conty#Hold         48
101 O                    ContyTotal    2    69
102 O                                        72 '**'
103 O          E         EofLine       0
104 O                                        44 'TOTAL VOTERS FOR STATE'
105 O                    StateTotal    2    69
    * * * * *  E N D   O F   S O U R C E  * * * * *
                                *>
```

Printed Report:

```
 8/05/98                      STATE OF CONFUSION                  PAGE    1
19:49:40             VOTERS REPORT BY DISTRICT, TOWN, & COUNTY


            DISTRICT      TOWN     COUNTY         VOTERS

              1000        100        10          215,625
              1010        100        10           82,784
              1020        100        10          104,716
              1030        100        10           12,899
              1040        100        10          267,004

            TOTAL VOTERS FOR TOWN 100           683,028 *

              2000        200        10           57,800
              2010        200        10           14,111
              2020        200        10          118,923
              2030        200        10           73,807

            TOTAL VOTERS FOR TOWN 200           264,641 *

            TOTAL VOTERS FOR COUNTY 10          947,669 **

              3000        300        30          200,749
              3010        300        30          111,111

            TOTAL VOTERS FOR TOWN 300           311,860 *

            TOTAL VOTERS FOR COUNTY 30          311,860 **

              4000        400        40           67,242
              4010        400        40          104,338
              4020        400        40           99,917
              4030        400        40          178,615
              4040        400        40          222,234
              4050        400        40           33,845
              4060        400        40          117,871
              4070        400        40           64,899
              4080        400        40           45,348
              4090        400        40          888,888

            TOTAL VOTERS FOR TOWN 400         1,823,197 *
```

```
┌─────────────────────────────────────────────────────────────┐
│                                                               │
│        TOTAL VOTERS FOR COUNTY 40        1,823,197 **         │
│                                                               │
│                                                               │
│        TOTAL VOTERS FOR STATE            3,082,726            │
│                                                               │
└─────────────────────────────────────────────────────────────┘
```

Programming Assignment 7-3: PLANT RAW MATERIALS REPORT

```
Line    <--------------------- Source Specifications --------------------><---- Comments ----> Do
Number  ....1....+....2....+....3....+....4....+....5....+....6....+....7....+....8....+....9....+...10 Nur
                               S o u r c e   L i s t i n g
    1 FP73psm    IF  E        K DISK
      *--------------------------------------------------------------------------------*
      *                           RPG name          External name                      *
      * File name. . . . . . . . : P73PSM           STAN/P73PSM                         *
      * Record format(s) . . . . : P73PSMR          P73PSMR                             *
      *--------------------------------------------------------------------------------*
    2 FQsysprt   O   F 132        PRINTER OFLIND(*INOF)
    3
    4 DJobHold       S          3
    5 DSectonHold    S          2
    6 DDeptHold      S          2
    7 DDollarAmt     S          9 2
    8 DJobTotal      S         10 2
    9 DSectnTotal    S         11 2
   10 DDeptTotal     S         12 2               **
   11 DPlantTotal    S         13 2
   12
   13=IP73PSMR
      *--------------------------------------------------------------------------------*
      * RPG record format . . . . : P73PSMR                                             *
      * External format . . . . . : P73PSMR : STAN/P73PSM                               *
      *--------------------------------------------------------------------------------*
   14=I                         A    1    4  PARTNO
   15=I                         A    5    7  JOBNO
   16=I                         A    8    9  SECTIONNO
   17=I                         A   10   11  DEPTNO
   18=I                         A   12   31  DESCRIPTON
   19=I                         P   32   34 0PARTSUSED
   20=I                         P   35   37 2PARTCOST
   21 C              EVAL       *INOF = *ON                      turn on OF indicator
   22 C              READ       P73psm                 ----LR    read first record
   23 C              EXSR       HousekepSR                       branch to subroutine
   24 C              DOW        *INLR = *OFF                     dow LR is off          BO
   25
   26 * Heading Control....
   27 C              IF         *INOF = *ON                      OF indicator on?       BO
   28 C              EXCEPT     Headings                         print heading lines    O
   29 C              EVAL       *INOF = *OFF                     turn off OF indicatr   O
   30 C              ENDIF                                       end IF group           EO
   31
   32 C              SELECT                                      begin SELECT group     BO
   33 C              WHEN       DeptNo <> DeptHold               dept break?            XO
   34 C              EXSR       JobSR                            branch to subroutine   O
   35 C              EXSR       SectionSR                        branch to subroutine   O
   36 C              EXSR       DeptSR                           branch to subroutine   O
   37 C              WHEN       SectionNo <> SectonHold          section break?         XO
   38 C              EXSR       JobSR                            branch to subroutine   O
   39 C              EXSR       SectionSR                        branch to subroutine   O
   40 C              WHEN       JobNo <> JobHold                 jobno break?           XO
   41 C              EXSR       JobSR                            branch to subroutine   O
   42 C              ENDSL                                       end SELECT group       EO
   43
   44 C              EVAL       DollarAmt = PartsUsed * PartCost  compute dollar amt    O
   45 C              EVAL       JobTotal = JobTotal + DollarAmt   accum jobtotal        O
   46 C              EXCEPT     DetailLine                       print record           O
   47 C              READ       P73psm                 ----LR    read next record       O
   48 C              ENDDO                                       end dow group          EO
   49
   50 C              EXSR       PlantSR                          branch to subroutine
   51 C              EVAL       *INLR = *ON                      turn on LR to end jb
   52
```

```
 53 * Begin subroutines...
 54 C    HousekepSR    BEGSR                                      begin subroutine
 55 C                  EVAL      JobHold = JobNo                  initialize jobhold
 56 C                  EVAL      SectonHold = SectionNo           initialize sectnhold
 57 C                  EVAL      DeptHold = DeptNo                initialize depthold
 58 C                  ENDSR                                      end subroutine
 59
 60 C    JobSR         BEGSR                                      begin subroutine
 61 C                  EVAL      SectnTotal = SectnTotal + JobTotal   accum section total
 62 C                  EXCEPT    JobLine                          print jobline
 63 C                  EVAL      JobHold = JobNo                  initialize jobhold
 64 C                  EVAL      JobTotal = *ZERO                 initialize jobtotal
 65 C                  ENDSR                                      end subroutine
 66
 67 C    SectionSR     BEGSR                                      begin subroutine
 68 C                  EVAL      DeptTotal = DeptTotal + SectnTotal   accum section total
 69 C                  EXCEPT    SectonLine                       print sectionline
 70 C                  EVAL      SectonHold = SectionNo           initialize sectnhold
 71 C                  EVAL      SectnTotal = *ZERO               initialize sectnTotl
 72 C                  ENDSR                                      end subroutine
 73
 74 C    DeptSR        BEGSR                                      begin subroutine
 75 C                  EVAL      PlantTotal = PlantTotal + DeptTotal   accum plant total
 76 C                  EXCEPT    DeptLine                         print plantline
 77 C                  EVAL      DeptHold = DeptNo                initialize depthold
 78 C                  EVAL      DeptTotal = *ZERO                initialize depttotal
 79 C                  ENDSR                                      end subroutine
 80
 81 C    PlantSR       BEGSR                              **      begin subroutine
 82 C                  EXSR      JobSR                            branch to subroutine
 83 C                  EXSR      SectionSR                        branch to subroutine
 84 C                  EXSR      DeptSR                           branch to subroutine
 85 C                  EXCEPT    PlantLine                        print plantline
 86 C                  ENDSR                                      end subroutine
 87
 88 OQsysprt   E       Headings         1 01
 89 O                  UDATE        Y        8
 90 O                                       36 'PART USAGE REPORT'
 91 O                                       51 'PAGE'
 92 O                  PAGE                  56
 93 O          E       Headings         3
 94 O                                       39 'BY JOB, SECTION, & DEPT'
 95 O          E       Headings         2
 96 O                                       11 'PART NO'
 97 O                                       26 'DESCRIPTION'
 98 O                                       47 'TOTAL COST'
 99 O          E       DetailLine       2
100 O                  PartNo                 9
101 O                  Descripton            31
102 O                  DollarAmt        1    47
103 O          E       JobLine        1 2
104 O                                       19 'JOB NO'
105 O                  JobHold               23
106 O                                       29 'TOTAL'
107 O                  JobTotal         1    47
108 O                                       49 '*'
109 O          E       SectonLine       2
110 O                                       20 'SECTION'
111 O                  SectonHold            23
112 O                                       29 'TOTAL'
113 O                  SectnTotal       2    47
114 O                                       50 '**'
115 O          E       DeptLine         2
116 O                                       17 'DEPT'
117 O                  DeptHold              20
118 O                                       26 'TOTAL'
119 O                  DeptTotal        2    47
120 O                                       51 '***'
121 O          E       PlantLine        0
122 O                                       24 'PLANT TOTAL'
123 O                  PlantTotal       2    47
      * * * * *  E N D   O F   S O U R C E  * * * * *
```

Printed Report:

```
8/06/98            PART USAGE REPORT          PAGE    1
                  BY JOB, SECTION, & DEPT


          PART NO    DESCRIPTION          TOTAL COST

            6278  CLOSER-WHITE                132.00
            6280  JAMB BRACKET-WHITE          17.52
            6284  DOOR BRACKET-WHITE          11.76


                  JOB NO 100 TOTAL           161.28 *

            6349  PHILP 12 X 1 SCREWS         15.36
            6350  PHILP 8 x 1 SCREWS           8.64
            6355  PHILP 6 X 1/2 SCREWS        48.00
            6364  THUMB SCREW                449.28


                  JOB NO 101 TOTAL           521.28 *

                  SECTION 20 TOTAL           682.56 **

                  DEPT 10 TOTAL              682.56 ***

            6461  36" SCREEN-WHITE           359.88
            6462  36" SCREEN-BLACK           719.76
            6463  32" SCREEN ALMOND     *?   329.90


                  JOB NO 102 TOTAL         1,409.54 *

                  SECTION 21 TOTAL         1,409.54 **

            6573  INSIDE HANDLE               76.80
            6574  OUTSIDE HANDLE              73.20
            6576  LATCH ASSEMBLY             298.56


                  JOB NO 103 TOTAL           448.56 *

                  SECTION 30 TOTAL           448.56 **

                  DEPT 20 TOTAL            1,858.10 ***

                  PLANT TOTAL              2,540.66
```

Programming Assignment 7-4: HOSPITAL BILLING REPORT

```
Line   <-------------------- Source Specifications --------------------------------><---- Comments ----> Do
Number ....1....+....2....+....3....+....4....+....5....+....6....+....7....+....8....+....9....+...10 Num
                        S o u r c e   L i s t i n g
    1 * PA 7-4: Hospital Billing Report....
    2 FP74psm    IF   E           K DISK
      *-----------------------------------------------------------------------------------------------*
      *                                  RPG name          External name                              *
      * File name. . . . . . . . :       P74PSM            STAN/P74PSM                                 *
      * Record format(s) . . . . . :     P74PSMR           P74PSMR                                     *
      *-----------------------------------------------------------------------------------------------*
    3 FQsysprt   O    F 132           PRINTER OFLIND(*INOF)
    4
    5 * Define work fields....
    6 DInCareRoom      S               8 2
    7 DPrivatRoom      S               8 2
    8 DSemiRoom        S               8 2
    9 DTotIcRooms      S               9 2
   10 DTotPrRooms      S               9 2
   11 DTotSeRooms      S               9 2
   12 DRoomCharge      S               8 2
   13 DExtraCharg      S               8 2
   14 DNurseBill       S               8 2
   15 DTVBill          S               7 2
```

```
16 DOxBill          S              7 2
17 DIVBill          S              7 2
18 DNoPatients      S              4 0
19 DTotExCharg      S              9 2
20 DRoom            S             14
21
22 * Define Named Constants....
23 DIcRoom          C                        'INTENSIVE CARE'
24 DPrRoom          C                        'PRIVATE       '
25 DSeRoom          C                        'SEMI-PRIVATE '
26
27=IP74PSMR
   *-------------------------------------------------------------------*
   * RPG record format .... : P74PSMR                                  *
   * External format ..... : P74PSMR : STAN/P74PSM                     *
   *-------------------------------------------------------------------*
28=I                         A    1    5 PATIENTNO
29=I                         A    6   25 PATNTNAME
30=I                         P   26   29 OADMITDATE
31=I                         P   30   33 OOUTDATE
32=I                         P   34   35 ODAYSIN
33=I                         A   36   36 ROOMTYPE
34=I                         A   37   37 PRIVTNURSE
35=I                         A   38   38 ROOMTV
36=I                         A   39   39 OXYGEN
37=I                         A   40   40 IVFEEDING
38 C        EVAL      *INOF = *ON                     turn on OF indicator
39 C        READ      p74psm                  *3   ----LR  read first record
40 C        DOW       *INLR = *OFF                   dow LR is off         B01
41
42 * Test for page overflow (OF indicator on)....
43 C        IF        *INOF = *ON                     page overflow        B02
44 C        EXCEPT    Headings                        print headings        02
45 C        EVAL      *INOF = *OFF                    turn off OF indicatr  02
46 C        ENDIF                                     end IF group         E02
47
48 C        SELECT                                    begin SELECT group   B02
49 C        WHEN      RoomType = 'I'                  Intensive Care Room? X02
50 C        EVAL      InCareRoom = 400 * DaysIn       compute ic room bill  02
51 C        EVAL      RoomCharge = InCareRoom         store in print field  02
52 C        EVAL      TotIcRooms = TotIcRooms + InCareRoom  accum InCarRoom bill 02
53 C        EVAL      Room = IcRoom                   init. with Named Cn    02
54 C        WHEN      RoomType = 'P'                  Private Room?        X02
55 C        EVAL      PrivatRoom = 300 * DaysIn       compute pr room bill  02
56 C        EVAL      RoomCharge = PrivatRoom         store in print field  02
57 C        EVAL      TotPrRooms = TotPrRooms + PrivatRoom  accum Privatoom bill 02
58 C        EVAL      Room = PrRoom                   init. with Named Cn    02
59 C        WHEN      RoomType = 'S'                  Private Room?        X02
60 C        EVAL      SemiRoom = 200 * DaysIn         compute pr room bill  02
61 C        EVAL      RoomCharge = SemiRoom           store in print field  02
62 C        EVAL      TotSeRooms = TotSeRooms + SemiRoom  accum Privatoom bill 02
63 C        EVAL      Room = SeRoom                   init. with Named Cn    02
64 C        ENDSL                                     end SLECT group      E02
65
66 * Add extra service charges (nurse, tv, oxygen, iv)....
67 C        IF        PrivtNurse = 'N'                Private Nurse?       B02
68 C        EVAL      NurseBill = 110 * DaysIn        compute nurse bill    02
69 C        EVAL      ExtraCharg = ExtraCharg + NurseBill  accum extra charges  02
70 C        ENDIF                                     end IF group         E02
71
72 C        IF        RoomTV = 'T'                    room tv?             B02
73 C        EVAL      TvBill = 10 * DaysIn            compute tv bill       02
74 C        EVAL      ExtraCharg = ExtraCharg + TvBill  Accum extra charges  02
75 C        ENDIF                                     end IF group         E02
76
77 C        IF        Oxygen = 'O'                    Private Nurse?       B02
78 C        EVAL      OxBill = 250 * DaysIn           compute nurse bill    02
79 C        EVAL      ExtraCharg = ExtraCharg + OxBill  accum extra charges  02
80 C        ENDIF                                     end IF group         E02
81
82 C        IF        IVFeeding = 'V'                 room tv?             B02
83 C        EVAL      IvBill = 105 * DaysIn           compute tv bill       02
84 C        EVAL      ExtraCharg = ExtraCharg + IvBill  Accum extra charges  02
85 C        ENDIF                                     end IF group         E02
```

```
86
87 C                    EXCEPT    DetailLine                                    print record              01
88 C                                                                                                      01
89 C                    EVAL      NoPatients = NoPatients + 1                   accum no of patients     01
90 C                    EVAL      TotExCharg = TotExCharg + ExtraCharg          accum totexcharg         01
91 C                    EVAL      ExtraCharg = *ZERO                            init. field to zero      01
92 C                                                                                                      01
93 C                    READ      P74psm                           ----LR      read next record         01
94 C                    ENDDO                                                   end dow group            E01
95
96 C                    EXCEPT    TotalLine                                     print totals
97 C                    EVAL      *INLR = *ON                                   end program
98
99  OQsysprt   E            Headings         1 01
100 O                                            59 'GET WELL HOSPITAL'
101 O                                           100 'PAGE'
102 O                        PAGE              105
103 O          E            Headings         1
104 O                                            61 'ROOM BILLING REPORT'
105 O          E            Headings         3
106 O                                            50 'AS OF'
107 O                        UDATE          Y   59
108 O          E            Headings         1
109 O                                             7 'PATIENT'
110 O                                            38 'ADMIT'
111 O                                            51 'CHECKOUT'
112 O                                            62 'BILLING'
113 O                                            87 'ROOM'
114 O                                           105 'EXTRA SERVICES'
115 O          E            Headings         2
116 O                                             6 'NUMBER'
117 O                                            25 'PATIENT NAME'
118 O                                            37 'DATE'
119 O                                            49 'DATE'
120 O                                            60 'DAYS'
121 O                                            75 'ROOM TYPE'
122 O                                            88 'CHARGE'
123 O                                           102 'CHARGE'
124 O          E            DetailLine       2
125 O                        PatientNo          5
126 O                        PatntName         29
127 O                        AdmitDate      Y   40
128 O                        OutDate        Y   51
129 O                        DaysIn         3   60
130 O                        Room              78
131 O                        RoomCharge     1   91
132 O                        ExtraCharg     1  103
133 O          E            TotalLine        2
134 O                                            12 'TOTALS'
135 O          E            TotalLine        1
136 O                                            31 'NUMBER OF PATIENTS......'
137 O                                            37 '......'
138 O                        NoPatients     1   42
139 O          E            TotalLine        1
140 O                                            27 'PRIVATE ROOM BILLING'
141 O                                            37 '..........'
142 O                                            38 '$'
143 O                        TotPrRooms     1   50
144
145 O          E            TotalLine        1
146 O                                            26 'INTENSIVE CARE ROOM'
147 O                                            37 'BILLING...'
148 O                                            38 '$'
149 O                        TotIcRooms     1   50
150
151 O          E            TotalLine        1
152 O                                            24 'SEMI-PRIVATE ROOM'
153 O                                            37 'BILLING.....'
154 O                                            38 '$'
155 O                        TotsERooms     1   50
156
157 O          E            TotalLine        1
158 O                                            29 'EXTRA SERVICES BILLING'
159 O                                            37 '........'
```

```
160 0                                      38 'S'
161 0                    TotExCharg    1    50
     * * * *  E N D   O F   S O U R C E  * * * *
```

Printed Report:

```
                              GET WELL HOSPITAL                          PAGE    1
                              ROOM BILLING REPORT
                               AS OF  1/30/95
```

PATIENT NUMBER	PATIENT NAME	ADMIT DATE	CHECKOUT DATE	BILLING DAYS	ROOM TYPE	ROOM CHARGE	EXTRA SERVICES CHARGE
10000	WALTER WINCHELL	1/05/95	1/15/95	10	PRIVATE	3,000.00	100.00
11000	EDGAR BERGEN	1/08/95	1/13/95	5	SEMI-PRIVATE	1,000.00	50.00
12000	ZAZU PITTS	1/02/95	1/19/95	17	INTENSIVE CARE	6,800.00	4,250.00
13000	LON CHANEY	1/06/95	1/15/95	9	INTENSIVE CARE	3,600.00	1,935.00
14000	FANNY BRICE	1/10/95	1/14/95	4	PRIVATE	1,200.00	40.00
15000	W.C. FIELDS	1/20/95	1/31/95	11	SEMI-PRIVATE	2,200.00	110.00
16000	JACK BENNY	1/22/95	1/30/95	8	INTENSIVE CARE	3,200.00	3,800.00

```
   TOTALS

      NUMBER OF PATIENTS............   7
      PRIVATE ROOM BILLING..........$   4,200.00
      INTENSIVE CARE ROOM BILLING...$  13,600.00
      SEMI-PRIVATE ROOM BILLING.....$   3,200.00
      EXTRA SERVICES BILLING........$  10,285.00
```

CHAPTER 8
QUESTION ANSWERS

1. The functions of Data Structures include:

   a. Divide a field into subfields.
   b. Change the format of a field.
   c. Group noncontiguous data into a contiguous format.
   d. Define an area of storage in more than one format.
   e. Define multiple occurrences of a data structure (introduced in Chapter 11).
   f. Special purpose data structures.

2. In the *Definition Specifications*.

3. a. The letters **DS** must be specified in columns 19-20.
   b. A field name cannot be used more than once.
   c. A field name cannot be specified as a field <u>and</u> data structure name.
   d. Overlapping subfields cannot be used as elements of a calculation statement.   **"**
   e. One subfield may redefine another subfield.
   f. Numeric subfields must be initialized with numeric data before they are used in calculations.

4. *Data Area Data Structure* - Implicitly access the values in a *data area* and implicitly update its value at the end of the controlling program. This data area is defined in the RPG IV program by specifying a **U** in position 23 and **DS** in columns 24-25.

   File Information Data Structure (**INFDS**) - Provides exception, error information that may occur when processing a <u>file</u> during program execution. This data structure contains predefined subfields that identify the file, record, and operation being processed when the error occurred. In addition, the status code number and RPG IV routine in which the error occurred may also be identified.

   Program Status Data Structures - Identify exception/errors that are generated by the RPG IV program and <u>not</u> by a file. This data structure is defined in an RPG IV program by the letter **S** in column 23 and **DS** in columns 24-25.

5.

```
.. 1 ...+... 2 ...+... 3 ...+... 4 ...+... 5 ...+... 6 ...+... 7 ...+... 8
DName++++++++++ETDsFrom+++To/L+++IDc.Keywords++++++++++++++++++++++++++++++++
* Data structure with subfields defined with absolute notation.

DCustno        DS
D  State                1     2
D  County               3    17
D  City                18    32
```

Note: Field sizes are randomly assigned.

6. **Note: Field sizes are based on the sizes in Question 5.**

```
* Data structure with subfields defined with length notation. Field being
* subdivided must be defined as a subfield-not as a data structure name

                    DS
DCustno
D State                        2    OVERLAY(Custno)
D County                      15    OVERLAY(Custno:3)
D City                        15    OVERLAY(ActNumber:18)
```

7.

```
.. 1 ...+... 2 ...+... 3 ...+... 4 ...+... 5 ...+... 6 ...+... 7 ...+... 8
DName++++++++++ETDsFrom+++To/L+++IDc.Keywords++++++++++++++++++++++++++++++++

* Definition Specification to subdivide a physical file field into
* subfields using absolute notatin.
DYyyyMmDd        DS
D  Yy                      1     4
D  Mm                      5     6
D  Dd                      7     8

* Definition Specification instructions to group the previous data
* structure's subfields into a different date format.
DMmDdYyyy        DS
D  Mm                      1     2
D  Dd                      3     4
D  Yyyy                    5     8
```

8. **Note: Physical file field sizes are randomly assigned.**

```
*.. 1 ...+... 2 ...+... 3 ...+... 4 ...+... 5 ...+... 6 ...+... 7 ...+... 8
A..........T.Name++++++RLen++TDpB.....Functions++++++++++++++++++++++++++++++
* Physical file record format

A          R CUSTRCD
A            CUSTNO         5
A            STATE          2
A            COUNTY        15
A            CITY          15
```

```
.. 1 ...+... 2 ...+... 3 ...+... 4 ...+... 5 ...+... 6 ...+... 7 ...+... 8
DName++++++++++ETDsFrom+++To/L+++IDc.Keywords++++++++++++++++++++++++++++++++
* Physical file's fields grouped in a different order to load the Cuskey
* data structure value

DCuskey          DS
D  Custno                  1     5
D  State                   6     7
D  County                  8    22
D  City                   23    37
```

9. *Record Identification Codes* identify a record format in one or more program described physical files. However, because externally described phyical files support only one record format they are seldom used.

They are specified in columns 24 through 46 of the *Record Description* area of the *Input Specifications* for a program described physical file.

In any position(s) in the body of the record format.

10. Any number in a continuing "and" relationship. Practically, however, only one character is commonly used.

11. Letter **C** - *Zone* and *digit* areas of the byte are tested.

    Letter **Z** - Only the *zone* area of the byte is tested.
    Letter **D** - Only the *digit* area of the byte is tested.

    Processing time is saved if the **C** (character) option is specified.

12. Saves memory during execution of the controlling program.

13. By defining the record formats in the physical (all must have exactly the same field configuration) as a program-defined file in the *Input Specifications* and redefining the record formats in a data structure with their related field parameters.

14.

```
.. 1 ...+... 2 ...+... 3 ...+... 4 ...*... 5 ...+... 6 ...+... 7 ...+... 8
DName++++++++++ETDsFrom++To/L+++IDc.Keywords++++++++++++++++++++++++++++++++
 * Data area data structure is defined with a U in the T field position 23
 * Data is implicitly read and updated.

DTermdt         UDS
D  TermDate            1      8 0
```

15. Any code greater than **00099**

16. a. By specifying a Resulting Indicator in the Lo field (positions 73-74) of a **CHAIN, UPDATE, WRITE, DELETE, READ, READE, READP,** or **READPE** RPG IV instruction.

    b. With a File Informatiion Data Structure.

    c. With a Program Status Data Structure.

17.

```
.. 1 ...+... 2 ...+... 3 ...+... 4 ...+... 5 ...+... 6 ...+... 7 ...+... 8 ...+... 9 ...+...10
FFilename++IPEASFRlen+LKlen+AIDevice+.Keywords++++++++++++++++++++++++++++++++Comments++++++++++++
 * File Information data structure (Infds1) is assigned to this input file with the INFDS key-
 * word. An internal subroutine (*PSSR) is provided by the INFSR keyword. *PSSR is an RPG IV
 * compiler-supplied subroutine that is automatically processed when an error occurs.

FStuMstr  IF  E           DISK      INFDS(Infds1)
F                                   INFSR(*PSSR)
```

```
.. 1 ...+... 2 ...+... 3 ...+... 4 ...+... 5 ...+... 6 ...+... 7 ...+... 8
DName++++++++++ETDsFrom++To/L+++IDc.Keywords++++++++++++++++++++++++++++++++

DInfds1         DS
D  Status           *STATUS
```

18. Some of the Program Status Data Structure codes include: Including:

    00101 - Negative square root

00102 - Divide by zero
00121 - Array index not valid
00122 - **OCCUR** outside of range

For the other Status Codes and their related conditions, refer to Figure 8-13 in the chapter.

19.

```
FFilename++IPEASFRLen+LKlen+AIDevice+.Keywords+++++++++++++++++++++++++++Comments+++++++++++++

FActMstr   IF  E           DISK     INFSR(*PSSR)
FQsysPrt   O   F  132      PRINTER
```

```
 .. 1 ...+... 2 ...+... 3 ...+... 4 ...+... 5 ...+... 6 ...+... 7 ...+... 8
DName++++++++++++ETDsFrom++To/L+++IDc.Keywords+++++++++++++++++++++++++++++++++

D              SDS
D  Procedure        *PROC
D  Statuscode       *STATUS
D  RPGRoutine       *ROUTINE
D  Parameters       *PARM
```

20. *Data Areas* are objects used to transfer data to one or more programs within a job or between jobs. They may be considered a one record storage area that is stored on disk.

21. **CRTDTAARA** (*Create Data Area*). Data area name, Library, Type (*DEC, *CHAR, or *LGL), Length, Decimal positions for *DEC type, Initial value, and Text 'description'.

22. **CHGDTAARA** (*Change Data Area*). **DSPDTAARA** (*Display Data Area*).

23. *DTAARA (*Factor 1* entry); **DEFINE** (*Operation*); and Data Area name in the *Result* field.

   IN - explicitly accesses the value in a data area.
   OUT - explicitly changes the value in a data area.

24. *LOCK - *Factor 1* entry of an **IN** statement prevents access (locks) of the data area.

   UNLOCK - Explicitly unlocks the data area. When *NAMVAR is specified in *Factor 2* of an **UNLOCK** statement, all of the data areas accessed by the RPG/400 program are unlocked.

25.

```
Number ....1....+....2....+....3....+....4....+....5....+....6....+....7....+....8....+....9....+...10 Num
  1 C   *DTAARA    DEFINE            RptDat               specify data area
  2 C   *LOCK      IN       RptDat                        access data area
  3 C              MOVE     UDATE    RptDat               move to data area
  4 C              OUT      RptDat                        update data area
  5 C              UNLOCK   RptDat                        unlock data area
  6 C              EVAL     *INLR = *ON                   end the job
```

PROGRAMMING ASSIGNMENTS

Programming Assignment 9-1: SCHEDULE OF ACCOUNTS RECEIVABLE

Notes to the Instructor:

1. A data area must be created and loaded with a 123197 date value and 5 zeros for the count of valid records. Because the values are to be separated for processing, inform students that the data area must be created as *CHAR type.

2. To illustrate the function of *Record Identifying* and how a *File Information Data Structure* can process unidentified record types, the record formats are defined as *Input Specification* instructions with the physical file defined as program described.

   Inform students that other methods of processing unidentified record tyes may provide more flexiblity. For example, a "dummy" record format could be included in the input instructions with no *Record Identifying Indicator* assigned to it. This would prevent cancellation of program execution and provide for additional processing of the invalid record type.

3. Explicitly define the data area in the RPG IV program and update the data area with a new 033198 + valid record count value (i.e. **03319800011**) at **LR** time.

CRTDTAARA Display (with original values):

```
                         Create Data Area (CRTDTAARA)

 Type choices, press Enter.

 Data area  . . . . . . . . . . > P81darea__    Name
   Library  . . . . . . . . . . >   STAN_____  Name, *CURLIB
 Type . . . . . . . . . . . . . > *CHAR____     *DEC, *CHAR, *LGL
 Length:
   Length . . . . . . . . . . . > 13___         1-2000
   Decimal positions  . . . . . > _____         0-9
 Initial value  . . . . . . . . > 1231199700000_____
 Text 'description' . . . . . . > pa 8-1 _____
 ____

                                                                  Bottom
 F3=Exit   F4=Prompt   F5=Refresh   F10=Additional parameters   F12=Cancel
 F13=How to use this display       F24=More keys
```

DSPDTAARA Display (after execution of the program):

```
                          Display Data Area
                                                  -System:   S1012CFA
 Data area . . . . . . . :   P81DAREA
   Library . . . . . . . :     STAN
 Type  . . . . . . . . . :   *CHAR
 Length  . . . . . . . . :   13
 Text  . . . . . . . . . :   pa 8-1 data area
 Value . . . . . . . . . :   '0331199800000'
```

```
                                                              Bottom
Press Enter to continue.
F3=Exit   F12=Cancel
```

DLTDTAARA (after student submits his/her assignment):

```
                    Delete Data Area (DLTDTAARA)

Type choices, press Enter.
Data area  . . . . . . . . . .   P81darea     Name, generic*
  Library  . . . . . . . . . .   . STAN       Name, *LIBL, *CURLIB...




                                                              Bottom
F3=Exit   F4=Prompt   F5=Refresh   F12=Cancel   F13=How to use this display
F24=More keys
```

Compile Listing:

```
Line    <-------------------- Source Specifications ---11----------------------><---- Comments ----> Do
Number  ....1....+....2....+....3....+....4....+....5....+....6....+....7....+....8....+....9....+...10 Num
                         S o u r c e   L i s t i n g
   1 FP81psm    IF   F   45        DISK     INFDS(Infds)              define data structur
   2 F                                      INFSR(*PSSR)              define error sr
   3 FQsysprt   O    F  132        PRINTER OFLIND(*INOF)
   4
   5  * Define field in the INFDS data structure....
   6 DInfds         DS
   7 D Status           *STATUS
   8
   9  * Define work fields....
  10 DTotBalance    S           9 2
  11 DRecordCnt     S           5 0
  12 DReadAgain     S           6
  13 DDateOut       S           8 0
  14 DTotRecords    S           5 0
  15
  16  * Define data area which stores report date and record count...
  17 DDSfordarea    DS                                                data area
  18 DReportDate          1    8                                      data area value
  19 DGoodRcds            9   13                                      data area value
  20
  21  * Define fields in program described physical file....
  22 IP81psm    SM  01   1 CA   2 CR
  23 I                           1    2  IdCode
  24 I                           3    7  CustNumber
  25 I                           8   37  CustName
  26 I                          38   45 2ActBalance
  27
  28  * Get report date and record count from data area...
  29 C     *DTAARA    DEFINE   P81darea      DSfordarea
  30 C     *LOCK      IN       DSfordarea                   extract d a data
  31 C                MOVE     ReportDate    DateOut        init. DateOut
  32 C                MOVE     GoodRcds      RecordCnt      init. RecordCnt
  33 C
  34 C                EVAL     *INOF = *ON                  turn on OF indicator
  35 C                READ     P81psm                ----LR read first record
  36 C                DOW      *INLR = *OFF                 dow LR is off        B01
  37
  38  * Heading control....
  39 C                IF       *INOF = *ON AND *IN50 = *OFF  OF indicator on?    B02
  40 C                EXCEPT   Headings                     print heading lines  02
  41 C                EVAL     *INOF = *OFF                 turn off OF indicatr  02
  42 C                EVAL     *IN50 = *OFF                 turn off indicatr 50 02
  43 C                ENDIF                                 end IF group         E02
```

79

```
44
45 C              IF        *IN01 = *ON                         valid id code?        B02
46 C              EXCEPT    GoodLine                            print valid record    02
47 C              EVAL      RecordCnt = RecordCnt + 1           increment record ctr  02
48 C              ENDIF                                         end IF group          E02
49
50 C              EVAL      TotBalance = TotBalance + ActBalance  increment TotBalance 01
51 C              EVAL      TotRecords = TotRecords + 1         increment RecordCnt   01
52 C              READ      P81psm                       ----LR read next record      01
53 C              ENDDO                                         end dow group         E01
54
55 C              MOVE      03311998       ReportDate           new data area value
56 C              MOVE      GoodRcds       RecordCnt            update data area fld
57 C              OUT       DSfordarea                          update data area
58 C              EXCEPT    TotalLine                           print total lines
59 C              EVAL      *INLR = *ON                         end program
60
61  * INFDS subroutine for unidentified record type....
62 C     *PSSR    BEGSR                                         begin error SR
63 C              IF        Status = 01011                      unidentified record   B01
64 C              EXCEPT    ErrorLine                           print error line      01
65 C              EVAL      *IN50 = *ON                         turn on indicator 50  01
66 C              EVAL      ReadAgain = '*GETIN'                RPG IV return point   01
67 C              ENDIF                                         end IF group          E01
68 C              ENDSR     ReadAgain                           return ctrl to RPG
69
70 OQsysprt  E          Headings      1 01
71 O                                        4 'PAGE'
72 O                     PAGE             9  *3
73 O                                       40 'EVERYBODY COMPANY'
74 O         E          Headings      1
75 O                                       37 'SCHEDULE OF ACCOUNTS'
76 O                                       48 'RECEIVABLE'
77 O         E          Headings      2
78 O                     DateOut      Y   35
79 O         E          Headings      2
80 O                                       18 'CUSTOMER NUMBER'
81 O                                       40 'CUSTOMER NAME'
82 O                                       65 'ACCOUNT BALANCE'
83 O         E          Headings      0
84 O                                       52 '$'
85 O         E          GoodLine      1
86 O                     CustNumber       12
87 O                     CustName         49
88 O                     ActBalance    1  64
89 O         E          ErrorLine     1
90 O                                       44 '...UNIDENTIFIED RECORD...'
91 O         E          TotalLine     1
92 O                                       64 '-------------'
93 O         E          TotalLine     1
94 O                                       52 '$'
95 O                     TotBalance    1  64
96 O         E          TotalLine     2
97 O                                       64 '============='
98 O         E          TotalLine     0
99 O                                       28 'RECORD PROCESSED = '
100 O                    TotRecords    1  34
     * * * * *  E N D   O F   S O U R C E  * * * *
```

Printed Report:

```
PAGE    1            EVERYBODY COMPANY
                SCHEDULE OF ACCOUNTS RECEIVABLE
                        3/31/1998

    CUSTOMER NUMBER        CUSTOMER NAME        ACCOUNT BALANCE

        11111        ALWAYS ABLE           $   2,192.15
        11121        MARY BEST                   513.22
                     ...UNIDENTIFIED RECORD...
        12345        LARS DEFICIT              7,977.88
        12356        HUGH DENT                   111.54
        13344        NEVER EARLY               4,856.73
```

```
14455        ONA TIME                         614.87
             ...UNIDENTIFIED RECORD...
16443        Y. HOLD                           41.28
17777        I. ITCH                        6,133.66
18123        H.I. JUMP                        324.46
19996        E.Z. KIDD                      4,444.44
20019        I.M.A. LUMOX                     567.84
                                          -------------
                                        $   27,778.07
                                          =============


             RECORD PROCESSED =      11
```

Programming Assignment 8-1: INCLUDING A PROGRAM STATUS DATA STRUCTURE IN AN RPG IV PROGRAM

```
Line   <--------------------- Source Specifications --------------------><---- Comments ----> Do
Number ....1....+....2....+....3....+....4....+....5....+....6....+....7....+....8....+....9....+...10 Num
                         S o u r c e   L i s t i n g
   1  * PA 8-2: Including a program status data structure in a program....
   2 FP65psm    IF  E           DISK   INFSR(*PSSR)
      *-------------------------------------------------------------------------------*
      *                                RPG name        External name                  *
      * File name. . . . . . . . :     P65PSM          ‚ŞTAN/P65PSM                   *
      * Record format(s) . . . . . :   P65PSMR         P65PSMR                        *
      *-------------------------------------------------------------------------------*
   3 FQsysprt   O   F 132        PRINTER OFLIND(*INOF)
   4
   5 DYear           S              4  0
   6 DDepAmount      S              7  0
   7 DAnnualDep      S              7  0
   8 DYrsCounter     S              2  0
   9 DAccumDep       S              7  0
  10 DBookValue      S              7  0
  11 DExcess         S              7  0
  12 DReadAgain      S              6
  13
  14  * Define Program Status Data Structure keywords....
  15 DPSDS           SDS
  16 D Procedure           *PROC
  17 D StatusCode          *STATUS
  18 D Routine             *ROUTINE
  19 D Parameters          *PARMS
  20
  21=IP65PSMR
      *-------------------------------------------------------------------------------*
      * RPG record format  . . . . :  P65PSMR                                         *
      * External format  . . . . . :  P65PSMR : STAN/P65PSM                           *
      *-------------------------------------------------------------------------------*
  22=I                        A    1   25 ASSETNAME
  23=I                        P   26   29 OPURCHDATE
  24=I                        P   30   34 2COST
  25=I                        P   35   36 OEUL
  26=I                        P   37   40 OSALVALUE
  27 C             EVAL      *INOF = *ON
  28 C             READ      P65psm                    ----LR   read first record
  29 C             DOW       *INLR = *OFF                       dow LR is off        B01
  30  * Heading print control....
  31 C             IF        *INOF = *ON                        OF indicator on?     B02
  32 C             EXCEPT    Headings                           print heading lines   02
  33 C             EVAL      *INOF = *OFF                       turn off OF indicatr  02
  34 C             ENDIF                                        end IF group         E02
  35
  36  * Housekeeping....
  37 C             MOVE      PurchDate   Year                   move yr to year       01
  38 C             MOVEL     19          Year                   compute fwt           01
  39 C             EVAL      DepAmount = Cost - SalValue        compute deprecbl amt  01
  40 C             EVAL      AnnualDep = DepAmount / Eul        compute annual dep    01
  41
  42  * Calculate AnnualDEp, AccumDep, and BookValue for the asset's eul....
```

82

```
43 C                    DO      Eul           YrsCounter         until counter > eul  B02
44 C                    EVAL    AccumDep = AccumDep + AnnualDep  accumm annualdep      02
45 C                    EVAL    BookValue = Cost - AccumDep      compute bookvalue     02
46
47 * Last year's depreciation computation....
48 C                    IF      YrsCounter = Eul AND BookValue > SalValue  compound test  B03
49 C                    EVAL    Excess = BookValue - SalValue    compute excess amt    03
50 C                    EVAL    AnnualDep = AnnualDep + Excess   increment AnnualDep   03
51 C                    EVAL    AccumDep = AccumDep + Excess     increment AccumDep    03
52 C                    EVAL    BookValue = SalValue             initialize book       03
53 C                    ENDIF                                    end IF group          E03
54
55 C                    EXCEPT  DetailLine                       print record          02
56 C                    EVAL    Year = Year + 1                  increment year        02
57 C                    ENDDO                                    end DO group          E02
58
59 C                    EVAL    AccumDep = *ZERO                 initialize AccumDep   01
60 C                    READ    P65psm                ----LR     read next record      01
61 C                    EVAL    *INOF = *ON                      new asset hdg contrl  01
62 C                    ENDDO                                    end dow group         E01
63
64 C                    EVAL    *INLR = *ON                      end job
65
66 * Begin error subroutine....
67 C     *PSSR          BEGSR                                    begin error routine
68 C                    IF      StatusCode = 00102               divide by zero error  B01
69 C                    EVAL    ReadAgain = '*GETIN'             compiler return pt     01
70 C                    EXCEPT  ErrorLine                *9      print error line       01
71 C                    ENDIF                                    end IF group          E01
72 C                    ENDSR   ReadAgain                        end SR & return
73
74 OQsysprt  E          Headings      1    01
75 O                    UDATE       Y      8
76 O                                       38 'DEPRECIATION SCHEDULE'
77 O                                       59 'PAGE'
78 O                    PAGE               64
79 O         E          Headings      3
80 O                                       37 'STRAIGHT-LINE METHOD'
81 O         E          Headings      2
82 O                                       10 'ASSET:'
83 O                    AssetName          36
84 O                                       52 'PURCHASE DATE:'
85 O                    PurchDate   Y      61
86 O         E          Headings      2
87 O                                        9 'COST:'
88 O                    Cost          1    22
89 O                                       32 'EUL:'
90 O                    Eul         Z      35
91 O                                       55 'SALVAGE VALUE:'
92 O                    SalValue      1    62
93 O         E          Headings      1
94 O                                       25 'ANNUAL'
95 O                                       42 'ACCUMULATED'
96 O                                       52 'BOOK'
97 O         E          Headings      2
98 O                                       12 'YEAR'
99 O                                       28 'DEPRECIATION'
100 O                                      43 'DEPRECIATION'
101 O                                      53 'VALUE'
102 O        E          DetailLine    2
103 O                   Year               12
104 O                   AnnualDep     1    28
105 O                   AccumDep      1    42
106 O                   BookValue     1    55
107 O        E          ErrorLine     2
108 O                                      17 'DIVIDE BY ZERO'    -
109 O                                      30 'PROCEDURE='
110 O                   Procedure          40
111 O                                      50 ' - STATUS='
112 O                   StatusCode         55
113 O                                      66 ' - ROUTINE='
114 O                   Routine            74
     * * * * *  E N D   O F   S O U R C E  * * * * *
```

Printed Report:

```
8/13/97          DEPRECIATION SCHEDULE              PAGE    1
                 STRAIGHT-LINE METHOD


   ASSET: BPT MILLING MACHINE       PURCHASE DATE:  5/14/97

   COST:    15,000.00      EUL:  7     SALVAGE VALUE:  3,000

                    ANNUAL      ACCUMULATED      BOOK
            YEAR    DEPRECIATION DEPRECIATION    VALUE

            1997         1,714        1,714      13,286

            1998         1,714        3,428      11,572

            1999         1,714        5,142       9,858

            2000         1,714        6,856       8,144

            2001         1,714        8,570       6,430

            2002         1,714       10,284       4,716

            2003         1,716       12,000       3,000
-------------------------------------------------------------
8/13/97          DEPRECIATION SCHEDULE      ••      PAGE    2
                 STRAIGHT-LINE METHOD


   ASSET: IBM AS/400 - MODEL E      PURCHASE DATE:  2/10/97

   COST:   375,000.00     EUL:        SALVAGE VALUE: 20,000

                    ANNUAL      ACCUMULATED      BOOK
            YEAR    DEPRECIATION DEPRECIATION    VALUE

   DIVIDE BY ZERO    PROCEDURE=P82RSM    - STATUS=00102 - ROUTIN =*DETC
-------------------------------------------------------------
8/13/97          DEPRECIATION SCHEDULE              PAGE    3
                 STRAIGHT-LINE METHOD


   ASSET: IBM MICRO - PENTIUM       PURCHASE DATE:  1/11/97

   COST:    2,800.00      EUL:  3     SALVAGE VALUE:    400

                    ANNUAL      ACCUMULATED      BOOK
            YEAR    DEPRECIATION DEPRECIATION    VALUE
            1997          800          800       2,000

            1998          800        1,600       1,200

            1999          800        2,400         400
-------------------------------------------------------------
8/13/97          DEPRECIATION SCHEDULE              PAGE    4
                 STRAIGHT-LINE METHOD


   ASSET: OFFICE FURNITURE          PURCHASE DATE:  10/01/97

   COST:    9,000.00      EUL: 10    SALVAGE VALUE:     600
                    ANNUAL      ACCUMULATED      BOOK

            YEAR    DEPRECIATION DEPRECIATION    VALUE

            1997          840          840       8,160

            1998          840        1,680       7,320

            1999          840        2,520       6,480

            2000          840        3,360       5,640
```

2001	840	4,200	4,800
2002	840	5,040	3,960
2003	840	5,880	3,120
2004	840	6,720	2,280
2005	840	7,560	1,440
2006	840	8,400	600

8/13/97   DEPRECIATION SCHEDULE   PAGE   5
STRAIGHT-LINE METHOD

ASSET: FACTORY BUILDING   PURCHASE DATE: 6/15/97

COST: 1,200,000.00   EUL: 18   SALVAGE VALUE: 0

YEAR	ANNUAL DEPRECIATION	ACCUMULATED DEPRECIATION	BOOK VALUE
1997	66,666	66,666	1,133,334
1998	66,666	133,332	1,066,668
1999	66,666	199,998	1,000,002
2000	66,666	266,664	933,336
2001	66,666	333,330	866,670
2002	66,666	399,996	800,004
2003	66,666	466,662	733,338
2004	66,666	533,328	666,672
2005	66,666	599,994	600,006
2006	66,666	666,660	533,340
2007	66,666	733,326	466,674
2008	66,666	799,992	400,008
2009	66,666	866,658	333,342
2010	66,666	933,324	266,676
2011	66,666	999,990	200,010
2012	66,666	1,066,656	133,344
2013	66,666	1,133,322	66,678
2014	66,678	1,200,000	0

Programming Assignment 9-2: CASH DISBURSEMENTS JOURNAL Instructor:

Notes to the Instructor:

1. The physical file is defined as program defined with the fields defined in two record types in the *Input Specifications*.

2. *Record Identification Codes* are included to identify the two record types in the file.

3. An *Informational Data Structure* is coded to control records that do not include an S or P in position 1 of the records.

4. Because the physical file is not processed by the *RPG Logic Cycle*, it is necessary that the *Record Identifying Indicator(s)* be turned off before the next record is read (see the **SETOFF** instruction on line 67.

```
Line    <-------------------- Source Specifications -------------------------><---- Comments ----> Do
Number  ....1....+....2....+....3....+....4....+....5....+....6....+....7....+....8....+....9....+...10 Num
                       S o u r c e   L i s t i n g
   1 FP83psm    IF   F   53        DISK    INFDS(Infds)              define data structur
   2 F                                     INFSR(*PSSR)              define error sr
   3 FQsysprt   O    F  132        PRINTER OFLIND(*INOF)
   4
   5  * Define field in the INFDS data structure....
   6 DInfds           DS
   7 D File               *FILE
   8 D Status             *STATUS
   9 D OpCode             *OPCODE
  10 D Routine            *ROUTINE
  11 D Record             *RECORD
  12
  13  * Define work fields....
  14 DTotSundry      S          7 2              **
  15 DCashOut        S          6 2
  16 DTotCash        S          7 2
  17 DDiscount       S          6 2
  18 DTotDiscont     S          7 2
  19 DTotActsPay     S          7 2
  20 DReadAgain      S          6
  21
  22  * Define fields in program described physical file....
  23 IP83psm      SM  01    1 CS
  24 I                            1    1 TransCode
  25 I                        P   2    5 0CheckDate
  26 I                        P   6    7 0CheckNum
  27 I                            8   27 Payee
  28 I                           28   47 ActDebit
  29 I                        P  48   49 0Folio
  30 I                        P  50   53 2SundryAmt
  31 I           SM  02    1 CP
  32 I                            1    1 TransCode
  33 I                        P   2    5 0CheckDate
  34 I                        P   6    7 0CheckNum
  35 I                            8   27 Payee
  36 I                           28   47 ActDebit
  37 I                        P  48   49 3Fol_Pct
  38 I                        P  50   53 2PurchAmt
  39
  40 C            EVAL      *INOF = *ON                    turn on OF indicator
  41 C            READ      P83psm                  ----LR read first record
  42 C            DOW       *INLR = *OFF                   dow LR is off        B01
  43
  44  * Heading control....
  45 C            IF        *INOF = *ON AND *IN50 = *OFF   OF indicator on?     B02
  46 C            EXCEPT    Headings                       print heading lines  02
  47 C            EVAL      *INOF = *OFF                   turn off OF indicatr 02
  48 C            EVAL      *IN50 = *OFF                   turn off indicatr 50 02
  49 C            ENDIF                                    end IF group         E02
  50
  51 C            SELECT                           -       begin SELECT group   B02
  52 C            WHEN      *IN01 = *ON                    01 record type?      X02
  53 C*           EVAL      Folio = Fol_Pct * 1000         convert to integer
  54 C            EVAL      TotSundry = TotSundry + SundryAmt accum TotSundry   02
  55 C            EVAL      CashOut = SundryAmt            Initialize CashOut   02
  56 C            EVAL      TotCash = TotCash + CashOut    accum TotCash        02
  57 C            EXCEPT    SundryLine                     print SundryLine     02
  58 C            WHEN      *IN02 = *ON                    02 record type?      X02
  59 C            EVAL      TotActsPay = TotActsPay + PurchAmt accum. TotActsPay 02
  60 C            EVAL      Discount = PurchAmt * Fol_Pct  compute discount     02
```

```
61 C                    EVAL      TotDiscont = TotDiscont + Discount        accum. TotDiscount   02
62 C                    EVAL      CashOut = PurchAmt - Discount             compute CashOut      02
63 C                    EVAL      TotCash = TotCash + CashOut               accum. TotCash       02
64 C                    EXCEPT    ActPayLine                                print ActPayLine     02
65 C                    ENDSL                                               end SELECT group    E02
66
67 C                    SETOFF                         0102--               housekeeping         01
68 C                    READ      P83psm               ----LR               read next record     01
69 C                    ENDDO                                               end dow group       E01
70 C                    EXCEPT    TotalLine                                 print total lines
71 C                    EVAL      *INLR = *ON                               end program
72
73 * INFDS subroutine for unidentified record type....
74 C       *PSSR        BEGSR                                               begin error SR
75 C                    IF        Status = 01011                           unidentified record  B01
76 C                    EXCEPT    ErrorLine                                 print error line     01
77 C                    EVAL      *IN50 = *ON                              turn on indicator 50  01
78 C                    EVAL      ReadAgain = '*GETIN'                      RPG IV return point   01
79 C                    ENDIF                                               end IF group        E01
80 C                    ENDSR     ReadAgain                                 return ctrl to RPG
81
82 OQsysprt    E        Headings         2 01
83 O                                             63 'CASH DISBURSEMENTS'
84 O                                            105 'PAGE'
85 O                    PAGE                     110
86 O           E        Headings         1
87 O                                             87 'ACCOUNTS'
88 O                                             99 'PURCHASE'
89 O           E        Headings         2                *3
90 O                                             14 'CHECK'
91 O                                             73 'SUNDRY'
92 O                                             86 'PAYABLE'
93 O                                             99 'DISCOUNT'
94 O                                            109 'CASH'
95 O           E        Headings         2
96 O                                              6 'DATE'
97 O                                             12 'NO'
98 O                                             28 'PAYEE'
99 O                                             54 'ACCOUNT DEBITED'
100 O                                            64 'FOLIO'
101 O                                            72 'DEBIT'
102 O                                            85 'DEBIT'
103 O                                            98 'CREDIT'
104 O                                           110 'CREDIT'
105 O           E        SundryLine       2
106 O                    CheckDate     Y         9
107 O                    CheckNum                13
108 O                    Payee                   35
109 O                    ActDebit                57
110 O                    Folio                   63
111 O                    SundryAmt     1         74
112 O                    CashOut       1        110
113 O           E        ActPayLine       2
114 O                    CheckDate     Y         9
115 O                    CheckNum                13
116 O                    Payee                   35
117 O                    ActDebit                57
118 O                    PurchAmt      1         86
119 O                    Discount      1         98
120 O                    CashOut       1        110
121 O           E        ErrorLine        2
122 O                                            20 'UNIDENTIFIED RECORD'
123 O                    File                    32
124 O                    Status                  42
125 O                    OpCode                  53
126 O                    Routine                 67
127 O                    Record                  80
128 O           E        TotalLine        1
129 O                    TotSundry     1         74
130 O                    TotActsPay    1         86
131 O                    TotDiscont    1         98
132 O                    TotCash       1        110
     * * * * *  E N D   O F   S O U R C E  * * * *
```

Chapter 8 - Data Structures and Data Areas

Printed Report:

CASH DISBURSEMENTS							PAGE 1
DATE	CHECK NO	PAYEE	ACCOUNT DEBITED	FOLIO	SUNDRY DEBIT	ACCOUNTS PAYABLE DEBIT	PURCHASE DISCOUNT CREDIT	CASH CREDIT
1/02/97	100	APEX REALTY	RENT EXPENSE	503	2,500.00			2,500.00
1/03/97	101	EASR SALES CO	EAST SALES CO			1,000.00	20.00	980.00
1/04/97	102	SAVO AND SONS	OFFICE EQUIPMENT	110	500.00			500.00
1/05/97	103	JERRY HALE	SALARIES EXPENSE	505	660.00			660.00
1/10/97	104	ACME MFG CO	ACME MFG CO			2,000.00	40.00	1,960.00
1/14/97	105	ELSIE TRUCKING CO	DELIVERY EXPENSES	590	57.98			57.98
1/18/97	106	SMITH AND SONS	SMITH AND SONS			300.00	7.50	292.50
1/22/97	107	ARIZONA SUPPLY CO	ARIZONA SUPPLY CO			950.10	14.25	935.85
UNIDENTIFIED RECORD	P83PSM		01011 READ F	*DETC				
1/25/97	109	WESTERN SUPPLY CO	WESTERN SUPPLY CO	*,		890.45	8.90	881.55
1/29/97	110	SHELTON FORD	CAR EXPENSE	511	450.93			450.93
1/31/97	111	MATCHLESS TOOL CO	MATCHLESS TOOL CO			600.00	18.00	582.00
UNIDENTIFIED RECORD	P83PSM		01011 READ F	*DETC				
					4,168.91	5,740.55	108.65	9,800.81

CHAPTER 9
QUESTION ANSWERS

1. For lists of relatively constant data that is to be accessed by other data.

2. State and Federal Income Tax and Federal Withholding Taxes determination.

3. *Definition Specifications*. After any File Description instructions.

4. In a contiguous order.

5. *Compile Time Table*. Data is included at the end of an RPG IV program.

   Prerun Time Table. Data is stored in one or more external files usually without a *Data Description Specification* format.

6.

Field Name	Position		Function

All of the following fields are used for *Compile* and *Prerun Time Tables*:

Name+++++++++	7-21	Table name must be entered here. All table name must begin with the letters **TAB**.
Ds	24-25	Table must be defined as a "stand-alone" field with an **S** in position 24.
Len+++	36-39	The length of the table's elements must be specified in this field.
I	40-40	Specifies the internal data type. **blank** for character data; **P** for packed-decimal numeric data; **S** for zoned decimal data; **B** for binary number; **D** for Date data; **T** for time data; **Z** for timestamp data; and **G** for Graphic data.
Dc	41-42	If the table elements are numeric, the number of decimal positions must be specified in this field. The entry cannot be larger than the *Len+++* field size.
Keywords	44-80	For Compile and PreRun time tables: **DIM** - Specifies the number of elements stored in the table.
		ASCEND - Specifies that the table data (elements) are stored in an

ascending order.

DESCEND - Specifies that the table data (elements) ares tored in a descending order.

PERRCD - Specifies the number of table elements stored on a record.

ALT - Specifies that the elements in this table are stored in an alternating format with another table.

For Compile time tables only:
CTDATA - Specifes that the table data is stored in the RPG IV program after the last program instruction. The data for each table must begin with a ****CTDATA** delimiter followed by the related table' name.

For Prerun time tables only:
FROMFILE - Specifies the input table file in which the table data is stored.

TOFILE - Specifies the file to which the table data will be written. Usually included if the table data is to be updated.

7. *Compile Time Tables* - No *File Description* entries required.

   Prerun Time Tables - The letter **I** must be specified in position 7, **T** in position 18, and depending on whether the file is program or externally described, an **F** or **E** in position 22 of the *File Description* definition. Because the table data will is often stored in a physical file without a DDS format, an **F** is the most common entry.

8. Table names must begin with the letters **TAB** and cannot be longer than ten characters.

9. *SEARCH ARGUMENT* - The field name, table name, array name or constant entered in *Factor 1* of a **LOOKUP** instruction.

   ARGUMENT TABLE - The table name entered in *Factor 2* of a **LOOKUP** instruction. Specifies the table that is to be searched by the *SEARCH ARGUMENT* value.

   FUNCTION TABLE - The table name entered in the *Result Field* of a **LOOKUP** instruction. Specifies a table related to the *ARGUMENT TABLE*.

LOOKUP - RPG IV operation required to access *ARGUMENT* and *FUNCTION TABLE* data as specified by the related *SEARCH ARGUMENT*.

10. a. Search Argument; b. Argument Table; c. Function Table;
     d. Factor 1, Operation, Factor 2 entries, and one or two
        Resulting Indicators.
     e. A maximum of two tables (one Argument and one Function)

11. Rule 1: All entries related to a table must be the same
             size.

     Rule 2: Smaller numeric entries must be padded with high-
             order zeros.

     Rule 3: Smaller character entries must be padded with
             low-order blanks.

     Rule 4: Pairs of alternating table data must not be split
             onto two records.

12. Tables that have their data stored in a format where one
     table's entry is immediately followed by another table's
     entry on a record. Only two tables may be defined in an
     alternating format. However, any number of "table pairs"
     may be included on a record.

13. a. At the first argument table entry.
     b. Yes, always at the first argument table entry.
     c. Consecutively
     d. At the last argument table entry. An unsuccessful table
        search (**LOOKUP**) will not cancel program execution.

14. If the data in an argument table is stored in an ascending
     sorted order and an <u>equal</u> **LOOKUP** condition is specified,
     program control will "early exit" when an argument table
     value is tested that is greater than the search argument
     value.

     If the argument table data is sorted in a descending
     order, program control will "early exit" when an argument
     table value is tested that is <u>less than</u> the search argu-
     ment value.

     "Early exit" processing is automatically provided for
     in an RPG IV program by specifing the keyword **ASCEND** or
     DESCEND in the *Definition Specification* instruction that
     defines the table.

15. A *compile time table* that is defined as sorted includes
     unsorted data will cause terminal errors during program
     compilation.

     A *prerun time table* that is defined as sorted includes
     unsorted data will cause program execution to halt or
     abort.

16. EQUAL lookup - Is specified by entering a *Resulting Indi-cator* in the **EQ** field (positions 75-76). An equal condition is tested when the value in the Search Argument (*Factor 1* entry) is equal to the value of the current Argument Table entry (*Factor 2*).

    HIGH RANGE - Is specified by entering the same *Resulting Indicator* in the **HI** (positions 71-72) and **EQ** (positions 75-76). A High Range condition is tested when the table data is sorted and the value in the Search Argument (*Factor 1* entry) is equal to or greater than the current Argument Table entry (*Factor 2*).

    LOW RANGE - Is specified by entering the same *Resulting Indicator* in the LO (positions 73-74) and **EQ** (positions 75-76). A Low Range condition is tested when the table data is sorted and the value in the Search Argument (*Factor 1* entry) is equal to or greater than the current Argument Table value (*Factor 2*). Program control will "back-up" and point to the previous argument table entry.

17. To support Low or High Range table processing, A sequence entry (**ASCEND** or **DESCEND**) must be specified in the *Definition Specification* instruction for the argument table. If the related keyword is omitted, the table will be specified in a default ascending order.

    For Calculation Specification instructions, refer to the answer for Question 16; Low and High Range processing.

18. For Low Range **LOOKUP**, entry 04750 will be accessed.
    For High Range **LOOKUP**, entry 07010 will be accessed.

19.   ┌──position 1
    **CTDATA TABCDE
    CTCONNECTICUT
    MAMASSACHUSETTS
    NHNEW HAMPSHIRE
    NJNEW JERSEY
    NYNEW YORK
    VTVERMONT
    **CTDATA TABTAX
    075060030060070050

20.

```
 .. 1 ...+... 2 ...+... 3 ...+... 4 ...+... 5 ...+... 6 ...+... 7 ...+... 8
DName++++++++++++ETDsFrom++To/L+++IDc.Keywords++++++++++++++++++++++++++++++
D TABCde        S            2    DIM(6) ASCEND CTDATA
D TABSta        S           13    DIM(6) ALT(TabCde)
D TABTax        S          3 3 DIM(6) CTDATA PERRCD(6)
```

```
*.. 1 ...+... 2 ...+... 3 ...+... 4 ...+... 5 ...+... 6 ...+... 7 ...+... 8
CL0N01Factor 1++++++Opcode(E)+Factor2++++++Result++++++++Len++D_HiLOEQ....
C     State     LOOKUP    TABCde      TabSta             30
C               IF        *IN30 = *ON
C     State     LOOKUP    TABCde      TABTax             30
C               ENDIF
```

91

21. Note: Because three tables are defined, two table files are required. An alternative solution may be to include the TABTax elements with the TABSta data and use **MOVE** and **MOVEL** instructions to separate the element values for the two tables. This would eliminate the need for a second table file and the second **LOOKUP** instruction.

```
.. 1 ...+... 2 ...+... 3 ...+... 4 ...+... 5 ...+... 6 ...+... 7 ...+... 8
FFilename++IPEASFRLen+LKLen+AIDevice+.Keywords++++++++++++++++++++++++++++++
FTableFile1IT   F   15        DISK
FTableFile2IT   F   18        DISK
```

```
.. 1 ...+... 2 ...+... 3 ...+... 4 ...+... 5 ...+... 6 ...+... 7 ...+... 8
DName+++++++++++ETDsFrom+++To/L+++IDc.Keywords++++++++++++++++++++++++++++++
D TABCde          S              2 0 DIM(6) ASCEND FROMFILE(TableFile1)
D TABSta          S             13   DIM(6) ALT(TabCde)
D TABTax          S              3 3 DIM(6) FROMFILE(TableFile2)
```

****Calculation instructions are identical to Question 21****

22.
```
**CTDATA TABLow
0007213549647892        Argument table entries
**CTDATA TABRate
0001020304050607        Function table entries
```

Entries begin in position 1 and follow last output instruction or calculation instruction if no output is included in the program.

23.
```
.. 1 ...+... 2 ...+... 3 ...+... 4 ...+... 5 ...+... 6 ...+... 7 ...+... 8
DName+++++++++++ETDsFrom+++To/L+++IDc.Keywords++++++++++++++++++++++++++++++
D TABLow          S              2 2 DIM(8) ASCEND CTDATA PERRCD(8)
D TABRate         S              2 2 DIM(8) ASCEND CTDATA PERRCD(8)
```

```
*.. 1 ...+... 2 ...+... 3 ...+... 4 ...+... 5 ...+... 6 ...+... 7 ...+... 8
CLON01Factor 1++++++Opcode(E)+Factor2+++++++Result++++++++Len++D_HiLOEQ....
C    Sales         LOOKUP    TABLow         TABRate              3030
```

24.
```
**CTDATA TABHigh
00702103504906407809210 7 Argument table entries
**CTDATA TABRate
0001020304050607         Function table entries
```

```
.. 1 ...+... 2 ...+... 3 ...+... 4 ...+... 5 ...+... 6 ...+... 7 ...+... 8
DName+++++++++++ETDsFrom+++To/L+++IDc.Keywords++++++++++++++++++++++++++++++
D TABHigh         S              3 2 DIM(8) ASCEND CTDATA PERRCD(8)
D TABRate         S              2 2 DIM(8) ASCEND CTDATA PERRCD(8)
```

```
*.. 1 ...+... 2 ...+... 3 ...+... 4 ...+... 5 ...+... 6 ...+... 7 ...+... 8
CLON01Factor 1++++++Opcode(E)+Factor2+++++++Result++++++++Len++D_HiLOEQ....
C    Sales         LOOKUP    TABHigh        TABRate             30 30
```

Note: The only change between low range and high range look up processing is the *Resulting Indicator* entries. Low range look up requires indicators in the *Lo* and *Eq* fields. High range look up requires indicators in the *Hi* and *Eq* fields.

PROGRAMMING ASSIGNMENTS

Programming Assignment 9-1: READ PROPERTY TAX REPORT

```
Line   <--------------------- Source Specifications ---------------------><---- Comments ----> Do
Number ....1....+....2....+....3....+....4....+....5....+....6....+....7....+....8....+....9....+...10 Num
                        S o u r c e   L i s t i n g
   1 * PA 9-1: Real Property Tax Report....
   2 FP91psm    IF  E           DISK
     *---------------------------------------------------------------------*
     *                          RPG name        External name              *
     * File name. . . . . . . . :  P91PSM        STAN/P91PSM                *
     * Record format(s) . . . . . :  P91PSMR       P91PSMR                  *
     *---------------------------------------------------------------------*
   3 FQsysprt   O   F 132       PRINTER OFLIND(*INOF)
   4
   5 * Define tables....
   6 DTABCode      S          2    DIM(9) CTDATA                    city code table
   7 DTABCity      S         10    DIM(9) ALT (TABCode)             City name tableN
   8 DTABMRate     S          3 1 DIM(9) CTDATA PERRCD(9)           mill rate table
   9
  10 * Define work fields....
  11 DHhMmSs       S          6 0                                   define time field
  12 DYes_No       S          3                                     yes if vet
  13 DMultiple     S          8 3                                   multiples of 1000
  14 DProprtyTax   S          9 2            **                     property tax
  15
  16 * Get system or job time value....
  17=IP91PSMR
     *---------------------------------------------------------------------*
     * RPG record format  . . . . :  P91PSMR                               *
     * External format  . . . . . :  P91PSMR : STAN/P91PSM                 *
     *---------------------------------------------------------------------*
  18=I                       A    1    2 CITYCODE
  19=I                       A    3   22 TAXPAYER
  20=I                       P   23   27 0ASSESSMENT
  21=I                       A   28   28 VETERAN
  22 C            EVAL      *INOF = *ON                   set on OF indicator
  23 C            TIME                 HhMmSs             get time value
  24 C            READ      P91psm                 ----LR read first record
  25
  26 C            DOW       *INLR = *OFF                  dow LR is off       B01
  27 C            IF        *INOF = *ON                   OF off?             B02
  28 C            EXCEPT    Headings                      print heading lines 02
  29 C            EVAL      *INOF = *OFF                  set off OF indicator 02
  30 C            ENDIF                                   end IF group        E02
  31
  32 C   CityCode LOOKUP    TABCode      TABCity    ----80 get city name      01
  33 C            IF        *IN80 = *ON                   TABCode value found? B02
  34 C   CityCode LOOKUP    TABCode      TABMRate   ----80 get mill rate      02
  35
  36 C            IF        Veteran = 'V'                 veteran?            B03
  37 C            EVAL      Assessment = Assessment - 1000 vet deduction      03
  38 C            EVAL      Yes_No = 'YES'                output constant     03
  39 C            ELSE                                    not a veteran       X03
  40 C            EVAL      Yes_No = 'NO'                 NO constant         03
  41 C            ENDIF                                   end inner IF group  E03
  42
  43 C            EVAL      Multiple = Assessment / 1000  compute multiples   02
  44 C            EVAL      ProprtyTax = Multiple * TABMRate compute property tax 02
  45 C            ENDIF                                   end outer IF group  E02
  46
  47 C            EXCEPT    DetailLine            -        print record       01
  48 C            READ      P91psm                 ----LR read next record    01
  49 C            ENDDO                                   end dow group       E01
  50
  51 C            EVAL      *INLR = *ON                   turn on LR to end jb
  52
  53 OQsysprt   E          Headings     1 01
  54 O                     UDATE        Y      8
  55 O                                         52 'PROPERTY TAX REPORT BY'
```

```
56 O                                    59 'CITIES'
57 O                                    80 'PAGE'
58 O                   PAGE             85
59 O        E          Headings    3
60 O                   HhMmSs          8 ' : : '
61 O        E          Headings    1
62 O                                    59 'MILL/'
63 O                                    78 'TAX'
64 O        E          Headings    2
65 O                                    16 'TAXPAYER'
66 O                                    33 'CITY'
67 O                                    50 'ASSESSMENT'
68 O                                    58 'RATE'
69 O                                    65 'VET'
70 O                                    81 'LIABILITY'
71 O        E          Headings    0
72 O                                    40 'S'
73 O        E          DetailLine  2
74 O                   TaxPayer        22
75 O                   TABCity         36
76 O                   Assessment  1   50
77 O                   TABMRate    1   58
78 O                   Yes_No          65
79 O                   ProprtyTax  1   83
80
   * * * * *  E N D   O F   S O U R C E  * * * * *

     ***Note: compile information has been deleted here***

        C o m p i l e   T i m e   D a t a
81 **CTDATA TABCode
   *-----------------------------------------------------*
   * Table . . . : TABCODE   Alternating Table . . . . : TABCITY  *
   *-----------------------------------------------------*
82 GHGREENWICH
83 SDSTAMFORD
84 NKNORWALK
85 BTBRIDGEPORT
86 STSTRATFORD
87 NHNEW HAVEN
88 MNMIDDLETOWN
89 HDHARTFORD
90 NLNEW LONDON
91 **CTDATA TABMRate
   *-----------------------------------------------------*
   * Table . . . : TABMRATE                               *
   *-----------------------------------------------------*
92 57252150748846547039 6423384
 * * * *  E N D   O F   C O M P I L E   T I M E   D A T A  * * * *
```

Report Design:

8/17/98 12:17:06	PROPERTY TAX REPORT BY CITIES				PAGE 1
TAXPAYER	CITY	ASSESSMENT	MILL/ RATE	VET	TAX LIABILITY
W.C. FIELDS	NEW LONDON	$ 124,000	38.4	YES	4,761.60
CLARK GABLE	STAMFORD	1,050,000	52.1	NO	54,705.00
MARILYN MONROE	STRATFORD	12,495,000	46.5	NO	581,017.50
CHARLIE CHAPLIN	GREENWICH	9,895,500	57.2	YES	566,022.60
STANLEY LAUREL	BRIDGEPORT	700,590	48.8	NO	34,188.79
BETTY BOOP	MIDDLETOWN	10,455,330	39.6	YES	414,031.06
JOHN WAYNE	NORWALK	15,000,000	50.7	NO	760,500.00
JAYNE MANSFIELD	NEW HAVEN	8,750,900	47.0	NO	411,292.30

TYRONE POWELL	HARTFORD	499,788	42.3	YES	21,141.03
ERROL FLYNN	STRATFORD	20,598,500	46.5	NO	957,830.25

Programming Assignment 9-2: WEEKLY SHIPPING REPORT

```
Line    <---------------------- Source Specifications ----------------------------><---- Comments ----> Do
Number  ....1....+....2....+....3....+....4....+....5....+....6....+....7....+....8....+....9....+...10 Num
                            S o u r c e   L i s t i n g
   1 FP92psm    IF   E         K DISK
     *----------------------------------------------------------------------------------------------*
     *                               RPG name        External name                                  *
     * File name. . . . . . . . :    P92PSM          STAN/P92PSM                                     *
     * Record format(s) . . . . :    P92PSMR         P92PSMR                                         *
     *----------------------------------------------------------------------------------------------*
   2 FQsysprt   O    F 132        PRINTER OFLIND(*INOA)
   3
   4 * Define tables....
   5 DTABPounds      S             2  0 DIM(20) CTDATA ASCEND PERRCD(20)
   6 DTABRate        S             3  2 DIM(20) CTDATA ASCEND PERRCD(4)
   7
   8 * Define work fields....
   9 DNewPounds      S             2  0
  10 DShipCharge     S             5  2
  11 DOverPounds     S             2  0           *
  12 DExcessChg      S             5  2
  13 DCodMsg         S             3
  14
  15 * Define Named Constants....
  16 DOverWgtMsg     C                    'OVER WEIGHT'
  17 DNoShipMsg      C                    '******'
  18
  19=IP92PSMR
     *----------------------------------------------------------------------------------------------*
     * RPG record format  . . . . :  P92PSMR                                                         *
     * External format . . . . . :   P92PSMR : STAN/P92PSM                                           *
     *----------------------------------------------------------------------------------------------*
  20=I                          A   1  20 CUSTNAME
  21=I                          P  21  23 0INVOICENO
  22=I                          P  24  27 2INVOICEAMT
  23=I                          P  28  29 0POUNDS
  24=I                          P  30  31 0OUNCES
  25=I                          A  32  32 COD
  26 C             EVAL      *INOA = *ON                        turn on OA indicator
  27 C             READ      P92psm                    ----LR   read first record
  28
  29 C             DOW       *INLR = *OFF                        dow LR is off         B01
  30
  31 * Heading control....
  32 C             IF        *INOA = *ON                         OA indicator on?      B02
  33 C             EXCEPT    Headings                            print headings        02
  34 C             EVAL      *INOA = *OFF                        turn off OA indicatr  02
  35 C             ENDIF                                         end IF group          E02
  36
  37 C             EXSR      HouseKepSR                          branch to subroutine  01
  38
  39 C             IF        NewPounds <= 70                     wgt > or = 70 pds?    B02
  40 C             EXSR      LookUpSR                            branch to subroutine  02
  41 C             ELSE                                          false action          X02
  42 C             EXCEPT    ErrorLine                           print error message   02
  43 C             ENDIF                                         end IF group          E02
  44
  45 C             READ      P92psm                    ----LR   read next record      01
  46 C             ENDDO                                         end dow group         E01
  47
  48 * Begin Subroutines....
  49 C   HouseKepSR  BEGSR                                       begin subroutine
  50 C             EVAL      NewPounds = Pounds                  init. NewPounds
  51 C             IF        Ounces > *ZERO                      Ounzes > zero?        B01
  52 C             EVAL      NewPounds = NewPounds + 1           increase NewPounds    01
  53 C             ENDIF                                         end IF group          E01
```

```
 54
 55 C                     EVAL      ShipCharge = *ZERO                              init. ShipCharge
 56 C                     ENDSR                                                     end subroutine
 57
 58 C     LookUpSR        BEGSR                                                     begin subroutine
 59 C                     IF        NewPounds > 20                                  NewPounds > 20?      B01
 60 C                     EVAL      NewPounds = 20                                  init. NewPounds      01
 61 C                     EVAL      OverPounds = Pounds - 20                        compute OverPounds   01
 62 C                     EVAL      ExcessChg = OverPounds * .06                    compute ExcessChg    01
 63 C                     EVAL      ShipCharge = ShipCharge + ExcessChg             increase ShipChargw  01
 64 C                     ENDIF                                                     end subroutine       E01
 65
 66 C     NewPounds       LOOKUP    TABPounds      TABRate             ----20       find table charge
 67 C                     IF        *IN20 = *ON                                     table element found? B01
 68 C                     EVAL      ShipCharge = TABRate + ShipCharge               increase ShipCharge  01
 69 C                     ENDIF                                                     end IF group         E01
 70
 71 * If COD sale, branch to subroutine....
 72 C     Cod             CASEQ     'Y'            CodSR                            Cod shipment?
 73 C                     ENDCS                                                     end CAS group
 74
 75 * If InvoiceAmt < $25, add shipping charge to InvoiceAmt....
 76 C                     IF        InvoiceAmt < 25                                 less than $25?       B01
 77 C                     EVAL      InvoiceAmt = InvoiceAmt + ShipCharge            increase InvoiceAmt  01
 78 C                     EXCEPT    NoChgLine                                       print output         01
 79 C                     ELSE                                                      false action         X01
 80 C                     EXCEPT    ShipChLine                                      print line           01
 81 C                     ENDIF                                              **     end IF group         E01
 82
 83 C                     EVAL      CodMsg = *BLANKS                                init. fld to blanks
 84 C                     ENDSR                                                     end subroutine
 85
 86 C     CodSR           BEGSR                                                     begin subroutine
 87 C                     IF        InvoiceAmt < 50                                 less than $50?       B01
 88 C                     EVAL      InvoiceAmt = InvoiceAmt + 1.50                  add $1.50            01
 89 C                     ENDIF                                                     end IF group         E01
 90 C                     EVAL      CodMsg = 'YES'                                  init. CodMsg field
 91 C                     ENDSR                                                     end subroutine
 92
 93 OQsysprt  E           Headings       2 01
 94 O                     UDATE          Y        8
 95 O                                             42 'FOB DESTINATION SHIPMENT'
 96 O                                             49 'REPORT'
 97 O                                             69 'PAGE'
 98 O                     PAGE                     74
 99 O        E           Headings       1
100 O                                             54 'WEIGHT'
101 O                                             73 'SHIPPING'
102 O        E           Headings       2
103 O                                             16 'CUSTOMER NAME'
104 O                                             30 'INVOICE'
105 O                                             44 'INVOICE AMT'
106 O                                             55 'PDS OZS'
107 O                                             61 'COD'
108 O                                             72 'CHARGE'
109 O        E           ShipChLine     2
110 O                     CustName                20
111 O                     InvoiceNo               28
112 O                     InvoiceAmt     1        42
113 O                     Pounds         1        50
114 O                     Ounces         1        54
115 O                     CodMsg                  61
116 O                     ShipCharge     1        72
117 O        E           NoChgLine      2
118 O                     CustName                20
119 O                     InvoiceNo               28
120 O                     InvoiceAmt     1        42
121 O                     Pounds         1        50
122 O                     Ounces         1        54
123 O                     CodMsg                  61
124 O                     NoShipMsg               72
125 O        E           ErrorLine      2
126 O                     CustName                20
127 O                     InvoiceNo               28
```

Chapter 9 - Table Processing

```
128 O                    InvoiceAmt   1    42
129 O                    Pounds       1    50
130 O                    Ounces       1    54
131 O                    OverWgtMsg        72
132
    * * * * *  E N D   O F   S O U R C E  * * * * *
                            .
                            .
    ****Note: Supplemented compile information deleted here****
                            .
                            .
                 C o m p i l e   T i m e   D a t a
133 **CTDATA TABPounds
    *---------------------------------------------------------------*
    * Table . . . : TABPOUNDS                                       *
    *---------------------------------------------------------------*
134 0102030405060708091011121314151617181920
135 **CTDATA TABRate
    *---------------------------------------------------------------*
    * Table . . . : TABRATE                                         *
    *---------------------------------------------------------------*
136 129137146154
137 163171180188
138 197205214222
139 231239248256
140 265273282290
    * * * * *  E N D   O F   C O M P I L E   T I M E   D A T A  * * * *
```

Printed Report:

```
8/18/98          FOB DESTINATION SHIPMENT REPORT              PAGE   1

                                               WEIGHT          SHIPPING
   CUSTOMER NAME     INVOICE   INVOICE AMT     PDS OZS   COD    CHARGE

DOROTHY PARTON        1235        100.00       20   0             2.90

ROBERT WARFIELD       1236         46.50        8   9    YES      1.97

MARIO LANZA           1237      1,200.00       70   0    YES      5.90

ENZIO PINZA           1238      2,450.00       82  12        OVER WEIGHT

NELSON EDDY           1239         12.79        1   0    YES     ******

HENRY JACKSON         1244         25.71        5   8            ******
```

Programming Assignment 9-3: FLEXIBLE BUDGET REPORT

```
Line   <--------------------- Source Specifications --------------------------><---- Comments ----> Do
Number ....1....+....2....+....3....+....4....+....5....+....6....+....7....+....8....+....9....+...10 Num
                    S o u r c e   L i s t i n g
  1  * PA 9-3: Flexible Budget Report....
  2 FP93psm    IF   E        K DISK
     *--------------------------------------------------------------------------*
     *                          RPG name      External name                     *
     * File name. . . . . . . . . :  P93PSM      STAN/P93PSM                     *
     * Record format(s) . . . . . :  P93PSMR     P93PSMR                         *
     *--------------------------------------------------------------------------*
  3 FQsysprt   O    F   132        PRINTER OFLIND(*INOC)
  4
  5
  6  * Define tables....
  7 DTABActNo       S            3     DIM(9) CTDATA ASCEND
  8 DTABActName     S           19     DIM(9) ALT(TABActNo)
  9 DTABFixAmt      S            5   0 DIM(9) CTDATA
 10 DTABVarRate     S            3   2 DIM(9) ALT (TABFixAmt)
```

```
11
12  * Define Data Area Data Structure....
13 DP93darea      UDS
14 D Date                    1      6 0
15 D StdHrs                  7     11 0
16
17  * Define Work Fields....
18 DVarAmt         S              8 2
19 DBudgetAmt      S              8 2
20 DVariance       S              8 2
21 DUorF           S              1
22
23=IP93PSMR
    *------------------------------------------------------------------*
    * RPG record format  . . . . :  P93PSMR                            *
    * External format  . . . . . :  P93PSMR : STAN/P93PSM              *
    *------------------------------------------------------------------*
24=I                          A    1    3 ACCOUNTNO
25=I                          P    4    8 2ACTUALCOST
26 C              EVAL      *INOC = *ON                    turn on OC indicator
27 C              READ      P93psm              ----LR     read first record
28
29 C              DOW       *INLR = *OFF                   dow LR is off        B01
30
31 * Heading Control....
32 C              IF        *INOC = *ON                    OC indicator on?     B02
33 C              EXCEPT    Headings                       print heading lines   02
34 C              EVAL      *INOC = *OFF         **        turn off OC indicatr  02
35 C              ENDIF                                    end IF group         E02
36
37 C   AccountNo  LOOKUP    TABActNo    TABActName  ----20 table look up         01
38 C              IF        *IN20 = *ON                    element found?       B02
39 C   AccountNo  LOOKUP    TABActNo    TABFixAmt   ----20 table look up         02
40 C   AccountNo  LOOKUP    TABActNo    TABVarRate  ----20 table look up         02
41 C              EVAL      VarAmt = StdHrs * TABVarRate   compute VarAmt        02
42 C              EVAL      BudgetAmt = VarAmt + TABFixAmt compute BudgetAmt     02
43 C              EVAL      Variance = ActualCost - BudgetAmt compute variance   02
44
45 * Test for unfavorable or favorable variance...
46 C              IF        Variance > 0                   variance test        B03
47 C              EVAL      UorF = 'U'                     unfavorable variance  03
48 C              ELSE                                     false action         X03
49 C              EVAL      UorF = 'F'                     favorable variance    03
50 C              ENDIF                                    end IF group         E03
51
52 C              EXCEPT    DetailLine                     print record          02
53 C              ENDIF                                                         E02
54
55 C              READ      P93psm              ----LR     read next record      01
56 C              ENDDO                                    end dow group        E01
57
58 OQsysprt    E          Headings     1 01
59 O                                        36 'VARIANCE ANALYSIS OF'
60 O                                        61 'FACTORY OVERHEAD EXPENSE'
61 O                                        66 'S FOR'
62 O                                        77 'PAGE'
63 O                       PAGE            82
64 O          E          Headings     2
65 O                       StdHrs      1   28
66 O                                        52 'DIRECT LABOR HRS ENDING'
67 O                       Date        Y   61
68 O          E          Headings     1
69 O                                         7 'ACCOUNT'
70 O                                        21 'ACCOUNT NAME'
71 O                                        36 'FIXED'
72 O                                        48 'VAR.RATE/'        -
73 O                                        56 'TOTAL'
74 O                                        68 'ACTUAL'
75 O                                        79 'VARIANCE'
76 O          E          Headings     2
77 O                                         6 'NUMBER'
78 O                                        37 'AMOUNT'
79 O                                        46 'DL HR'
80 O                                        57 'BUDGET'
```

```
81 O                                        67 'COST'
82 O                                        78 'AMOUNT'
83 O          E          DetailLine    2
84 O                     AccountNo          4
85 O                     TABActName         28
86 O                     TABFixAmt     2    37
87 O                     TABVarRate    2    45
88 O                     BudgetAmt     1    58
89 O                     ActualCost    1    69
90 O                     Variance      1    79
91 O                     UorF               81
   * * * *   E N D   O F   S O U R C E   * * * *
```

****Note: Compile information deleted here****

```
                   C o m p i l e   T i m e   D a t a
 92 **CTDATA TABActNo
    *-------------------------------------------------------------*
    * Table . . . : TABACTNO    Alternating Table . . . . : TABACTNAME *
    *-------------------------------------------------------------*
 93 600INDIRECT LABOR
 94 601FACTORY SUPPLIES
 95 602FACTORY ELECTRICITY
 96 603MACHINE REPAIRS
 97 604PLANT MAINTENANCE\
 98 605FACTORY HEATING OIL
 99 606FACTORY CUSTODIAL                              *3
100 607TOOL CRIB LABOR
101 608COST CLERKS
102 **CTDATA TABFixAmt
    *-------------------------------------------------------------*
    * Table . . . : TABFIXAMT   Alternating Table . . . . : TABVARRATE *
    *-------------------------------------------------------------*
103 20000015
104 02000100
105 03000006
106 01000010
107 04000020
108 02700004
109 05000010
110 04500011
111 04000008
   * * * *   E N D   O F   C O M P I L E   T I M E   D A T A   * * * *
```

Printed Report:

VARIANCE ANALYSIS OF FACTORY OVERHEAD EXPENSES FOR					PAGE	1
50,000 DIRECT LABOR HRS ENDING 11/30/98						
ACCOUNT NUMBER	ACCOUNT NAME	FIXED AMOUNT	VAR.RATE/ DL HR	TOTAL BUDGET	ACTUAL COST	VARIANCE AMOUNT
600	INDIRECT LABOR	20,000	.15	27,500.00	30,000.90	2,500.90 U
601	FACTORY SUPPLIES	2,000	1.00	52,000.00	51,000.10	999.90 F
602	FACTORY ELECTRICITY	3,000	.06	6,000.00	5,500.68	499.32 F
603	MACHINE REPAIRS	1,000	.10	6,000.00	8,400.00	2,400.00 U
604	PLANT MAINTENANCE\	4,000	.20	14,000.00	15,000.25	1,000.25 U
605	FACTORY HEATING OIL	2,700	.04	4,700.00	5,500.10	800.10 U
606	FACTORY CUSTODIAL	5,000	.10	10,000.00	10,000.00	.00 F
607	TOOL CRIB LABOR	4,500	.11	10,000.00	9,500.00	500.00 F
608	COST CLERKS	4,000	.08	8,000.00	7,050.78	949.22 F

Programming Assignment 9-4:

```
Line    <-------------------- Source Specifications --------------------><---- Comments ----> Do
Number  ....1....+....2....+....3....+....4....+....5....+....6....+....7....+....8....+....9....+...10 Num
                          S o u r c e   L i s t i n g
    1  * PA 9-4: Weekly Payroll Checks....
    2  FP94psm    IF E         K DISK
       *------------------------------------------------------------------------------------*
       *                                                                                    *
       *                              RPG name           External name                      *
       * File name. . . . . . . . :   P94PSM             STAN/P94PSM                         *
       * Record format(s) . . . . :   P94PSMR            P94PSMR                             *
       *------------------------------------------------------------------------------------*
    3  FQsysprt   O  F 132       PRINTER
    4
    5  * Define Tables....
*RNF2318 00      3 000300  Overflow indicator OA is assigned to PRINTER file QSYSPRT.
    6  DTABLowSing      S            4  0 DIM(5) CTDATA ASCEND
    7  DTABFixSing      S            5  2 DIM(5) ALT(TABLowSing)
    8  DTABLowMar       S            4  0 DIM(5) CTDATA ASCEND
    9  DTABFixMar       S            6  2 DIM(5) ALT(TABLowMar)
   10  DTABPercent      S            2  2 DIM(5) CTDATA PERRCD(5)
   11
   12  * Define Data Area Data Structure....
   13  DP94darea        UDS
   14  D CheckDate             1      8  0
   15  D CheckNo              9     12  0
   16                                              **
   17  * Define work fields....
   18  DFactor          S            5  2
   19  DNetWages        S            6  2
   20  DNet             S            4  0
   21  DDifference      S            6  2
   22  DExcessAmt       S            5  2
   23  DFwtax           S            6  2
   24  DUnderAmt        S            9  2
   25  DSSTax           S            6  2
   26  DMedicarTax      S            5  2
   27
   28=IP94PSMR
       *------------------------------------------------------------------------------------*
       * RPG record format   . . . . :  P94PSMR                                             *
       * External format     . . . . :  P94PSMR : STAN/P94PSM                               *
       *------------------------------------------------------------------------------------*
   29=I                        P    1    5 OSSNUMBER
   30=I                        A    6   27 EMPNAME
   31=I                        P   28   32 2YTDWAGES
   32=I                        P   33   36 2YTDFWT
   33=I                        P   37   40 2YTDSS
   34=I                        P   41   44 2YTDMEDICAR
   35=I                        P   45   48 2WEEKWAGES
   36=I                        P   49   50 0EXEMPTIONS
   37=I                        A   51   51 MAR_STATUS
   38 C                  READ  P94psm                      ----LR   read first record
   39 C                  DOW   *INLR = *OFF                         dow LR is off       B01
   40 C                  EVAL  CheckNo = CheckNo + 1                increment BegCheckNo 01
   41 C                  EVAL  Factor = Exemptions * 38.46          statutory amount     01
   42 C                  EVAL  NetWages = WeekWages - Factor        base wages           01
   43 C                  EVAL  Net = NetWages                       init. NetWages       01
   44
   45 C  Mar_Status      CASEQ 'S'          SingleSR               single wage earner?  01
   46 C                  CAS               MarriedSR               married wage earner  01
   47 C                  ENDCS                                     end cas group        01
   48
   49 C                  EVAL  NetWages = WeekWages - Fwtax         compute NetWages     01
   50 C                  EVAL  YtdFwt = YtdFwt + Fwtax              add to YtdFwt        01
   51 C                  EXSR  SSSR                                 branch to subroutine 01
   52 C                  EVAL  YtdWages = YtdWages + WeekWages      add to YtdWages      01
   53
   54 * Compute Medicare Withheld....
   55 C                  EVAL  MedicarTax = WeekWages * .0145       compute MedicarTax   01
   56 C                  EVAL  NetWages = NetWages - MedicarTax     deduct MedicarTax    01
   57 C                  EVAL  YTDMediCar = YTDMediCar + MedicarTax increment YTDMediCar 01
   58
```

```
59  * Print check....
60 C                    EXCEPT    PrintCheck                               print a check         01
61 C                    READ      P94psm                          ----LR   read next record      01
62 C                    ENDDO                                              end dow group         E01
63
64 C                    EVAL      *INLR = *ON                              end program
65
66  * Begin subroutines....
67 C      SingleSR      BEGSR                                              begin subroutine
68 C      Net           LOOKUP    TABLowSing    TABFixSing       --2020    gey fixed amount
69 C                    IF        *IN20 = *ON                              successful look up?   B01
70 C      Net           LOOKUP    TABLowSing    TABPercent       --2020    get table percent     01
71 C                    EVAL      Difference = NetWages - TABLowSing       compute Difference    01
72 C                    EVAL(H)   ExcessAmt = Difference * TABPercent      compute ExcessAmt     01
73 C                    EVAL      Fwtax = TABFixSing + ExcessAmt           compute fwtax         01
74 C                    ENDIF                                              end IF group          E01
75 C                    ENDSR                                             end subroutine
76
77 C      MarriedSR     BEGSR                                              begin subroutine
78 C      Net           LOOKUP    TABLowMar     TABFixMar        --2020    get fixed amount
79 C                    IF        *IN20 = *ON                              successful look up?   B01
80 C      Net           LOOKUP    TABLowMar     TABPercent       --2020    get table percent     01
81 C                    EVAL      Difference = NetWages - TABLowMar        compute Difference    01
82 C                    EVAL(H)   ExcessAmt = Difference * TABPercent      compute ExcessAmt     01
83 C                    EVAL      Fwtax = TABFixMar + ExcessAmt            compute fwtax         01
84 C                    ENDIF                                              end IF group          E01
85 C                    ENDSR                                             end subroutine
86
87 C      SSSR          BEGSR                             *)               begin subroutine
88 C                    IF        YTDWages < 62700                         less than $62,700?    B01
89 C                    EVAL      UnderAmt = 62700 - YTDWages              compute UnderAmt      01
90 C                    IF        UnderAmt < WeekWages                     less than WeekWages?  B02
91 C                    EVAL      SSTax = UnderAmt * .0620                 compute ss withheld   02
92 C                    ELSE                                               false action          X02
93 C                    EVAL      SSTax = WeekWages * .0620                compute ss withheld   02
94 C                    ENDIF                                              end inner IF group    E02
95 C                    EVAL      YTDss = YTDss + SSTax                    increment YTDss       01
96 C                    EVAL      NetWages = NetWages - SSTax              deduct SSTax          01
97 C                    ENDIF                                              end outer IF group    E01
98 C                    ENDSR                                             end subroutine
99
100 OQsysprt    E           PrintCheck     2 01
101 O                       SSNumber              12 '0  -  -  '
102 O                       CheckNo        Z      60
103 O           E           PrintCheck     2
104 O                       CheckDate      Y      60
105 O           E           PrintCheck     2
106 O                       EmpName               35
107 O           E           PrintCheck            14
108 O                       NetWages              31 '$  ,  *.  '
109 O           E           PrintCheck     2
110 O                       CheckNo               60
111 O           E           PrintCheck            20
112 O                       SSNumber              12 '0  -  -  '
113 O                       CheckDate      Y      60
114 O           E           PrintCheck            25
115 O                       WeekWages      1      11
116 O                       Fwtax          1      23
117 O                       SSTax          1B     35
118 O                       MedicarTax     1      46
119 O                       NetWages       J      59
120 O           E           PrintCheck     0
121 O                       YTDWages       1      17
122 O                       YTDSS          1      29
123 O                       YTDMedicar     1      40
124 O                       YTDFwt         1      55
125
     * * * * *  E N D   O F   S O U R C E  * * * *
                          .
                          .
         ****Note: Compile time information deleted****
                          .
                          .
```

```
                    C o m p i l e   T i m e   D a t a
126 **CTDATA TABLowSing
    *----------------------------------------------------------------*
    * Table . . . : TABLOWSING   Alternating Table . . . . : TABFIXSING *
    *----------------------------------------------------------------*
127 000000000
128 002100000
129 037805355
130 088519551
131 202857270
132 **CTDATA TABLowMar
    *----------------------------------------------------------------*
    * Table . . . : TABLOWMAR    Alternating Table . . . . : TABFIXMAR *
    *----------------------------------------------------------------*
133 0000000000
134 0062000000
135 0657008925
136 1501032557
137 3695104959
138 **CTDATA TABPercent
    *----------------------------------------------------------------*
    * Table . . . : TABPERCENT                                        *
    *----------------------------------------------------------------*
139 0015283328
    * * * *   E N D   O F   C O M P I L E   T I M E   D A T A   * * * *
```

Printed Report:

```
┌──────────────────────────────────────────────────┐
│ 020-31-5555                                   1001 │
│                                                    │
│                                        12/17/1998  │
│                                                    │
│              ALEXANDER BELL                        │
│                                                    │
│                 $*1,986.45                         │
│                                                    │
│                                                    │
│                                                    │
│                                                    │
│                                                    │
│  - - - - - - - - - - - - - - - - - - - - - - - -   │
│                                               1001 │
│                                                    │
│ 020-31-5555                            12/17/1998  │
│                                                    │
│                                                    │
│   2,694.00     668.49        .00    39.06  1,986.45│
│                                                    │
│                                                    │
│                                                    │
│     137,394.00   3,887.40  1,992.21   33,992.99    │
├──────────────────────────────────────────────────┤
│ 030-21-6532                                   1002 │
│                                                    │
│                                        12/17/1998  │
│                                                    │
│              THOMAS EDISON                         │
│                                                    │
│                $***449.16                          │
│                                                    │
│                                                    │
│                                                    │
│  - - - - - - - - - - - - - - - - - - - - - - - -   │
│                                               1002 │
│                                                    │
│ 030-21-6532                            12/17/1998  │
│                                                    │
│                                                    │
└──────────────────────────────────────────────────┘
```

600.00	104.94	37.20	8.70	449.16
30,600.00	1,897.20	443.70		5,346.94

040-50-3871	1003
	12/17/1998

ROBERT FULTON

$***985.73

- -

	1003
040-50-3871	12/17/1998

1,250.00	233.75	12.40	18.12	985.73
		•?		
63,750.00	3,887.40	924.37		9,287.25

050-70-3302	1004
	12/17/1998

WALTER CHRYSLER

$***888.45

- -

	1004
050-70-3302	12/17/1998

1,200.00	219.75	74.40	17.40	888.45
61,200.00	3,794.40	887.40		11,207.25

060-54-8754	1005
	12/17/1998

HENRY FORD

$***961.38   -

- -

	1005

Chapter 9 - Table Processing

060-54-8754				12/17/1998
1,300.00	319.77	.00	18.85	961.38
66,300.00	3,887.40	961.35		15,371.27

CHAPTER 10
QUESTION ANSWERS

1. Data loaded in a contiguous area in storage that is defined so that it may be processed by indexing.

2. The elements in a <u>one</u>-dimensional array are stored next to each other in <u>one</u> row. Elements are referenced by <u>one</u> index item.

   The elements in a <u>two</u>-dimensional array are stored in <u>two</u> rows and require <u>two</u> indexes to access a value.

   For any dimension, the elements are accessed according to their relative position in the array (i.e. first element, 1st position; tenth element, 10th position; and so forth).

   RPG only supports one-dimensional array structure and processing. However, two or more dimension arrays may be simulated by a programmer-supplied routine or with a multiple occurrence data structure.

3. a. How the data for the array or table is organized.
   b. How the data for the array or table will be processed.

4.

<u>Arrays</u>	<u>Tables</u>
Data to load to a run time array on input or in calculations may be stored anywhere in the body of the records.	Data to load tables must be stored consecutively beginning in the first byte of the records.
Arrays may be searched randomly.	Table are consecutively searched.
All of the elements in an array may be accessed by one instruction.	Only one or two table elements may be accessed at a time.
Additional **LOOKUP** statements are not required to reference the element values from related arrays.	Additional **LOOKUP**s are required to access the values from three or more related tables.

5. *Compile time, prerun time,* and *runtime* (loaded on input or calculations).

6.

Array Type	Where Stored
COMPILE TIME	Internally in the program after the last output (O) instruction and preceded by a **CTDATA control instruction.
PRERUN TIME	Externally from the program in a physical file defined as a table file.

RUN TIME	Externally from the program in a phys-
	ical file. Data is loaded by input or calculation statements in the RPG IV program.

7. <u>Array Type</u>   <u>When Used</u>

COMPILE TIME	Arrays have few elements that are not subject to frequent changes.
PRERUN TIME	Arrays have many elements and/or are subject to frequent changes.
RUN TIME	Array data is not loaded beginning in the first position of every re- cord and/or each record or group of data records changes the values for array.

8. *Definition Specifications.*   **

9. **DIM** - Defines the number of array elements.

   ALT - Array element data is in an alternating format with the data in a related array.

   DESCEND - Specifies that the array data is in a descending order.

   XFOOT - Crossfoots (adds) the contiguous elements in a numeric array.

   PERRCD - Specifies the number of elements per record.

   FROMFILE - Specifies the input table file in which the array data is stored.

   OVERLAY - Redefines the attributes with another array so that sorting may begin on an element other than the first in the array.

   LOOKUP - Randomly access an element value from an array.

   CTDATA - Defines a compile time array.

   ASCEND - Specifies that the array element values are in an ascending order.

   TOFILE - Specifies the file to which the array data will be written.

10. **DIM(50)** - Defines the array with 50 elements.

    DESCEND - specifies that the array elements are in a descending order.

CTDATA - Defines the array as compile time.

PERRCD(5) - Specifies that five elements are stored on a record.

11. **DIM(50)** - Defines the array with 50 elements.

ALT((ArrayOne) - Specifies that the elements are in an alternating format with ArrayOne. The data for an ArrayOne elements will be followed with the data for an ArrayTwo element with five pairs per record.

12. ArrayThree is defiens as a runtIme array. The data will be loaded as each record is read from the physical file.

13. Prerun Time array.

14. Defines the array as Prerun Time and specifies the table file (ArrayFile) in which the data for the array is stored.

15. The data for Prerun Time arrays is stored in a physical file.

16. **TOFILE** defines the file to which the array data will be loaded when the program ends.

17. With *Definition, Input,* or *Calculation Specification* instructions.

18. Crossfoots (adds) the contiguous elements in a numeric array.

19. b - an array name.

20. c - either a field or an array name (element).

21. All arithmetic operations. All of the elements may be accessed with one instruction.

22. An *index* (numeric field or literal) stores a value that may be used to randomly access an element from an array.

An *index* (numeric literal or field) must be defined as a numeric integer.

An *index* may be defined as an input field, data structure item, array element, table name, or a result field from a calculation instruction.

23. The integer value in the **X** index will determine the element accessed from the CustName array.

24. The **LOOKUP** operation randomly accesses an element from an array based on the value in the *Factor 1* item. The **LOOKUP** operation for table processed the table sequentially whereas it processes arrays randomly.

25. The index is incremented automatically.

26. One **LOOKUP** instruction. Related values from the MthName and MthDays arrays are accessed by specifying the *index* name, N, used with the MthNo array with the MthName and MthDays arrays.

27. Extracts an array element randomly by its index value <u>without</u> a **LOOKUP** instruction.

28. a. Index value zero, b. index value negative, c. Index value cannot be greater than the number of elements defined as the array size in the *Definition Specifications*.

29. The **MOVEA** operation will move values to or from an array or field until the data is moved the target array or field is filled. Data movement may begin at a specified array element. The **MOVE** or **MOVEL** operations will only move one array element.

30. 123456; DUCK,DONALD; DEVON NY; 0100009; 14

31. Simulates multiple dimension array processing. The data structure must be defined in the *Definition Specifications* with a **DS** in the *Ds* field and the **OCCURS()** keyword in the *Keyword* field.

32. The **OCCUR** operation.

33.

```
.. 1 ...+... 2 ...+... 3 ...+... 4 ...+... 5 ...+... 6 ...+... 7 ...+... 8
DName++++++++++ETDsFrom+++To/L+++IDc.Keywords+++++++++++++++++++++++++++++
 *
D Model            DS                    OCCURS(4)
D  Deluxe                        4
D  Standard                      4
```

34.

```
*.. 1 ...+... 2 ...+... 3 ...+... 4 ...+... 5 ...+... 6 ...+... 7 ...+... 8
CLON01Factor1++++++++Opcode&ExtFactor2+++++++Result++++++++Len++D+HiLoEq....
C     *IN10         CASEQ    *OFF           LoadSR
C                   ENDCS
C     Models        OCCUR    Model
C                   IF       Type = 'D'
C                   EVAL     SellPrice = Deluxe
C                   ELSE
C                   EVAL     SellPrice = Standard
C                   ENDIF
C
C     LoadSR        BEGSR
C     1             OCCUR    Model
C                   MOVE     12001000       Model
C     2             OCCUR    Model
C                   MOVE     13501175       Model
C     3             OCCUR    Model
C                   MOVE     16001450       Model
C     4             OCCUR    Model
C                   MOVE     12001790       Model
C                   EVAL     *IN10 = *ON
C                   ENDSR
```

Note: Models (stores model number) and Type (stores D or S for Deluxe o Standard)

are fields from an externally defined physical file. SellPrice i a standalone
field defined in the Definition Specifications.

35. The *OpCode&Ext* and *Factor2* fields.

36. At the first byte (character) of the array's elements. The
sort may be modified to begin at a different position within
the array's elements with the **OVERLAY** keyword used in the
definition of the array.

37. **ASCEND**, **DESCEND**, and **OVERLAY**. If **ASCEND** or **DESCEND** is not
specified, the sort will default to an ascending sorted order.

38. **DIM(3)** defines the DEFArray with three elements. **ASCEND**
specifies that the array will be sorted in ascending order.

    The HIGArray stores the characters from the DEFArray to be
    sorted. The **OVERLAY(DEFArray:4)** keyword specifies that the
    elements in the DEFArray will be sorted beginning in the fourth
    position.

    Note that the HIGArray name is included with the **SORTA** calcu-
    lation instruction and not the DEFArray. However, after the
    sort, the DEFArray array will be in the same order as the
    HIGArray.

39. 123ABC 234MNO 456XYZ

PROGRAMMING ASSIGNMENTS

Programming Assignment 10-1: FACTORY OVERHEAD BUDGET

Notes to the Instructor:

1. This assignment requires students to define two runtime arrays;
   one loaded on input and the other in calculations.

2. Two **XFOOT** statements are required; one for expense account
   totals and a second for total overhead cost for the year.

3. The program solution loads the expense array from the related
   physical file's fields using the *Input Specification* method.

```
|Line   <--------------------- Source Specifications --------------------------><---- Comments ----> Do |
|Number ....1....+....2....+....3....+....4....+....5....+....6....+....7....+....8....+....9....+...10 Num|
                          S o u r c e   L i s t i n g
   1  * PA 10-1 Factory Overhead Budget....
   2 FP101psm  IF  E           DISK
     *--------------------------------------------------------------------------------------*
     *                              RPG name          External name                          *
     * File name. . . . . . . . :  P101PSM           STAN/P101PSM                             *
     * Record format(s) . . . . :  P101PSMR          P101PSMR                                 *
     *--------------------------------------------------------------------------------------*
   3 FQsysprt   O   F  132      PRINTER OFLIND (*INOF)
   4
   5 * Define arrays....
   6 DOverExpAry      S              6 0 DIM(4)
   7 DTotOverAry      S              7 0 DIM(4)
```

```
 8
 9  * Define work fields....
10 DTotalExp          S              7 0
11 DTotalYear         S              8 0
12
13  * Load runtime array (OverExpAry)....
14 IP101psmr
15 I            QtrOne                    OverExpAry(1)
16 I            QtrTwo                    OverExpAry(2)
17 I            QtrThree                  OverExpAry(3)
18 I            QtrFour                   OverExpAry(4)
19
     *-----------------------------------------------------------------*
     * RPG record format  . . . . :  P101PSMR                          *
     * External format  . . . . . :  P101PSMR : STAN/P101PSM           *
     *-----------------------------------------------------------------*
20=I                       A   1   24 ACTNAME
21=I                       P  25   28 OOVEREXPARY(1)
22=I                       P  29   32 OOVEREXPARY(2)
23=I                       P  33   36 OOVEREXPARY(3)
24=I                       P  37   40 OOVEREXPARY(4)
25 C           EVAL      *INOF = *ON                       seton OF indicator
26 C           READ      P101Psm               ----LR     read first record
27 C           DOW       *INLR = *OFF                      dow LR is off          B01
28
29  * Test for page overflow....
30 C           IF        *INOF = *ON                       OF indicator on?       B02
31 C           EXCEPT    Headings              **         print heading lines     02
32 C           ENDIF                                       end IF group           E02
33
34 C           XFOOT     OverExpAry   TotalExp             add qtrs for expense   01
35 C           EVAL      TotOverAry = TotOverAry + OverExpAry   accum array elements  01
36 C           EXCEPT    DetailLine                        print a record         01
37 C           READ      P101Psm               ----LR     read next record       01
38 C           ENDDO                                       end dow group          E01
39
40 C           XFOOT     TotOverAry   TotalYear            compute TotalYear
41 C           EXCEPT    TotalLine                         print TotalLine
42
43 OQsysprt  E         Headings    1 01
44 O                                   48 'PROJECTO MANUFACTURING'
45 O                                   56 'COMPANY'
46 O                                   77 'PAGE'
47 O                   PAGE           82
48 O        E         Headings    1
49 O                                   46 'BUDGETED FACTORY OVER'
50 O                                   61 'HEAD COST BY QUARTERS'
51 O        E         Headings    3
52 O                                   48 'FOR BUDGET YEAR 19'
53 O                   UYEAR          50
54 O        E         Headings    2
55 O                                   19 'EXPENSE ACCOUNT'
56 O                                   31 '10'
57 O                                   42 '20'
58 O                                   53 '30'
59 O                                   63 '40'
60 O                                   78 'YEAR'
61 O        E         DetailLine  2
62 O                   ActName        24
63 O                   OverExpAry     71 '   ,   0&&&&'
64 O                   TotalExp     2 80
65 O        E         TotalLine   0
66 O                                   20 'TOTAL OVERHEAD COST'
67 O                   TotOverAry     69 '   ,   0&&'
68 O                   TotalYear    2 80
    * * * * *  E N D   O F   S O U R C E  * * * * *
```

Printed Report:

```
              PROJECTO MANUFACTURING COMPANY            PAGE     1
              BUDGETED FACTORHEAD COST BY QUARTERS
                    FOR BUDGET YEAR 1998
```

EXPENSE ACCOUNT	1Q	2Q	3Q	4Q	YEAR
INDIRECT LABOR	250,000	190,000	201,910	186,750	828,660
FACTORY SUPPLIES	86,000	70,000	103,480	93,100	352,580
HEAT, LIGHT, POWER	67,440	79,000	80,500	71,330	298,270
SUPERVISION	150,000	150,000	165,000	167,000	632,000
MAINTENANCE	90,000	87,000	89,000	77,900	343,900
TAXES AND INSURANCE	110,000	110,000	110,000	110,000	440,000
DEPRECIATION	125,000	125,000	125,000	125,000	500,000
TOTAL OVERHEAD COST	878,440	811,000	874,890	831,080	3,395,410

Programming Assignment 10-2: INCOME STATEMENT BY QUARTERS

Notes to the Instructor:

1. The program solution loads a work array (DataAry) by the *Input Specification's* method from the related fields in the physical file. In calculation the Salesrt, CostAry, and ExpenseAry arrays are loaded from the data in the Datary array with MOVEA instructions (lines 42, 45, and 48).

    Eight arrays are defined in the program.

2. Remind students that any of the arithmetic functions may be used with an array.

3. Printer spacing chart is formatted so that an equal number of spaces is specified between an array's elements. Consequently, three edit word formats may be defined to control the printing of the related array's values. One for the quarterly values that include $; another for the quarterly values that do not include $; and, an edit word for the percent array (last line of the report).

```
|Line   <--------------------- Source Specifications -------------------------><---- Comments ----> Do
|Number ....1....+....2....+....3....+....4....+....5....+....6....+....7....+....8....+....9....+...10 Num
                        S o u r c e   L i s t i n g
    1 * PA 10-2 Income Statement by Quarters....
    2 FP102psm   IF  E           DISK
    *-----------------------------------------------------------------------------------------------*
    *                              RPG name          External name                                  *
    * File name. . . . . . . . :   P102PSM           STAN/P102PSM                                    *
    * Record format(s) . . . . . :  P102PSMR          P102PSMR                                       *
    *-----------------------------------------------------------------------------------------------*
    3 FQsysprt   O   F 132       PRINTER
    4
    5 * Define arrays....                                                    -
*RNF2318 00    3 000300 Overflow indicator OA is assigned to PRINTER file QSYSPRT.
    6 DDataAry        S            6  0 DIM(4)
    7 DSalesAry       S            6  0 DIM(4)
    8 DCostAry        S            6  0 DIM(4)
    9 DGProfitAry     S            6  0 DIM(4)
   10 DExpenseAry     S            6  0 DIM(4)
   11 DNProfitAry     S            6  0 DIM(4)
   12 DDecPctAry      S            4  4 DIM(4)
```

```
13 DPercentAry         S              4  2 DIM(4)
14
15  * Define work fields....
16 DTotalSales         S              7  0
17 DTotalCost          S              7  0
18 DTotalExp           S              7  0
19 DTotalGross         S              7  0
20 DTotalNet           S              7  0
21 DTotDecPct          S              4  4
22 DTotPercent         S              4  2
23
24  * Load runtime array (DataAry)....
25 IP102psmr
26 I              Qtr1Amt                   DataAry(1)
27 I              Qtr2Amt                   DataAry(2)
28 I              Qtr3Amt                   DataAry(3)
29 I              Qtr4Amt                   DataAry(4)
30
    *-------------------------------------------------------------------------*
    * RPG record format  . . . . :  P102PSMR                                  *
    * External format  . . . . . :  P102PSMR : STAN/P102PSM                   *
    *-------------------------------------------------------------------------*
31=I                           A   1   1 ACTCODE
32=I                           P   2   3 OYEAR
33=I                           P   4   7 ODATAARY(1)
34=I                           P   8  11 ODATAARY(2)
35=I                           P  12  15 ODATAARY(3)
36=I                           P  16  19 ODATAARY(4)
37 C            READ     P102Psm                    ----LR   read first record
38 C            DOW      *INLR = *OFF                         dow LR is off      B01
39
40 C            SELECT                                        begin select group B02
41 C            WHEN     ActCode = 'S'                        ActCode = S?       X02
42 C            MOVEA    DataAry      SalesAry                load salesary      02
43 C            XFOOT    SalesAry     TotalSales              crossfoot for total 02
44 C            WHEN     ActCode = 'C'                        ActCode = C?       X02
45 C            MOVEA    DataAry      CostAry                 load costary       02
46 C            XFOOT    CostAry      TotalCost               crossfoot for total 02
47 C            WHEN     ActCode = 'E'                        ActCode = E?       X02
48 C            MOVEA    DataAry      ExpenseAry              load expenseary    02
49 C            XFOOT    ExpenseAry   TotalExp                crossfoot for total 02
50 C            ENDSL                                         end select group   E02
51
52 C            READ     P102Psm                    ----LR   read next record   01
53 C            ENDDO                                         end dow group      E01
54
55 C            EVAL     GProfitAry = SalesAry - CostAry      compute gross profit
56 C            XFOOT    GProfitAry   TotalGross              cross foot array
57 C            EVAL     NProfitAry = GProfitAry - ExpenseAry compute net profit
58 C            XFOOT    NProfitAry   TotalNet                cross foot array
59 C            EVAL     TotDecPct = TotalNet / TotalSales    compute totpercent
60 C            EVAL     TotPercent = TotDecPct * 100         compute totpercent
61 C            EVAL(H)  DecPctAry = NProfitAry / SalesAry    compute decimal pct
62 C            EVAL     PercentAry = DecPctAry * 100         compute percents
63 C            EXCEPT   PrintLine                            print TotalLine
64
65 OQsysprt  E        PrintLine       1 01
66 O                                      48 'DAGWOOD COMPANY'
67 O         E        PrintLine       1
68 O                                      49 'INCOME STATEMENT'
69 O         E        PrintLine       2
70 O                                      51 'FOR THE YEAR ENDING 12/31/'
71 O                      Year            53
72 O         E        PrintLine       2
73 O                                      33 '10'
74 O                                      44 '20'
75 O                                      55 '30'
76 O                                      66 '40'
77 O                                      80 'TOTAL'
78 O         E        PrintLine       1
79 O                                       6 'SALES'
80 O                      SalesAry        71 '$$   ,   &&'
81 O                                      72 '$'
82 O                      TotalSales    2 82
```

```
83 O          E        PrintLine      1
84 O                                     19 'LESS COST OF SALES'
85 O                   CostAry            73 '  ,  0&&&&'
86 O                   TotalCost     2    82
87 O          E        PrintLine      1
88 O                                     15 'GROSS PROFIT'
89 O                   GProfitAry         71 '$&  ,  0&&'
90 O                                      72 '$'
91 O                   TotalGross    2    82
92 O          E        PrintLine      1
93 O                                     24 'LESS OPERATING EXPENSES'
94 O                   ExpenseAry         73 '  ,  0&&&&'
95 O                   TotalExp      2    82
96 O          E        PrintLine      2
97 O                                     22 'NET INCOME (LOSS -)'
98 O                   NProfitAry         71 '$&  ,  0-&'
99 O                                      72 '$'
100 O                  TotalNet      2    82
101 O         E        PrintLine      1
102 O                                    28 'PCT OF NET INCOME TO SALES'
103 O                  PercentAry         74 ' 0.  -&&&&&'
104 O                  TotPercent    J    81
    * * * *  E N D   O F   S O U R C E  * * * *
```

Printed Report:

```
                    DAGWOOD COMPANY
                    INCOME STATEMENT
                  FOR YEAR ENDING 12/31/98

                 1Q        2Q        3Q        4Q        TOTAL

SALES          $ 200,000 $ 175,000 $ 210,000 $ 309,000 $  894,000
LESS COST OF SALES 100,000    92,000   120,000   209,000    521,000
  GROSS PROFIT  $ 100,000 $  83,000 $  90,000 $ 100,000 $  373,000
LESS OPERATING EXPENSES 70,000  52,000    89,000   105,000    316,000
  NET INCOME (LOSS-)  $ 30,000 $ 31,000 $   1,000 $   5,000- $  57,000

PCT OF NET INCOME TO  SALES 15.00    17.71      .47      1.61-     6.38
```

Programming Assignment 10-3: SHIPPING CHARGE REPORT

Notes to the Instructor:

1. Because this program requires use of a multiple occurrence data structure and the OCCUR operation, required that students review that section of the chapter.

2. Indicate that the 1-day and 2-day rates are to be "hard-coded" in the program into a multiple occurrence data structure. Lines 96-115 in the program example.

3. Refer students to the printer spacing chart and identify when the OVERWEIGHT message is printed and the when the six asterisks are printed. Note that the error message and the asterisks are defined as *Named Constants* (lines 5 and 6 in the program example).

```
Line  <--------------------- Source Specifications -------------------------><---- Comments ----> Do
Number ....1....+....2....+....3....+....4....+....5....+....6....+....7....+....8....+....9....+...10 Num
                      S o u r c e   L i s t i n g
    1 * PA 10-3 Shipping charge Report....
    2 FP103psm  IF  E            DISK
```

```
    *-------------------------------------------------------------------------*
    *                               RPG .name         External name           *
    * File name. . . . . . . . . :  P103PSM           STAN/P103PSM            *
    * Record format(s) . . . . . :  P103PSMR          P103PSMR               *
    *-------------------------------------------------------------------------*
  3 FQsysprt   O   F  132        PRINTER OFLIND (*INOF)
  4
  5 DOverWeight       C                    'OVER WEIGHT'
  6 DUnder$25         C                    '  ******'
  7
  8 * Define work fields....
  9 DMessage          S            11
 10 DNewPounds        S             2 0
 11 DShipCharge       S             5 2
 12 DOverPounds       S             2 0
 13 DExtraChg         S             5 2
 14
 15 * Define multiple occurrence data structure.....
 16 DRates            DS                   OCCURS(10)
 17 D OneDayRate              1      3 2
 18 D TwoDayRate              4      6 2
 19
 20=IP103PSMR
    *-------------------------------------------------------------------------*
    * RPG record format  . . . . :  P103PSMR                                  *
    * External format  . . . . . :  P103PSMR : STAN/P103PSM                   *
    *-------------------------------------------------------------------------*
 21=I                          A    1   20  CUSTNAME
 22=I                          A   21   24  INVNUMBER **
 23=I                          P   25   28 2INVAMOUNT
 24=I                          P   29   30 OPOUNDS
 25=I                          P   31   32 2OUNCES
 26=I                          P   33   33 ODELDAYS
 27 C                EVAL      *INOF = *ON                    seton OF indicator
 28
 29 * Branch to subroutine to load multiple occurrence data structure....
 30 C                EXSR      LoadSR                         branch to load SR
 31
 32 C                READ      P103Psm               ----LR  read first record
 33 C                DOW       *INLR = *OFF                   dow LR is off        B01
 34
 35 * Test for page overflow....
 36 C                IF        *INOF = *ON                    OF indicator on?     B02
 37 C                EXCEPT    Headings                       print heading lines  02
 38 C                ENDIF                                    end IF group         E02
 39
 40 C                EXSR      HouseKepSR                     branch to subroutine 01
 41
 42 C                IF        NewPounds <= 20                < or = to 20 pds?    B02
 43 C                EXSR      ChargeSR                       branch to subroutine 02
 44 C                ELSE                                     pds over 20          X02
 45 C                EVAL      Message = OverWeight           init. message        02
 46 C                EVAL      *IN30 = *ON                    set on indicator 30  02
 47 C                ENDIF                                    end IF group         E02
 48
 49 C                EXCEPT    DetailLine                     print a record       01
 50 C                READ      P103Psm               ----LR  read next record     01
 51 C                ENDDO                                    end dow group        E01
 52
 53 * Begin subroutines....
 54 C      HouseKepSR BEGSR                                   begin subroutine
 55 C                EVAL      NewPounds = Pounds             initialize NewPounds
 56
 57 C                IF        Ounces > *ZERO                 ounces > zero?       B01
 58 C                EVAL      NewPounds = NewPounds + 1      add 1 to NewPounds   01
 59 C                ENDIF                                    end IF group         E01
 60
 61 C                EVAL      ShipCharge = *ZERO             init. ShipCharge
 62 C                EVAL      *IN30 = *OFF                   set off indicator 30
 63 C                ENDSR                                    end subroutine
 64
 65 C      ChargeSR   BEGSR                                   begin subroutine
 66 C                IF        NewPounds > 10                 NewPounds > 10 pds?  B01
 67 C                EVAL      NewPounds = 10                 init. NewPounds      01
```

```
 68 C                    EXSR      ExcessSR                            branch to subroutine  01
 69 C                    ENDIF                                         end IF group          E01
 70
 71 * Compute shipping charge....
 72 C       NewPounds    OCCUR     Rates                               access data struct
 73 C                    IF        DelDays = 1                         DelDays = 1?          B01
 74 C                    EVAL      ShipCharge = ShipCharge + OneDayRate increment ShipCharge  01
 75 C                    ELSE                                          not 1 day shipment    X01
 76 C                    EVAL      ShipCharge = Shipcharge + TwoDayRate increment Shipcharge  01
 77 C                    ENDIF                                         end IF group          E01
 78
 79 * If InvAmount is less than $25, add shipping charge to InvAmount....
 80 C                    IF        InvAmount < 25                      InvAmount < $25?      B01
 81 C                    EVAL      InvAmount = InvAmount + Shipcharge   increase InvAmount     01
 82 C                    EVAL      Message = Under$25                   init. Message          01
 83 C                    EVAL      *IN30 = *ON                         set on indicator 30    01
 84 C                    ENDIF                                         end IF group          E01
 85 C                    ENDSR                                         end subroutine
 86
 87 * Compute excess shipping charge for items over 20 pounds...
 88 C       ExcessSR     BEGSR                                         begin subroutine
 89 C                    EVAL      OverPounds = Pounds - 10            compute excess pds
 90 C                    EVAL      ExtraChg = OverPounds * .06         compute extrachg
 91 C                    EVAL      ShipCharge = Shipcharge + ExtraChg  increase Shipcharge
 92 C                    ENDSR                                         end subroutine
 93
 94 * Load Multiple Occurrence Data Structure....
 95 C       LoadSR       BEGSR                              *)         begin subroutine
 96 C       1            OCCUR     Rates                               access 1st occurence
 97 C                    MOVE      129161    Rates                     load 1st occurrence
 98 C       2            OCCUR     Rates                               access 2nd occurence
 99 C                    MOVE      137171    Rates                     load 2nd occurrence
100 C       3            OCCUR     Rates                               access 3rd occurence
101 C                    MOVE      146183    Rates                     load 3rd occurrence
102 C       4            OCCUR     Rates                               access 4th occurence
103 C                    MOVE      154192    Rates                     load 4th occurrence
104 C       5            OCCUR     Rates                               access 5th occurence
105 C                    MOVE      163204    Rates                     load 5th occurrence
106 C       6            OCCUR     Rates                               access 6th occurence
107 C                    MOVE      171213    Rates                     load 6th occurrence
108 C       7            OCCUR     Rates                               access 7th occurence
109 C                    MOVE      180225    Rates                     load 7th occurrence
110 C       8            OCCUR     Rates                               access 8th occurence
111 C                    MOVE      188235    Rates                     load 8th occurrence
112 C       9            OCCUR     Rates                               access 9th occurence
113 C                    MOVE      197246    Rates                     load 9th occurrence
114 C       10           OCCUR     Rates                               access 10th occurenc
115 C                    MOVE      205257    Rates                     load 10th occurrenc
116 C                    ENDSR                                         end subroutine
117
118 OQsysprt  E          Headings         2 01
119 O                    UDATE          Y      8
120 O                                        49 'FOB DESTINATION SHIPMENT'
121 O                                        56 'REPORT'
122 O                                        78 'PAGE'
123 O                    PAGE                 83
124 O         E          Headings         1
125 O                                        31 'INVOICE'
126 O                                        61 'WEIGHT'
127 O                                        72 ' 1 OR 2'
128 O                                        83 'SHIPPING'
129 O         E          Headings         2
130 O                                        16 'CUSTOMER NAME'
131 O                                        30 'NUMBER'
132 O                                        50 'INVOICE AMOUNT'
133 O                                        62 'PDS OZS'
134 O                                        70 'DAY'
135 O                                        82 'CHARGE'
136 O         E          DetailLine       2
137 O                    CustName            20
138 O                    InvNumber           29
139 O                    InvAmount        1  47
140 O                    Pounds           1  57
141 O                    Ounces              61 '0 '
```

Chapter 10 - Array Processing

```
142 O                    DelDays         69
143 O                    ShipCharge  1B  82           blank after printing
144 O              30     Message         82           print when 30 is on
        * * * * *  E N D  O F  S O U R C E  * * * *
```

Printed Report:

```
1/06/98              FOB DESTINATION SHIPMENT REPORT              PAGE   1

                    INVOICE                      WEIGHT    1 OR 2   SHIPPING
   CUSTOMER NAME     NUMBER    INVOICE AMOUNT     PDS OZS    DAY      CHARGE

HENRY JACKSON        1234          25.71          5   8      1      ******

DOROTHY PARTNER      1235         100.00         10   0      2        2.57

ROBERT WARFIELD      1236          45.00          9   9      1        2.05

MARIO LANZA          1237       1,200.00         20   0      1        2.65

ENZIO PINZA          1238       2,450.00         20  12      2   OVER WEIGHT

NELSON EDDY          1239          11.61          1   0      2      ******
```

Programming Assignment 10-4: MAILING LABELS

Notes to the Instructor:

1. Indicate to the students that four *prerun time* arrays should be defined in their programs and loaded with data in calculations.

2. If the arrays are defined as four elements each with a length of 33 bytes, the required space between the labels will be provided.

3. If Address2 field from the physical file record is blank, the value from the CityStZip field is to be moved to that array. Otherwise, the values from the Address2 and CityStZip fields are to be moved into their related array elements.

4. Control must be included in the RPG IV program to print the last group of labels at LR time when there are less than four. See line 41.

```
Line   <-------------------- Source Specifications --------------------><---- Comments ----> Do
Number ....1....+....2....+....3....+....4....+....5....+....6....+....7....+....8....+....9....+...10 Num
                     S o u r c e   L i s t i n g
   1 * PA 10-4 Mailing Labels....
   2 FP104psm  IF  E           DISK
     *--------------------------------------------------------------------------------------*
     *                           RPG name          External name                           *
     * File name. . . . . . . . :  P104PSM          STAN/P104PSM                            *
     * Record format(s) . . . . :  P104PSMR         P104PSMR                                *
     *--------------------------------------------------------------------------------------*
   3 FQsysprt  O   F  132      PRINTER
   4
   5 * Define Arrays....
*RNF2318 00     3 000300  Overflow indicator OA is assigned to PRINTER file QSYSPRT.
   6 DNameAry         S            33    DIM(4)
   7 DAddrs1Ary       S            33    DIM(4)
   8 DAddrs2Ary       S            33    DIM(4)
   9 DCtStZpAry       S            33    DIM(4)
  10
```

116

```
11  * Define index for the arrays....
12 DCtr             S              1  0                          labels/line counter
13
14=IP104PSMR
    *--------------------------------------------------------------------------------*
    * RPG record format  . , . . :  P104PSMR                                         *
    * External format  . . . . . :  P104PSMR : STAN/P104PSM                          *
    *--------------------------------------------------------------------------------*
15=I                             A    1   18  CUSTNAME
16=I                             A   19   36  ADDRESS1
17=I                             A   37   47  ADDRESS2
18=I                             A   48   78  CITYSTZIP
19 C           READ       P104psm                       ----LR   read first record
20 C           DOW        *INLR = *OFF                            dow LR is off          B01
21 C           EVAL       Ctr = Ctr + 1                           increment counter       01
22 C           MOVEA      CustName      NameAry(Ctr)              load array element       01
23 C           MOVEA      Address1      Addrs1Ary(Ctr)            load array element       01
24 C           IF         Address2 > *BLANKS                      field value blank?l     B02
25 C           MOVEA      Address2      Addrs2Ary(Ctr)            load array element       02
26 C           MOVEA      CityStZip     CtStZpAry(Ctr)            load array element       02
27 C           ELSE                                               address2 blank          X02
28 C           MOVEA      CityStZip     Addrs2Ary(Ctr)            load array element       02
29 C           ENDIF                                              end IF group            E02
30
31  * If four labels are loaded, print line of four labels....
32 C           IF         Ctr = 4                                 four labels loaded?     B02
33 C           EXCEPT     PrintLine                               print line of labels    02
34 C           EVAL       Ctr = *ZERO              **              init. counter to 0      02
35 C           ENDIF                                              end IF group            E02
36
37 C           READ       P104psm                       ----LR   read next record         01
38 C           ENDDO                                              end dow group           E01
39
40  * Print last line of labels at LR time....
41 C           EXCEPT     PrintLine                               print last labels
42
43 OQsysprt  E              PrintLine       1
44 O                          NameAry        B  132
45 O         E              PrintLine       1
46 O                          Addrs1Ary      B  132
47 O         E              PrintLine       1
48 O                          Addrs2Ary      B  132
49 O         E              PrintLine       2
50 O                          CtStZpAry      B  132
    * * * * *  E N D   O F   S O U R C E  * * * * *
```

Printed Labels:

```
KAREL APPEL              GEORGES BRAQUE          PAUL CEZANNE            MARC CHAGALL
20 AMSTERDAM AVE         300 ST CLAIR ST         44 RUE PIGALLE          222 QUAIL AVENUE
APT 35                   NEW JERSEY, NJ 055011234 BLDG 10                BRIDGEPORT, CT 066661000
NEW YORK, NY 074500000                           STAMFORD, CT 065180010


EDGAR DEGAS             MAX ERNST                BUCKMINSTER FULLER      JULIO GONZALEZ
10 ROSE TERRACE         1 FRANKFURT DRIVE        999 PARK AVENUE         101 SMITH LANE
WESTPORT, PA 077770000  LOT 14                   APT 201                 GREENWICH, CT 064440000
                        FRANKFORT, KY 055510111  NEW YORK, NY 075500000


HECTOR HYPPOLITE        PIERRE JEANERET          WASSILY KANDINSKY       CHARLES CORBUSIER
888 PEACHTREE AVE       90 CHATEAU DRIVE         13 WARSAW LANE          10 PARIS PLACE
ATLANTA, GA 033322200   GENEVA, NY 077774000     LOS ANGELES, CA 099900000  ENGLEWOOD CLIFFS, NJ 076320000


PABLO PICASSO
1784 BASTILLE BLD
FRANCE, KY 088800000
```

Programming Assignment 10-5: SORTING AN ARRAY

Notes to the Instructor:

1. A physical file without a DDS format must be created and

loaded with the array data. It will be processed as a
a program described table file in the RPG IV program.

2. The array is to be sorted beginning at the first character
   of each element.

3. After sorting three SUBST instructions separate the 26 characte
   elements into SalPerNo, SalesAmt, and SalPName fields.

```
Line    <--------------------- Source Specifications --------------------------><---- Comments ----> Do
Number  ....1....+....2....+....3....+....4....+....5....+....6....+....7....+....8....+....9....+...10 Num
                    S o u r c e   L i s t i n g
    1 * PA 10-5  Sorting an array....
    2 FP105psm   IT  F   26        DISK
    3 FQsysprt   O   F  132        PRINTER OFLIND(*INOF)
    4
    5 * Define prerun time array....
    6 DSalesAry       S           26    DIM(6) FROMFILE(P105psm)
    7
    8 * Define array index....
    9 DX              S            1 0
   10
   11 * Define work fields....
   12 DSalPerNo       S            4                      **
   13 DSalesAmt       S            8 2
   14 DHoldAmt        S            8
   15 DSalPName       S           14
   16
   17 C                   EVAL      *INOF = *ON              set on OF indicator
   18
   19 * Sort SalesAry in ascending order beginning at first character....
   20 C                   SORTA     SalesAry                 sort on 1st charater
   21
   22 * Separate array into fields for printing....
   23 C                   DOU       X = 6                    dou X is equal to 6  B01
   24
   25 C                   IF        *INOF = *ON              OF indicator on?     B02
   26 C                   EXCEPT    Headings                 print heading lines  02
   27 C                   ENDIF                              end IF group         E02
   28
   29 C                   EVAL      X = X + 1                increment index X    01
   30 C        4          SUBST     SalesAry(X):1 SalPerNo   extract SalPerNo     01
   31 C        8          SUBST     SalesAry(X):5 HoldAmt    extract SalPerName   01
   32 C                   MOVE      Holdamt       SalesAmt   move to numeric fld  01
   33 C       14          SUBST     SalesAry(X):13SalPName   extract SalPerNo     01
   34 C                   EXCEPT    DetailLine               print record         01
   35 C                   ENDDO                              end dow group        E01
   36
   37 C                   EVAL      *INLR = *ON              set on LR indicator
   38
   39 OQsysprt   E            Headings       1 01
   40 O                                           33 'SALESPERSON PERFORMANCE'
   41 O                                           40 'REPORT'
   42 O                        PAGE             49
   43 O          E            Headings       3
   44 O                                           22 'AS OF'
   45 O                        *DATE          Y  33
   46 O          E            Headings       1
   47 C                                           12 'SALESPERSON'
   48 O                                           49 'YEAR-TO-DATE'
   49 O          E            Headings       2
   50 O                                            9 'NUMBER'
   51 O                                           32 'SALESPERSON NAME'
   52 O                                           46 'SALES'
   53 O          E            DetailLine     2
   54 O                        SalPerNo          8
   55 O                        SalPName         31
   56 O                        SalesAmt       1 49
      * * * * *  E N D   O F   S O U R C E  * * * * *
```

Printed Report:

```
┌────────────────────────────────────────────────────────┐
│          SALESPERSON PERFORMANCE REPORT        1         │
│                AS OF  9/08/1997                          │
│                                                          │
│  SALESPERSON                           YEAR-TO-DATE      │
│    NUMBER      SALESPERSON NAME           SALES          │
│                                                          │
│     1100       HENRY SMITH              12,567.84        │
│                                                          │
│     2200       WALTER CHANG            100,032.19        │
│                                                          │
│     3300       JEROME WALDRON           3,109.86         │
│                                                          │
│     4400       MARGARET STERN          34,685.62         │
│                                                          │
│     5500       JOSE GONZALEZ            4,988.55         │
│                                                          │
│     6600       KALMAN COHEN            67,589.74         │
└────────────────────────────────────────────────────────┘
```

Programming Assignment 10-6: SORTING AN ARRAY BEGINNING ON A SELECT POSITION IN AN ELEMENT

Notes to the Instructor:

1. A second array (OverAry) is defined on line 9 that holds the characters the character from the SalesAry to be sorted.

2. The **OVERLAY(SalesAry:5)** keyword specifies on the position in the elements in the SalesAry where the sort is to begin.

3. Note that the OverAry is specified in the SORTA instruction on line 23 and not the SalesAry. However, the sorted SalesAry is used in the three **SUBST** instructions on lines 33, 34, and 36.

```
|Line   <---------------------- Source Specifications ----------------------------><---- Comments ----> Do
|Number ....1....+....2....+....3....+....4....+....5....+....6....+....7....+....8....+....9....+...10 Num
                           S o u r c e    L i s t i n g
    1 * PA 10-6  Sorting an array beginning on a
    2 * select position within an element....
    3 FP105psm   IT  F   26        DISK
    4 FQsysprt   O   F  132        PRINTER OFLIND(*INOF)
    5
    6 * Define prerun time array and overlay array....
    7 D              DS
    8 DSalesAry               26    DIM(6) FROMFILE(P105psm)
    9 DOverAry                22    OVERLAY(SalesAry:5)
   10
   11 * Define array index....
   12 DX             S         1 0
   13
   14 * Define work fields....
   15 DSalPerNo      S         4
   16 DSalesAmt      S         8 2
   17 DHoldAmt       S         8
   18 DSalPName      S        14
   19
   20 C              EVAL      *INOF = *ON                          set on OF indicator
   21
   22 * Sort the OverAry in ascending order beginning at fifth character....
   23 C              SORTA     OverAry                              sort on 1st charater
   24
   25 * Separate the SalesAry array into fields for printing....
   26 C              DOU       X = 6                                dou X is equal to 6  B01
```

119

```
27
28 C                    IF        *INOF = *ON              OF indicator on?      B02
29 C                    EXCEPT    Headings                 print heading lines    02
30 C                    ENDIF                              end IF group          E02
31
32 C                    EVAL      X = X + 1                increment index X      01
33 C        4           SUBST     SalesAry(X):1 SalPerNo   extract SalPerNo       01
34 C        8           SUBST     SalesAry(X):5 HoldAmt    extract SalPerName     01
35 C                    MOVE      Holdamt       SalesAmt   move to numeric fld    01
36 C        14          SUBST     SalesAry(X):13SalPName   extract SalPerNo       01
37 C                    EXCEPT    DetailLine               print record           01
38 C                    ENDDO                              end dow group         E01
39
40 C                    EVAL      *INLR = *ON              set on LR indicator
41
42 OQsysprt   E         Headings       1 01
43 O                                       33 'SALESPERSON PERFORMANCE'
44 O                                       40 'REPORT'
45 O                    PAGE               49
46 O          E         Headings       3
47 O                                       22 'AS OF'
48 O                    *DATE        Y     33
49 O          E         Headings       1
50 O                                       12 'SALESPERSON'
51 O                                       49 'YEAR-TO-DATE'
52 O          E         Headings       2
53 O                                        9 'NUMBER'
54 O                                       32 'SALESPERSON NAME'
55 O                                       46 'SALES'
56 O          E         DetailLine     2
57 O                    SalPerNo            8
58 O                    SalPName           31
59 O                    SalesAmt      1     49
      * * * * *  E N D   O F   S O U R C E  * * * * *
```

Printed Report:

```
        SALESPERSON PERFORMANCE REPORT        1
              AS OF   9/08/1998

SALESPERSON
  NUMBER      SALESPERSON NAME      YEAR-TO-DATE
                                       SALES

   3300       JEROME WALDRON          3,109.86

   5500       JOSE GONZALEZ           4,988.55

   1100       HENRY SMITH            12,567.84

   4400       MARGARET STERN         34,685.62

   6600       KALMAN COHEN           67,589.74

   2200       WALTER CHANG          100,032.19
```

CHAPTER 11
RPG IV CHARACTER MANIPULATION OPERATIONS, BUILT-IN FUNCTIONS (BIFs), and DATE/TIME OPERATIONS

1. **CHECK** *(Check)*, **CHECKR** *(Check Reverse)*, **SCAN** *(Scan String)*, **SUBST** *(Substring)*, **XLATE** *(Translate)*.

2. The **XLATE** operation.

3. The **CHECKR** operation.

4. The **SUBST** operation.

5. The **SCAN** operation.

6. The **CHECK** operation.

7. The position of the first non-blank character in the StudntName field.

8. The position of any characters not in the *Named Constant* AlphaChars.

9. The position of the first , (comma) in the StudntName field.

10. The position of nay blanks in the CitStZip field.

11. The number of characters to be extracted from the ClientName field.

12. The beginning position in the ClientName field from which the four characters will be extracted.

13. If an error occurs when the instruction is executed. An error may occur if the start position is greater than the length of the *Factor 2* item; or if the *Factor 1* entry is larger than the *Result* field item.

14. Pads the low-order positions of the *Result* field item with blanks.

15. 20 characters.

16. Uppercase characters for the StudntName value.

17. Translate the comma in the CityStZip field to a blank and stores the new format in the NewAddress field.

18. %SUBST Function - Extracts a substring or portion of a substring. Has the same function as the RPG IV **SUBST** operation but provides more flexibility.

    %TRIM Function - Strings both leading a trailing blanks in the item specified.

%TRIML Function - Strips leading blanks in the item specified and stores the new value left-justified in the character field to the left of the equal sign in the **EVAL** instruction.

%TRIMR Function - Strips trailing blanks in the item specified and stores the new value right-justified in the character field to the left of the equal sign in the **EVAL** instruction.

%SIZE Function - Determines the number of bytes stored in the array, data structure, field, literal, or named constant.

%ELEM Function - Returns the number of elements in an array or table; or the number of occurrences in a multiple-occurrence data structure.

19. New to RPG, a pointer points to an address in memory indicating where an item may be found: it does <u>not</u> point to the value of an item.

20. **Basing pointer** - Points to the address of a data item.

   Procedure pointer - Points to the address of a procedure or function.

21. A pointer is defined in *Definition Specifications* instruction with an asterisk in the *internal data type* field (position 40).

22. The **%ADDR** function stores the address of an array element, variable, or an expression defined as a pointer.

   The **%PADDR** function store the address of a procedure in an item defined as a pointer.

23. The address of the CodeTable item.

24. Initializes the Location field with the address of the CodeTable item.

25. The address of the Address1 procedure.

26. The address of a procedure.

27. Initializes the Address1 item with the address of the Billing procedure.

28. ADDDUR, SUBDUR, EXTRCT operations.

29. *YEARS (*Y), *MONTHS (*M), *DAYS (*D), *HOURS (*H), *MINUTES (*MN), *SECONDS (*S), *MSECONDS (*MS)

30. 12

31. 97

32. 35

33. *ISO (yyyy-mm-dd) format

34. Tests the validity of a date, time, or timestamp field value before it is subsequently used in a RPG IV program.

PROGRAMMING ASSIGNMENTS

Programming Assignment 11-1: CUSTOMER LISTING BY LAST NAME

Notes to the Instructor:

1. Stress that students should review the syntax and function of the **SCAN** and **SUBST** operations.

2. Indicate that a **SCAN** instruction and **SUBST** instruction are required to separate the last name value form the CustName field. Refer to lines 26 through 29 in the compile listing.

3. Indicate that a **SCAN** instruction and **SUBST** instruction are required to separate the State field value from the CityState field. Refer to lines 32 through 34 in the compile listing.

```
Line    <------------------ Source Specifications ------------------><---- Comments ----> Do
Number  ....1....+....2....+....3....+....4....+....5....+....6....+....7....+....8....+....9....+...10 Num
                        S o u r c e   L i s t i n g
    1  * PA 11-1: Customer Listing By Last Name....
    2  FP111psm   IF  E            DISK
       *-------------------------------------------------------------------------------*
       *                            RPG name           External name                  *
       * File name. . . . . . . . :  P111PSM           STAN/P111PSM                    *
       * Record format(s) . . . . :  P111PSMR          P111PSMR                        *
       *-------------------------------------------------------------------------------*
    3  FQsysprt   O   F  132        PRINTER OFLIND(*INOC)
    4
    5  DLastName         S            17
    6  DState            S             2
    7  DNoOfCustrs       S             4 0
    8  DX                S             2 0                             counter
    9  DLength           S             2 0
   10  DHhmmss           S             6 0
   11
   12=IP111PSMR
       *-------------------------------------------------------------------------------*
       * RPG record format  . . . . :  P111PSMR                                         *
       * External format  . . . . . :  P111PSMR : STAN/P111PSM                          *
       *-------------------------------------------------------------------------------*
   13=I                        A    1   20  CUSTNAME
   14=I                        A   21   45  STREET
   15=I                        A   46   60  CITYSTATE
   16=I                        P   61   63 0ZIPCODE
   17 C           TIME                       Hhmmss            get system time
   18 C           EVAL       *INOC = *ON                       set on OC indicator
   19 C           READ       P111Psm                     ----LR  read first record
   20 C           DOW        *INLR = *OFF                      dow LR is off        B01
   21 C           IF         *INOC = *ON                       overlow ind. on?     B02
   22 C           EXCEPT     Headings                          print heading lines  02
   23 C           ENDIF                                        end IF group         E02
   24
   25 * Extract LastName from CustName field....
   26 C    ' '    SCAN       CustName     X                    find pos of space    01
   27 C           EVAL       X = X + 1                          beg pos of lastname  01
   28 C           EVAL       Length = 20 - X                    determine length     01
   29 C    Length SUBST      CustName:X   LastName             extract LastName     01
   30
   31 * Extract State code from Citystate field....
   32 C    ','    SCAN       CityState    X                    find pos of comma    01
   33 C           EVAL       X = X + 2                          beg pos of state cod 01
   34 C    2      SUBST      CityState:X  State                extract state code   01
```

```
35
36 C                    EXCEPT    DetailLine                          print record             01
37 C                    EVAL      NoOfCustrs = NoOfCustrs + 1         increment record ctr     01
38 C                    READ      P111psm                    ----LR   read next record         01
39 C                    ENDDO                                         end dow group           E01
40
41 C                    EXCEPT    TotalLine                           print totalline
42 C                    EVAL      *INLR = *ON                         end program
43 OQsysprt   E         Headings      1 01
44 O                    Hhmmss              8 ' : : '
45 O                                       35 'CUSTOMER LISTING IN LAST'
46 O                                       46 'NAME ORDER'
47 O                                       53 'PAGE'
48 O                    PAGE               58
49 O         E         Headings      3
50 O                                       27 'AS OF'
51 O                    UDATE         Y    36
52 O         E         Headings      2
53 O                                       23 'CUSTOMER NAME'
54 O                                       48 'STATE'
55 O         E         DetailLine    2
56 O                    LastName           26
57 O                    State              47
58 O         E         TotalLine     1
59 O                                       23 'NUMBER OF CUSTOMERS:'
60 O                    NoOfCustrs    1    29
     * * * * *  E N D   O F   S O U R C E   * * * * *
```

Printed Report: *2

```
15:35:16   CUSTOMER LISTING IN LAST NAME ORDER    PAGE     1
                     AS OF   9/17/98


           CUSTOMER NAME                      STATE

           HAMILTON                           NY

           JAY                                NY

           JEFFERSON                          VA

           KENSINGTON                         FL

           ROOSEVELT                          NY

           WASHINGTON                         VA


   NUMBER OF CUSTOMERS:     6
```

Programming Assignment 11-2: PATIENT MAILING LABELS

Notes to the Instructor:

1. Stress that students should refer catenation with the **EVAL** operations and the syntax and use of the **%TRIMR** function.

2. Indicate when a customer does not have an Address2 field] value, the CitStZip field value must be printed on the third line of the label and not the fourth. Refer to lines 30 through 34 of the compile listing.

```
Line   <-------------------- Source Specifications -------------------------><---- Comments ----> Do
Number ....1....+....2....+....3....+....4....+....5....+....6....+....7....+....8....+....9....+...10 Num
                   S o u r c e   L i s t i n g
   1 * PA 11-2: Patient Mailing Labels....
   2 FP112psm  IF  E            DISK
```

```
    *------------------------------------------------------------------------*
    *  ·                          RPG name        External name               *
    * File name. . . . . . . . :  P112PSM         STAN/P112PSM                *
    * Record format(s) . . . . :  P112PSMR        P112PSMR                    *
    *------------------------------------------------------------------------*
 3 FQsysprt    O    F  132          PRINTER
 4
 5 DPatientNam        S            29
 6 DCitStZip          S            29
 7 DHoldField         S            29
 8 DHoldZip           S             5
 9
10=IP112PSMR
    *------------------------------------------------------------------------*
    * RPG record format  . . . . :  P112PSMR                                   *
    * External format  . . . . . :  P112PSMR : STAN/P112PSM                    *
    *------------------------------------------------------------------------*
11=I                        A   1  12  FIRST_NAME
12=I                        A  13  27  LAST_NAME
13=I                        A  28  47  ADDRESS1
14=I                        A  48  59  ADDRESS2
15=I                        A  60  79  CITY
16=I                        A  80  81  STATE
17=I                        P  82  84 0ZIP_CODE
18 C            READ      P112psm                    ----LR  read first record
19 C            DOW       *INLR = *OFF                       dow LR is off        B01
20
21 * Concatenate First_Name and Last_Name into PatientNam field....
22 C            EVAL      PatientNam = %TRIMR(First_Name) + ' ' +                01
23 C                      %TRIMR(Last_Name)      **          concatenate fields  01
24
25 * Concatenate City, State, and Zip_Code fields....
26 C            MOVE      Zip_Code      HoldZip            move to char. field    01
27 C            EVAL      CitStZip = %TRIMR(City) + ', ' + State +               01
28 C                      ' ' + HoldZip                    concatenate fields     01
29
30 C            IF        Address2 > *BLANKS                blank value?          B02
31 C            EVAL      HoldField = Address2              init. holdfield       02
32 C            ELSE                                                              X02
33 C            EVAL      HoldField = CitStZip              move to hold field    02
34 C            EVAL      CitStZip = *BLANKS                init.fld to blanks    02
35 C            ENDIF                                       end IF group          E02
36
37 C            EXCEPT    LabelLine                         print label           01
38
39 C            READ      P112psm                    ----LR  read next record     01
40 C            ENDDO                                       end dow group         E01
41
42 C            EVAL      *INLR = *ON                       end program
43
44 OQsysprt  E           LabelLine        1     03
45 O                     PatientNam            29
46 O         E           LabelLine        1
47 O                     Address1              20
48 O         E           LabelLine        1
49 O                     HoldField             29
50 O         E           LabelLine        3
51 O                     CitStZip              29
    * * * * *  E N D   O F   S O U R C E  * * * * *
```

Printed Report:

```
-----------------------------
|
| WASSILY KANDINSKY
| 20 AMSTERDAM AVE
| APT 35
| FRANCE, KY 07450
-----------------------------
|
| GEORGES BRAQUE
| 300 ST CLAIR ST
| NEW JERSEY, NJ 05501
|
-----------------------------
```

```
PAUL CEZANNE
44 RUE PIGALLE
BLDG 10
STAMFORD, CT 06666
-----------------------

MARK CHAGALL
222 QUAIL AVENUE
BRIDGEPORT, CT 06666

-----------------------

EDGAR DEGAS
10 ROSE TERRACE
WESTPORT, PA 07777

-----------------------

BUCKMINISTER FULLER
999 PARK AVENUE
APT 201
RYE, NY 07550

-----------------------
```

Programming Assignment 11-3: AGING ACCOUNTS RECEIVABLE

Notes to the Instructor:

1. Stress that INV_DATE was defined as a date field in the physica
   file (see line 40) in an **MDY** format.

2. Stress that the Datefield was defined as a date field and initialized to 05/01/97 in the *Definition Specification* instruction
   on line 28 with an **MDY** format.

3. Indicate that the **DATFMT(*MDY)** keyword must be specified in the
   Control Specifications (H type instruction) to control the matc
   ing of the Inv_Date and Datefield field formats. Without this
   keyword, **ISO** would be the default format and not be compatible
   with the required **MDY** date formats. The omission of the DATFM
   keyword will cause an error during compilation of the program.

4. Explain that a **SUBDUR** instruction subtracts the different betwe
   two fields with date formats and stores the requested *Y, *M, o
   *D value in the *Result* field item. The **SUBDUR** instruction on l
   56 stores the number of dats between the DateField field value
   the Inv_Date field value.

5. The program is written considering that there are 30 days in a
   month. Using **WHEN** instructions (lines 61, 65, 69, and 73), a D
   field value <u>less than or equal to 30</u> is considered Current; <u>les
   than or equal to 60</u>, OneMthOvr; <u>less than or equal to 90</u>, TwoMth
   <u>greater than 90</u>, ThreMthOvr. The Inv_Amount value from each inv
   is stored and accumulated in the related fields based on the Da
   field value.

6. A CompanyNo control break is included in the program to control
   the printing of a Company Total line when a changed in the
   CompanyNo field value is detected (see line 50). A HoldCompNo
   field is defined in the *Definition Specifications* to hold the
   current CompanyNo field value for the control break test. Afte

a control break occurs, the HoldCompNo field is initialized with the CompanyNo field value from the record that generated the control break (the current record being processed).

```
Line    <--------------------- Source Specifications ------------------------------><---- Comments ----> Do
Number  ....1....+....2....+....3....+....4....+....5....+....6....+....7....+....8....+....9....+...10 Num
                         S o u r c e   L i s t i n g
   1  * PA 11-3: Aging Accounts Receivable....
   2
   3  HDATFMT(*MDY)
   4  FP113psm   IF   E        K DISK
      *------------------------------------------------------------------------------------------*
      *                            RPG name         External name                                *
      * File name. . . . . . . . :  P113PSM          STAN/P113PSM                                 *
      * Record format(s) . . . . . :  P113PSMR        P113PSMR                                    *
      *------------------------------------------------------------------------------------------*
   5  FQsysprt   O   F 132        PRINTER OFLIND(*INOO)
   6
   7  * Define status fields for invoice amounts due....
   8  DCurrent          S          7  2
   9  DOneMthOvr        S          7  2
  10  DTwoMthOvr        S          7  2
  11  DThreMthOvr       S          7  2
  12
  13  * Define company total fields....
  14  DTotInvoice       S          8  2
  15  DTotCurrent       S          8  2                     *3
  16  DTot1MthOvr       S          8  2
  17  DTot2MthOvr       S          8  2
  18  DTot3MthOvr       S          8  2
  19
  20  * Define grand total fields....
  21  DGrnInvoice       S          8  2
  22  DGrnCurrent       S          8  2
  23  DGrn1MthOvr       S          8  2
  24  DGrn2MthOvr       S          8  2
  25  DGrn3MthOvr       S          8  2
  26
  27  * Define given date field and value....
  28  DDateField        S             D  DATFMT(*MDY) INZ(D'05/01/97')    init. a date field
  29
  30  * Define the field for number of days between dates....
  31  DDays             S          3  0
  32
  33  * Define hold field for CompanyNo used for control break test....
  34  DHoldCompNo       S          5
  35
  36=IP113PSMR
      *------------------------------------------------------------------------------------------*
      * RPG record format . . . . :  P113PSMR                                                     *
      * External format  . . . . . :  P113PSMR : STAN/P113PSM                                     *
      *------------------------------------------------------------------------------------------*
  37=I                         A    1    5  COMPANYNO
  38=I                         A    6   30  COMPNYNAME
  39=I                         A   31   34  INVOICENO
  40=I                    *MDY/D   35   42  INV_DATE
  41=I                         P   43   46 2INV_AMOUNT
  42 C            EVAL      *INOO = *ON                      set on overflow ind.
  43 C            READ      P113psm                ----LR    read first record
  44 C            EVAL      HoldCompNo = CompanyNo           init. holdcompno fld
  45 C            DOW       *INLR = *OFF                     dow LR is off         B01
  46 C            IF        *INOO = *ON                      overflow ind. on?     B02
  47 C            EXCEPT    Headings                         print heading lines    02
  48 C            ENDIF                                      end IF group          E02
  49
  50 C            IF        CompanyNo <> HoldCompNo          control break?        B02
  51 C            EXCEPT    ComTotLine                       print company totals   02
  52 C            EVAL      HoldCompNo = CompanyNo           move in current no     02
  53 C            ENDIF                                      false action          E02
  54
  55  * Compute number of days between dates...
  56 C  DateField  SUBDUR    Inv_Date   Days:*D             deter. overdue mths    01
  57
```

```
 58 * Determine whether current, 1 month, 2 months, or 3 months or
 59 * greater over due....
 60 C              SELECT                                          begin select group   B02
 61 C              WHEN      Days <= 30                            current              X02
 62 C              EVAL      Current = Inv_Amount                  init. output field    02
 63 C              EVAL      TotCurrent = TotCurrent + Inv_Amount  accum total field     02
 64 C              EVAL      GrnCurrent = GrnCurrent + Inv_Amount  accum total           02
 65 C              WHEN      Days <= 60                            current              X02
 66 C              EVAL      OneMthOvr = Inv_Amount                1 mth over date       02
 67 C              EVAL      Tot1MthOvr = Tot1MthOvr + Inv_Amount  accum total           02
 68 C              EVAL      Grn1MthOvr = Grn1MthOvr + Inv_Amount  accum totals          02
 69 C              WHEN      Days <= 90                            current              X02
 70 C              EVAL      TwoMthOvr = Inv_Amount                init. output field    02
 71 C              EVAL      Tot2MthOvr = Tot2MthOvr + Inv_Amount  accum total           02
 72 C              EVAL      Grn2MthOvr = Grn2MthOvr + Inv_Amount  accum totals          02
 73 C              WHEN      Days > 90                             current              X02
 74 C              EVAL      ThreMthOvr = Inv_Amount               init. output field    02
 75 C              EVAL      Tot3MthOvr = Tot3MthOvr + Inv_Amount  accum total           02
 76 C              EVAL      Grn3MthOvr = Grn3MthOvr + Inv_Amount  accum totals          02
 77 C              ENDSL                             .             end select group     E02
 78
 79 C              EVAL      TotInvoice = TotInvoice + Inv_Amount                        01
 80 C              EVAL      GrnInvoice = GrnInvoice + Inv_Amount                        01
 81 C              EXCEPT    DetailLine                            print record          01
 82 C              READ      P113psm                       ----LR  read next record      01
 83 C              ENDDO                                           end dow group        E01
 84
 85 C              EXCEPT    ComTotLine                            print company totals
 86 C              EXCEPT    GrnTotLine                            print grand totals
 87 C              EVAL      *INLR = *ON               *1          end program
 88
 89 OQsysprt   E      Headings       3 01
 90 O              *DATE          Y   10
 91 O                                 64 'ACCOUNTS RECEIVABLE AGING'
 92 O                                 71 'REPORT'
 93 O                                103 'PAGE'
 94 O              PAGE              108
 95 O          E      Headings       1
 96 O                                  8 'COMPANY'
 97 O                                 46 'INVOICE'
 98 O                                 57 'INVOICE'
 99 O                                 81 '1 MONTH'
100 O                                 95 '2 MONTHS'
101 O                                107 '3 MONTHS'
102 O          E.     Headings       2
103 O                                  7 'NUMBER'
104 O                                 27 'COMPANY NAME'
105 O                                 45 'NUMBER'
106 O                                 56 'AMOUNT'
107 O                                 69 'CURRENT'
108 O                                 81 'OVERDUE'
109 O                                 94 'OVERDUE'
110 O                                106 ' & OVER'
111 O          E      DetailLine     2
112 O              CompanyNo          6
113 O              CompnyName        33
114 O              InvoiceNo         44
115 O              Inv_Amount     2  58
116 O              Current        2B 70
117 O              OneMthOvr      2B 82
118 O              TwoMthOvr      2B 95
119 O              ThreMthOvr     2B 107
120 O          E      ComTotLine     2
121 O                                 32 'COMPANY TOTALS'
122 O                                 45 '.............'
123 O              TotInvoice     2B 58
124 O              TotCurrent     2B 70
125 O              Tot1MthOvr     2B 82
126 O              Tot2MthOvr     2B 95
127 O              Tot3MthOvr     2B 107
128 O          E      GrnTotLine   1
129 O                                 43 'GRAND TOTALS.............'
130 O              GrnInvoice     2  58
131 O              GrnCurrent     2  70
132 O              Grn1MthOvr     2  82
133 O              Grn2MthOvr     2  95
```

```
 134 0              Grn3MthOvr    2    107
     * * * *  E N D   O F   S O U R C E  * * * *
```

Printed Report:

9/21/1997			ACCOUNTS RECEIVABLE AGING REPORT					PAGE 1
COMPANY NUMBER	COMPANY NAME	INVOICE NUMBER	INVOICE AMOUNT	CURRENT	1 MONTH OVERDUE	2 MONTHS OVERDUE	3 MONTHS & OVER	
50006	THERMAL AIR SYSTEMS	2002	500.00	500.00				
	COMPANY TOTALS.............		500.00	500.00				
60000	MILFORD AUTO SUPPLY	3500	23,400.98		23,400.98			
60000	MILFORD AUTO SUPPLY	3700	50.37		50.37			
60000	MILFORD AUTO SUPPLY	3750	300.00	300.00				
60000	MILFORD AUTO SUPPLY	3761	2,575.78	2,575.78				
	COMPANY TOTALS.............		26,327.13	2,875.78	23,451.35			
65005	DAVID MARINE ENGINEERING	4000	3,527.50		3,527.50			
65005	DAVID MARINE ENGINEERING	4010	40.25				40.25	
65005	DAVID MARINE ENGINEERING	4200	730.00		730.00			
65005	DAVID MARINE ENGINEERING	4290	950.33	950.33				
	COMPANY TOTALS.............		5,248.08	950.33	4,257.50		40.25	
70000	AMERICAN HOME CARE	5000	44.27			44.27		
70000	AMERICAN HOME CARE	5052	157.89				157.89	
70000	AMERICAN HOME CARE	5100	9,456.78		9,456.78			
70000	AMERICAN HOME CARE	5300	10,237.60	10,237.60				
	COMPANY TOTALS.............		19,896.54	10,237.60	9,456.78	44.27	157.89	
	GRAND TOTALS.............		51,971.75	14,563.71	37,165.63	44.27	198.14	

129

CHAPTER 12
QUESTION ANSWERS

1. External or internal processes of insuring that the data input to the storage medium is accurate.

2. a. Batch procedures external to a data entry program.
   b. Batch procedures internal to a data entry program.
   c. Interactive procedures internal to a data entry program.

3. <u>External batch data validation procedures</u> are controlled by recording data on key-to-diskette, key-to-disk, or key-to-magnetic tape units which usually have a separate verification mode.

   <u>Internal batch data validation procedures</u> are controlled by coding routines included in an RPG IV program.

   <u>Interactive data validation procedures</u> are controlled by the screen utility software and the related RPG IV program.

4. In the strictest terms, and **error rejection file** stores records that do no pass a validation test for identification only. On the other hand, an **error abeyance file** stores records that do not pass data validation for subsequent corrections.

5. Validation functions in data type testing are:

   a. Numeric or alphabetic value
   b. Arithmetic sign or zero

6. In a batch processing environment, under control of an RPG I program, fields may be tested as having valid numeric characters by the **TESTN** operation.

   In an interactive environment, field values are usually tested as numeric by controls included in the syntax of a screen format generator. Any attempt to enter anything other than a 0 through 9 into a field defined as numeric will be prevented by the utility software before processing by the RPG IV program.

7. 0 through 9.

8. *Resulting Indicator* 20 will turn on if the value in AM contains valid numeric digits.

   Resulting Indicator 21 will turn on if the value in AM contains one or more leading blanks.

   Resulting Indicator 22 will turn on if the value in AM contains all blanks.

9. Redefined as character.

10. Because RPG IV does not have an operation for alphabetic validation, a *compile time* array or table that includes any alphabetic characters that the user may want to consider as valid alphabetic may be specified in the validation program. Or, the characters may be included in a *Named Constant* defined as a *Definition Specifications* instruction.

11. In the *Field Indicator* fields (columns 69-74) on the *Input Specifications* or in the *Resulting Indicator* fields (columns 71-76) in the *Calculation Specifications*. Or, with an **IF** instruction.

12. Over the low-order digit. The numeric value is identified as positive on IBM minicomputers by the letter **F** over (zone area) the low-order digit and negative by the letter **D**.

    On IBM mainframes, a numeric value is identified as positive by the letter **C** over (zone area) the low-order digit and negative by the letter **D**.

13. Any numeric field used as the divisor in a division instruction must be tested for zero to prevent cancellation (or a halt on some systems) of program execution.

14. Data field checking includes:

    a. Presence or absence of data
    b. Justification of data
    c. Acceptability of data
    d. Relationship of other data
    e. Structure of the data

15. Presence checking of an input field may be controlled in an RPG IV program by entering an indicator in the Zero/ Blank field (positions 69-70) of the *Input Specifications*. If the related numeric field has a zero value, the indicator will turn on which may be used to condition subsequent processing. An indicator specified with an alphanumeric field will turn on if the field value is blank.

    In lieu of indicator control, the input field may be tested for zero or blank with one of the structured operations that provide for relational testing (IF, WHEN, CAS, DO, DOU, DOW).

16. The absence of data could be supported by the procedures explained in question 15.

17. Only on alphanumeric fields. Because RPG IV automatically initializes all input and work fields to zeros when the program is executed, it is impossible to check the low-order digit for the absence of a valid numeric value.

    However, if an alphanumeric field or unused field follows a numeric field, may be justification tested.

18. Functions related to the acceptability of data testing include: a. Range checking; b. Check digits; c. Limit checking.

19. Checking of transaction dates to insure that they meet predetermined month, day, and year parameters. The RPG IV **TEST** operation tests the validity of date, time, or time-stamp fields. Consequently, unless a valid date is to be checked for specifc values, RPG IV routines are no longer needed to check for a valid date.

20. By an instruction that validates the a range of a sales amount for a cash or trade discount.

21. A check digit may be included in an account number or such to mathematically identify substitution or transpositional errors in the value. With a standardized Modulus-10 or Modulus-11 formula an invalid entry may be identified. Check digits are usually stored in the low-order byte of the field value.

22. Account number: 12000

Step 1:   Step 2:

$$
\begin{array}{ccccc}
1 & 2 & 0 & 0 & 0 \\
\underline{\text{x6}} & \underline{\text{x5}} & \underline{\text{x4}} & \underline{\text{x3}} & \underline{\text{x2}} \\
\end{array}
$$

6 +10 + 0 + 0 + 0 = 16

$$
\begin{array}{r}
1 \\
\hline
11 \big| 16 \\
\underline{11} \\
5
\end{array}
$$

Step 3:

11 - 5 = 6 Check digit

Account number with check digit is 120006

* * * * * * * * * * * * *

Account number: 123456

Step 1:   Step 2:

$$
\begin{array}{cccccc}
1 & 2 & 3 & 4 & 5 & 6 \\
\underline{\text{x7}} & \underline{\text{x6}} & \underline{\text{x5}} & \underline{\text{x4}} & \underline{\text{x3}} & \underline{\text{x2}} \\
\end{array}
$$

7 + 12 + 15 + 16 + 15 + 12 = 77

$$
\begin{array}{r}
7 \\
\hline
11 \big| 77 \\
\underline{77} \\
0
\end{array}
$$

Step 3:

If remainder is 0 use it as check digit

Account number with check digit is 1234560

23. Account number: 130003

Step 1:

```
  1     3     0     0     0     3
 x6    x5    x4    x3    x2    x1
  6 + 15 + 0 + 0 + 0 + 3 = 24
```

Step 2:

```
         2
     11|24
        22
         2   Not a valid account number
         * * * * * * * * * * * * *
```

Account number: 77003

Step 1:

```
  7     7     0     0     3
 x5    x4    x3    x2    x1
 35 + 28 + 0 + 0 + 3 = 66      ••
```

Step 2:
```
          6
     11|66
         66
          0  Valid account number
```

24. Maximum balance for a credit card account. It is imple-
    mented in a program by adding the current sale amount to
    the account balance and then checking the total with the
    maximum balance allowed for the related account.

25. A cross reference of data. For example, a birth of a
    child is related to a female patient and not a male.

26. A total for a group of transactions. In an interactive
    environment, a batch total is entered before the trans-
    actions are recorded. The total of the transactions is
    compared with the batch total. If it is the same, the
    numeric amounts have been entered correctly. On the
    other hand, if the totals do not agree, either the batch
    value is wrong or more likely, the data entered.

PROGRAMMING ASSIGNMENTS

Programming Assignment 12-1: BATCH VALIDATION OF SAVINGS
                            ACCOUNT TRANSACTIONS

Notes to the Instructor:

1. A DATFMT(*MDY) keyword is specified in as a *Control Specification* instruction so that the TRANSDATE date field from the
   physical (see line 21=I is in a compatible format with the

EXTRCT instruction on line 41.

The **EXTRCT** instruction extracts the TransDate year value and
stores it in the TransYr field, so it may be compared to the
ReportYr (see line 63).

2. A *Named Constant*, which includes the valid transaction codes
   is defined on line 6. The validation test for a valid code is
   specified on line 35. Note that the *Named Constant* (ValidCodes)
   is entered in *Factor 1* and the physical file's field name in
   Factor 2.

3. A *Data Area Data Structure*, with subfield, is defined on lines
   15 and 16. Note that the subfield must be defined as character. The data area (P121da) was created as character.

4. Note the complex **EVAL** instruction on lines 50-52 that includes
   AND and **OR** logical operators. This may be difficult for the
   students to format.

5. Other than the Headings lines, note that two other line types
   are specified. The DetailLine controls the printing of a valid
   record (no validation errors) and the ErrorLine controls the
   printing of the record information with its related validation
   error.

   The related error message from the compile time array
   (MsgArray) is accessed by the integer value in the X index.

```
Line     <--------------------- Source Specifications --------------------------------><---- Comments ----> Do
Number   ....1....+....2....+....3....+....4....+....5....+....6....+....7....+....8....+....9....+...10 Num
                        S o u r c e   L i s t i n g
    1  * Batch validation of savings account transactions....
    2  HDATFMT(*MDY)
    3  FP121psm   IF   E        K DISK
       *--------------------------------------------------------------------------------------*
       *                         RPG name         External name                               *
       * File name. . . . . . . . : P121PSM        STAN/P121PSM                                *
       * Record format(s) . . . . . : P121PSMR      P121PSMR                                   *
       *--------------------------------------------------------------------------------------*
    4  FQsysprt   O   F 132        PRINTER OFLIND(*INOA)
    5
    6  DValidCodes       C              'ACDIW'
    7  DMsgArray         S         38   DIM(5) CTDATA              define MsgArray
    8
    9  DTransYr          S          2 0                           define TransYr field
   10  DReportYr         S          2 0                           define subfield
   11  DDateOut          S          6 0
   12  DX                S          1 0                           define array index
   13
   14  * Access data area data structure for report date....
   15  DP121da           UDS                                      access data area
   16  D ReportDate            1      6                           define field
   17
   18=IP121PSMR
       *--------------------------------------------------------------------------------------*
       * RPG record format  . . . . : P121PSMR                                                *
       * External format  . . . . . : P121PSMR : STAN/P121PSM                                 *
       *--------------------------------------------------------------------------------------*
   19=I                         A    1    1  TRANSCODE
   20=I                         A    2    7  ACTNUMBER
   21=I                       *MDY/D   8   15  TRANSDATE
```

```
22=I                            P   16   19 2TRANSAMT
23 C              EVAL          *INOA = *ON                            turn on overflow ind
24 C              MOVE          ReportDate    DateOut                  move to numeric fld
25 C              MOVE          DateOut       ReportYr                 access ReportYr
26 C              READ          P121psm                      ----LR    read first record
27 C              DOW           *INLR = *OFF                           dow LR is off           B01
28
29 C              IF            *INOA = *ON                            overflow ind. on?       B02
30 C              EXCEPT        Headings                               print heading lines      02
31 C              ENDIF                         .                      end IF group            E02
32
33 * Begin validation tests....
34 * Test for valid transaction code....
35 C    ValidCodes CHECK        TransCode                    ----40    validate TransCode       01
36 C              IF            *IN40 = *ON                            invalid TransCode?      B02
37 C              EVAL          X = 1                                  initialize index         02
38 C              EXCEPT        ErrorLine                              print ErrorLine          02
39 C              ELSE                                                 end IF group            X02
40 * Extract year from TransDate field....
41 C              EXTRCT        TransDate:*Y  TransYr                  extract year value       02
42
43 C              SELECT                                               begin select group      B03
44 * Test for zero value in TransAmt....
45 C              WHEN          TransAmt = *ZERO                       TransAmt zero?          X03
46 C              EVAL          X = 2                                  access second msg        03
47 C              EXCEPT        ErrorLine                              print record             03
48                                                    **
49 * Test for positive TransAmt and valid D, I, or C TransCode....
50 C              WHEN          TransAmt < 0 AND TransCode = 'D'                               X03
51 C                            OR TransAmt < 0 AND TransCode = 'C'                            X03
52 C                            OR TransAmt < 0 AND TransCode = 'I'    test related code?      X03
53 C              EVAL          X = 3                                  access array msg         03
54 C              EXCEPT        ErrorLine                              print record             03
55
56 * Test for negative TransAmt and valid W or A TransCode....
57 C              WHEN          TransAmt > 0 AND TransCode = 'W'       test related code       X03
58 C                            OR TransAmt > 0 AND TransCode = 'A'    related code            X03
59 C              EVAL          X = 4                                  access array msg         03
60 C              EXCEPT        ErrorLine                              print record             03
61
62 * Test if TransYr is not equal to ReportYr (from data structure)
63 C              WHEN          TransYr <> ReportYr                    test for valid year     X03
64 C              EVAL          X = 5                                  access array msg         03
65 C              EXCEPT        ErrorLine                              print record             03
66 C              OTHER                                                no validation errors    X03
67 C              EXCEPT        DetailLine                             print no errors line     03
68 C              ENDSL                                                end select group        E03
69 C              ENDIF                                                end IF group            E02
70
71 C              READ          P121psm                      ----LR    read next record         01
72 C              ENDDO                                                end dow group           E01
73
74 C              EVAL          *INLR = *ON                            end program
75
76 OQsysprt  E         Headings        1 01
77 O                                        51 'QUARTERLY SAVINGS ACCOUNT'
78 O                                        64 'TRANSACTIONS'
79 O                                        86 'PAGE'
80 O              PAGE            91
81 O         E         Headings        3
82 O                                        49 'FOR QUARTER ENDING'
83 O              DateOut       Y   58
84 O         E         Headings        2
85 O                                        13 'ACCOUNT NO'
86 O                                        22 'DATE'
87 O                                        33 'CODE'
88 O                                        45 'AMOUNT'
89 O                                        75 'ERROR MESSAGES'
90 O         E         DetailLine      2
91 O              ActNumber         11
92 O              TransDate         24
93 O              TransCode         32
94 O              TransAmt      J   46
```

Chapter 12 - Data Validation (Batch Mode)

```
 95 O           E          ErrorLine      2
 96 O                      ActNumber            11
 97 O                      TransDate            24
 98 O                      TransCode            32
 99 O                      TransAmt       J     46
100 O                      MsgArray(X)          87
    * * * *   E N D   O F   S O U R C E   * * * *
                              .
                              .
       ****Note: Compile time information deleted****
                              .
                              .
                    C o m p i l e   T i m e   D a t a
101 **CTDATA MsgArray
    *------------------------------------------------------------*
    * Array . . . : MSGARRAY                                     *
    *------------------------------------------------------------*
102 INVALID TRANSACTION CODE
103 TRANSACTION AMOUNT ZERO
104 CODE INDICATES AMOUNT MUST BE POSITIVE
105 CODE INDICATES AMOUNT MUST BE NEGATIVE
106 TRANSACTION YEAR INVALID
    * * * *   E N D   O F   C O M P I L E   T I M E   D A T A   * * * *
```

Printed Report:

```
                 QUARTERLY SAVINGS ACCOUNT TRANSACTIONS              PAGE   1
                    FOR QUARTER ENDING  2/28/97


ACCOUNT NO    DATE     CODE      AMOUNT           ERROR MESSAGES

 100000     02/01/96    D       840.00    TRANSACTION YEAR INVALID

 200000     02/28/97    W     12,500.00   CODE INDICATES AMOUNT MUST BE NEGATIVE

 300000     02/10/97    T        92.50    INVALID TRANSACTION CODE

 400000     02/28/97    A       245.67-

 500000     02/15/97    I     9,000.00

 600000     02/01/97    C       678.99

 700000     02/11/97    D          .00    TRANSACTION AMOUNT ZERO

 800000     02/28/97    W       120.94-

 900000     02/28/97    D        25.00-   CODE INDICATES AMOUNT MUST BE POSITIVE

 910000     02/08/97    D     1,000.00

 980000     02/28/98    C       700.00-   CODE INDICATES AMOUNT MUST BE POSITIVE
```

Programming Assignment 12-2: BATCH VALIDATION OF ITEM PURCHASES

Notes to the Instructor:

1. A *Named Constant*, which includes the valid alphabetic characters (programmer determined), is defined on line 5. The validation test for valid alphabetic characters in the Item_Name field is entered on line 69. Note that the *Named Constant* (AlphaChars) is entered in *Factor 1* and the physical file's field name in *Factor 2*.

2. Two compile time arrays are defined on lines 6 and 7. The VendorAry array includes valid vendor codes and the MsgArray,

the five eror messages.

3. The **SCAN** instruction on line 76 tests the Item_Name field for left-justification. If a blank character is tested in position 1, it indicates that the field value is not left-justified.

4. When an error is detected in a field, a branch is made to the PrintSR from which it is printed. The first error is printed with the related field data. Any other errors tested in the record are printed on the following lines without the field data. PrintLine1 controls printing of the first error and PrintLine2 of any other errors for the current record processed.

```
Line    <--------------------- Source Specifications --------------------------><---- Comments ----> Do
Number  ....1....+....2....+....3....+....4....+....5....+....6....+....7....+....8....+....9....+...10 Num
                         S o u r c e    L i s t i n g
  1  * PA 12-2: Batch Validation of Item Purchases....
  2 FP122Psm   IF   E           K DISK
     *----------------------------------------------------rf-------------------------------------*
     *                                  RPG name          External name                          *
     * File name. . . . . . . . . :     P122PSM           STAN/P122PSM                            *
     * Record format(s) . . . . . :     P122PSMR          P122PSMR                                *
     *--------------------------------------------------------------------------------------------*
  3 FQsysprt   O    F  132        PRINTER OFLIND(*INOF)
  4
  5 DAlphaChars      C                       ' -ABCDEFGHIJKLMNOPQRSTUVWXYZ'     specify AlphaChars
  6 DVendorAry       S              1    DIM(6) CTDATA PERRCD(6)               define vendor no ary
  7 DMsgArray        S             37    DIM(5) CTDATA
  8 D                DS
  9 DNumArray                      1  0 DIM(5)                                 define mod-11 array
 10 DItemNumber             1      5                                           field to load array
 11
 12  * Define Modulus-11 items....
 13
 14 DSum             S              3  0
 15 DQuotient        S              3  0
 16 DRemainder       S              3  0
 17
 18 DTotalCost       S              8  2
 19 DLocation        S              1  0
 20 DX               S              1  0
 21
 22=IP122PSMR
     *--------------------------------------------------------------------------------------------*
     * RPG record format . . . . . :    P122PSMR                                                  *
     * External format  . . . . . :    P122PSMR : STAN/P122PSM                                    *
     *--------------------------------------------------------------------------------------------*
 23=I                             A    1    5  ITEMNUMBER
 24=I                             A    6   31  ITEM_NAME
 25=I                             P   32   35  OPURCHDATE
 26=I                             A   36   36  VENDERNO
 27=I                             P   37   38  OQUANTITY
 28=I                             P   39   42  2UNITCOST
 29=I                             A   43   48  UNOFMEASUR
 30 C           EVAL      *INOF = *ON                      turn on OF indicator
 31 C           READ      P122Psm                  ----LR  read first record
 32 C           DOW       *INLR = *OFF                     dow LR is off          B01
 33
 34 C           IF        *INOF = *ON                      overflow ind. on?      B02
 35 C           EXCEPT    Headings                         print heading lines    02
 36 C           EVAL      *INOF = *OFF                     turn off overflow in   02
 37 C           ENDIF                                      end IF group          E02
 38
 39 C           EVAL      TotalCost = UnitCost * Quantity  compute totalcost      01
 40
```

137

```
41 C                    EXSR      Mod11SR                              branch to subroutine   01
42 C                    EXSR      NameSR                               branch to subroutine   01
43 C                    EXSR      VendorSR                             branch to subroutine   01
44 C                    EXSR      CostSR                               branch to subroutine   01
45
46 C                    EVAL      *IN60 = *OFF                         turn control indictr   01
47 C                    READ      P122Psm                    ----LR    read first record      01
48 C                    ENDDO                                          end dow group          E01
49
50  * Modulus-11 check digit validation of ItemNumber....
51 C    Mod11SR         BEGSR                                          begin subroutine
52 C                    EVAL      Sum =                                compute sum
53 C                              NumArray(5) * 1                      5th element * 1
54 C                              + NumArray(4) * 2                    4th element * 2
55 C                              + NumArray(3) * 3                    3rd element * 3
56 C                              + NumArray(2) * 4                    2nd element * 4
57 C                              + NumArray(1) * 5                    1st element * 5
58 C    Sum             DIV       11          Quotient                 compute quotient
59 C                    MVR                   Remainder                save remainder
60
61 C                    IF        Remainder > 0                        remainder > 0?         B01
62 C                    EVAL      X = 1                                initialize ary index   01
63 C                    EXSR      PrintSR                              branch to subroutine   01
64 C                    ENDIF                                          end IF group           E01
65 C                    ENDSR                                          end subroutine
66
67 C    NameSR          BEGSR                             *?           begin subroutine
68  * Validate Item_Name for alphabetic characters....
69 C    AlphaChars      CHECK     Item_Name                  ----30    validate Item_Name
70 C                    IF        *IN30 = *ON                          invalid alpha char?    B01
71 C                    EVAL      X = 2                                intialize index        01
72 C                    EXSR      PrintSR                              branch to subroutine   01
73 C                    ENDIF                                          end IF group           E01
74
75  * Validate Item_Name for left_justification....
76 C    ' '             SCAN      Item_Name   Location       ----40    scan for blank char.
77 C                    IF        Location = 1                         blank in first char    B01
78 C                    EVAL      X = 3                                intialize index        01
79 C                    EXSR      PrintSR                              branch to subroutine   01
80 C                    ENDIF                                          end IF group           E01
81 C                    ENDSR                                          end subroutine
82
83  * Validate VenderNo value for valid code....
84 C    VendorSR        BEGSR                                          begin subroutine
85 C    VenderNo        LOOKUP    VendorAry                  ----80    search array
86 C                    IF        *IN80 = *OFF                         invalid vendorno?      B01
87 C                    EVAL      X = 4                                initialize index       01
88 C                    EXSR      PrintSR                              branch to subroutine   01
89 C                    ENDIF                                          end IF group           E01
90 C                    ENDSR                                          end subroutine
91
92  * Validate that cost does not exceed $2,000....
93 C    CostSR          BEGSR                                          begin subroutine
94 C                    IF        TotalCost > 2000                     greater than $2000?    B01
95 C                    EVAL      X = 5                                initialize index       01
96 C                    EXSR      PrintSR                              branch to subroutine   01
97 C                    ENDIF                                          end IF group           E01
98 C                    ENDSR                                          end subroutine
99
100  * Controls printing of record values on the first line and any
101  * other error messages for the record on subsequent lines....
102 C   PrintSR         BEGSR                                          begin subroutine
103 C                    IF        *IN60 = *OFF                         indicator 60 off?      B01
104 C                    EXCEPT    PrintLine1                           print first error ms   01
105 C                    EVAL      *IN60 = *ON                          turn onindicator 60    01
106 C                    ELSE                                           other error msgs       X01
107 C                    EXCEPT    PrintLine2                           print other error ms   01
108 C                    ENDIF                                          end IF group           E01
109 C                    ENDSR                                          end subroutine
110
111 OQsysprt   E              Headings      3 06
112 C                          UDATE         Y      9
113 O                                             74 'ITEM PURCHASES VALIDATION'
```

```
114 O                                         81 'REPORT'
115 O                                        126 'PAGE'
116 O                          PAGE          131
117 O          E              Headings     2
118 O                                          5 'ITEM'
119 O                                         26 'ITEM NAME'
120 O                                         43 'DATE'
121 O                                         53 'VENDOR'
122 O                                         73 'COST/ITEM'
123 O                                         88 'UNIT OF MEAS.'
124 O                                        103 'ERROR MESSAGES'
125 O          E              PrintLine1    2
126 O                          ItemNumber       6
127 O                          Item_Name       34
128 O                          PurchDate    Y  45
129 O                          VenderNo        51
130 O                          Quantity     1  60
131 O                          TotalCost    1  72
132 O                          UnOfMeasur      83
133 O                          MsgArray(X)    127
134 O          E              PrintLine2    2
135 O                          MsgArray(X)    127
      * * * * *   E N D   O F   S O U R C E   * * * * *



          ****Note: Compile time information deleted****
                                                     +3
               C o m p i l e   T i m e   D a t a
136 **CTDATA MsgArray
    *-----------------------------------------------------------*
    * Array . . . : MSGARRAY                                    *
    *-----------------------------------------------------------*
137 ITEM NUMBER DOES NOT CHECK
138 ITEM NAME NOT ALPHABETIC
139 ITEM NAME NOT LEFT-JUSTIFIED
140 VENDOR NUMBER NOT VALID
141 COST EXCEEDS $2,000
142 **CTDATA VendorAry
    *-----------------------------------------------------------*
    * Array . . . : VENDORARY                                   *
    *-----------------------------------------------------------*
143 124568
    * * * * *   E N D   O F   C O M P I L E   T I M E   D A T A   * * * * *
```

Printed Report: (Only records that have validation errors are printed).

5/01/97			ITEM PURCHASES VALIDATION REPORT					PAGE 1
ITEM	ITEM NAME	DATE	VENDOR		COST/ITEM	UNIT OF MEAS.	ERROR MESSAGES	
11184	BLACK TRUFFLES	4/01/97	1	24	2,040.00	JAR/OZ	ITEM NUMBER DOES NOT CHECK COST EXCEEDS $2,000	
11206	SHARK FIN SOUP	4/05/97	4	120	1,200.00	CAN/OZ	ITEM NUMBER DOES NOT CHECK	
11304	PICKLED TRIPE	4/10/97	3	36	144.00	JAR/OZ	VENDOR NUMBER NOT VALID	
11509	SMOKED PHEASANT	4/15/97	8	12	144.00	CAN/PK	ITEM NAME NOT LEFT-JUSTIFIED	
11606	BLACK CAVIAR	4/18/97	5	60	2,340.00	CAN/OZ	COST EXCEEDS $2,000	
11800	SEA WATER EEL9 SPROUTS	4/28/97	2	144	2,880.00	JAR/OZ	ITEM NAME NOT ALPHABETIC COST EXCEEDS $2,000	
12009	REINDEER MILK YOGURT	4/30/97	9	10	70.00	JAR/QT	VENDOR NUMBER NOT VALID	

CHAPTER 13
QUESTION ANSWERS

1. a) Addition of records, b) update of existing records, c) logical deletion of records, d) inquiry, and e) reorganization.

Function	File Description Entries
2. Addition	Defined as an output (**O** in column 17) or update (**U** in column 17 and **F** in column 18) and **A** in column 20.
Update	Defined as update (**U** in column 17 and **F** in column 18).
Logical Deletion	Defined as update (**U** in column 17 and **F** in column 18).
Inquiry	Defined as input (I in column 17 and F in column 18).
Reorganization	**RGZPFM** (Reorganize Physical File Member) command.

3. Function	RPG/400 Operation
Addition	**WRITE** operation
Update	**CHAIN** (to get the record) and **UPDATE** (to update the record with changed values).
Logical Deletion	**CHAIN** (to get the record) and **DELETE** (to delete the record).
Inquiry	**CHAIN** (to get the record).
Reorganization	**RGZPFM** command.

4. Addition of records to an existing physical file.

5. A physical file's record name.

6. When an error occurs when the **WRITE** statement is executed. Typical errors on a write included duplicate key for a unique file, file is full, or file is not available.

7. May be defined as output (O in column 17) or update (**U** in column 17) and an **A** in column 20.

8. After the last record stored in the physical file.

9. **CPYF** (*Copy File*) command. **DSPPFM** (*Display Physical File Member*) command.

10. A ***HEX** listing presents the data in an over-and-under or side-by-side byte format. A ***CHAR** listing presents the data in a single character format. The values for numeric fields that are defined as packed are not readable in a ***CHAR** listing.

11. The **SETLL** operation positions the file at a record that has a key value or relative record number equal to or greater than the value stored in the *Factor 1* item.

12. The *Factor 1* entry may be a field name, named constant, a literal, figurative constant, or **KLIST** name. The AAA for this example could be a field name, named constant, or **KLIST** name.

13. A file name or, for externally described files, a record name.

14. *Resulting indicator* 80 in columns 73-74 is set on if an error occurs when the **SETLL** statement is executed.

15. *Resulting indicator* 81 in column 75-76 is set on when the *Factor 1* value is equal to a key value or relative record number in the physical file.

16. Assuming AAA contains a key value, a record in the physical file will be "pointed to" that has a value equal to or the first record with a key greater than the AAA value.

17. The **CHAIN** operation randomly retrieves a record from a file that has a key value or relative record number stored in the item specified in *Factor 1*.

18. A key value or relative record number.

19. May be a file name, or for externally described files, a record name.

20. The *Resulting Indicator* 90 in columns 54-55 will be set on when the chain is <u>not</u> successful (key value or relative record number <u>not</u> found).

21. As an input (**I** in column 17) or update (**U** in column 17) file with an **F** (full-procedural) in column 18.

22. The **UPDATE** operation writes the current record, which was accessed by a **CHAIN** or one of the **READ** operations, back to its original storage position.

23. A record name for **externally described** files or a file name for **program described** files. In addition, if *Factor 2* contains a file name, a data structure name must be specified in the *Result Field*.

24. When a error occurs as the **UPDATE** statement is executed.

25. With a **U** in column 17 and an **F** in column 18.

26. The record to be updated must have been retrieved by a **CHAIN**

or one of the **READ** operations.

27. The **DELETE** operation "logically" deletes record from a physical file. A record "logically" deleted cannot be subsequently retrieved.

28. A record name for *externally described* files or a file name for *program described* physical files.

29. The *Resulting Indicator* in columns 73-74 will be set on if an error occurs when the **DELETE** statement is executed.

30. With a **U** in column 17 and an **F** in column 18.

31. The record to be "logically" deleted must have been retrieved by a **CHAIN** or one of the **READ** operations.

32. The **READ** operation reads and accesses a record without any relational test criteria. The **READE** operation reads and accesses a record based on the key or relative record number value in the *Factor 1* item. To read more than one record, the related **READ** or **READE** statement must be included in an iterative procedure controlled by a **DO**, **DOU**, or **DOW** group.

33. A key or relative record number value.

34. A record name for *externally described* physical files or a file name for *program described* files.

35. The required *Resulting Indicator* in column 75-76 will be set on if an equal key is not found in the file or if an end-of-file condition is tested.

36. A key or relative record number value.

37. A record name for *externally described* physical files or a file name for *program described* files.

38. The required *Resulting Indicator* in column 75-76 will be set on if an equal key is not found in the file or if the beginning of the file condition is tested.

39. The **OPEN** operation. The **CLOSE** operation.

40. The **USROPN** keyword must be enteredin the Keywords field of the related File Description statement for the physical file.

41. The **SETGT** operation automatically points to the first record in the physical file that has a key or relative record value greater than the one stored in the *Factor 1* item. Whereas, the **SETLL** operation will point first to a record that has an equal key or relative record number value and then to the next higher record if the equal test is not satisfied.

42. **KLIST** is a declarative operation that stores the values from

the related **KFLD** operations in its *Factor 1* item.

The declarative **KFLD** operation identifies the field values that are to be stored in the **KLIST** *Factor 1* item.

43. The value in PlantNo, BinNo, and ItemNo in that order.

44. Most likely in the fields in a physical file.

45. When the first statement that is not a **KFLD** statement is encountered.

46. **RGZPFM** (Reorganize Physical File Mbr).

47. a. Removes deleted records.
    b. Compresses the file which changes the relative record numbers.
    c. Resequences keyed physical files in an ascending key value order.

PROGRAMMING ASSIGNMENTS

Programming Assignment 13-1 SAVINGS ACCOUNT MASTER FILE ADDITION

Notes to the Instructor:

1. Three physical files must be created for this assignment. A master file with records that must be entered; a transaction file with records that must be entered, and an error file in the same record format as the transaction file.

2. Transaction records that have a duplicate key (same as a record already stored in the master file) are to be written to the error file.

3. Three hexadecimal listings are required. A CPYF listing of the master file <u>before</u> adding records; a listing of the master file <u>after</u> record addition; and a listing of the error file to which records with duplicate keys are written.

Compiled Program Listing:

```
Line    <-------------------- Source Specifications -------------------><---- Comments ----> Do
Number  ....1....+....2....+....3....+....4....+....5....+....6....+....7....+....8....+....9....+...10 Num
                        S o u r c e   L i s t i n g
    1  * This program adds records to an existing physical file from a
    2  * transaction physical file defined as nonkeyed.  Duplicate add
    3  * records are loaded to an error file with the same format as
    4  * the transaction file.
    5
    6  FP131ptr   IF   E          DISK
       *----------------------------------------------------------------------------*
       *                              RPG name          External name               *
       * File name. . . . . . . . . :  P131PTR          STAN/P131PTR                *
       * Record format(s) . . . . . :  P131PTRR         P131PTRR                    *
       *----------------------------------------------------------------------------*
    7  FP131pmr   O  A E          K DISK
```

```
      *----------------------------------------------------------------------*
      *                           RPG name          External name            *
      * File name. . . . . . . . . :  P131PMR        STAN/P131PMR             *
      * Record format(s) . . . . . :  P131PMRR       P131PMRR                 *
      *----------------------------------------------------------------------*
  8 FP131per   O  A E            DISK
  9
      *----------------------------------------------------------------------*
      *                           RPG name          External name            *
      * File name. . . . . . . . :   P131PER        STAN/P131PER              *
      * Record format(s) . . . . . :  P131PERR       P131PERR                 *
      *----------------------------------------------------------------------*
 10=IP131PTRR
      *----------------------------------------------------------------------*
      * RPG record format  . . . . :  P131PTRR                                *
      * External format  . . . . . :  P131PTRR : STAN/P131PTR                 *
      *----------------------------------------------------------------------*
 11=I                             A    1    5  ACCTNUMBER
 12=I                             A    6   36  NAME
 13=I                             A   37   56  STREET
 14=I                             A   57   72  CITY
 15=I                             A   73   74  STATE
 16=I                             P   75   77 0ZIPCODE
 17=I                             P   78   81 2DEPOSIT
 18 C              READ      p131ptr                          ----LR   read first record
 19 C              DOW       *INLR = *OFF                               dow LR is off          B01
 20 C              EXSR      Trans2Mstr                                 branch to SR            01
 21 C              WRITE     p131pmrr                         --90--   add record to mstr       01
 22 C              IF        *IN90 = *ON                                duplicate record?      B02
 23 C              EXSR      Trans2Err                                  write to Ch13errs       02
 24 C              WRITE     p131perr                                   add to error file       02
 25 C              ENDIF                                                end IF group           E02
 26 C              READ      p131ptr                          ----LR   read next record         01
 27 C              ENDDO                                                end DOW group          E01
 28
 29 C   Trans2Mstr BEGSR                                                begin SR
 30 C              MOVE      AcctNumber    AcctNumber                   move to mstr field
 31 C              MOVE      Name          Name
 32 C              MOVE      Street        Street                       move to mstr field
 33 C              MOVE      City          City                         move to mstr field
 34 C              MOVE      State         State                        move to mstr field
 35 C              MOVE      ZipCode       ZipCode                      move to mstr field
 36 C              MOVE      Deposit       ActBalance
 37 C              ENDSR                                                end SR
 38
 39 C   Trans2Err  BEGSR                                                begin SR
 40 C              MOVE      AcctNumber    AcctNumber                   move to mstr field
 41 C              MOVE      Name          Name
 42 C              MOVE      Street        Street                       move to mstr field
 43 C              MOVE      City          City                         move to mstr field
 44 C              MOVE      State         State                        move to mstr field
 45 C              MOVE      ZipCode       ZipCode                      move to mstr field
 46 C              MOVE      Deposit       Deposit
 47 C              ENDSR                                                end SR
 48=OP131PMRR
      *----------------------------------------------------------------------*
      * RPG record format  . . . . :  P131PMRR                                *
      * External format  . . . . . :  P131PMRR : STAN/P131PMR                 *
      *----------------------------------------------------------------------*
 49=O                        DELETECODE       1A CHAR      1
 50=O                        ACCTNUMBER       6A CHAR      5
 51=O                        NAME            37A CHAR     31
 52=O                        STREET          57A CHAR     20
 53=O                        CITY            73A CHAR     16
 54=O                        STATE           75A CHAR      2
 55=O                        ZIPCODE         78P PACK    5,0
 56=O                        ACTBALANCE      82P PACK    6,2
 57=OP131PERR
      *----------------------------------------------------------------------*
      * RPG record format  . . . . :  P131PERR                                *
      * External format  . . . . . :  P131PERR : STAN/P131PER                 *
      *----------------------------------------------------------------------*
 58=O                        ACCTNUMBER       5A CHAR      5
```

```
59=0                    NAME           36A CHAR    31
60=0                    STREET         56A CHAR    20
61=0                    CITY           72A CHAR    16
62=0                    STATE          74A CHAR     2
63=0                    ZIPCODE        77P PACK   5,0
64=0                    DEPOSIT        81P PACK   6,2
     * * * *  E N D   O F   S O U R C E  * * * *
```

Master File Hexidecimal Listing (Before Adds):

```
RCDNBR  *...+... 1 ...+... 2 ...+... 3 ...+... 4 ...+... 5 ...+... 6 ...+... 7 ...+... 8 .

    1   21345JOHN DOE                   212 ELM STREET     BRIDGEPORT    CT /
        4FFFFFDDCD4CDC4444444444444444444444444FFF4CDD4EEDCCE444444CDCCCCDDDE444444CE0600200
        0213451685046500000000000000000000000002120534023955300000029947576930000003361F100F

    2   31121LOUISE LESSER              12 APPLES ROAD     BAHA          CAk   a ⊥
        4FFFFFDDECEC4DCEECD4444444444444444444444FF4CDDDCE4DDCC444444CCCC4444444444444CC9100829
        0311213649250352259000000000000000000000120177352096140000002181000000000003120F019F

    3   48891JUDY JOHNSON               114 EASY DRIVE     RALEIGH       NCà    "
        4FFFFFDECE4DDCDEDD4444444444444444444444FFF4CCEE4CDCEC444444DCDCCCC444444444DC4400007
        0488911448016852650000000000000000000001140512804995500000091359780000000005341F061F

    4   5000DAVE HOOTEN                 8 STRIKE LANE      LOS ANGELES   CA°   ⌐
        4FFFFCCEC4CDDECD4444444444444444444444F4EEDCDC4DCDC4444444DDE4CDCCDCE444444CC9000611
        0500004155086635500000000000000000000008023992503155000000362015753520000031100F041F

    5   51540MARIE BLAKE                GREEN PASTURE RD   NEWARK        NJ L
        4FFFFFDCDCC4CDCDC4444444444444444444444CDCCD4DCEEEDC4DC4444DCECDD444444444DD0730403
        0515404199502312500000000000000000000007955507123495094000055619200000000005173F901F

    6   63141JOSEPH WELCH               110 DILL STREET    NEW YORK      NY  ╫"
        4FFFFFDDECDC4ECDCC4444444444444444444444FFF4CCDD4EEDCCE444444DCE4EDDD4444444DE1000777
        0631411625780653380000000000000000000001100493302395530000055608692000000005800F077F

    7   71510JOHN HINES                 220 HIGH DRIVE     KEENE         NDìd"  m
        4FFFFFDDCD4CCDCE4444444444444444444444FFF4CCCC4CDCEC444444DCCDC4444444444DC5870090
        0715101685089552000000000000000000000002200897804995500000025555000000000005484F004F
```

└─Relative record number indicates location of the record in the file

Master File Hexidecimal Listing (After Adds):

```
RCDNBR  *...+... 1 ...+... 2 ...+... 3 ...+... 4 ...+... 5 ...+... 6 ...+... 7 ...+... 8 .

    8   10000PETER LORRE                9 DREARY DRIVE     HUNGRY        ALrr⊥ &
        4FFFFFDCECD4DDDDC4444444444444444444444F4CDCCDE4CDCEC444444CEDCDE444444444CD9990050
        0100007535903699500000000000000000000009049519804995500000084579800000000001399F040F

    1   21345JOHN DOE                   212 ELM STREET     BRIDGEPORT    CT /
        4FFFFFDDCD4CDC4444444444444444444444444FFF4CDD4EEDCCE444444CDCCCCDDDE444444CE0600200
        0213451685046500000000000000000000000002120534023955300000029947576930000003361F100F

    2   31121LOUISE LESSER              12 APPLES ROAD     BAHA          CAk   a ⊥
        4FFFFFDDECEC4DCEECD4444444444444444444444FF4CDDDCE4DDCC444444CCCC4444444444444CC9100829
        0311213649250352259000000000000000000000120177352096140000002181000000000003120F019F

    3   48891JUDY JOHNSON               114 EASY DRIVE     RALEIGH       NCà    "
        4FFFFFDECE4DDCDEDD4444444444444444444444FFF4CCEE4CDCEC444444DCDCCCC444444444DC4400007
        0488911448016852650000000000000000000001140512804995500000091359780000000005341F061F

    4   50000DAVE HOOTEN                8 STRIKE LANE      LOS ANGELES   CA°   ⌐
        4FFFFFCCEC4CDDECD4444444444444444444444F4EEDCDC4DCDC4444444DDE4CDCCDCE444444CC9000611
        0500004155086635500000000000000000000008023992503155000000362015753520000031100F041F

    5   51540MARIE BLAKE                GREEN PASTURES ROAD NEWARK       NJ L
        4FFFFFDCDCC4CDCDC4444444444444444444444CDCCD4DCEEEDCE4DDCC4DCECDD444444444DD0730403
        0515404199502312500000000000000000000007955507123495209614055619200000000005173F901F
```

```
 9   60000BORIS KARLOFF                    1 INNER SANCTUM    MISERABLE    AK    ñ
     4FFFFFCDDCE4DCDDDCC4444444444444444444F4CDDCD4ECDCEED44444DCECDCCDC4444444CD1000400
     06000026992021936660000000000000000001095559021533440000049259123500000001200F590F

 6   63141JOSEPH WELCH                   110 DILL STREET     NEW YORK     NY    ⊞"
     4FFFFFDDECDC4ECDCC4444444444444444444FFF4CCDD4EEDCCE44444DCE4EDDD4444444DE1000777
     06314116257806533800000000000000000001100493302395530000055608692000000005800F077F

 7   71510JOHN HINES                     220 HIGH DRIVE      KEENE        NDìd"  m
     4FFFFFDDCD4CCDCE4444444444444444444444FFF4CCCC4CDCEC444444DCCDC4444444444DC5870090
     07151016850895520000000000000000000000220089780499550000002555500000000005484F004F

10   80000SIDNEY GREENSTREET              10 CASTLE LANE     ALCATRAZ     CAk
     4FFFFFECCDCE4CDCCDEEDCCE4444444444444FF4CCEEDC4DCDC444444CDCCEDCE4444444CC9200000
     08000029455807955523955300000000000001003123350315500000013313919000000003122F100F
```

└── Indicates relative record number of record in the file. The CPYF utility lists
    a keyed file in ascending key value order.

Error File (After program execution):

```
RCDNBR  *...+... 1 ...+... 2 ...+... 3 ...+... 4 ...+... 5 ...+... 6 ...+... 7 ...+... 8

  1   71510JOHN HINES                     220 HIGH DRIVE     KEENE        NDìd"  ⌐n
      FFFFFDDCD4CCDCE4444444444444444444444FFF4CCCC4CDCEC444444DCCDC4444444444DC5870790
      07151016850895520000000000000000000000220089780499550000002555500000000005484F055F
```

Programming Assignment 13-2: SAVINGS ACCOUNT MASTER FILE UPDATE AND LOGICAL DELETION OF RECORDS

Notes to the Instructor:

1. The master file for assignment 13-1 must have been created
   and loaded with the orginal and add data before this assignment is started.

2. Require that students print a hexadecimal listing of the
   master file before this program is executed so that they
   can see the results of their updates and deletions after
   the program is executed and another hexidecimal listing
   is generated (see hexidecimal listing (after adds) above).

3. The edit report must only include output of the master file
   record before and after update.

Compiled Program Listing:

```
Line  <-------------------- Source Specifications -------------------><---- Comments ----> Do
Number ....1....+....2....+....3....+....4....+....5....+....6....+....7....+....8....+....9....+...10 Num
                    S o u r c e   L i s t i n g
  1 * PA 13-2: Savings Account Master Update & Logical Deletion....
  2 FP132ptr   IF   E        K DISK
    *-------------------------------------------------------------------------------------*
    *                         RPG name           External name                           *
    * File name. . . . . . . . . :  P132PTR       STAN/P132PTR                            *
    * Record format(s) . . . . . :  P132PTRR      P132PTRR                                *
    *-------------------------------------------------------------------------------------*
  3 FP131pmr   UF   E        K DISK
    *-------------------------------------------------------------------------------------*
    *                         RPG name           External name                           *
    * File name. . . . . . . . . :  P131PMR       STAN/P131PMR                            *
    * Record format(s) . . . . . :  P131PMRR      P131PMRR                                *
    *-------------------------------------------------------------------------------------*
```

```
  4 FQsysprt   O   F  132        PRINTER OFLIND(*INOF)
  5
  6=IP132PTRR
      *-------------------------------------------------------------------*
      * RPG record format  . . . . :  P132PTRR                            *
      * External format  . . . . . :  P132PTRR : STAN/P132PTR             *
      *-------------------------------------------------------------------*
  7=I                        A    1    1  TRCODE
  8=I                        A    2    6  TACTNO
  9=I                        A    7   37  TNAME
 10=I                        A   38   57  TSTREET
 11=I                        A   58   73  TCITY
 12=I                        A   74   75  TSTATE
 13=I                        P   76   78 0TZIPCODE
 14=I                        P   79   82 2TAMOUNT
 15=IP131PMRR
      *-------------------------------------------------------------------*
      * RPG record format  . . . . :  P131PMRR                            *
      * External format  . . . . . :  P131PMRR : STAN/P131PMR             *
      *-------------------------------------------------------------------*
 16=I                        A    1    1  DELETECODE
 17=I                        A    2    6  ACCTNUMBER
 18=I                        A    7   37  NAME
 19=I                        A   38   57  STREET
 20=I                        A   58   73  CITY
 21=I                        A   74   75  STATE
 22=I                        P   76   78 0ZIPCODE
 23=I                        P   79   82 2ACTBALANCE
 24 C              EVAL      *INOF = *ON              turn on OF indicator
 25 C              READ      P132ptr            ----LR read first trans rcd
 26 C              DOW       *INLR = *OFF              dow LR is off        B01
 27
 28 C              IF        *INOF = *ON               overflow ind. on?    B02
 29 C              EXCEPT    Heading                   print heading line    02
 30 C              ENDIF                               end IF group         E02
 31
 32 C    TactNo    CHAIN     P131pmr            90---- find master record    01
 33 C              IF        *IN90 = *ON               record not found?    B02
 34 C              EXCEPT    PrintError                print error message   02
 35 C              ELSE                                false action         X02
 36 C              EXCEPT    PrintBefor                print before update   02
 37
 38 C              SELECT                              begin select group   B03
 39 C              WHEN      TrCode = 'U'              udate transaction?   X03
 40 C              EXSR      UpdateSR                  branch to subroutine  03
 41 C              WHEN      TrCode = 'D'              delete transaction?  X03
 42 C              EXSR      DeleteSR                  branch to subroutine  03
 43 C              ENDSL                               end select group     E03
 44 C              ENDIF                               end IF group         E02
 45
 46 C              READ      P132ptr            ----LR read first trans rcd  01
 47 C              ENDDO                               end dow group        E01
 48
 49 * Begin subroutines....
 50 C    UpdateSR  BEGSR                               begin subroutine
 51 C              IF        TName <> *BLANK           field blank?         B01
 52 C              EVAL      Name = TName              udate master field    01
 53 C              ENDIF                               end IF group         E01
 54
 55 C              IF        TStreet <> *BLANKS        field not blank?     B01
 56 C              EVAL      Street = TStreet          update master field   01
 57 C              ENDIF                               end IF group         E01
 58
 59 C              IF        TCity <> *BLANKS          field not blank?     B01
 60 C              EVAL      City = TCity              update master field   01
 61 C              ENDIF                               end IF group         E01
 62
 63 C              IF        TState <> *BLANKS         field not blank?     B01
 64 C              EVAL      State = TState            update master field   01
 65 C              ENDIF                               end IF group         E01
 66
 67 C              IF        TZipCode <> *ZEROS        field not blank?     B01
 68 C              EVAL      ZipCode = TZipCode        update master field   01
 69 C              ENDIF                               end IF group         E01
```

```
 70
 71 C                EVAL      ActBalance = ActBalance + TAmount        add to ActBalance
 72
 73 C                UPDATE    P131pmrr                        --60--   update master record
 74 C                EXCEPT    PrintAfter                               orint after update
 75 C                ENDSR                                              end subroutine
 76
 77 C     DeleteSR   BEGSR                                              begin subroutine
 78 C                DELETE    P131pmrr                        --60--   delete master record
 79 C                ENDSR                                              end subroutine
 80
 81 OQsysprt   E              Heading       3 01
 82 O                         UDATE         Y    8
 83 O                                           59 'SAVINGS ACCOUNTS EDIT'
 84 O                                           66 'REPORT'
 85 O                                           99 'PAGE'
 86 O                         PAGE              104
 87 O          E              PrintBefor    2
 88 O                                           16 'BEFORE UPDATING:'
 89 O          E              PrintBefor    2
 90 O                         DeleteCode         3
 91 O                         AcctNumber        10
 92 O                         Name              43
 93 O                         Street            65
 94 O                         City              83
 95 O                         State             87
 96 O                         ZipCode           94
 97 O                         ActBalance    1  104
 98 O          E              PrintError    2
 99 O                         TrCode             3
100 O                         TactNo            10
101 O                                           36 '....ACCOUNT NOT FOUND....'
102 O          E              PrintAfter    2
103 O                                           15 'AFTER UPDATING'
104 O          E              PrintAfter    2
105 O                         TrCode             3
106 O                         AcctNumber        10
107 O                         Name              43
108 O                         Street            65
109 O                         City              83
110 O                         State             87
111 O                         ZipCode           94
112 O                         ActBalance    1  104
113=OP131PMRR
    *-----------------------------------------------------------------------------*
    * RPG record format . . . . : P131PMRR                                        *
    * External format . . . . . : P131PMRR : STAN/P131PMR                         *
    *-----------------------------------------------------------------------------*
114=O                          DELETECODE         1A CHAR      1
115=O                          ACCTNUMBER         6A CHAR      5
116=O                          NAME              37A CHAR     31
117=O                          STREET            57A CHAR     20
118=O                          CITY              73A CHAR     16
119=O                          STATE             75A CHAR      2
120=O                          ZIPCODE           78P PACK    5,0
121=O                          ACTBALANCE        82P PACK    6,2
    * * * * *  E N D   O F   S O U R C E  * * * *
```

Printed Report:

```
 1/11/98                         SAVING ACCOUNTS EDIT REPORT                        PAGE    1

BEFORE UPDATING:

   21345   JOHN DOE                      212 ELM STREET       BRIDGEPORT     CT  06610  1,200.00
AFTER UPDATING:

   21345   JOHN DOEST                    10 ROSE TERRACE      TRUMBULL       VT  07779  1,200.00
```

```
 U  40000 ....ACCOUNT NOT FOUND....

BEFORE UPDATING:

    48891  JUDY JOHNSON                 114 EASY DRIVE        RALEIGH        NC  44410     60.17


 D  61000 ....ACCOUNT NOT FOUND....

BEFORE UPDATING:

    63141  JOSEPH WELCH                 110 DILL STREET       NEW YORK       NY  10000    777.77

AFTER UPDATING:

    63141  JOSEPH WELCH                 110 DILL STREET       NEW YORK       NY  10000       .00


BEFORE UPDATING:

    80000  SIDNEY GREENSTREET           10 CASTLE LANE        ALCATRAZ       CA  92220  1,000.00


AFTER UPDATING:

    80000  SIDNEY GREENSTREET           10 CASTLE LANE        ALCATRAZ       CA  92220  3,000.00
```

Hexidecimal Listing of the Master File After Update and Deletion Processing:

```
RCDNBR   *...+... 1 ...+... 2 ...+... 3 ...+... 4 ...+... 5 ...+... 6 ...+... 7 ...+... 8 .

     8   10000PETER LORRE              9 DREARY DRIVE     HUNGRY       ALrr⊥  &
         4FFFFFDCECD4DDDDC4444444444444444444F4CDCCDE4CDCEC444444CEDCDE444444444CD9990050
         0100007535903699500000000000000000000904951980499550000008457980000000001399F040F

     1   21345JOHN DOEST              10 ROSE TERRACE    TRUMBULL     VT ⊥
         4FFFFFDDCD4CDCEE4444444444444444444444FF4DDEC4ECDDCCC44444EDEDCEDD4444444EE0790200
         0213451685046523000000000000000000000100962503599135000003944243300000005377F100F

     2   31121LOUISE LESSER           12 APPLES ROAD     BAHA         CAk    a ⊥
         4FFFFFDDECEC4DCEECD4444444444444444444FF4CDDDCE4DDCC444444CCCC44444444444CC9100829
         0311213649250352259000000000000000000012017735209614000002181000000000003120F019F

     4   50000DAVE HOOTEN             8 STRIKE LANE      LOS ANGELES  CA°  ⌐
         4FFFFFCCEC4CDDECD4444444444444444444444F4EEDCDC4DCDC4444444DDE4CDCCDCE44444CC9000611
         0500004155086635500000000000000000000080239925031550000003620157535200003100F041F

     5   51540MARIE BLAKE             GREEN PASTURES ROAD NEWARK      NJ ⌐
         4FFFFFDCDCC4CDCDC4444444444444444444444CDCCD4DCEEEDCE4DDCC4DCECDD4444444444DD0730403
         0515404199502312500000000000000000000079555071234952096140556192000000000005173F901F

     9   60000BORIS KARLOFF           1 INNER SANCTUM    MISERABLE    AK   ñ
         4FFFFFCDDCE4DCDDDCC4444444444444444444F4CDDCD4ECDCEED44444DCECDCDC4444444CD1000400
         0600002699202193666000000000000000000109555902153344000004925912350000001200F590F

     6   63141JOSEPH WELCH            110 DILL STREET    NEW YORK     NY
         4FFFFFDDECDC4ECDCC4444444444444444444FFF4CCDD4EEDCCE44444DCE4EDDD4444444DE1000000
         0631411625780653380000000000000000000110049330239553000005560869200000005800F000F

     7   71510JOHN HINES              220 HIGH DRIVE     KEENE        NDîd"  m
         4FFFFFDDCD4CCDCE4444444444444444444444FFF4CCCC4CDCEC44444DCĊDC4444444444DC5870090
         0715101685089552000000000000000000000022008978049955000002555500000000005484F004F

    10   80000SIDNEY GREENSTREET      10 CASTLE LANE     ALCATRAZ     CAk
         4FFFFFECCDCE4CDCCDEEDCCE4444444444444FF4CCEEDC4DCDC444444CDCCEDCE4444444CC9200000
         0800002945580795552395530000000000000100312335031550000001331391900000003122F300F
```

records updated⟶

149

Programming Assignment 13-3: CEREAL BRANDS MASTER FILE ADDITION

Notes to the Instructor:

1. The master and transaction files must be created and loaded
   with data before the RPG IV program is compiled and executed.

2. Because the master file is defined as **UNIQUE**, any duplicate
   keys in the transaction file are to be printed on the report.

Compiled Program Listing:

```
Line    <---------------------- Source Specifications ----------------------------><---- Comments ----> Do
Number  ....1....+....2....+....3....+....4....+....5....+....6....+....7....+....8....+....9....+...10 Num
                        S o u r c e   L i s t i n g
   1  * PA 13-3 - Cereal brands master file addition....
   2
   3 FP133ptr   IF   E        K DISK
      *------------------------------------------------------------------------------------------------*
      *                                    RPG name          External name                             *
      * File name. . . . . . . . . :       P133PTR           STAN/P133PTR                               *
      * Record format(s) . . . . . :       P133PTRR          P133PTRR                                   *
      *------------------------------------------------------------------------------------------------*
   4 FP133pmr   UF A E        K DISK
      *------------------------------------------------------------------------------------------------*
      *                                    RPG name          External name                             *
      * File name. . . . . . . . . :       P133PMR           STAN/P133PMR                               *
      * Record format(s) . . . . . :       P133PMRR          P133PMRR                                   *
      *------------------------------------------------------------------------------------------------*
   5 FQsysprt   O   F 132      PRINTER
   6
*RNF2318 00     5 000500 Overflow indicator OA is assigned to PRINTER file QSYSPRT.
   7 DRcdsLoaded      S           4 0
   8 DErrorRcds       S           4 0
   9
  10=IP133PTRR
      *------------------------------------------------------------------------------------------------*
      * RPG record format  . . . . :       P133PTRR                                                     *
      * External format  . . . . . :       P133PTRR : STAN/P133PTR                                      *
      *------------------------------------------------------------------------------------------------*
  11=I                              A    1    5  ABRANDNO
  12=I                              A    6   25  ANAME
  13=I                              P   26   27 0ASIZE
  14=I                              A   28   29  AMEASURE
  15=I                              A   30   44  AMFGR
  16=I                              P   45   48 0APURDATE
  17=I                              P   49   52 4ALASTPRICE
  18=I                              P   53   55 0AQTYONHND
  19=I                              P   56   59 4AUNITCOST
  20=I                              P   60   62 2AUNITSP
  21=IP133PMRR
      *------------------------------------------------------------------------------------------------*
      * RPG record format  . . . . :       P133PMRR                                                     *
      * External format  . . . . . :       P133PMRR : STAN/P133PMR                                      *
      *------------------------------------------------------------------------------------------------*
  22=I                              A    1    1  DELCODE
  23=I                              A    2    6  BRANDNO
  24=I                              A    7   26  BRANDNAME
  25=I                              P   27   28 0SIZE
  26=I                              A   29   30  UNIT
  27=I                              A   31   45  MFGR
  28=I                              P   46   49 0LASTPDATE
  29=I                              P   50   53 4UNITCOST
  30=I                              P   54   56 0QTYONHAND
  31=I                              P   57   60 4AVGCOST
  32=I                              P   61   63 2UNITSP
  33 C                 EXCEPT    Heading                            print heading line
  34 C                 READ      P133ptr                   ----LR   read first record
  35
```

```
36 C              DOW        *INLR = *OFF                    dow LR is off          B01
37 C   ABrandNo   SETLL      p133pmr            ----50       check for dup key      01
38 C              IF         *IN50 = *OFF                    duplicat record?       B02
39 C              EVAL       BrandNo = ABrandNo              load to mr field       02
40 C              EVAL       BrandName = AName               load to mr field       02
41 C              EVAL       Size = ASize                    load to mr field       02
42 C              EVAL       Unit = AMeasure                 load to mr field       02
43 C              EVAL       MFGR = AMFGR                    load to mr field       02
44 C              EVAL       LastPdate = APurDate            load to mr field       02
45 C              EVAL       UnitCost = ALastPrice           load to mr field       02
46 C              EVAL       QtyOnHand = AQtyOnHnd           load to mr field       02
47 C              EVAL       AvgCost = AUnitCost             load to mr field       02
48 C              EVAL       UnitSp = AUnitSp                load to mr field       02
49 C              WRITE      P133pmrr                        add rcd to mstr file   02
50 C              EVAL       RcdsLoaded = RcdsLoaded + 1     increment counter      02
51 C              ELSE                                       begin false action     X02
52 C              EXCEPT     DuprcdLine                      print duplicate rcd    02
53 C              EVAL       ErrorRcds = ErrorRcds + 1       increment counter      02
54 C              ENDIF                                      end IF group           E02
55
56 C              READ       P133ptr            ----LR       read next record       01
57 C              ENDDO                                      end dow group          E01
58
59 C              EXCEPT     SummryLine                      print summryline
60
61 OQsysprt  E              Heading      3 01
62 O                        UDATE        Y    8
63 O                                         33 'DUPLICATE RECORDS'
64 O                                         44 'PAGE'
65 O                        PAGE              48
66 O         E              DupRcdLine   2
67 O                        ABrandNo          26
68 O         E              SummryLine   1
69 O                                         17 'RECORDS LOADED'
70 O                        RcdsLoaded   1    23
71 O                                         39 'ERROR RECORDS'
72 O                        ErrorRcds    1    45
73=OP133PMRR
   *------------------------------------------------------------------------------------*
   * RPG record format  . . . . :  P133PMRR                                             *
   * External format  . . . . . :  P133PMRR : STAN/P133PMR                              *
   *------------------------------------------------------------------------------------*
74=O                        DELCODE      1A CHAR     1
75=O                        BRANDNO      6A CHAR     5
76=O                        BRANDNAME   26A CHAR    20
77=O                        SIZE        28P PACK   3,0
78=O                        UNIT        30A CHAR     2
79=O                        MFGR        45A CHAR    15
80=O                        LASTPDATE   49P PACK   6,0
81=O                        UNITCOST    53P PACK   6,4
82=O                        QTYONHAND   56P PACK   5,0
83=O                        AVGCOST     60P PACK   6,4
84=O                        UNITSP      63P PACK   4,2
   * * * * *   E N D   O F   S O U R C E   * * * * *
```

Hexidecimal listing of file after records are added:

```
RCDNBR   *...+... 1 ...+... 2 ...+... 3 ...+... 4 ...+... 5 ...+... 6 ..

    1   C1100TOTAL             OZGENERAL MILLS   -'¬        /
        4CFFFFEDECD4444444444444444402DECCDCDCD4DCDDE440675011103006110013
        031100363130000000000000001F69755591304933200009F061F06F111F08F

    2   C1134kix              !OZGENERAL MILLS   -'¬  r  ç   r¬  ⊥
        4CFFFFF98A444444444444444444404DECCDCDCD4DCDDE440675019004001900299
        03113429700000000000000000001F69755591304933200009F099F08F099F03F

    3   C1200TREATS           !OZKELLOGG'S       c ¬ i¬  i¬ ⊥
        4CFFFFEDCCEE4444444444444444404DEDCDDDCC7E4444440805028502002850399
        0312003951320000000000000000C1F69253367702000000039F089F70F089F04r
```

```
4    C4889BRAN CHEX            ¦OZRALSTON          É ¬  i⊥ d   i⊥   ⊥
     4CFFFFCDCD4CCCE444444444404DEDCDEEDD4444444071501890800189019
     0348892915038570000000000001F69913236500000000019F029F04F029F04F

5    C5150RICE CHEX             OZRALSTON          é ¬   f      f   ⊥
     4CFFFFDCCC4CCCE444444444402DEDCDEEDD4444444051501500200150019
     0351509935038570000000000001F69913236500000000019F045F10F045F06F

6    C5200SUN FLAKES           ¬OZRALSTON          b ¬   °   -   °   ⊥
     4CFFFFEED4CDCDCE444444444405DEDCDEEDD4444444082501900600190029
     0352002450631252000000000001F69913236500000000029F090F00F090F01F

7    C6314RAISN BRAN            OZKELLOGG          É ¬  d   o   d   ⊥
     4CFFFFDCCED4CDCD44444444400DEDCDDDCC4444444072501800900180029
     0363149192502915000000000002F69253367700000000019F084F06F084F00F

8    C6550CORN FLAKES          ±OZKELLOGG          /B¬              ±
     4CFFFFCDDD4CDCDCE444444408DEDCDDDCC4444444065501000400100018
     0365503695063125200000000001F69253367700000000019F000F20F000F01F

9    C6900FROSTED FLAKES        OZKELLOGG          /B¬  j  ⅃  j   ⊥
     4CFFFFCDDEECC4CDCDCE44444400DEDCDDDCC4444444065501900800190019
     0369006962354063125200000001F69253367700000000019F001F10F001F02F

10   C7000GRAPE-NUT FLAKES      OZPOST             /Ñ¬  ╞     ╞   ⊥
     4CFFFFCDCDC6DEE4CDCDCE44402DEDDEE4444444444066501780400178019
     0370007917505430631252000001F69762300000000000019F028F20F028F03F

11   C7100FRUIT & FIBER        ¦OZPOST             éì¬              ⊥
     4CFFFFCDECE454CCCCD444444404DEDDEE4444444444058501200200120019
     0371006949300069259000000001F69762300000000000019F062F10F062F08F

12   C7440ALPHA-BITS           ¬OZPOST             ê ¬    ⅃        ¬
     4CFFFFCDDCC6CCEE44444444405DEDDEE4444444444050501000800100015
     0374401378102932000000000001F69762300000000000029F075F40F075F09F

13   C8000CAP'N CRUNCH         ?OZQUAKER           ⊤ ¬            ⊥
     4CFFFFCCD7D4CDEDCC444444406DEDECDCD4444444444071501230000123019
     038000317D50394538000000001F69841259000000000029F073F60F073F09F

14   C8100PUFFED WHEAT         ?OZQUAKER           ⅃ ¬            ⊥
     4CFFFFDECCCC4ECCCE44444446DEDECDCD4444444444062501001000100019
     038100746654068513000000000F69841259000000000029F000F20F000F01F

15   C9000SHREDDED WHEAT SS     OZNABISCO          bñ¬  &   &   ¬
     4CFFFFECDCCCCC4ECCCE4EE44402DEDCCCECD4444444084501500000150015
     0390002895445406851302200001F69512923600000000029F010F18F010F02F
```

Printed Report:

```
8/31/98          DUPLICATE RECORDS          PAGE    1


                        C1134

                        C8100

RECORDS LOADED     3    ERROR RECORDS     2
```

**Programming Assignment 13-4: CEREAL BRANDS MASTER FILE UPDATE
AND LOGICAL DELETION OF RECORDS**

1. Remind students that the master file must have been created
   (Assignment 13-3) and all of the records added before this
   program is started.

2. Require that students print a **CPYF** listing in ***HEX** <u>before</u> their update/delete program is executed.

3. Two transaction files must be created and loaded with data. One file is for sales and purchase transactions and the other for changes and logical delete transactions.

4. Require that students print a **CPYF** listing in ***HEX** <u>after</u> the RPG IV program is executed and identify the sales, purchase, change, and delete transactions.

5. Refer to the hexidecimal listing of the file on pages 151-152 of this manual <u>before</u> this program is run.

6. The program example includes two **DOW** groups. One processes the Sales/Purchases file with two **READ** statements. The second processes the Changes/Deletes file with two **READ** statements.

   The three physical files are defined as *full-procedural* and *externally described*.

<u>Compiled Program Listing</u>:

```
Line    <--------------------- Source Specifications -------------------------><---- Comments ----> Do
Number  ....1....+....2....+....3....+....4....+....5....+....6....+....7....+....8....+....9....+...10 Num
                        S o u r c e   L i s t i n g
    1  * Cereal brands master file update & logical deletion....
    2
    3 FP134trsp  IF   E        K DISK
      *-------------------------------------------------------------------------------------------*
      *                          RPG name            External name                                *
      * File name. . . . . . . . : P134TRSP          STAN/P134TRSP                                 *
      * Record format(s) . . . . : P134TRSPR         P134TRSPR                                     *
      *-------------------------------------------------------------------------------------------*
    4 FP134trcd  IF   E        K DISK
      *-------------------------------------------------------------------------------------------*
      *                          RPG name            External name                                *
      * File name. . . . . . . . : P134TRCD          STAN/P134TRCD                                 *
      * Record format(s) . . . . : P134TRCDR         P134TRCDR                                     *
      *-------------------------------------------------------------------------------------------*
    5 FP133Pmr   UF   E        K DISK
      *-------------------------------------------------------------------------------------------*
      *                          RPG name            External name                                *
      * File name. . . . . . . . : P133PMR           STAN/P133PMR                                  *
      * Record format(s) . . . . : P133PMRR          P133PMRR                                      *
      *-------------------------------------------------------------------------------------------*
    6 FQsysprt   O    F  132      PRINTER
    7
*RNF2318 00    6 000600  Overflow indicator OA is assigned to PRINTER file QSYSPRT.
    8 DHhMmSs        S           6 0                             stores system time
    9 DUpdatercds    S           4 0                             records updated
   10 DErrorRcds     S           4 0                             error records
   11 DTotalRcds     S           4 0                             total rcds processed
   12
   13  * Housekeeping....
   14=IP134TRSPR
      *-------------------------------------------------------------------------------------------*
      * RPG record format  . . . . : P134TRSPR                                                    *
      * External format  . . . . . : P134TRSPR : STAN/P134TRSP                                    *
      *-------------------------------------------------------------------------------------------*
   15=I                            A     1    1 TRANSCODE
   16=I                            A     2    6 BRANDNO
   17=I                            P     7    9 0SORPQTY
   18=I                            P    10   13 2PURCOST
   19=I                            P    14   17 0PURDATE
```

```
20=IP134TRCDR
      *-----------------------------------------------------------------------*
      *  RPG record format  . . . . :  P134TRCDR                              *
      *  External format  . . . . . :  P134TRCDR : STAN/P134TRCD             *
      *-----------------------------------------------------------------------*
21=I                          A    1    1  CCODE
22=I                          A    2    6  CBRANDNO
23=I                          A    7   26  CNAME
24=I                          P   27   28  OCSIZE
25=I                          A   29   30  CMEASURE
26=I                          A   31   45  CMFGR
27=I                          P   46   49  OCLPDATE
28=I                          P   50   53 4CUNITCOST
29=I                          P   54   56  OCQTYONHAND
30=I                          P   57   60 4CAVGCOST
31=I                          P   61   63 2CUNITSP
32=IP133PMRR
      *-----------------------------------------------------------------------*
      *  RPG record format  . . . . :  P133PMRR                              *
      *  External format  . . . . . :  P133PMRR : STAN/P133PMR              *
      *-----------------------------------------------------------------------*
33=I                          A    1    1  DELCODE
34=I                          A    2    6  BRANDNO
35=I                          A    7   26  BRANDNAME
36=I                          P   27   28  OSIZE
37=I                          A   29   30  UNIT
38=I                          A   31   45  MFGR
39=I                          P   46   49  OLASTPDATE
40=I                          P   50   53 4UNITCOST
41=I                          P   54   56  OQTYONHAND
42=I                          P   57   60 4AVGCOST
43=I                          P   61   63 2UNITSP
44 C           IF        *IN10 = *OFF                    indicator 10 off?    B01
45 C           TIME                    HhMmSs            access system time    01
46 C           EVAL      *IN10 = *ON                     turn on indicator 10  01
47 C           EXCEPT    Heading                         print heading line    01
48 C           ENDIF                                     end IF group         E01
49
50  * Process sales and purchases transaction file....
51 C           READ      P134trsp              ----80    read first record
52 C           DOW       *IN80 = *OFF                    dow ind. 90 is off   B01
53 C  BrandNo  CHAIN     P133pmr               99----    get master record     01
54
55 C           IF        *IN99 = *OFF                    master rcd found?    B02
56 C  TransCode CASEQ    'S'         SorPSR              transcode = S?        02
57 C  TransCode CASEQ    'P'         SorPSR              or P?                 02
58 C           ENDCS                                     end case group        02
59 C           ELSE                                                          X02
60 C           EVAL      Errorrcds = Errorrcds + 1       increment counter     02
61 C           EXCEPT    ErrorLine1                      print errorline       02
62 C           ENDIF                                     end IF group         E02
63
64 C           EVAL      Totalrcds = Totalrcds + 1       increment counter     01
65 C           READ      P134trsp              ----80    read next record'     01
66 C           ENDDO                                     end dow group        E01
67
68  * Process changes & deletes transaction file....
69 C           READ      P134trcd              ----80    read first record
70 C           DOW       *IN80 = *OFF                    dow ind. 90 is off   B01
71 C  CBrandNo CHAIN     P133pmr               99----    get master record     01
72
73 C           IF        *IN99 = *OFF                    master rcd found?    B02
74 C  CCode    CASEQ     'C'         CorDSR              transcode = S?        02
75 C  CCode    CASEQ     'D'         CorDSR              or P?                 02
76 C           ENDCS                                     end case group        02
77 C           ELSE                                -                         X02
78 C           EVAL      Errorrcds = Errorrcds + 1       increment counter     02
79 C           EXCEPT    ErrorLine2                      print errorline       02
80 C           ENDIF                                     end IF group         E02
81
82 C           EVAL      Totalrcds = Totalrcds + 1       increment counter     01
83 C           READ      P134trcd              ----80    read next record'     01
84 C           ENDDO                                     end dow group        E01
```

```
 85
 86 C           EXCEPT    TotalLine                    print totalline
 87 C           EVAL      *INLR = *ON                  end job
 88
 89  * Begin Sales and Purchases subroutine....
 90 C    SorPSR BEGSR                                  begin sales & pur SR
 91 C           SELECT                                 begin select group   B01
 92 C           WHEN      TransCode = 'S'              trancode = S?        X01
 93 C           EVAL      QtyOnHand = QtyOnHand - SorPQty   reduce QtyOnHand  01
 94 C           WHEN      Transcode = 'P'              trandcode = P?       X01
 95 C           EVAL      QtyOnHand = QtyOnHand + SorPQty   comput new QtyOnHand 01
 96 C           EVAL      AvgCost = (QtyOnHand * AvgCost +                   01
 97 C                     SorPQty * PurCost) / QtyOnHand  compute new AvgCost  01
 98 C           IF        PurDate <> *ZERO             not equal to zero?   B02
 99 C           EVAL      LastPDate = PurDate          new LastPDate        02
100 C           ENDIF                                  end IF group         E02
101 C           ENDSL                                  end select group     E01
102
103 C           UPDATE    P133pmrr                     update master record
104 C           EVAL      Updatercds = Updatercds + 1  increment counter
105 C           ENDSR                                  end subroutine
106
107  * Begin Changes and Deletions subroutine....
108 C    CorDSR BEGSR                                  begin sales & pur SR
109 C           SELECT                                 begin select group   B01
110 C           WHEN      CCode = 'C'                  trancode = S?        X01
111 C           IF        CName <> *BLANKS             field blank?         B02
112 C           EVAL      BrandName = CName            update BrandName     02
113 C           ENDIF                                  end IF group         E02
114
115 C           IF        CSize <> *ZERO              field not blank?     B02
116 C           EVAL      Size = CSize                change Size field     02
117 C           ENDIF                                  end IF group         E02
118
119 C           IF        CMeasure <> *BLANKS         field not blank?     B02
120 C           EVAL      Unit = CMeasure             change Size field     02
121 C           ENDIF                                  end IF group         E02
122
123 C           IF        CMfgr <> *BLANKS            field not blank?     B02
124 C           EVAL      Mfgr = CMfgr                change Size field     02
125 C           ENDIF                                  end IF group         E02
126
127 C           IF        CLPDate <> *ZERO            field not blank?     B02
128 C           EVAL      LastPDate = CLPDate         change Size field     02
129 C           ENDIF                                  end IF group         E02
130
131 C           IF        CUnitCost <> *ZERO          field not blank?     B02
132 C           EVAL      UnitCost = CUnitCost        change Size field     02
133 C           ENDIF                                  end IF group         E02
134
135 C           IF        CQtyOnHand <> *ZERO         field not blank?     B02
136 C           EVAL      QtyOnHand = CQtyOnHand      change Size field     02
137 C           ENDIF                                  end IF group         E02
138
139 C           IF        CAvgCost <> *ZERO           field not blank?     B02
140 C           EVAL      AvgCost = CAvgCost          change Size field     02
141 C           ENDIF                                  end IF group         E02
142
143 C           IF        CUnitSP <> *ZERO            field not blank?     B02
144 C           EVAL      UnitSP = CUnitSP            change Size field     02
145 C           ENDIF                                  end IF group         E02
146
147 C           UPDATE    P133pmrr                     update master record  01
148 C           EVAL      UpDatercds = UpDatercds + 1  increment counter    01
149
150 C           WHEN      CCode = 'D'                  CCode = D?           X01
151 C           DELETE    P133pmrr                     delete master record  01
152
153 C           ENDSL                                  end select group     E01
154 C           ENDSR                                  end subroutine
155
156 OQsysprt E            Heading       1 01
157 O                                   26 'UPDATE/DELETE'
```

```
158 O                                        39 'TRANSACTIONS'
159 O                    UDATE          Y      8
160 O                    HhMmSs               52 '  :  :  '
161 O        E           Heading        2
162 O                                        38 'WITH NO MASTER FILE KEY'
163 O        E           Heading        1
164 O                                        19 'CODE'
165 O                                        36 'KEY'
166 O        E           Heading        2
167 O                                        37 'VALUE'
168 O        E           ErrorLine1     1
169 O                    TransCode            17
170 O                    BrandNo              37
171 O        E           ErrorLine2     1
172 O                    CCode                17
173 O                    CBrandNo             37
174 O        E           TotalLine      2
175 O                                        26 'TRANSACTIONS PROCESSED:'
176 O                    Totalrcds      3     31
177 O        E           TotalLine      2
178 O                                        26 'MASTER RECORDS UPDATED:'
179 O                    UpdateRcds     3     31
180 O        E           TotalLine      0
181 O                                        17 'ERROR RECORDS:'
182 O                    ErrorRcds      3     22
183=OP133PMRR
      *---------------------------------------------------------------------------------*
      * RPG record format . . . . : P133PMRR                                            *
      * External format . . . . . : P133PMRR : STAN/P133PMR                             *
      *---------------------------------------------------------------------------------*
184=O                    DELCODE             1A CHAR        1
185=O                    BRANDNO             6A CHAR        5
186=O                    BRANDNAME          26A CHAR       20
187=O                    SIZE               28P PACK      3,0
188=O                    UNIT               30A CHAR        2
189=O                    MFGR               45A CHAR       15
190=O                    LASTPDATE          49P PACK      6,0
191=O                    UNITCOST           53P PACK      6,4
192=O                    QTYONHAND          56P PACK      5,0
193=O                    AVGCOST            60P PACK      6,4
194=O                    UNITSP             63P PACK      4,2
     * * * *  E N D  O F  S O U R C E  * * * *
```

Printed Report:

```
┌──────────────────────────────────────────────────────┐
│  1/11/95      UPDATE/DELETE TRANSACTIONS    13:34:47   │
│               WITH NO MASTER FILE KEY                  │
│                                                        │
│               CODE              KEY                    │
│                                 VALUE                  │
│                                                        │
│                P                C2121                  │
│                S                C8900                  │
│                C                C1300                  │
│                                                        │
│                                                        │
│   TRANSACTIONS PROCESSED:    12                        │
│                                                        │
│   MASTER RECORDS UPDATED:     9                        │
│                                                        │
│   ERROR RECORDS:    3                                  │
└──────────────────────────────────────────────────────┘
```

Hexidecimal Listing of the Master File
Before the Program is executed:

```
RCDNBR  *...+... 1 ...+... 2 ...+... 3 ...+... 4 ...+... 5 ...+... 6 ..
    1   C1100TOTAL              OZGENERAL MILLS    - ¼
        4CFFFFEDECD444444444444402DECCDCDCD4DCDDE44067501110300111013
        03110036313000000000000001F6975559130493320000F061F06F061F08F
```

```
  2   C1134KIX                  ¦0ZGENERal MILLS   -'¼  r  T  r  -
     4CFFFFDCE4444444444444444404FECCDCD894DCDDE44067501900400190029
     0311342970000000000000000001F09755591304933200009F099F08F099F03F

  3   C1200TREATS               ¦0ZKELLOGG'S        c ¼  i¼    i¼ -
     4CFFFFEDCCEE4444444444444404DEDCDDDCC7E444444080502850200285039
     031200395132000000000000001F692533677D20000000039F089F70F089F04F

  4   C4889BRAN CHEX            ¦0ZRALSTON          r ¼  i- d  i-  -
     4CFFFFCDCD4CCCE4444444444404DEDCDEEDD44444444071501890800189019
     034889291503857000000000001F699132365000000000019F029F04F029F04F

  5   C5150RICE CHEX             0ZRALSTON          θ ¼  ¢     ¢   -
     4CFFFFDCCC4CCCE4444444444402DEDCDEEDD44444444051501500200150019
     035150993503857000000000001F699132365000000000019F045F10F045F06F

  6   C5200SUN FLAKES           %0ZRALSTON          b ¼     -      -
     4CFFFFEED4CDCDCE444444444405DEDCDEEDD44444444082501900600190029
     03520024506312520000000001F699132365000000000029F090F00F090F01F

  7   C6314RAISIN BRAN           0ZKELLOGG          r ¼  d  o  d   -
     4CFFFFDCCECD4CDCD44444444400DEDCDDDCC44444444072501800900180029
     036314919295029150000000002F692533677000000000019F084F06F084F00F

  8   C6550CORN FLAKES           0ZKELLOGG          /¼
     4CFFFFCDDD4CDCDCE44444444408DEDCDDDCC44444444065501000400100018
     036550369506312520000000001F692533677000000000019F000F20F000F01F

  9   C6900FROSTED FLAKES        0ZKELLOGG          /¼  j  +  j   -
     4CFFFFCDDEECC4CDCDCE44444400DEDCDDDCC44444444065501900800190019
     036900696235406312520000001F692533677000000000019F001F10F001F02F

 10   C7000GRAPE-NUT FLAKES      0ZPOST             /┬¼            -
     4CFFFFCDCDC6DEE4CDCDCE444402DEDDEE44444444444066501780400178019
     037000791750543063125200001F697623000000000000019F028F20F028F03F

 11   C7100FRUIT & FIBER        ¦0ZPOST             θi¼            -
     4CFFFFCDECE454CCCCD444444404DEDDEE44444444444058501200200120019
     037100694930006925900000001F697623000000000000019F062F10F062F08F

 12   C7440ALPHA-BITS           %0ZPOST             Ω ¼     +      ¼
     4CFFFFCDDCC6CCEE444444444405DEDDEE44444444444050501000800100015
     03744013781029320000000001F697623000000000000029F075F40F075F09F

 13   C8000CAP'N CRUNCH         ?0ZQUAKER           - ¼            -
     4CFFFFCCD7D4CDEDCC4444444406DEDECDCD444444444071501230000123019
     038000317D50394538000000001F698412590000000000029F073F60F073F09F

 14   C8100PUFFED WHEAT         ?0ZQUAKER           ▪ ¼            -
     4CFFFFDECCCC4ECCCE4444444406DEDECDCD444444444062501001000100019
     038100746654068513000000000F698412590000000000029F000F20F000F01F

 15   C9000SHREDDED WHEAT SS     0ZNABISCO          b±¼  &     &  ¼
     4CFFFFECDCCCCC4ECCCE4EE44402DEDCCCECD44444444084501500000150015
     039000289544540685130220001F695129236000000000029F010F18F010F02F
```

Hexidecimal Listing of the Master File
After the Program is executed:

```
RCDNBR *...+... 1 ...+... 2 ...+... 3 ...+... 4 ...+... 5 ...+... 6 ..
     1   C1100TOTAL                0ZGENERAL MILLS   -'¼
        4CFFFFEDECD44444444444444402DECCDCDCD4DCDDE44067501000300111010
        031100363130000000000000001F69755591304933200009F070F06F061F09F

     2   C1134KIX                  ¦0ZGENERal MILLS   -'¼  r  T  r  -
        4CFFFFDCE4444444444444444404FECCDCD894DCDDE44067501900400190029
        0311342970000000000000000001F09755591304933200009F099F08F099F03F

     3   C1200TREATS               ¦0ZKELLOGG'S        c ¼  i¼    i¼ -
        4CFFFFEDCCEE4444444444444404DEDCDDDCC7E444444080502850400285039
        031200395132000000000000001F692533677D20000000039F089F00D089F04F
```

```
 4    C4889BRAN CHEX          OZRALSTON       a██" i- d  i- -
      4CFFFFCDCD4CCCE4444444444402DEDCDEEDD4444444444085701890800189019
      03488929150385700000000000001F699132365000000000019F029F04F029F04F

 5    C5150RICE CHEX          OZRALSTON       θ ¼  φ     φ  -
      4CFFFFDCCC4CCCE4444444444402DEDCDEEDD4444444444051501500200150019
      03515099350385700000000000001F699132365000000000019F045F10F045F06F

 6    C5200SUN FLAKES         ¼OZRALSTON      b ¼  ▦  -  ▦
      4CFFFFFEED4CDCDCE4444444444405DEDCDEEDD4444444444082501900600190029
      03520024506312520000000000001F699132365000000000029F090F00F090F01F

 7    C6314RAISIN BRAN        OZKELLOGG       ┌ ¼  d  o   d  -
      4CFFFFDCCECD4CDCD4444444444400DEDCDDDCC4444444444072501800900180029
      03631491929502915000000000002F692533677000000000019F084F06F084F00F

 8    C6550CORN FLAKES        ▉OZKELLOGG      /▉¼     ▦        ▉
      4CFFFFCDDD4CDCDCE4444444444408DEDCDDDCC4444444444065501000900100018
      03655036950631252000000000001F692533677000000000019F000F10F000F01F

 9    C6900FROSTED FLAKES     OZKELLOGG       /▉¼  j  +   j  -
      4CFFFFCDDEECC4CDCDCE4444444400DEDCDDDCC4444444444065501900800190019
      03690069623540631252000000001F692533677000000000019F001F10F001F02F

10    C7000GRAPE-NUT FLAKES   OZPOST          /┬¼  ▉        ▉  -
      4CFFFFCDCDC6DEE4CDCDCE444402DEDDEE4444444444444066501780400178019
      03700079175054306312520000001F697623000000000000019F028F20F028F03F

13    C8000CAP'N CRUNCH       ?OZQUAKER       k "    ┌   -
      4CFFFFCCD7D4CDEDCC4444444406DEDECDCD4444444444091701230000423019
      03800031705039453800000000001F698412590000000000029F073F80F423F09F

14    C8100PUFFED RICE        ?OZQUAKER       ⁙ ¼         -
      4CFFFFDECCCC4DCCC4444444406DEDECDCD4444444444062501001000100019
      03810074665409935000000000000F698412590000000000029F000F20F000F01F

15    C9000SHREDDED WHEAT SS  OZNABISCO       b±¼  &     &   ¼
      4CFFFFECDCCCCC4ECCCE4EE44402DEDCCCECD4444444444084501500000150015
      03900028954454540685130220001F695129236000000000029F010F18F010F02F
```

Note: Records 7100 and 7440 were deleted   After change transactions ─┘
                                            After sales & purchase transactions ──┘

CHAPTER 14
QUESTION ANSWERS

1. Display files are files that include record formats for the input, output, or input/output of data to and from a work station. Their function is to support interactive inquiry, file addition, update, and deletion of records in a physical file via workstation control.

2. With **SEU** (Source Entry Utility) or with **SDA** (Screen Design Aid).

3. 1024 separate record formats.

4. When using **SEU**, the screen record should be formatted on a CRT layout form or printer spacing chart. The completed form (or chart) is referenced to enter file, record, and field level entries via **SEU**.

   When using **SDA**, the screen record may be designed directly on the CRT and the constants and variable field placed as required.

5. **PRINT**   - Including this keyword at the file or record level enables the PRINT key. When the operator presses the PRINT key, the image of the screen record is printed.

   CAnn   - *Command Attention Key* passes status of an indicator to the RPG program. **nn** specifies the command key and the related indicator is included in parenthesis after the **nn** entry (i.e. **CA01(01)**).

   CFnn   - *Command Function Key* passes the status of an indicator <u>and</u> field values to the RPG program. **nn** specifies the command key and the related indicator is included in parenthesis after the **nn** entry (i.e. **CF02(02)**).

   DSPATR - Specifies one or more display attributes related to the constant or field value.

   ERRMSG - Controls the display of the error message included in the format of this keyword. **ERRMSG** must immediately follow the field it relates to. One or more conditioning indicators are required to control the display (and nondisplay) of the message. Default location is position 1 line 24. Line number location (not position) may be changed by a **MSGLOC** keyword.

   EDTCDE - Any of the RPG IV supported edit codes (1, 2, 3, 4, A, B, C, D, J, K, L, M, Y, and Z) may be specified with this keyword to control the editing of numeric fields when displayed.

> **EDTWRD** - Any acceptable RPG IV edit word format may be speci-
> fied with this keyword.
>
> **REF** - *File level* keyword that references a Physical or
> Field Reference file for field attributes.
>
> **REFFLD** - *Field level* keyword that references a Physical or
> Field Reference file for a specified field attri-
> bute.
>
> **DATE** - Accesses the system or job date.
>
> **TIME** - Accesses the system time.
>
> **CHGINPDFT** - Supports the change of the default underline attri-
> bute for variables to one of the other optional
> display attributes.

6. **CAnn** keyword passes only the status of the related indicator
to the controlling RPG program. **CFnn** passes the status of
related indicator and the variable field values included in
the screen record format to the controlling RPG program.

7. CA04(04 'update record')

```
  |         |            |
  |         |            └─Text entry (optional)
  |         └──────────────Indicator turned on by command key
  └────────────────────────Command key referenced
```

8. NO. The **CA02** entry must be **CF02** to pass data from the
display file to the RPG IU program. Note that any indicator (01-99) may be specified, not only 02.

9. In the record format or externally in one or more physical
or field reference files.

10. MMDDYY. HH:MM:SS (note that colons are included in the TIME
value.

11. Underlining for the variable field sizes. By the **CHGINPDFT**
command followed by a display attribute in parenthesis at the
file or record level (i.e. **CHGINPDFT(RI)**).

12. Normal intensity. By specifying the **CHGINPDFT** command with
each constant.

13. <u>DSPATR</u>   <u>Function</u>

   <u>For all fields</u>:

None	Remove default underlining of variable fields.
BL	Blinking field
CS	Column separators (dots)
HI	High intensity
UL	Underline
PC	Position cursor

| ND | Non-display |
| RI | Reverse image |

For Input-Capable Fields Only:

MDT	Set modified data tag
OID	Operator identification
PR	Protect field
SP	Select by light pen

14. **CHGINPDFT(RI)**

15. **DSPATR(PC BL)**

16. O - Output from the RPG IV program to the CRT.
    I - Input from the CRT to the RPG IV program.
    B - Input and output to and from the RPG IV program.

17. O - for inquiry processing.
    I - for addition processing.
    B - for update/deletion processing.

18. Entries in this field limit what the user may enter in the field. It does not determine the type of data; Decimal Positions (36-37) defines the data type.

    A - All characters are valid for data type

    P - Packed numeric value.

    S - Only digits are valid. Display length is one more than the field size. The low-order position is reserved for a minus sign.

    X - Alphabetic characters only.

    D - Digits only.

    Y - Number 0-9, plus (+), minus (-), period (.), comma (,), and space ( ) are valid entries for this field type.

19. **Line** - specifies the CRT line on which the constant or variable will be displayed.

    Pos - specifies the CRT column on which the first character of the constant or variable will be placed for display.

20. *File, Record,* and *Field*.

21. REF(PARTS/INVENTRY)

22. REFFLD(PTNAME PARTS/INVENTRY)

23. The letter R.

24. Conditions the **ERRMSG** keyword so that the text will display on when 90 is on. Because it refers to a DUPLICATE KEY error, it will be turned on in the RPG IV program by a **WRITE** statement indicator (columns 73-74) when an attempt to add a duplicate record to a unique file is detected.

25. When 90 is turned on in the RPG program, the error message DUPLICATE KEY will display on line 24 or on some other line specified by a **MSGLOC** keyword.

26. By specifying the indicator after the error message text as shown in the coding and pressing RESET on the keyboard.

27. YES. However, only the text for one ERRMSG keyword can display at a time.

28. Line 24 Position 1. Line number may be changed by a **MSGLOC** (*Message Location*) keyword. However, all **ERRMNSG** text will always display beginning in position 1.

29. **CHECK, COMP, VALUES, RANGE.**

30. **CHECK(M11 AB)**

31. **RANGE(25.00 3000.00)**

32. **CHECK(MF)**

33. **VALUES(10 15 20 25)**

34. **COMP(LT 9)**

PROGRAMMING ASSIGNMENTS

General Notes to the Instructor:

1. Create the required physical file so that its field attributes can be referenced by the display file.

2. Note that the data will not be entered until the related programs are completed in Chapter 15.

3. Students should be required to test their display files using **SDA**. Consequently, an introduction to Appendix D is a must.

4. If time permits, students should be required to complete one of this chapter's display files using **SDA**. This will require a comprehensive discussion of Appendix D.

Programming Assignment 14-1: VALIDATION OF NEW CUSTOMER ACCOUNTS

Notes to the Instructor:

1. The **CA** and **CF** keywords are included at the record level.

Specifying at the file level would enable the keys for all of the record types in the file (when there are more).

2. **X's** in column 35 for the CUSTNAME, CITY, STATE, and CREDRATING fields restrict the entry of only alphabetic data.

3. **D's** in column 35 for the CUSTNUMBER, ZIPCODE, and CREDLIMIT fields will eliminate the low-order sign position when the variable is displayed and restrict the entry to digits (0-9).

Display File Listing (Expanded not shown):

```
                               Data Description Source
SEQNBR  *...+....1....+....2....+....3....+....4....+....5....+....6....+....7....+....8
  100   A                                        REF(STAN/PA141P)
  200   A              R ENTRY                    CA03(03 'EOJ')
  300   A                                         CF02(02 'ENTER')
  400   A                                         CA05(05 'IGNORE')
  500   A                                         CHGINPDFT(RI)
  600   A                                    1  3DATE EDTCDE(Y) DSPATR(HI)
  700   A                                    1 33'CUSTOMER ENTRY' DSPATR(UL HI)
  800   A                                    1 73TIME DSPATR(HI)
  900   A                                    4  5'CUSTOMER NUMBER:' DSPATR(HI)
 1000   A              CUSTNUMBERR   D  B     4 22
 1100   A  99                                    ERRMSG('RECORD ALREADY EXITS' 99)
 1200   A                                    4 34'NAME:' DSPATR(HI)
 1300   A              CUSTNAME  R   X  B     4 40
 1400   A                                    6  5'STREET:' DSPATR(HI)
 1500   A              STREET    R      B     6 13
 1600   A                                    8  5'CITY:' DSPATR(HI)
 1700   A              CITY      R   X  B     8 11
 1800   A                                    8 37'STATE:' DSPATR(HI)
 1900   A              STATE     R   X  B     8 44
 2000   A                                    8 52'ZIP:' DSPATR(HI)
 2100   A              ZIPCODE   R   D  B     8 57
 2200   A                                   10  5'CREDIT LIMIT:' DSPATR(HI)
 2300   A              CREDLIMIT R   D  B    10 19
 2400   A                                   10 62'CREDIT RATING:' DSPATR(HI)
 2500   A              CREDRATINGR   X  B    10 77
 2600   A                                   13  8'CMD KEY 3 - EOJ' DSPATR(HI)
 2700   A                                   13 31'CMD KEY 2 - ENTER' DSPATR(HI)
 2800   A                                   13 58'CMD KEY 5 - IGNORE' DSPATR(HI)
               * * * * *  E N D   O F   S O U R C E  * * * * *
```

SDA Test Display):

1. **Bs** indicate an input/output character field.
2. **9s** indicate an input/output numeric field.

```
 12/28/97                CUSTOMER ENTRY                15:52:04

   CUSTOMER NUMBER: BBBBB      NAME: BBBBBBBBBBBBBBBBBBBBBBBBBBBB

   STREET: BBBBBBBBBBBBBBBBBBBBBB

   CITY: BBBBBBBBBBBBBBBBBBBBBB     STATE: BB    ZIP: 99999

   CREDIT LIMIT: 9999999                        CREDIT RATING: BB


     CMD KEY 3 - EOJ        CMD KEY 2 - ENTER        CMD KEY 5 - IGNORE
```

Programming Assignment 14-2: VALIDATION OF NEW CUSTOMER ACCOUNTS

Notes to the Instructor:

1. The **CA** and **CF** keywords are included at the record level.
   Specifying at the file level would enable the keys for
   all of the record types in the file (when there are more).

3. **D's** in column 35 for the CUSTNUMBER, ZIPCODE, and CREDLIMIT
   fields restricts data keyed to numeric (0-9) and suppresses
   the low-order sign position.

4. **X** in column 35 for the CUSTNAME, STREET, CITY, STATE, and
   CREDRATING restricts the data keyed to alphabetic.

5. Validation keywords, **CHECK** (mandatory entry and mandatory
   fill), **VALUES**, and **RANGE** are specified for select fields as
   required for the assignment.

Display File Listing (Expanded not shown):

```
                              Data Description Source
SEQNBR  *...+....1....+....2....+....3....+....4....+....5....+....6....+....7....+....8
  100   A                                             REF(STAN/PA141P)
  200   A               R ENTRY                       CA03(03 'EOJ')
  300   A                                             CF02(02 'ENTER')
  400   A                                             CA05(05 'IGNORE')
  500   A                                             CHGINPDFT(RI)
  600   A                                      1  3DATE EDTCDE(Y) DSPATR(HI)
  700   A                                      1 33'CUSTOMER ENTRY' DSPATR(UL HI)
  800   A                                      1 73TIME DSPATR(HI)
  900   A                                      4  5'CUSTOMER NUMBER:' DSPATR(HI)
 1000   A               CUSTNUMBERR   D B      4 22CHECK(AB M11)
 1100   A  99                                    ERRMSG('RECORD ALREADY EXITS' 99)
 1200   A                                      4 34'NAME:' DSPATR(HI)
 1300   A               CUSTNAME  R   X B      4 40CHECK(ME)
 1400   A                                      6  5'STREET:' DSPATR(HI)
 1500   A               STREET    R     B      6 13CHECK(ME)
 1600   A                                      8  5'CITY:' DSPATR(HI)
 1700   A               CITY      R   X B      8 11CHECK(ME)
 1800   A                                      8 37'STATE:' DSPATR(HI)
 1900   A               STATE     R     B      8 44VALUES('OH' 'MI' 'NY' 'IL' 'PA' -
 2000   A                                         'NJ' 'CA')
 2100   A                                      8 52'ZIP:' DSPATR(HI)
 2200   A               ZIPCODE   R   D B      8 57CHECK(MF)
 2300   A                                     10  5'CREDIT LIMIT:' DSPATR(HI)
 2400   A               CREDLIMIT R   D B     10 19RANGE(500 5000)
 2500   A                                     10 62'CREDIT RATING:' DSPATR(HI)
 2600   A               CREDRATINGR     B     10 77VALUES('A' 'A-' 'B' 'B-' 'C')
 2700   A                                     13  8'CMD KEY 3 - EOJ' DSPATR(HI)
 2800   A                                     13 31'CMD KEY 2 - ENTER' DSPATR(HI)
 2900   A                                     13 58'CMD KEY 5 - IGNORE' DSPATR(HI)
        * * * * *  E N D  O F  S O U R C E  * * * * *
```

SDA Test Display:

1. **Bs** indicate an input/output character field.
2. **9s** indicate an input/output numeric field.
3. **6s** indicate an output numeric field.

```
 12/28/97              CUSTOMER ENTRY              15:52:04


 CUSTOMER NUMBER: BBBBB      NAME: BBBBBBBBBBBBBBBBBBBBBBBBBB

 STREET: BBBBBBBBBBBBBBBBBBBBBB
```

```
┌─────────────────────────────────────────────────────────────────────┐
│                                                                       │
│   CITY: BBBBBBBBBBBBBBBBBBBBB      STATE: BB      ZIP: 99999           │
│                                                                       │
│   CREDIT LIMIT: 9999999                        CREDIT RATING: BB       │
│                                                                       │
│                                                                       │
│      CMD KEY 3 - EOJ        CMD KEY 2 - ENTER      CMD KEY 5 - IGNORE  │
│                                                                       │
└─────────────────────────────────────────────────────────────────────┘
```

Programming Assignment 14-3: MODIFICATION OF ASSIGNMENT 14-1 OR 14-2
TO INCLUDE A SECOND RECORD FORMAT

1. A second record format (PROMPT) is included in the display
   file for programming assignment 14-2. This format will be
   displayed first to initiate the related maintenance function.

2. The **CA** and **CF** keywords are included at the record level to
   control the functions supported by that record type. Specifying these keywords at the file level would enable the keys
   for both of the record types. Undersirable for this scenario.

Display File Listing: (Expanded not shown)

```
                            Data Description Source
SEQNBR  *...+....1....+....2....+....3....+....4....+....5....+....6....+....7....+....8
  100    A                                    REF(STAN/PA141P)
  200    A                                    CHGINPDFT(RI)
  300    A              R PROMPT
  400    A                                    CA03(03 'EOJ')
  500    A                                    CF02(02 'ADD')
  600    A                                    CF07(07 'INQUIRY')
  700    A                                    CF11(11 'UPDATE')
  800    A                                    CF23(23 'DELETE')
  900    A                                1  2DATE EDTCDE(Y) DSPATR(HI)
 1000    A                                1 25'CUSTOMER FILE MAINTENANCE'
 1100    A                                     DSPATR(HI)
 1200    A                                1 71TIME DSPATR(HI)
 1300    A                                3  8'ENTER CUSTOMER NUMBER:' DSPATR(HI)
 1400    A              CUST#       5D 0I  3 31CHECK(M11 AB)
 1500    A 98                                 ERRMSG('DUPLICATE RECORD' 98)
 1600    A 99                                 ERRMSG('RECORD NOT FOUND' 99)
 1700    A                                6 16'F3 - EOJ' DSPATR(HI)
 1800    A                                6 30'F2 - ADD' DSPATR(HI)
 1900    A                                6 43'F11 - UPDATE' DSPATR(HI)
 2000    A                                7 21'F23 - DELETE' DSPATR(HI)
 2100    A                                7 38'F7 - INQUIRY' DSPATR(HI)
 2200    A              R ENTRY
 2300    A                                    CA03(05 'IGNORE')
 2400    A                                    CF02(02 'ENTER')
 2400    A                                1  3DATE EDTCDE(Y) DSPATR(HI)
 2500    A                                1 33'CUSTOMER ENTRY' DSPATR(UL HI)
 2600    A                                1 73TIME DSPATR(HI)
 2700    A                                4  5'CUSTOMER NUMBER:' DSPATR(HI)
 2800    A              CUSTNUMBERR   D B  4 22DSPATR(PR)
 2900    A                                4 34'NAME:' DSPATR(HI)
 3000    A              CUSTNAME  R   X B  4 40CHECK(ME) DSPATR(PC)
 3100    A                                6  5'STREET:' DSPATR(HI)
 3200    A              STREET    R     B  6 13CHECK(ME)
 3300    A                                8  5'CITY:' DSPATR(HI)
 3400    A              CITY      R   X B  8 11CHECK(ME)
 3500    A                                8 37'STATE:' DSPATR(HI)
 3600    A              STATE     R     B  8 44VALUES('OH' 'MI' 'NY' 'IL' 'PA' -
 3700    A                                   'NJ' 'CA')
 3800    A                                8 52'ZIP:' DSPATR(HI)
 3900    A              ZIPCODE   R   D B  8 57CHECK(MF)
 4000    A                               10  5'CREDIT LIMIT:' DSPATR(HI)
 4100    A              CREDLIMIT R   D B 10 19RANGE(500 5000)
 4200    A                               10 62'CREDIT RATING:' DSPATR(HI)
 4300    A              CREDRATINGR     B 10 77VALUES('A' 'A-' 'B' 'B-' 'C')
```

165

```
4400    A                              13 16'CMD KEY 2 - ENTER' DSPATR(HI)
4500    A                              13 50'CMD KEY 5 - IGNORE' DSPATR(HI)
                * * * *  E N D   O F   S O U R C E  * * * *
```

SDA Test Display:

PROMPT record format:

```
┌──────────────────────────────────────────────────────────────────────┐
│  1/11/98                 CUSTOMER MAINTENANCE              16:08:55     │
│                                                                        │
│                                                                        │
│          ENTER CUSTOMER NUMBER: IIIII                                  │
│                                                                        │
│                                                                        │
│              F3 - EOJ          ENTER - TO DISPLAY ENTRY SCREEN         │
│                                                                        │
└──────────────────────────────────────────────────────────────────────┘
```

ENTRY record format:

```
┌──────────────────────────────────────────────────────────────────────┐
│  1/11/98                 CUSTOMER MAINTENANCE              16:12:40     │
│                               OOOOOOO                                  │
│      CUSTOMER NUMBER: 33333      NAME: IIIIIIIIIIIIIIIIIIIIIIIII        │
│                                                                        │
│      STREET: IIIIIIIIIIIIIIIIIIII                                      │
│                                                                        │
│      CITY: IIIIIIIIIIIIIIIIIIII     STATE: II      ZIP: 33333          │
│                                                                        │
│      CREDIT LIMIT: 3333333                      CREDIT RATING: II       │
│                                                                        │
│              F2 - ENTER                    F5 - IGNORE                 │
└──────────────────────────────────────────────────────────────────────┘
```

Programming Assignment 14-4: STUDENT COURSE FILE MAINTENANCE

Notes to the Instructor:

1. Each display file design form for this assignment details the requirements for the related record format.

Display File Listing:

```
                              Data Description Source
SEQNBR  *...+....1....+....2....+....3....+....4....+....5....+....6....+....7....+....8
   100  A                              REF(STAN/PA144)
   200  A                              MSGLOC(8)
   300  A                              PRINT
   400  A                              CHGINPDFT(RI)
   500  A           R PROMPT
   600  A                              CA03(03 'EOJ')
   700  A                              CF02(02 'ADD')
   800  A                              CF11(11 'UPDATE')
   900  A                              CF23(23 'DELETE')
  1000  A                              CF07(07 'INQUIRY')
  1100  A                            1  2DATE EDTCDE(Y) DSPATR(HI)
  1200  A                            1 27'COURSE FILE MANTENANCE'
  1300  A                              DSPATR(HI UL)
  1400  A                            1 71TIME DSPATR(HI)
  1500  A                            4  5'ENTER:' DSPATR(HI)
  1600  A                            6  5'SS NUMBER:' DSPATR(HI)
  1700  A           SSNUMBER  R     B  6 16
  1800  A                            6 32'COURSE NUMBER:' DSPATR(HI)
  1900  A           COURSENO  R     B  6 47
```

```
2000      A                                      6 60'TERM DATE:' DSPATR(HI)
2100      A              TERMDATE  R          B  6 71
2200      A  98                                     ERRMSG('DUPLICATE RECORD' 98)
2300      A  99                                     ERRMSG('RECORD NOT FOUND' 99)
2400      A                                      9 17'F3 - EOJ' DSPATR(HI)
2500      A                                      9 31'F2 - ADD' DSPATR(HI)
2600      A                                      9 44'F11 - UPDATE' DSPATR(HI)
2700      A                                     10 22'F23 - DELETE' DSPATR(HI)
2800      A                                     10 44'F7 - INQUIRY' DSPATR(HI)
2900      A              R MAINTRCD
3000      A                                        CF02(02 'ENTER')
3100      A                                        CA10(10 'IGNORE')
3200      A                                      1  2DATE EDTCDE(Y) DSPATR(HI)
3300      A                                      1 27'COURSE FILE MAINTENANCE'
3400      A                                        DSPATR(HI UL)
3500      A                                      1 71TIME DSPATR(HI)
3600      A              MODE         7    O     2 36
3700      A                                      5  9'STUDENT NO:' DSPATR(HI)
3800      A              SSNUMBER  R      D   B  5 21DSPATR(PR)
3900      A                                      5 53'COURSE NO:' DSPATR(HI)
4000      A              COURSENO  R          B  5 64DSPATR(PR)
4100      A                                      7  9'COURSE NAME:' DSPATR(HI)
4200      A              DOURSENAME  20       B  7 22DSPATR(PC)
4300      A                                      7 53'TERM DATE:' DSPATR(HI)
4400      A              TERMDATE  R      D   B  7 64DSPATR(PR)
4500      A                                      9  9'INSTRUCTOR CODE:' DSPATR(HI)
4600      A              DNSTCODE    3D   OB   9 26
4700      A                                      9 39'CREDITS:' DSPATR(HI)
4800      A              DREDIT      1D   OB   9 48
4900      A                                      9 63'MARK:' DSPATR(HI)
5000      A              DARK        1     B   9 69
5100      A                                     12 15'F2 - ENTER' DSPATR(HI)
5200      A                                     12 55'F10 - IGNORE' DSPATR(HI)
          * * * * *  E N D   O F   S O U R C E  * * * * *
```

SDA Test Displays:

PROMPT record format:

```
 1/01/98               COURSE FILE MANTENANCE                   12:01:03

   ENTER:

   SS NUMBER: 999999999      COURSE NUMBER: BBBBBB      TERM DATE: 999999


                F3 - EOJ     F2 - ADD     F11 - UPDATE
                         F23 - DELETE     F7 - INQUIRY
```

MAINTRCD record format:

```
 1/01/98               COURSE FILE MAINTENANCE                  12:02:07
                            OOOOOOO


     STUDENT NO: 999999999                  COURSE NO: BBBBBB

     COURSE NAME: BBBBBBBBBBBBBBBBBBBB       TERM DATE: 999999

     INSTRUCTOR CODE: 999        CREDITS: 9              MARK: B


          F2 - ENTER                        F10 - IGNORE
```

Programming Assignment 14-5: PARTS INVENTORY MASTER FILE MAINTENANCE

Notes to the Instructor:

1. Each display file design form for this assignment details the requirements for the related record format.

2. A variable for the job date (MMDDYYYY) is specified on line 2 of both display file record formats. The job date value will be accessed from the *DATE special word and loaded to the field in the RPG IV program.

Display File listing (expanded not shown):

```
                                    Data Description Source
SEQNBR  *...+....1....+....2....+....3....+....4....+....5....+....6....+....7....+....8
  100   A                                        PRINT
  200   A                                        CHGINPDFT(RI)
  300   A                                        MSGLOC(15)
  400   A              R PROMPT
  500   A                                        CA03(03 'EOJ')
  600   A                                        CF02(02 'ADD')
  700   A                                        CF11(11 'UPDATE')
  800   A                                        CF23(23 'DELETE')
  900   A                                        CF07(07 'INQUIRY')
 1000   A                                      1  2TIME
 1100   A                                      1 26'PARTS INVENTORY MAINTENANCE'
 1200   A                                        DSPATR(HI)
 1300   A                MMDDYYYY      8  00    2 34EDTWRD('0 / /    ')
 1400   A                                      4  9'ENTER PART NUMBER:' DSPATR(HI)
 1500   A                PART#         5   I    4 28
 1600   A   99                                    ERRMSG('DUPLICATE RECORD' 99)
 1700   A   98                                    ERRMSG('PART NUMBER NOT FOUND' 98)
 1800   A                                      7 16'F3 - EOJ' DSPATR(HI)
 1900   A                                      7 30'F2 - ADD' DSPATR(HI)
 2000   A                                      7 44'F11 - UPDATE' DSPATR(HI)
 2100   A                                      8 21'F23 - DELETE' DSPATR(HI)
 2200   A                                      8 38'F7 - INQUIRY' DSPATR(HI)
 2300   A              R ENTRY
 2400   A                                        CA03(03 'EOJ')
 2500   A                                        CA12(12 'IGNORE')
 2600   A                                        CF02(02 'ENTER')
 2700   A                                      1  4TIME DSPATR(HI)
 2800   A                                      1 26'PARTS INVENTORY MAINTENANCE'
 2900   A                                        DSPATR(HI UL)
 3000   A                MODE          7         1 71
 3100   A                MMDDYYYY      8  00    2 34EDTWRD('0 / /    ')
 3200   A                                      4 15'PART NUMBER:' DSPATR(HI)
 3300   A                PART#         5   B    4 28CHECK(ME)
 3400   A                                      6 15'PART NAME:' DSPATR(HI)
 3500   A                DARTNAME     20   B    6 26CHECK(ME)
 3600   A                                      8 15'AMT-ON-HAND:' DSPATR(HI)
 3700   A                DMTONHAND    6O  OB    8 28CHECK(ME)
 3800   A                                      8 50'AVG COST:' DSPATR(HI)
 3900   A                DVGCOST      7D  OB    8 60CHECK(ME)
 4000   A                                     10 15'AMT-ON-ORDER:' DSPATR(HI)
 4100   A                DMTORDERED   6O  OB   10 29CHECK(ME)
 4200   A                                     10 51'AMT ALLOCATED:' DSPATR(HI)
 4300   A                DMTALLOCTD   6O  OB   10 66CHECK(ME)
 4400   A                                     12 15'EOQ:' DSPATR(HI)
 4500   A                DOQ          6O  OB   12 20CHECK(ME)
 4600   A                                     12 50'SAFETY STOCK:' DSPATR(HI)
 4700   A                DAFTYSTOCK   6O  OB   12 64CHECK(ME)
 4800   A                                     14 15'LEAD TIME:' DSPATR(HI)
 4900   A                DEADTIME     3D  OB   14 26CHECK(ME)
 5000   A                                     14 30'DAYS' DSPATR(HI)
 5100   A                                     14 50'WAREHOUSE LOCATION:' DSPATR(HI)
 5200   A                DAREHLOCTN   3X   B   14 70CHECK(ME)
 5300   A                                     17 16'F3 - EOJ' DSPATR(HI)
 5400   A                                     17 53'F12 - IGNORE' DSPATR(HI)
 5500   A                                     18 32'F2 - ENTER' DSPATR(HI)
```

Chapter 14 - Display Files

SDA Test Display:

PROMPT record format:

```
12:03:11              PARTS INVENTORY MAINTENANCE
                             OOOOOOOOOO

    ENTER PART NUMBER:


         F3 - EOJ     F2 - ADD     F11 - UPDATE
            F23 - DELETE     F7 - INQUIRY
```

ENTRY record format:

```
12:03:46              PARTS INVENTORY MAINTENANCE              OOOOOOO
                             OOOOOOOOOO

         PART NUMBER: BBBBB

         PART NAME: BBBBBBBBBBBBBBBBBBBBB

         AMT-ON-HAND: 999999          AVG COST: 9999999

         AMT-ON-ORDER: 999999         AMT ALLOCATED: 999999

         EOQ: 999999                  SAFETY STOCK: 999999

         LEAD TIME: 999 DAYS          WAREHOUSE LOCATION: BBB


            F3 - EOJ                      F12 - IGNORE
                     F2 - ENTER
```

CHAPTER 15
QUESTION ANSWERS

1. Defines the WORKSTN file as *combined*, supporting input and output.

2. **I** for input only or **O** for output only.

3. **F** in column 17 defines the display file as a full-procedural file for which any RPG IV file processing (**CHAIN, READ, READ, READP, READPE, SETLL, SETGT, WRITE, UPDATE, DELETE,** etc.) operation is supported.

4. **E** in column 22 defines the file as *externally described*. An **F** in this position would define the file as *program-described* (not supported for WORKSTN files).

5. A workstation (keyboard and CRT).

6. Writes and reads a display file record to and from the CRT. The **EXFMT** operation is only functional with DSPFs.

   Separate **WRITE** and **READ** operations will provide the same controls.

7. For *externally described* display file's, a record name.

   For *program described* display file's, the file name and a data structure name in the *Result Field* (unlikely coding for a display file). Syntax of the **WRITE** operation was explained in Chapter 13.

8. If an error is detected when writing the screen record to the CRT. Prevents program execution from aborting.

9. The related display file's record format will display waiting for an operator's response.

10. As an *externally defined* (E in column 22) output or update file (O or U in column 17) that supports the addition of records (A in column 20).

    If a UNIQUE physical file was to be checked for a duplicate key condition in a prompt screen before the entry screen was displayed and filled with data. Thereby, saving data entry labor.

11. **WRITE** operation. Duplicate key error for keyed physical files defined as unique, a file full error, or a device error.

    By an **ERRMSG** keyword conditioned by the indicator specified in columns 73-74 of the related **WRITE** statement. If this control is not included in the display file, the system will supply an error message.

12. A record name for externally described display files or a file name for program described display files.

13. **U** in column 16, **F** in column 17, **E** in column 22, and an **A** in column 20 of the related *File Description* statement.

14. **CHAIN** or a **READ** operation to <u>get</u> the record and an **UPDATE** operation to <u>update</u> the record. Refer to syntax of the **CHAIN, UPDATE,** and **READ** operations in Chapter 13.

    RECORD NOT FOUND error with the **CHAIN** operation or a device error with the **CHAIN** or **UPDATE** operations.

    The **CHAIN** operation.

15. The physical file name for the **CHAIN** or **READ** operation and the physical file's record name for the **UPDATE** operation.

16. As an update (**U** in column 16), full-procedural (**F** in column 17), externally described (**E** in column 22) file in the related *File Description* statement.

17. **CHAIN** or a **READ** operation to <u>get</u> the record and a **DELETE** operation to <u>logically delete</u> the record. Refer to syntax of the **CHAIN, DELETE,** and **READ** operations in Chapter 13.

    Record not found with the **CHAIN** or **READ** operation or a device error with the **CHAIN** or **DELETE** operations.

    The **CHAIN** operation.

18. The physical file's record name.

19. As an input (**I** in column 16), full-procedural (**F** in column 17) externally defined (**E** in column 22) file in the related *File Description* statement.

20. The **CHAIN** or one of the **READ** operations.

    RECORD NOT FOUND or device error.

21. The physical file name.

22. Clears the fields and/or elements in a record format, data structure, array, table, or subfield to blanks for character field or zeros for numeric fields. All specified indicators are set "off".

    Factor 1 may contain *NOKEY which will prevent any key fields from being cleared.

    May be used with any RPG IV supported file type.

23. *ALL may be entered in *Factor 2* which will clear all occurr-

ences of a multiple occurrence data structure.

PROGRAMMING ASSIGNMENTS

Programming Assignment 15-1: VALIDATION OF NEW CUSTOMER ACCOUNTS

Notes to the Instructor for assignments 15-1 through 15-4:

1. Students must refer to their completed programming assignment 14-3 and the physical file PA141p. Remind students that may have used different names for their display and physical files.

2. Note that assignment 14-3 includes a PROMPT and an ENTRY record format. Because assignment 15-1 through 15-4 support only one maintenance function, all of the command keys included in the PROMPT record will not be functional for each assignment. Only the related command key(s) will support an individual program.

2. Execution of the RPG IV program must display the PROMPT record first. If a duplicate key is not entered the ENTRY format will display in which field values may be entered.

3. Note that with the exception of the modulus-11, all other field validation is supported in the ENTRY display.

4. After the data is added, a hexadecimal listing should be printed (using CPYF) to verify the results of the adds processing.

Compiled Program Listing (Adds Maintenance):

```
Line    <--------------------- Source Specifications --------------------------><----- Comments ----> Do
Number  ....1....+....2....+....3....+....4....+....5....+....6....+....7....+....8....+....9....+...10 Num
                    S o u r c e   L i s t i n g
    1  * PA15-1: Validation of New Customers Accounts...
    2 FPa141p    UF A E          K DISK
      *-----------------------------------------------------------------------------------------------*
      *                          RPG name         External name                                       *
      * File name. . . . . . . . : PA141P          STAN/PA141P                                         *
      * Record format(s) . . . . : PA141PR         PA141PR                                             *
      *-----------------------------------------------------------------------------------------------*
    3 FPA143d    CF  E           WORKSTN
    4
      *-----------------------------------------------------------------------------------------------*
      *                          RPG name         External name                                       *
      * File name. . . . . . . . : PA143D          STAN/PA143D                                         *
      * Record format(s) . . . . : PROMPT          PROMPT          -                                  *
      *                           ENTRY            ENTRY                                               *
      *-----------------------------------------------------------------------------------------------*
    5=IPA141PR
      *-----------------------------------------------------------------------------------------------*
      * RPG record format  . . . . : PA141PR                                                           *
      * External format  . . . . . : PA141PR : STAN/PA141P                                             *
      *-----------------------------------------------------------------------------------------------*
    6=I                           P    1    3 OCUSTNUMBER
    7=I                           A    4   27 CUSTNAME
```

```
  8=I                        A   28  47  STREET
  9=I                        A   48  67  CITY
 10=I                        A   68  69  STATE
 11=I                        P   70  72  OZIPCODE
 12=I                        P   73  76  OCREDLIMIT
 13=I                        A   77  78  CREDRATING
 14=IPROMPT
   *-------------------------------------------------------------------------*
   * RPG record format  . . . . :  PROMPT                                    *
   * External format  . . . . . :  PROMPT : STAN/PA143D                      *
   *-------------------------------------------------------------------------*
 15=I                        A    2   2  *IN02            ADD
 16=I                        A    1   1  *IN03            EOJ
 17=I                        A    3   3  *IN07            INQUIRY
 18=I                        A    4   4  *IN11            UPDATE
 19=I                        A    5   5  *IN23            DELETE
 20=I                        A    6   6  *IN98            DUPLICATE RECORD
 21=I                        A    7   7  *IN99            RECORD NOT FOUND
 22=I                        S    8  12  OCUST#
 23=IENTRY
   *-------------------------------------------------------------------------*
   * RPG record format  . . . . :  ENTRY                                     *
   * External format  . . . . . :  ENTRY : STAN/PA143D                       *
   *-------------------------------------------------------------------------*
 24=I                        A    2   2  *IN02            ENTER
 25=I                        A    1   1  *IN05            IGNORE
 26=I                        S    3   7  OCUSTNUMBER
 27=I                        A    8  31  CUSTNAME
 28=I                        A   32  51  STREET
 29=I                        A   52  71  CITY
 30=I                        A   72  73  STATE
 31=I                        S   74  78  OZIPCODE
 32=I                        S   79  85  OCREDLIMIT
 33=I                        A   86  87  CREDRATING
 34 C           DOU       *IN03 = *ON              dou ind 03 is on     B01
 35 C           CLEAR              Entry           clear Entry record    01
 36 C           EXFMT     Prompt                   display prompt scrn   01
 37 C  *IN03    CASEQ     *OFF       AddSR         branch to subroutine  01
 38 C           ENDCS                              end CAS group         01
 39 C           ENDDO                              end dou group        E01
 40
 41 C           EVAL      *INLR = *ON              end program
 42
 43 C  AddSR    BEGSR                              begin subroutine
 44 C  Cust#    SETLL     Pa141P            ----98 does record exist?
 45 C           IF        *IN98 = *OFF             duplicate record?    B01
 46 C           EVAL      CustNumber = Cust#       prompt fld to PF fld  01
 47 C           EXFMT     Entry                    display Entry scrn    01
 48 C           IF        *IN02 = *ON              ignore entry or add  B02
 49 C           WRITE     Pa141pr                  add record to file    02
 50 C           ENDIF                              end line 18 line grp E02
 51 C           ENDIF                              end line 1600 IF grp E01
 52 C           ENDSR                              end subroutine
 53=OPA141PR
   *-------------------------------------------------------------------------*
   * RPG record format  . . . . :  PA141PR                                   *
   * External format  . . . . . :  PA141PR : STAN/PA141P                     *
   *-------------------------------------------------------------------------*
 54=0              CUSTNUMBER        3P PACK   5,0
 55=0              CUSTNAME         27A CHAR    24
 56=0              STREET           47A CHAR    20
 57=0              CITY             67A CHAR    20
 58=0              STATE            69A CHAR     2
 59=0              ZIPCODE          72P PACK   5,0
 60=0              CREDLIMIT        76P PACK   7,0
 61=0              CREDRATING       78A CHAR     2          -
 62=OPROMPT
   *-------------------------------------------------------------------------*
   * RPG record format  . . . . :  PROMPT                                    *
   * External format  . . . . . :  PROMPT : STAN/PA143D                      *
   *-------------------------------------------------------------------------*
 63=0              *IN98             1A CHAR     1          DUPLICATE RECORD
 64=0              *IN99             2A CHAR     1          RECORD NOT FOUND
 65=OENTRY
   *-------------------------------------------------------------------------*
```

```
     * RPG record format  . . . . :  ENTRY                                         *
     * External format  . . . . . :  ENTRY : STAN/PA143D                           *
     *-----------------------------------------------------------------------------*
  66=0                    CUSTNUMBER        5S ZONE       5,0
  67=0                    CUSTNAME         29A CHAR        24
  68=0                    STREET           49A CHAR        20
  69=0                    CITY             69A CHAR        20
  70=0                    STATE            71A CHAR         2
  71=0                    ZIPCODE          76S ZONE       5,0
  72=0                    CREDLIMIT        83S ZONE       7,0
  73=0                    CREDRATING       85A CHAR         2
     * * * *   E N D   O F   S O U R C E   * * * *
```

PROMPT Display:

```
  1/05/98              CUSTOMER FILE MAINTENANCE                14:25:51

      ENTER CUSTOMER NUMBER: 65005


          F3 - EOJ      F2 - ADD      F11 - UPDATE
          F23 - DELETE     F7 - INQUIRY
```

Note: If a modulus-11 error is detected for the customer number value, the following system supplied error message will display:

The value for this field does not meet the modulus 10 or 11 check.

For this condition, ignore the record, do not display the ENTRY screen, and continue to the next record. **Customer number 14100 does not meet the** modulus-11 check digit check.

ENTRY Display:

```
  1/05/98                   CUSTOMER ENTRY                      14:26:16


   CUSTOMER NUMBER: 65005      NAME: HENRY ATLAS

   STREET: 210 LUG AVENUE

   CITY: GREENWICH           STATE: CT      ZIP: 06649

   CREDIT LIMIT: 3000                          CREDIT RATING: B


           CMD KEY 2 - ENTER              CMD KEY 5 - IGNORE
```

Notes within the ENTRY screen the following errors will be detected:

1. The Credit limit value for CUSTOMER NUMBER 35009 and 47104 are not within the 500 to 5000 range. The following system-supplied error message will display for each record:

   valid range for field is 500 to 5000

2. The characters for the NAME and CITY fields are not alphabetic. The following system-supplied error message will display for each field:

   name invalid (Field requires alphabetic characters)

3. The state field value for customer number 65005 is not valid. The following error message will display:

Value entered for field is not valid. Valid values listed in message help.

To access message help from a PC keyboard, press the **Shift** and **Scroll Lock** keys for a list of valid values.

In any case, do not enter a record with substitute values (contrary to the assignment specifications).

HEX Listing of physical file **after valid data is loaded:**

```
RCDNBR  *...+... 1 ...+... 2 ...+... 3 ...+... 4 ...+... 5 ...+... 6 ...+... 7 ...+...
   1      JOHN FIRESTONE        20 TYRE LANE      AKRON           OH B?    B
         133DDCD4CCDCEEDDC444444444FF4EEDC4DCDC4444444CDDDD44444444444444DC0460000C4
         24F1685069952365500000000002003895031550000000012965000000000000006855F020F20

   2      %WILLIAM GOODYEAR     19 TUBE ROAD      DETROIT         MI -?    A
         105ECDDCCD4CDDCECCD44444444FF4EECC4DDCC4444444CCEDDCE44444444444DC0660000C4
         30F693391407664851900000000190342509614000000004539693000000000000004960F050F10

   3      █JAMES GOODRICH       81 VALVE TERRACE  CHICAGO         IL ¦     B
         208DCDCE4CDDCDCCC444444444FF4ECDEC4ECDDCCC4444CCCCCCD44444444444CD0440000C4
         10F1145207664993800000000081051355035991350000389317600000000000009340F030F20

   4      α █ANTHONY PIRELLI    33 FIAT BOULEVARD ROME            NY -█    A-
         408CDECDDE4DCDCDDC444444444FF4CCCE4CDEDCECDC444DDDC44444444444444DE0680000C6
         40F1538658079953390000000003306913026435519400096450000000000000005860F040F10

   7      & █JAMES COOPER       55 FLAT STREET    COOPERSTOWN     NY ▪     & C
         508DCDCE4CDDDCD4444444444444FF4CDCE4EEDCCE444444CDDDCDEEDED4444444DE0600050C4
         00F11452036675900000000000000550631302395530000003667592366500000005862F000F30

   6      - WILLIAM BRIDGESTONE 80 WHEEL DRIVE    AGOURA          CA m     B-
         603ECDDCCD4CDCCCCEEDDC44444FF4ECCCD4CDCEC444444CCDEDC44444444444CC0900000C6
         00F6933914029947523655000080068553049955000000176491000000000000003194F020F20
```

Programming Assignment 15-2: CUSTOMER FILE INQUIRY

Notes to the Instructor:

1. The constants in the display file for assignment 15-1 have been modified to support inquiry processing and a new display file created.

2. Validation functions for inquiry processing are not initiated for inquiry processing.

Compiled Program Listing:

```
Line   <-------------------- Source Specifications --------------------><---- Comments ----> Do
Number ....1....+....2....+....3....+....4....+....5....+....6....+....7....+..8....+....9....+...10 Num
                    S o u r c e   L i s t i n g
   1 * PA15-2: Customer File Inquiry....
   2 FPa141p   IF  E      K DISK
     *-------------------------------------------------------------------------------*
     *                          RPG name        External name                       *
     * File name. . . . . . . . :  PA141P        STAN/PA141P                         *
     * Record format(s) . . . . :  PA141PR       PA141PR                            *
     *-------------------------------------------------------------------------------*
   3 FPA143di  CF  E             WORKSTN
```

175

```
    4
      *----------------------------------------------------------------------*
      *                                   RPG name         External name      *
      * File name. . . . . . . . :         PA143DI          STAN/PA143DI       *
      * Record format(s) . . . . :         PROMPT           PROMPT             *
      *                                    ENTRY            ENTRY              *
      *----------------------------------------------------------------------*
    5=IPA141PR
      *----------------------------------------------------------------------*
      * RPG record format  . . . . :  PA141PR                                  *
      * External format  . . . . . :  PA141PR : STAN/PA141P                    *
      *----------------------------------------------------------------------*
    6=I                          P    1    3 0CUSTNUMBER
    7=I                          A    4   27  CUSTNAME
    8=I                          A   28   47  STREET
    9=I                          A   48   67  CITY
   10=I                          A   68   69  STATE
   11=I                          P   70   72 0ZIPCODE
   12=I                          P   73   76 0CREDLIMIT
   13=I                          A   77   78  CREDRATING
   14=IPROMPT
      *----------------------------------------------------------------------*
      * RPG record format  . . . . :  PROMPT                                   *
      * External format  . . . . . :  PROMPT : STAN/PA143DI                    *
      *----------------------------------------------------------------------*
   15=I                          A    2    2 *IN02                    ADD
   16=I                          A    1    1 *IN03                    EOJ
   17=I                          A    3    3 *IN07                    INQUIRY
   18=I                          A    4    4 *IN11                    UPDATE
   19=I                          A    5    5 *IN23                    DELETE
   20=I                          A    6    6 *IN98                    DUPLICATE RECORD
   21=I                          A    7    7 *IN99                    RECORD NOT FOUND
   22=I                          S    8   12 0CUST#
   23=IENTRY
      *----------------------------------------------------------------------*
      * RPG record format  . . . . :  ENTRY                                    *
      * External format  . . . . . :  ENTRY : STAN/PA143DI                     *
      *----------------------------------------------------------------------*
   24=I                          A    2    2 *IN02                    ENTER
   25=I                          A    1    1 *IN05                    IGNORE
   26=I                          S    3    7 0CUSTNUMBER
   27=I                          A    8   31  CUSTNAME
   28=I                          A   32   51  STREET
   29=I                          A   52   71  CITY
   30=I                          A   72   73  STATE
   31=I                          S   74   78 0ZIPCODE
   32=I                          S   79   85 0CREDLIMIT
   33=I                          A   86   87  CREDRATING
   34 C                   DOU       *IN03 = *ON                  dou ind 03 is on     B01
   35 C                   CLEAR               Entry              clear Entry record    01
   36 C                   EXFMT     Prompt                       display prompt scrn   01
   37 C         *IN03     CASEQ     *OFF      InquirySR          branch to subroutine  01
   38 C                   ENDCS                                  end CAS group         01
   39 C                   ENDDO                                  end dou group        E01
   40
   41 C                   EVAL      *INLR = *ON                  end program
   42
   43 C         InquirySR BEGSR                                  begin subroutine
   44 C         Cust#     CHAIN     Pa141P                99----  search for record
   45 C                   IF        *IN99 = *OFF                 record found?        B01
   46 C                   EVAL      CustNumber = Cust#           prompt fld to PF fld  01
   47 C                   EXFMT     Entry                        display Entry scrn    01
   48 C                   ENDIF                                  end line 1600 IF grp E01
   49 C                   ENDSR                                  end subroutine
   50=OPROMPT
      *----------------------------------------------------------------------*
      * RPG record format  . . . . :  PROMPT                                   *
      * External format  . . . . . :  PROMPT : STAN/PA143DI                    *
      *----------------------------------------------------------------------*
   51=O              *IN98              1A CHAR       1           DUPLICATE RECORD
   52=O              *IN99              2A CHAR       1           RECORD NOT FOUND
   53=OENTRY
      *----------------------------------------------------------------------*
      * RPG record format  . . . . :  ENTRY                                    *
```

```
    * External format . . . . . : ENTRY : STAN/PA143DI                              *
    *------------------------------------------------------------------------------*
  54=0                    CUSTNUMBER          5S ZONE      5,0
  55=0                    CUSTNAME           29A CHAR       24
  56=0                    STREET             49A CHAR       20
  57=0                    CITY               69A CHAR       20
  58=0                    STATE              71A CHAR        2
  59=0                    ZIPCODE            76S ZONE      5,0
  60=0                    CREDLIMIT          83S ZONE      7,0
  61=0                    CREDRATING         85A CHAR        2
     * * * * *  E N D   O F   S O U R C E  * * * * *
```

PROMPT Display):

> (Same as PROMPT   screen for assignment 15-1)

ENTRY Display):

```
 _____
| 1/02/98              CUSTOMER INQUIRY                  16:18:55 |
|                                                                |
|                                                                |
|  CUSTOMER UPDATE: 60003      NAME: WILLIAM BRIDGESTONE         |
|                                                                |
|  STREET: 99 BALANCE LANE                                       |
|                                                                |
|  CITY: PITTSBURGH          STATE: PA      ZIP: 07701           |
|                                                                |
|  CREDIT LIMIT: 0003000                    CREDIT RATING: A-    |
|                                                                |
|                                                                |
|          CMD KEY 2 - ENTER            CMD KEY 5 - IGNORE       |
|_____|
```

Programming Assignment 15-3: CUSTOMER FILE UPDATE

Notes to the Instructor:

1. Suggest that students create a copy of the physical file data, the display file for assignment 15-2, and the RPG IV program completed for assignment 15-2.

2. Modify the constants in the copied display file to identify update processing.

3. Modify the copied RPG IV program to support update processing.

Compiled Program Listing:

```
|Line  <------------------- Source Specifications --------------------------><---- Comments ----> Do
|Number ....1....+....2....+....3....+....4....+....5....+....6....+....7....+....8....+....9....+...10 Num
|                       S o u r c e   L i s t i n g
|   1 * PA15-3: Customer File Update....
|   2 FPa141p    UF  E           K DISK
|     *--------------------------------------------------------------------------------*
|     *                          RPG name         External name       -                *
|     * File name. . . . . . . . . :  PA141P      STAN/PA141P                           *
|     * Record format(s) . . . . . :  PA141PR     PA141PR                               *
|     *--------------------------------------------------------------------------------*
|   3 FPA143du   CF  E             WORKSTN
|   4
|     *--------------------------------------------------------------------------------*
|     *                          RPG name         External name                        *
|     * File name. . . . . . . . . :  PA143DU     STAN/PA143DU                          *
|     * Record format(s) . . . . . :  PROMPT      PROMPT                                *
```

```
    *                                    ENTRY           ENTRY                                           *
    *------------------------------------------------------------------------------------------*
 5=IPA141PR
    *------------------------------------------------------------------------------------------*
    * RPG record format  . . . . :  PA141PR                                                    *
    * External format  . . . . . :  PA141PR : STAN/PA141P                                      *
    *------------------------------------------------------------------------------------------*
 6=I                          P   1    3 OCUSTNUMBER
 7=I                          A   4   27  CUSTNAME
 8=I                          A  28   47  STREET
 9=I                          A  48   67  CITY
10=I                          A  68   69  STATE
11=I                          P  70   72 OZIPCODE
12=I                          P  73   76 OCREDLIMIT
13=I                          A  77   78  CREDRATING
14=IPROMPT
    *------------------------------------------------------------------------------------------*
    * RPG record format  . . . . :  PROMPT                                                     *
    * External format  . . . . . :  PROMPT : STAN/PA143DU                                      *
    *------------------------------------------------------------------------------------------*
15=I                          A   2    2 *IN02                         ADD
16=I                          A   1    1 *IN03                         EOJ
17=I                          A   3    3 *IN07                         INQUIRY
18=I                          A   4    4 *IN11                         UPDATE
19=I                          A   5    5 *IN23                         DELETE
20=I                          A   6    6 *IN98                         DUPLICATE RECORD
21=I                          A   7    7 *IN99                         RECORD NOT FOUND
22=I                          S   8   12 OCUST#
23=IENTRY
    *------------------------------------------------------------------------------------------*
    * RPG record format  . . . . :  ENTRY                                                      *
    * External format  . . . . . :  ENTRY : STAN/PA143DU                                       *
    *------------------------------------------------------------------------------------------*
24=I                          A   2    2 *IN02                         ENTER
25=I                          A   1    1 *IN05                         IGNORE
26=I                          S   3    7 OCUSTNUMBER
27=I                          A   8   31  CUSTNAME
28=I                          A  32   51  STREET
29=I                          A  52   71  CITY
30=I                          A  72   73  STATE
31=I                          S  74   78 OZIPCODE
32=I                          S  79   85 OCREDLIMIT
33=I                          A  86   87  CREDRATING
34 C             DOU      *IN03 = *ON              dou ind 03 is on      B01
35 C             CLEAR              Entry          clear Entry record     01
36 C             EXFMT    Prompt                   display prompt scrn    01
37 C    *IN03    CASEQ    *OFF      UpdateSR       branch to subroutine   01
38 C             ENDCS                             end CAS group          01
39 C             ENDDO                             end dou group         E01
40
41 C             EVAL     *INLR = *ON              end program
42
43 C   UpdateSR  BEGSR                             begin subroutine
44 C   Cust#     CHAIN    Pa141P          99----   search for record
45 C             IF       *IN99 = *OFF             record found?         B01
46 C             EVAL     CustNumber = Cust#       prompt fld to PF fld   01
47 C             EXFMT    Entry                    display Entry scrn     01
48 C             IF       *IN11 = *ON              update indicator on?  B02
49 C             UPDATE   Pa141pr                  update current recd    02
50 C             ENDIF                             end inner IF groupf   E02
51 C             ENDIF                             end line 1600 IF grp  E01
52 C             ENDSR                             end subroutine
53=OPA141PR
    *------------------------------------------------------------------------------------------*
    * RPG record format  . . . . :  PA141PR                                                    *
    * External format  . . . . . :  PA141PR : STAN/PA141P                                      *
    *------------------------------------------------------------------------------------------*
54=O             CUSTNUMBER       3P PACK   5,0
55=O             CUSTNAME        27A CHAR    24
56=O             STREET          47A CHAR    20
57=O             CITY            67A CHAR    20
58=O             STATE           69A CHAR     2
59=O             ZIPCODE         72P PACK   5,0
60=O             CREDLIMIT       76P PACK   7,0
61=O             CREDRATING      78A CHAR     2
```

```
 62=0PROMPT
    *---------------------------------------------------------------------*
    * RPG record format  . . . . :  PROMPT                                 *
    * External format . . . . . :  PROMPT : STAN/PA143DU                   *
    *---------------------------------------------------------------------*
 63=0                      *IN98           1A CHAR       1       DUPLICATE RECORD
 64=0                      *IN99           2A CHAR       1       RECORD NOT FOUND
 65=0ENTRY
    *---------------------------------------------------------------------*
    * RPG record format  . . . . :  ENTRY                                  *
    * External format . . . . . :  ENTRY : STAN/PA143DU                    *
    *---------------------------------------------------------------------*
 66=0              CUSTNUMBER           5S ZONE       5,0
 67=0              CUSTNAME            29A CHAR       24
 68=0              STREET              49A CHAR       20
 69=0              CITY                69A CHAR       20
 70=0              STATE               71A CHAR       2
 71=0              ZIPCODE             76S ZONE       5,0
 72=0              CREDLIMIT           83S ZONE       7,0
 73=0              CREDRATING          85A CHAR       2
       * * * *  E N D   O F   S O U R C E  * * * *
```

PROMPT Display:

(Same as assignment 15-1)

ENTRY Display:

```
+------------------------------------------------------------+
| 1/02/98              CUSTOMER UPDATE              16:34:24  |
|                                                            |
|  CUSTOMER NUMBER: 60003     NAME: WILLIAM BRIDGESTONE      |
|                                                            |
|  STREET: 99 BALANCE LANE                                   |
|                                                            |
|  CITY: PITTSBURGH          STATE: PA     ZIP: 07701        |
|                                                            |
|  CREDIT LIMIT: 0003000                  CREDIT RATING: A-  |
|                                                            |
|                                                            |
|         CMD KEY 2 - ENTER          CMD KEY 5 - IGNORE      |
+------------------------------------------------------------+
```

Programming Assignment 15-4: CUSTOMER FILE RECORD DELETION

Notes to the Instructor:

1. Suggest that students create a copy of the display file, the physical file data, and the RPG IV program from assignment 15-3.

2. Modify the constants in the ENTRY record format to support deletion maintenance.

3. Modify the RPG IV program to support logical deletion processing.

Compiled Program Listing:

```
|Line  <---------------------- Source Specifications ----------------------><---- Comments ----> Do|
|Number ....1....+....2....+....3....+....4....+....5....+....6....+....7....+....8....+....9....+...10 Num|
                           S o u r c e   L i s t i n g
   1 * PA15-3: Customer file record deletion....
   2 FPa141p   UF   E          K DISK
    *----------------------------------------------------------------------------*
```

```
     *                                RPG name        External name                            *
     * File name. . . . . . . . :     PA141P          STAN/PA141P                              *
     * Record format(s) . . . . . :   PA141PR         PA141PR                                  *
     *------------------------------------------------------------------------------------------*
  3 FPA143dd   CF   E              WORKSTN
  4
     *------------------------------------------------------------------------------------------*
     *                                RPG name        External name                            *
     * File name. . . . . . . . :     PA143DD         STAN/PA143DD                             *
     * Record format(s) . . . . . :   PROMPT          PROMPT                                   *
     *                                ENTRY           ENTRY                                    *
     *------------------------------------------------------------------------------------------*
  5=IPA141PR
     *------------------------------------------------------------------------------------------*
     * RPG record format  . . . . :   PA141PR                                                  *
     * External format  . . . . . :   PA141PR : STAN/PA141P                                    *
     *------------------------------------------------------------------------------------------*
  6=I                         P    1    3 OCUSTNUMBER
  7=I                         A    4   27 CUSTNAME
  8=I                         A   28   47 STREET
  9=I                         A   48   67 CITY
 10=I                         A   68   69 STATE
 11=I                         P   70   72 OZIPCODE
 12=I                         P   73   76 OCREDLIMIT
 13=I                         A   77   78 CREDRATING
 14=IPROMPT
     *------------------------------------------------------------------------------------------*
     * RPG record format  . . . . :   PROMPT                                                   *
     * External format  . . . . . :   PROMPT : STAN/PA143DD                                    *
     *------------------------------------------------------------------------------------------*
 15=I                         A    2    2 *IN02                        ADD
 16=I                         A    1    1 *IN03                        EOJ
 17=I                         A    3    3 *IN07                        INQUIRY
 18=I                         A    4    4 *IN11                        UPDATE
 19=I                         A    5    5 *IN23                        DELETE
 20=I                         A    6    6 *IN98                        DUPLICATE RECORD
 21=I                         A    7    7 *IN99                        RECORD NOT FOUND
 22=I                         S    8   12 OCUST#
 23=IENTRY
     *------------------------------------------------------------------------------------------*
     * RPG record format  . . . . :   ENTRY                                                    *
     * External format  . . . . . :   ENTRY : STAN/PA143DD                                     *
     *------------------------------------------------------------------------------------------*
 24=I                         A    2    2 *IN02                        ENTER
 25=I                         A    1    1 *IN05                        IGNORE
 26=I                         S    3    7 OCUSTNUMBER
 27=I                         A    8   31 CUSTNAME
 28=I                         A   32   51 STREET
 29=I                         A   52   71 CITY
 30=I                         A   72   73 STATE
 31=I                         S   74   78 OZIPCODE
 32=I                         S   79   85 OCREDLIMIT
 33=I                         A   86   87 CREDRATING
 34 C              DOU        *IN03 = *ON                       dou ind 03 is on      B01
 35 C              CLEAR                  Entry                 clear Entry record     01
 36 C              EXFMT      Prompt                            display prompt scrn    01
 37 C    *IN03     CASEQ      *OFF        DeleteSR              branch to subroutine   01
 38 C              ENDCS                                        end CAS group          01
 39 C              ENDDO                                        end dou group         E01
 40
 41 C              EVAL       *INLR = *ON                       end program
 42
 43 C  DeleteSR    BEGSR                                        begin subroutine
 44 C  Cust#       CHAIN      Pa141P                   99----   search for record
 45 C              IF         *IN99 = *OFF                      record found?         B01
 46 C              EVAL       CustNumber = Cust#            -   prompt fld to PF fld   01
 47 C              EXFMT      Entry                             display Entry scrn     01
 48 C              IF         *IN23 = *ON                       update indicator on?  B02
 49 C              DELETE     Pa141pr                           update current recd    02
 50 C              ENDIF                                        end inner IF groupf   E02
 51 C              ENDIF                                        end line 1600 IF grp E01
 52 C              ENDSR                                        end subroutine
 53=OPROMPT
     *------------------------------------------------------------------------------------------*
     * RPG record format  . . . . :   PROMPT                                                   *
```

```
        * External format . . . . . :  PROMPT : STAN/PA143DD                                    *
        *-------------------------------------------------------------------------------*
  54=0                      *IN98          1A CHAR      1          DUPLICATE RECORD
  55=0                      *IN99          2A CHAR      1          RECORD NOT FOUND
  56=OENTRY
        *-------------------------------------------------------------------------------*
        * RPG record format . . . . :  ENTRY                                            *
        * External format . . . . . :  ENTRY : STAN/PA143DD                             *
        *-------------------------------------------------------------------------------*
  57=0                      CUSTNUMBER     5S ZONE    5,0
  58=0                      CUSTNAME      29A CHAR     24
  59=0                      STREET        49A CHAR     20
  60=0                      CITY          69A CHAR     20
  61=0                      STATE         71A CHAR      2
  62=0                      ZIPCODE       76S ZONE    5,0
  63=0                      CREDLIMIT     83S ZONE    7,0
  64=0                      CREDRATING    85A CHAR      2
     * * * *  E N D   O F   S O U R C E  * * * *
```

Prompt Display:

Same as PROMPT screen for assignment 15-1

Deletion Display:

```
 ┌──────────────────────────────────────────────────────────────────┐
 │ 1/03/98              COURSE FILE MAINTENANCE              9:06:58   │
 │                            DELETE                                   │
 │                                                                    │
 │     STUDENT NO: 033445555              COURSE NO: MTH201            │
 │                                                                    │
 │     COURSE NAME: CALCULUS I            TERM DATE: 052297            │
 │                                                                    │
 │     INSTRUCTOR CODE: 167      CREDITS: 5        MARK: D             │
 │                                                                    │
 │                                                                    │
 │         F2 - ENTER                     F10 - IGNORE                 │
 └──────────────────────────────────────────────────────────────────┘
```

Note: the result of update and deletion processing may be checked by executing either assignment 15-2 or 15-3. A hexidecimal listing is not required.

Programming Assignment 15-5: STUDENT COURSE FILE MAINTENANCE

Notes to the Instructor:

1. Indicate to the students that this assignment includes adds, update, logical deletion, and inquiry processing in one display file controlled by one RPG IV program.

3. File addition, update, and record deletion may be checked by selecting the inquiry or update option. A hexidecimal list is not required.

Compiled Program Listing:

```
Line   <--------------------- Source Specifications ----------------------><---- Comments ----> Do
Number ....1....+....2....+....3....+....4....+....5....+....6....+....7....+....8....+....9....+...10 Num
                               S o u r c e   L i s t i n g
   1 * PA15-5: Student course file maintenance...
   2 FPa144    UF A E          K DISK
        *-------------------------------------------------------------------------------*
```

```
        *                               RPG name        External name              *
        * File name. . . . . . . . :     PA144           STAN/PA144                 *
        * Record format(s) . . . . . :   PA144R          PA144R                     *
        *--------------------------------------------------------------------------*
  3 FPA144d    CF   E              WORKSTN
  4
        *--------------------------------------------------------------------------*
        *                               RPG name        External name              *
        * File name. . . . . . . . :     PA144D          STAN/PA144D                *
        * Record format(s) . . . . . :   PROMPT          PROMPT                     *
        *                                MAINTRCD        MAINTRCD                    *
        *--------------------------------------------------------------------------*
  5=IPA144R
        *--------------------------------------------------------------------------*
        * RPG record format  . . . . :   PA144R                                     *
        * External format  . . . . . :   PA144R : STAN/PA144                        *
        *--------------------------------------------------------------------------*
  6=I                           P    1    5 OSSNUMBER
  7=I                           A    6   11 COURSENO
  8=I                           A   12   31 COURSENAME
  9=I                           P   32   35 OTERMDATE
 10=I                           P   36   37 OINSTCODE
 11=I                           P   38   38 OCREDIT
 12=I                           A   39   39 MARK
 13=IPROMPT
        *--------------------------------------------------------------------------*
        * RPG record format  . . . . :   PROMPT                                     *
        * External format  . . . . . :   PROMPT : STAN/PA144D                       *
        *--------------------------------------------------------------------------*
 14=I                           A    2    2 *IN02                  ADD
 15=I                           A    1    1 *IN03                  EOJ
 16=I                           A    5    5 *IN07                  INQUIRY
 17=I                           A    3    3 *IN11                  UPDATE
 18=I                           A    4    4 *IN23                  DELETE
 19=I                           A    6    6 *IN98                  DUPLICATE RECORD
 20=I                           A    7    7 *IN99                  RECORD NOT FOUND
 21=I                           S    8   16 OSSNUMBER
 22=I                           A   17   22 COURSENO
 23=I                           S   23   28 OTERMDATE
 24=IMAINTRCD
        *--------------------------------------------------------------------------*
        * RPG record format  . . . . :   MAINTRCD                                   *
        * External format  . . . . . :   MAINTRCD : STAN/PA144D                     *
        *--------------------------------------------------------------------------*
 25=I                           A    1    1 *IN02                  ENTER
 26=I                           A    2    2 *IN10                  IGNORE
 27=I                           S    3   11 OSSNUMBER
 28=I                           A   12   17 COURSENO
 29=I                           A   18   37 DOURSENAME
 30=I                           S   38   43 OTERMDATE
 31=I                           S   44   46 ODNSTCODE
 32=I                           S   47   47 ODREDIT
 33=I                           A   48   48 DARK
 34 C                 DOU       *IN03 = *ON                dou ind 03 is on      B01
 35 C                 CLEAR               MaintRcd         clear Entry record      01
 36 C                 EXFMT     Prompt                     display prompt scrn     01
 37
 38 * Load composite key....
 39 C      Key        KLIST                                begin KLIST             01
 40 C                 KFLD                SSNumber         1st field of key        01
 41 C                 KFLD                CourseNo         2nd field of key        01
 42 C                 KFLD                TermDate         3rd field of key        01
 43
 44 C      *IN02      CASEQ     *ON       AddSR            branch to subroutine    01
 45 C      *IN11      CASEQ     *ON       UpdateSR         branch to subroutine    01
 46 C      *IN23      CASEQ     *ON       DeleteSR         branch to subroutine    01
 47 C      *IN07      CASEQ     *ON       InquirySR        branch to subroutine    01
 48 C                 ENDCS                                end CAS group           01
 49 C                 ENDDO                                end dou group          E01
 50
 51 C                 EVAL      *INLR = *ON                end program
 52
 53 C      AddSR      BEGSR                                begin subroutine
 54 C      Key        SETLL     Pa144                 ----98 does record exist?
 55 C                 IF        *IN98 = *OFF               duplicate record?     B01
```

```
56 C              EVAL      Mode = 'ADDS    '                    initialize field       01
57 C              EXFMT     MaintRcd                             display Entry scrn     01
58 C              IF        *IN02 = *ON                          branch to subroutine  B02
59 C              EXSR      DftoPfSR                             branch to subroutine   02
60 C              WRITE     Pa144r                               add record to file     02
61 C              ENDIF                                          end line 18 line grp  E02
62 C              ENDIF                                          end line 1600 IF grp  E01
63 C              ENDSR                                          end subroutine
64
65 C    UpdateSR  BEGSR                                          begin subroutine
66 C    Key       CHAIN     pA144                        99----  get record
67 C              IF        *IN99 = *OFF                         record found?         B01
68 C              EVAL      Mode = 'UPDATE '                     initialize field       01
69 C              EXSR      PftoDfSR                             branch to subroutine   01
70 C              EXFMT     MaintRcd                             display rcd format     01
71 C              IF        *IN02 = *ON                                                B02
72 C              EXSR      DftoPfSR                             branch to subroutine   02
73 C              UPDATE    Pa144r                               update current recrd   02
74 C              ENDIF                                          end inner IF group    E02
75 C              ENDIF                                          end inner IF group    E01
76 C              ENDSR                                          end subroutine
77
78 C    DeleteSR  BEGSR                                          begin subroutine
79 C    Key       CHAIN     pA144                        99----  get record
80 C              IF        *IN99 = *OFF                         record found?         B01
81 C              EVAL      Mode = 'DELETE '                     initialize field       01
82 C              EXSR      PftoDfSR                             branch to subroutine   01
83 C              EXFMT     MaintRcd                             display rcd format     01
84 C              IF        *IN02 = *ON                                                B02
85 C              DELETE    Pa144r                               update current recrd   02
86 C              ENDIF                                          end inner IF group    E02
87 C              ENDIF                                          end outer IF group    E01
88 C              ENDSR                                          end subroutine
89
90 C    InquirySR BEGSR                                          begin subroutine
91 C    Key       CHAIN     pA144                        99----  get record
92 C              IF        *IN99 = *OFF                         record found?         B01
93 C              EVAL      Mode = 'INQUIRY'                     initialize field       01
94 C              EXSR      PftoDfSR                             branch to subroutine   01
95 C              EXFMT     MaintRcd                             display rcd format     01
96 C              ENDIF                                          end IF group          E01
97 C              ENDSR                                          end subroutine
98
99  * Move Display file fields to Physical file fields....
100 C   DftoPfSR  BEGSR                                          begin subroutine
101 C             EVAL      CourseName = DourseName              move to pf field
102 C             EVAL      InstCode = DnstCode                  move to pf field
103 C             EVAL      Credit = Dredit                      move to pf field
104 C             EVAL      Mark = Dark                          move to pf field
105 C             ENDSR                                          end outer IF group
106
107 * Move Physical file fields to Display file fields....
108 C   PftoDfSR  BEGSR                                          begin subroutine
109 C             EVAL      DourseName = CourseName              move to pf field
110 C             EVAL      DnstCode = InstCode                  move to pf field
111 C             EVAL      Dredit = Credit                      move to pf field
112 C             EVAL      Dark = Mark                          move to pf field
113 C             ENDSR                                          end outer IF group
114=OPA144R
    *-------------------------------------------------------------------------*
    * RPG record format  . . . . :  PA144R                                    *
    * External format  . . . . . :  PA144R : STAN/PA144                       *
    *-------------------------------------------------------------------------*
115=O                  SSNUMBER        5P PACK      9,0
116=O                  COURSENO       11A CHAR      6
117=O                  COURSENAME     31A CHAR     20
118=O                  TERMDATE       35P PACK      6,0
119=O                  INSTCODE       37P PACK      3,0
120=O                  CREDIT         38P PACK      1,0
121=O                  MARK           39A CHAR      1
122=OPROMPT
    *-------------------------------------------------------------------------*
    * RPG record format  . . . . :  PROMPT                                    *
    * External format  . . . . . :  PROMPT : STAN/PA144D                      *
    *-------------------------------------------------------------------------*
```

```
123=0                    *IN98          1A CHAR       1         DUPLICATE RECORD
124=0                    *IN99          2A CHAR       1         RECORD NOT FOUND
125=0                    SSNUMBER      11S ZONE       9,0
126=0                    COURSENO      17A CHAR       6
127=0                    TERMDATE      23S ZONE       6,0
128=OMAINTRCD
      *--------------------------------------------------------------------*
      * RPG record format  . . . . :  MAINTRCD                             *
      * External format  . . . . . :  MAINTRCD : STAN/PA144D              *
      *--------------------------------------------------------------------*
129=0                    MODE           7A CHAR       7
130=0                    SSNUMBER      16S ZONE       9,0
131=0                    COURSENO      22A CHAR       6
132=0                    DOURSENAME    42A CHAR      20
133=0                    TERMDATE      48S ZONE       6,0
134=0                    DNSTCODE      51S ZONE       3,0
135=0                    DREDIT        52S ZONE       1,0
136=0                    DARK          53A CHAR       1
      * * * * *  E N D   O F   S O U R C E  * * * * *
```

PROMPT Display:

```
 ----------------------------------------------------------------
| 1/07/98              COURSE FILE MANTENANCE         18:25:26   |
|                                                                |
|                                                                |
|   ENTER:                                                       |
|                                                                |
|   SS NUMBER: 011111111    COURSE NUMBER: ACD101   TERM DATE: 052297 |
|                                                                |
|                                                                |
|          F3 - EOJ    F2 - ADD    F11 - UPDATE                  |
|              F23 - DELETE        F7 - INQUIRY                  |
 ----------------------------------------------------------------
```

Update Display (similar for inquiry, adds, and deletion):

```
 ----------------------------------------------------------------
| 1/07/98              COURSE FILE MAINTENANCE        18:25:58   |
|                            UPDATE                              |
|                                                                |
|                                                                |
|    STUDENT NO: 011111111          COURSE NO: ACD101           |
|                                                                |
|    COURSE NAME: ENGLISH I         TERM DATE: 052297           |
|                                                                |
|    INSTRUCTOR CODE: 300    CREDITS: 3        MARK: B          |
|                                                                |
|        F2 - ENTER                      F10 - IGNORE           |
 ----------------------------------------------------------------
```

Programming Assignment 15-6: PARTS INVENTORY MASTER FILE MAINTENANCE

Notes to the Instructor:

1. Indicate to the students that this assignment includes adds, update, logical deletion, and inquiry processing in one display file controlled by one RPG IV program.

2. The maintenance screen will display only if the key entered is valid for the function. As indicated, it must display the maintenance function currently processed.

Compiled Program Listing:

```
Line   <--------------------- Source Specifications --------------------------><---- Comments ----> Do
Number ....1....+....2....+....3....+....4....+....5....+....6....+....7....+....8....+....9....+...10 Num
                         S o u r c e   L i s t i n g
    1 * PA15-6: Part inventory master file maintenance....
    2 FPa145p   UF A E          K DISK
      *-------------------------------------------------------------------------------------*
      *                              RPG name          External name                        *
      * File name. . . . . . . . :  PA145P           STAN/PA145P                            *
      * Record format(s) . . . . :  PA145PR          PA145PR                                *
      *-------------------------------------------------------------------------------------*
    3 FPA145d   CF  E             WORKSTN
    4
      *-------------------------------------------------------------------------------------*
      *                              RPG name          External name                        *
      * File name. . . . . . . . :  PA145D           STAN/PA145D                            *
      * Record format(s) . . . . :  PROMPT           PROMPT                                 *
      *                              ENTRY            ENTRY                                  *
      *-------------------------------------------------------------------------------------*
    5=IPA145PR
      *-------------------------------------------------------------------------------------*
      * RPG record format  . . . :  PA145PR                                                 *
      * External format . . . . . :  PA145PR : STAN/PA145P                                  *
      *-------------------------------------------------------------------------------------*
    6=I                            A    1    5  PARTNUMBER
    7=I                            A    6   25  PARTNAME
    8=I                            P   26   29 0AMTONHAND
    9=I                            P   30   33 0AMTORDERED
   10=I                            P   34   37 2AVGCOST
   11=I                            P   38   41 0AMTALLOCTD
   12=I                            P   42   45 0EOQ
   13=I                            P   46   49 0SAFTYSTOCK
   14=I                            P   50   51 0LEADTIME
   15=I                            A   52   54  WAREHLOCTN
   16=IPROMPT
      *-------------------------------------------------------------------------------------*
      * RPG record format  . . . :  PROMPT                                                  *
      * External format . . . . . :  PROMPT : STAN/PA145D                                   *
      *-------------------------------------------------------------------------------------*
   17=I                            A    2    2 *IN02                       ADD
   18=I                            A    1    1 *IN03                       EOJ
   19=I                            A    5    5 *IN07                       INQUIRY
   20=I                            A    3    3 *IN11                       UPDATE
   21=I                            A    4    4 *IN23                       DELETE
   22=I                            A    7    7 *IN98                       PART NUMBER NOT FOUND
   23=I                            A    6    6 *IN99                       DUPLICATE RECORD
   24=I                            A    8   12  PART#
   25=IENTRY
      *-------------------------------------------------------------------------------------*
      * RPG record format  . . . :  ENTRY                                                   *
      * External format . . . . . :  ENTRY : STAN/PA145D                                    *
      *-------------------------------------------------------------------------------------*
   26=I                            A    3    3 *IN02                       ENTER
   27=I                            A    1    1 *IN03                       EOJ
   28=I                            A    2    2 *IN12                       IGNORE
   29=I                            A    4    8  PART#
   30=I                            A    9   28  DARTNAME
   31=I                            S   29   34 0DMTONHAND
   32=I                            S   35   41 0DVGCOST
   33=I                            S   42   47 0DMTORDERED
   34=I                            S   48   53 0DMTALLOCTD
   35=I                            S   54   59 0DOQ
   36=I                            S   60   65 0DAFTYSTOCK
   37=I                            S   66   68 0DEADTIME
   38=I                            A   69   71  DAREHLOCTN
   39 C                DOU        *IN03 = *ON              -        dou ind 03 is on      B01
   40 C                CLEAR                 Entry                  clear Entry record     01
   41 C                EVAL       Mmddyyyy = *DATE                  access job date        01
   42 C                EXFMT      Prompt                            display prompt scrn    01
   43 C     *IN02      CASEQ      *ON         AddSR                 branch to subroutine   01
   44 C     *IN11      CASEQ      *ON         UpdateSR              branch to subroutine   01
   45 C     *IN23      CASEQ      *ON         DeleteSR              branch to subroutine   01
   46 C     *IN07      CASEQ      *ON         InquirySR             branch to subroutine   01
   47 C                ENDCS                                        end CAS group          01
   48 C                ENDDO                                        end dou group         E01
```

```
49
50 C                 EVAL      *INLR = *ON                              end program
51
52 C    AddSR        BEGSR                                             begin subroutine
53 C    Part#        SETLL     Pa145p                        ----99    does record exist?
54 C                 IF        *IN99 = *OFF                            duplicate record?     B01
55 C                 EVAL      Mode = 'ADDS   '                        initialize field      01
56 C                 EXFMT     Entry                                   display Entry scrn    01
57 C                 IF        *IN02 = *ON                             branch to subroutine B02
58 C                 EXSR      DftoPfSR                                branch to subroutine  02
59 C                 WRITE     Pa145pr                                 add record to file    02
60 C                 ENDIF                                             end line 18 line grp E02
61 C                 ENDIF                                             end line 1600 IF grp E01
62 C                 ENDSR                                             end subroutine
63
64 C    UpdateSR     BEGSR                                             begin subroutine
65 C    Part#        CHAIN     pA145p                        98----    get record
66 C                 IF        *IN98 = *OFF                            record found?         B01
67 C                 EVAL      Mode = 'UPDATE '                        initialize field      01
68 C                 EXSR      PftoDfSR                                branch to subroutine  01
69 C                 EXFMT     Entry                                   display rcd format    01
70 C                 IF        *IN02 = *ON                                                   B02
71 C                 EXSR      DftoPfSR                                branch to subroutine  02
72 C                 UPDATE    Pa145pr                                 update current recrd  02
73 C                 ENDIF                                             end inner IF group    E02
74 C                 ENDIF                                             end inner IF group    E01
75 C                 ENDSR                                             end subroutine
76
77 C    DeleteSR     BEGSR                                             begin subroutine
78 C    Part#        CHAIN     pA145p                        98----    get record
79 C                 IF        *IN98 = *OFF                            record found?         B01
80 C                 EVAL      Mode = 'DELETE '                        initialize field      01
81 C                 EXSR      PftoDfSR                                branch to subroutine  01
82 C                 EXFMT     Entry                                   display rcd format    01
83 C                 IF        *IN02 = *ON                                                   B02
84 C                 DELETE    Pa145pr                                 update current recrd  02
85 C                 ENDIF                                             end inner IF group    E02
86 C                 ENDIF                                             end outer IF group    E01
87 C                 ENDSR                                             end subroutine
88
89 C    InquirySR    BEGSR                                             begin subroutine
90 C    Part#        CHAIN     pA145p                        98----    get record
91 C                 IF        *IN98 = *OFF                            record found?         B01
92 C                 EVAL      Mode = 'INQUIRY'                        initialize field      01
93 C                 EXSR      PftoDfSR                                branch to subroutine  01
94 C                 EXFMT     Entry                                   display rcd format    01
95 C                 ENDIF                                             end IF group          E01
96 C                 ENDSR                                             end subroutine
97
98  * Move Display file fields to Physical file fields....
99 C    DftoPfSR     BEGSR                                             begin subroutine
100 C                EVAL      PartNumber = Part#                      move to pf field
101 C                EVAL      PartName = DartName                     move to pf field
102 C                EVAL      AmtOnHand = DmtOnHand                   move to pf field
103 C                EVAL      AvgCost = DvgCost                       move to pf field
104 C                EVAL      AmtOrdered = DmtOrdered
105 C                EVAL      AmtAlloctd = DmtAlloctd                 move to pf field
106 C                EVAL      EOQ = DOQ                               move to pf field
107 C                EVAL      SaftyStock = DaftyStock
108 C                EVAL      LeadTime = DeadTime                     move to pf field
109 C                EVAL      WareHLoctn = DareHLoctn                 move to pf field
110 C                ENDSR                                             end outer IF group
111
112 * Move Physical file fields to Display file fields....
113 C    PftoDfSR     BEGSR                                             begin subroutine
114 C                EVAL      Part# = PartNumber                  -    move to pf field
115 C                EVAL      DartName = PartName                     move to pf field
116 C                EVAL      DmtOnHand = AmtOnHand                   move to pf field
117 C                EVAL      DvgCost = AvgCost                       move to pf field
118 C                EVAL      DmtOrdered = AmtOrdered                 move to df field
119 C                EVAL      DmtAlloctd = AmtAlloctd                 move to df field
120 C                EVAL      Doq = Eoq                               move to df field
121 C                EVAL      DaftyStock = SaftyStock                 move to df field
122 C                EVAL      DeadTime = LeadTime                     move to df field
123 C                EVAL      DareHLoctn = WareHLoctn                 move to df field
```

```
124 C                     ENDSR                                    end outer IF group
125=OPA145PR
      *----------------------------------------------------------------------------*
      * RPG record format  . . . . :  PA145PR                                       *
      * External format  . . . . . :  PA145PR : STAN/PA145P                         *
      *----------------------------------------------------------------------------*
126=O                     PARTNUMBER        5A CHAR        5
127=O                     PARTNAME         25A CHAR       20
128=O                     AMTONHAND        29P PACK        6,0
129=O                     AMTORDERED       33P PACK        6,0
130=O                     AVGCOST          37P PACK        7,2
131=O                     AMTALLOCTD       41P PACK        6,0
132=O                     EOQ              45P PACK        6,0
133=O                     SAFTYSTOCK       49P PACK        6,0
134=O                     LEADTIME         51P PACK        3,0
135=O                     WAREHLOCTN       54A CHAR        3
136=OPROMPT
      *----------------------------------------------------------------------------*
      * RPG record format  . . . . :  PROMPT                                        *
      * External format  . . . . . :  PROMPT : STAN/PA145D                          *
      *----------------------------------------------------------------------------*
137=O                     *IN98             2A CHAR        1       PART NUMBER NOT FOUND
138=O                     *IN99             1A CHAR        1       DUPLICATE RECORD
139=O                     MMDDYYYY         10S ZONE        8,0
140=OENTRY
      *----------------------------------------------------------------------------*
      * RPG record format  . . . . :  ENTRY                                         *
      * External format  . . . . . :  ENTRY : STAN/PA145D                           *
      *----------------------------------------------------------------------------*
141=O                     MODE              7A CHAR        7
142=O                     MMDDYYYY         15S ZONE        8,0
143=O                     PART#            20A CHAR        5
144=O                     DARTNAME         40A CHAR       20
145=O                     DMTONHAND        46S ZONE        6,0
146=O                     DVGCOST          53S ZONE        7,0
147=O                     DMTORDERED       59S ZONE        6,0
148=O                     DMTALLOCTD       65S ZONE        6,0
149=O                     DOQ              71S ZONE        6,0
150=O                     DAFTYSTOCK       77S ZONE        6,0
151=O                     DEADTIME         80S ZONE        3,0
152=O                     DAREHLOCTN       83A CHAR        3
      * * * *   E N D   O F   S O U R C E   * * * *
```

PROMPT Display:

```
15:36:35               PARTS INVENTORY MAINTENANCE
                              1/03/1998

    ENTER PART NUMBER: E3459


        F3 - EOJ    F2 - ADD      F11 - UPDATE
            F23 - DELETE     F7 - INQUIRY
```

Adds Display (similar for inquiry, update, and deletion):

```
15:36:58              PARTS INVENTORY MAINTENANCE         ADDS
                             1/03/1998

        PART NUMBER: E3459                         -

        PART NAME: LIQUID CAR WASH

        AMT-ON-HAND: 10224              AVG COST: 125

        AMT-ON-ORDER: 0                 AMT ALLOCATED: 50000

        EOQ: 4000                       SAFETY STOCK: 3000

        LEAD TIME: 15  DAYS             WAREHOUSE LOCATION: BBB
```

```
┌─────────────────────────────────────────────────────────────────────┐
│                                                                       │
│        F3 - EOJ                                 F12 - IGNORE          │
│                        F2 - ENTER                                     │
│                                                                       │
└─────────────────────────────────────────────────────────────────────┘
```

CHAPTER 16
QUESTION ANSWERS

1. A *subfile* is a temporary area in the computer for the storage of records. Storage area is like an array or direct file.

2. Any, including file inquiry, record addition, record deletion, and update.

3. With SEU or SDA.

4. Two, including the *subfile record* and the *control record*. *Subfile record* must be specified first.

5. *Subfile record* format defines the variable fields. The *control record* format defines constants and controls the subfile size, records per page, initialization, clearing, display, and so forth.

6. **SFL, SFLCTL. SFLSIZ, SFLPAG,** and **SFLDSP.**

7. h - SFLDLT

8. i - SFLRNA

9. l - SFLLIN

10. c - SFLSIZ

11. d - SFLPAG

12. b - SFL

13. e - SFLDSP

14. g - SFLINZ

15. n - SFLDROP

16. a - SFLCTL

17. j - SFLDSPCTL

18. k - SFLEND

19. m - SFLMSG

20. o - SFLNXTCHG

21. f - SFLCLR

22. Inquiry - O; Addition - I; and B for Update.

23. **READC** (Read Change Record). Optional indicator in columns 73-74 (less than field) tests for an error conditions.

Required indicator in columns 75-76 (equal to field) tests
for the end of the subfile.

24. The WORKSTN file supports the specified subfile.

25. The subfile record name which is defined in the display file.

26. Delineating symbol.

27. Programmer-supplied *subfile record* counter defined in the RPG IV
program.

28. *Control record format.*.

29. Control record format.

30. **WRITE.** Indicator specified in columns 75-76 (equal to field)
turns on when subfile is full.

31. *Windowing* is the superimposing of one or more displays within
the body of an existing display.

32. <u>Keyword</u>   <u>Function</u>

     WINDOW   Defines the display record as a window format
                   with row, column, width, and height specified.

     WDWBORDER   Defines the window's border characters and
                   display attributes.

     RMVWDW   Clears all window formats from a display and then
                   the window format specified is displayed.

     USRRSTDSP   Reduces blanking and blinking when displays
                   overlap.

33.   WINDOW(10 30 8 40)

     Starting line
     Starting column
     number of lines
     number of columns

34.   WDWBORDER((*CHAR '12345678') (*DSPATR RI))

     First border character   Eighth border character
     Second border character   Seventh border character
     Third border character   Sixth border character
     Fourth border character   Fifth border character

     *DSPATR RI keyword will display window in reverse image

35.   12222222222222222222222222222222222223
           4   5
           4   5
           4   5

```
            4                                              5
            67777777777777777777777777777777777777778
```

36. None. The previously discussed **WRITE** operation which must
    reference the control record displays the window in the body
    of the current display. Windowing may be included in any
    display file not with only subfiles.

PROGRAMMING ASSIGNMENTS

Before the assignments for this chapter are started, the physical
file specified at the beginning of these assignments must be created and loaded with the data supplied.

Programming Assignment 16-1: INQUIRY PROCESSING WITH A SUBFILE

Notes to the Instructor:

1. Display file includes four record formats: a prompt screen
   to enter the beginning part number, subfile record format,
   subfile control record format, and a command line record
   format.

2. Subfile record fields are defined as O (output) usage and
   use the physical file's field names.

3. Because subfile fields are defined as O usage, initialization of screen fields is not required in the RPG IV
   program.

Display File Listing:

```
                          Data Description Source
SEQNBR  *...+....1....+....2....+....3....+....4....+....5....+....6....+....7....+....8
  100   A                              REF(STAN/PA161P)
  200   A                              PRINT
  300   A                              CHGINPDFT(RI)
  400   A         R PROMPT
  500   A                              CA03(03 'EOJ')
  600   A                            1  2DATE EDTCDE(Y)
  700   A                            1 26'PARTS INVENTORY MASTER INQUIRY'
  800   A                              DSPATR(HI UL)
  900   A                            4 10'ENTER PART NO:' DSPATR(HI)
 1000   A           PART#     5   I  4 26
 1100   A                            8 20'F3-EOJ' DSPATR(HI)
 1200   A                            8 39'ENTER - TO DISPLAY' DSPATR(HI)
 1300
 1400   * Define subfile record....
 1500   A         R SFRECORD           SFL
 1600   A           PARTNO    R      O 6  3
 1700   A           PARTNAME  R      O 6 12
 1800   A           AMTONHAND R      O 6 39EDTCDE(1)
 1900   A           AMTONORDER R     O 6 50EDTCDE(1)
 2000   A           AMTALCATED R     O 6 60EDTCDE(1)
 2100   A           AVGCOST   R      O 6 68EDTCDE(1)
 2200
 2300   * Define subfile control record....
 2400   A         R CTRLRECORD         SFLCTL(SFRECORD)
 2500   A                              SFLSIZ(10)
 2600   A                              SFLPAG(5)
 2700   A  80                          SFLCLR
```

```
2800      A  81                                        SFLDSP
2900      A  81                                        SFLDSPCTL
3000      A  81                                        SFLEND
3100      A                                            OVERLAY
3200      A                                    1  2TIME DSPATR(HI)
3300      A                                    1 26'PARTS INVENTORY MASTER INQUIRY'
3400      A                                           DSPATR(HI UL)
3500      A                                    1 73DATE EDTCDE(Y) DSPATR(HI)
3600      A                                    4  3'PART#' DSPATR(HI)
3700      A                                    4 17'PART NAME' DSPATR(HI)
3800      A                                    4 38'ON HAND' DSPATR(HI)
3900      A                                    4 49'ON ORDER' DSPATR(HI)
4000      A                                    4 59'ALLOCATED' DSPATR(HI)
4100      A                                    4 70'AVG COST' DSPATR(HI)
4200
4300         * Command record....
4400      A         R CMDRECORD
4500      A  70                             13  1'*NO RECORDS IN DATA FILE'
4600      A                                           DSPATR(HI)
4700      A                                    16 32'ENTER TO CONTINUE' DSPATR(HI)
                       * * * * *  E N D   O F   S O U R C E  * * * * *
```

Compiled Program Listing:

```
Line   <--------------------- Source Specifications --------------------------><---- Comments ----> Do
Number ....1....+....2....+....3....+....4....+....5....+....6....+....7....+....8....+....9....+...10 Num
                         S o u r c e   L i s t i n g
    1 * Inquiry processing with a subfile...
    2 FPa161sf   CF  E              WORKSTN SFILE(Sfrecord:Sfrrno)
      *-----------------------------------------------------------------------------------------*
      *                            RPG name          External name                              *
      * File name. . . . . . . . :  PA161SF          STAN/PA161SF                                *
      * Record format(s) . . . . :  PROMPT           PROMPT                                      *
      *                             SFRECORD         SFRECORD                                    *
      *                             CTRLRECORD       CTRLRECORD                                  *
      *                             CMDRECORD        CMDRECORD                                   *
      *-----------------------------------------------------------------------------------------*

    3 FPa161p    IF  E          K DISK
    4
      *-----------------------------------------------------------------------------------------*
      *                            RPG name          External name                              *
      * File name. . . . . . . . :  PA161P           STAN/PA161P                                 *
      * Record format(s) . . . . :  PA161PR          PA161PR                                     *
      *-----------------------------------------------------------------------------------------*

    5 DSfrrno           S          4 0                            subfile rcrd counter
    6
    7=IPROMPT
      *-----------------------------------------------------------------------------------------*
      * RPG record format  . . . . :  PROMPT                                                     *
      * External format  . . . . . :  PROMPT : STAN/PA161SF                                      *
      *-----------------------------------------------------------------------------------------*

    8=I                              A     1    1  *IN03                        EOJ
    9=I                              A     2    6  PART#
   10=ISFRECORD
      *-----------------------------------------------------------------------------------------*
      * RPG record format  . . . . :  SFRECORD                                                   *
      * External format  . . . . . :  SFRECORD : STAN/PA161SF                                    *
      *-----------------------------------------------------------------------------------------*

   11=I                              A     1    5  PARTNO
   12=I                              A     6   25  PARTNAME
   13=I                              S    26   31  0AMTONHAND
   14=I                              S    32   37  0AMTONORDER
   15=I                              S    38   43  0AMTALCATED
   16=I                              S    44   50 2AVGCOST
   17=ICTRLRECORD
      *-----------------------------------------------------------------------------------------*
      * RPG record format  . . . . :  CTRLRECORD                                                 *
      * External format  . . . . . :  CTRLRECORD : STAN/PA161SF                                  *
      *-----------------------------------------------------------------------------------------*

   18=ICMDRECORD
      *-----------------------------------------------------------------------------------------*
      * RPG record format  . . . . :  CMDRECORD                                                  *
```

```
        * External format  . . . . : CMDRECORD : STAN/PA161SF              *
        *-------------------------------------------------------------------*
     19=IPA161PR
        *-------------------------------------------------------------------*
        * RPG record format  . . . . : PA161PR                              *
        * External format  . . . . . : PA161PR : STAN/PA161P               *
        *-------------------------------------------------------------------*
     20=I                       A    1    5 PARTNO
     21=I                       A    6   25 PARTNAME
     22=I                       P   26   29 OAMTONHAND
     23=I                       P   30   33 OAMTONORDER
     24=I                       P   34   37 2AVGCOST
     25=I                       P   38   41 OAMTALCATED
     26=I                       P   42   45 OEOQ
     27=I                       P   46   49 OSAFTYSTOCK
     28=I                       P   50   51 OLEADTIME
     29=I                       A   52   54 WARELOCATN
     30 C           EXFMT    Prompt                         display prompt scrn
     31 C           DOW      *IN03 = *OFF                   dow ind 30 is off    B01
     32 C           EVAL     *IN80 = *ON                    sfl clear control    01
     33 C           WRITE    CtrlRecord                     clear subfile        01
     34 C           EVAL     *IN80 = *OFF                   turn off indicator   01
     35 C           EVAL     Sfrrno = *ZERO                 initialize counter   01
     36 C           SETOFF                        7071--    turn off program ind 01
     37 C    Part#  SETLL    Pa161p                         positn to = or > key 01
     38 C           READ     Pa161p                 ----70  read a pf record     01
     39
     40  * If one or more records are stored in the physical file, load the
     41  * subfile until end of the physical file is read or subfile is full..
     42
     43 C           IF       *IN70 = *OFF                   no pf record test    B02
     44 C           DOW      *IN71 = *OFF                   sf load control      B03
     45 C           EVAL     Sfrrno = Sfrrno + 1            increment counter    03
     46 C           WRITE    SfRecord               ----71  write rcd to subfile 03
     47 C           IF       *IN71 = *OFF                   subfile full?        B04
     48 C           READ     Pa161p                 ----71  read next pf record  04
     49 C           ENDIF                                   end inner IF group   E04
     50 C           ENDDO                                   end inner dow group  E03
     51 C           ENDIF                                   end outer dow group  E02
     52
     53  * Display subfile or message if no records in the physical file...
     54
     55 C           WRITE    CmdRecord                      display constants    01
     56 C           EVAL     *IN81 = *ON                    turn on display ind  01
     57 C           EXFMT    CtrlRecord                     dsp sf & constants   01
     58 C           EVAL     *IN81 = *OFF                   turn off display ind 01
     59 C           EXFMT    Prompt                         dsp prompt screen    01
     60 C           ENDDO                                   end outer dow group  E01
     61
     62 C           EVAL     *INLR = *ON                    end program
     63=OPROMPT
        *-------------------------------------------------------------------*
        * RPG record format  . . . . : PROMPT                               *
        * External format  . . . . . : PROMPT : STAN/PA161SF               *
        *-------------------------------------------------------------------*
     64=OSFRECORD
        *-------------------------------------------------------------------*
        * RPG record format  . . . . : SFRECORD                             *
        * External format  . . . . . : SFRECORD : STAN/PA161SF             *
        *-------------------------------------------------------------------*
     65=O             PARTNO           5A CHAR       5
     66=O             PARTNAME        25A CHAR      20
     67=O             AMTONHAND       31S ZONE     6,0
     68=O             AMTONORDER      37S ZONE     6,0
     69=O             AMTALCATED      43S ZONE     6,0
     70=O             AVGCOST         50S ZONE     7,2
     71=OCTRLRECORD
        *-------------------------------------------------------------------*
        * RPG record format  . . . . : CTRLRECORD                           *
        * External format  . . . . . : CTRLRECORD : STAN/PA161SF           *
        *-------------------------------------------------------------------*
     72=O             *IN80            1A CHAR       1
     73=O             *IN81            2A CHAR       1
     74=OCMDRECORD
```

```
*-----------------------------------------------------------------*
* RPG record format . . . . :  CMDRECORD                          *
* External format . . . . . :  CMDRECORD : STAN/PA161SF           *
*-----------------------------------------------------------------*
  75=0                      *IN70            1A CHAR          1
    * * * *  E N D   O F   S O U R C E  * * * *
```

PROMPT record display (with response entered):

```
 2/25/98              PARTS INVENTORY MASTER INQUIRY


         ENTER PART NO: A2345




                 F3 - EOJ           ENTER - TO DISPLAY
```

Subfile display (first page):

```
 11:13:50            PARTS INVENTORY MASTER INQUIRY           2/25/98


    PART#        PART NAME       ON HAND   ON ORDER  ALLOCATED  AVG COST

    A2345     AC SPARK PLUGS          0     18,000     5,000      .75
    B6789     FRAM OIL FILTRS     4,000      1,200       480     3.25
    C5555     POINT SETS            600          0         0     8.50
    D9876     LOCKING GAS CAP        24         12        12     4.99
    E3459     LIQUID CAR WASH       360        120       480     1.79   +




                    ENTER TO CONTINUE
```

Subfile display (second page):

```
 11:13:50            PARTS INVENTORY MASTER INQUIRY           2/25/98


    PART#        PART NAME       ON HAND   ON ORDER  ALLOCATED  AVG COST

    E4555     TURTLE WAX          1,200        480       900     2.36
    F6666     CHAMOIS (LARGE)       600        120       240     3.97
    G7800     ARMOR ALL           2,800        840     1,400     2.19
    H1000     NO TOUCH FOAM       1,350        360       800     2.75
    H2100     GAS LINE AF         4,000      1,200     3,000      .51




                    ENTER TO CONTINUE
```

Programming Assignment 16-2: UPDATE PROCESSING WITH A SUBFILE

Notes to the Instructor:

1. Display file includes four record formats: a prompt screen to enter the beginning part number, subfile record format, subfile control record format, and a command line record format.

2. Subfile record fields are defined as **B** (input/output) usage. Fields must be defined with names different than the physical file's. **REFFLD** keyword is used in example to access the same field attributes.

3. Because the program supports update maintenance, the physical field values must be moved to separately defined subfile fields before display of the subfile and then after any subfile values are updated, from subfile fields to physical file's fields before the physical file's record is updated.

Display File Listing:

```
                              Data Description Source
SEQNBR  *...+....1....+....2....+....3....+....4....+....5....+....6....+....7....+....8
  100    A                                   REF(STAN/PA161P)
  200    A                                   PRINT
  300    A                                   CHGINPDFT(RI)
  400    A          R PROMPT
  500    A                                   CA03(03 'EOJ')
  600    A                                 1  2DATE EDTCDE(Y)
  700    A                                 1 26'PARTS INVENTORY MASTER UPDATE'
  800    A                                   DSPATR(HI UL)
  900    A                                 4 10'ENTER PART NO:' DSPATR(HI)
 1000    A          PART#       5  I  4 26
 1100    A                                 8 20'F3-EOJ' DSPATR(HI)
 1200    A                                 8 39'ENTER - TO DISPLAY' DSPATR(HI)
 1300
 1400       * Define subfile record....
 1500    A          R SFRECORD               SFL
 1600    A            SARTNO    R    B  6  3REFFLD(PARTNO) DSPATR(PR)
 1700    A            SARTNAME  R    B  6 12REFFLD(PARTNAME) DSPATR(PC)
 1800    A            SMTONHAND R    B  6 39REFFLD(AMTONHAND)
 1900    A            SMTONORDERR    B  6 50REFFLD(AMTONORDER)
 2000    A            SMTALCATEDR    B  6 60REFFLD(AMTALCATED)
 2100    A            SVGCOST   R    B  6 68REFFLD(AVGCOST)
 2200
 2300       * Define subfile control record....
 2400    A          R CTRLRECORD             SFLCTL(SFRECORD)
 2500    A                                   SFLSIZ(10)
 2600    A                                   SFLPAG(5)
 2700    A 80                                SFLCLR
 2800    A 81                                SFLDSP
 2900    A 81                                SFLDSPCTL
 3000    A 81                                SFLEND
 3100    A                                   OVERLAY
 3200    A                                   CA05(05 'IGNORE UPDATE')
 3300    A                                 1  2TIME DSPATR(HI)
 3400    A                                 1 26'PARTS INVENTORY MASTER UPDATE'
 3500    A                                   DSPATR(HI UL)
 3600    A                                 1 73DATE EDTCDE(Y) DSPATR(HI)
 3700    A                                 4  3'PART#' DSPATR(HI)
 3800    A                                 4 17'PART NAME' DSPATR(HI)
 3900    A                                 4 38'ON HAND' DSPATR(HI)
 4000    A                                 4 49'ON ORDER' DSPATR(HI)
 4100    A                                 4 59'ALLOCATED' DSPATR(HI)
 4200    A                                 4 70'AVG COST' DSPATR(HI)
 4300
 4400       * Command record....
 4500    A          R CMDRECORD
 4600    A 70                             13  1'*NO RECORDS IN DATA FILE'
 4700    A                                   DSPATR(HI)
 4800    A                                16 20'ENTER TO UPDATE' DSPATR( HI)
 4900    A                                16 49'F5-IGNORE UPDATE' DSPATR(HI)
                   * * * * *  E N D   O F   S O U R C E  * * * *
```

Compile Program Listing:

```
Line------------------------ Source Specifications --------------------------><---- Comments ----> Do
Number ....1....+....2....+....3....+....4....+....5....+....6....+....7....+....8....+....9....+...10 Num
                          S o u r c e   L i s t i n g
   1 * Update processing with a subfile...
   2 FPa162sf   CF  E              WORKSTN SFILE(Sfrecord:Sfrrno)
     *-------------------------------------------------------------------------------*
     *                              RPG name            External name                *
     * File name. . . . . . . . :   PA162SF            STAN/PA162SF                   *
     * Record format(s) . . . . :   PROMPT             PROMPT                         *
     *                              SFRECORD           SFRECORD                       *
     *                              CTRLRECORD         CTRLRECORD                      *
     *                              CMDRECORD          CMDRECORD                       *
     *-------------------------------------------------------------------------------*
   3 FPa161p    UF  E          K DISK
   4
     *-------------------------------------------------------------------------------*
     *                              RPG name            External name                *
     * File name. . . . . . . . :   PA161P             STAN/PA161P                    *
     * Record format(s) . . . . :   PA161PR            PA161PR                        *
     *-------------------------------------------------------------------------------*
   5 DSfrrno         S         4 0                      subfile rcrd counter
   6
   7=IPROMPT
     *-------------------------------------------------------------------------------*
     * RPG record format . . . . :  PROMPT                                           *
     * External format . . . . . :  PROMPT : STAN/PA162SF                            *
     *-------------------------------------------------------------------------------*
   8=I                          A     1    1 *IN03                   EOJ
   9=I                          A     2    6 PART#
  10=ISFRECORD
     *-------------------------------------------------------------------------------*
     * RPG record format . . . . :  SFRECORD                                         *
     * External format . . . . . :  SFRECORD : STAN/PA162SF                          *
     *-------------------------------------------------------------------------------*
  11=I                          A     1    5 SARTNO
  12=I                          A     6   25 SARTNAME
  13=I                          S    26   31 OSMTONHAND
  14=I                          S    32   37 OSMTONORDER
  15=I                          S    38   43 OSMTALCATED
  16=I                          S    44   50 2SVGCOST
  17=ICTRLRECORD
     *-------------------------------------------------------------------------------*
     * RPG record format . . . . :  CTRLRECORD                                       *
     * External format . . . . . :  CTRLRECORD : STAN/PA162SF                        *
     *-------------------------------------------------------------------------------*
  18=I                          A     1    1 *IN05                   IGNORE UPDATE
  19=ICMDRECORD                                                      IGNORE UPDATE
     *-------------------------------------------------------------------------------*
     * RPG record format . . . . :  CMDRECORD                                        *
     * External format . . . . . :  CMDRECORD : STAN/PA162SF                         *
     *-------------------------------------------------------------------------------*
  20=IPA161PR                                                        IGNORE UPDATE
     *-------------------------------------------------------------------------------*
     * RPG record format . . . . :  PA161PR                                          *
     * External format . . . . . :  PA161PR : STAN/PA161P                            *
     *-------------------------------------------------------------------------------*
  21=I                          A     1    5 PARTNO
  22=I                          A     6   25 PARTNAME
  23=I                          P    26   29 OAMTONHAND
  24=I                          P    30   33 OAMTONORDER
  25=I                          P    34   37 2AVGCOST
  26=I                          P    38   41 OAMTALCATED
  27=I                          P    42   45 OEOQ
  28=I                          P    46   49 OSAFTYSTOCK
  29=I                          P    50   51 OLEADTIME
  30=I                          A    52   54 WARELOCATN
  31 C             EXFMT    Prompt                        display prompt scrn
  32 C             DOW      *IN03 = *OFF                  dow ind 30 is off    B01
  33 C             EVAL     *IN80 = *ON                   sfl clear control     01
  34 C             WRITE    CtrlRecord                    clear subfile         01
  35 C             EVAL     *IN80 = *OFF                  turn off indicator    01
  36 C             EVAL     Sfrrno = *ZERO                initialize counter    01
  37 C             SETOFF                        707172   turn off program ind  01
```

```
38 C      Part#        SETLL      Pa161p                              positn to = or > key  01
39 C                   READ       Pa161p                    ----70    read a pf record      01
40
41 * If one or more records are stored in the physical file, load the
42 * subfile until end of the physical file is read or subfile is full..
43
44 C                   IF         *IN70 = *OFF                        no pf record test     B02
45 C                   DOW        *IN71 = *OFF                        sf load control       B03
46 C                   EXSR       Pf2Sf                               branch to subroutine  03
47 C                   EVAL       Sfrrno = Sfrrno + 1                 increment counter     03
48 C                   WRITE      SfRecord                  ----71    write rcd to subfile  03
49 C                   IF         *IN71 = *OFF                        subfile full?         B04
50 C                   READ       Pa161p                    ----71    read next pf record   04
51 C                   ENDIF                                          end inner IF group    E04
52 C                   ENDDO                                          end inner dow group   E03
53 C                   ENDIF                                          end outer dow group   E02
54
55 * Display subfile or message if no records in the physical file...
56
57 C                   WRITE      CmdRecord                           display constants     01
58 C                   EVAL       *IN81 = *ON                         turn on display ind   01
59 C                   EXFMT      CtrlRecord                          dsp sf & constants    01
60 C                   EVAL       *IN81 = *OFF                        turn off display ind  01
61
62 * Update physical file record(s) with modified subfile record(s).
63
64 C                   DOW        *IN72 = *OFF AND *IN70 = *OFF        end of sf and pf?     B02
65 C                   READC      SfRecord                  ----72    read changed sf recd  02
66 C                   IF         *IN72 = *ON                         sf at end?            B03
67 C                   LEAVE                                          exit dow group        03
68 C                   ENDIF                                          end IF group          E03
69
70 * Update physical file with changed subfile records...
71
72 C      SartNo       CHAIN      Pa161p                    99----    get pf record         02
73 C                   IF         *IN99 = *ON                         pf record not found?  B03
74 C                   LEAVE                                          exit dow group        03
75 C                   ENDIF                                          end IF group          E03
76 C                   EXSR       Sf2Pf                               branch to subroutine  02
77 C                   UPDATE     Pa161pr                                                   02
78 C                   ENDDO                                          end inner dow group   E02
79
80 C                   EXFMT      Prompt                              dsp prompt screen     01
81 C                   ENDDO                                          end outer dow group   E01
82
83 C                   EVAL       *INLR = *ON                         end program
84
85 * Move physical file field values to display file fields....
86
87 C      Pf2Sf        BEGSR                                          begin subroutine
88 C                   EVAL       Sartno = Partno                     from pf to df fields
89 C                   EVAL       SartName = PartName                 move pf to df fields
90 C                   EVAL       SmtOnHand = AmtOnHand               move pf to df fields
91 C                   EVAL       SmtOnOrder = AmtOnOrder             move df to pf field
92 C                   EVAL       SmtAlCated = AmtAlCated             move pf to df field
93 C                   EVAL       SvgCost = AvgCost                   move pf to df field
94 C                   ENDSR                                          end subroutine
95
96 * Move display file field values to physical file fields....
97
98 C      Sf2Pf        BEGSR                                          begin subroutine
99 C                   EVAL       Partno = Sartno                     from pf to df fields
100 C                  EVAL       PartName = SartName                 move pf to df fields
101 C                  EVAL       AmtOnHand = SmtOnHand               move pf to df fields
102 C                  EVAL       AmtOnOrder = SmtOnOrder             move df to pf field
103 C                  EVAL       AmtAlCated = SmtAlCated             move pf to df field
104 C                  EVAL       AvgCost = SvgCost                   move pf to df field
105 C                  ENDSR                                          end subroutine
106=OPROMPT
    *-------------------------------------------------------------------------*
    * RPG record format  . . . . :  PROMPT                                    *
    * External format  . . . . . :  PROMPT : STAN/PA162SF                     *
    *-------------------------------------------------------------------------*
107=OSFRECORD
```

```
    *-------------------------------------------------------------------------*
    * RPG record format  . . . . :  SFRECORD                                  *
    * External format  . . . . . :  SFRECORD : STAN/PA162SF                   *
      *-----------------------------------------------------------------------*
108=O                        SARTNO         5A CHAR        5
109=O                        SARTNAME      25A CHAR       20
110=O                        SMTONHAND     31S ZONE        6,0
111=O                        SMTONORDER    37S ZONE        6,0
112=O                        SMTALCATED    43S ZONE        6,0
113=O                        SVGCOST       50S ZONE        7,2
114=OCTRLRECORD
    * External format  . . . . . :  CTRLRECORD : STAN/PA162SF                 *
      *-----------------------------------------------------------------------*
115=O                        *IN80          1A CHAR        1
116=O                        *IN81          2A CHAR        1
117=OCMDRECORD
      *-----------------------------------------------------------------------*
    * RPG record format  . . . . :  CMDRECORD                                 *
    * External format  . . . . . :  CMDRECORD : STAN/PA162SF                  *
      *-----------------------------------------------------------------------*
118=O                        *IN70          1A CHAR        1
119=OPA161PR
      *-----------------------------------------------------------------------*
    * RPG record format  . . . . :  PA161PR                                   *
    * External format  . . . . . :  PA161PR : STAN/PA161P                     *
      *-----------------------------------------------------------------------*
120=O                        PARTNO         5A CHAR        5
121=O                        PARTNAME      25A CHAR       20
122=O                        AMTONHAND     29P PACK        6,0
123=O                        AMTONORDER    33P PACK        6,0
124=O                        AVGCOST       37P PACK        7,2
125=O                        AMTALCATED    41P PACK        6,0
126=O                        EOQ           45P PACK        6,0
127=O                        SAFTYSTOCK    49P PACK        6,0
128=O                        LEADTIME      51P PACK        3,0
129=O                        WARELOCATN    54A CHAR        3
     * * * *  E N D   O F   S O U R C E  * * * *
```

PROMPT record display (with response entered):

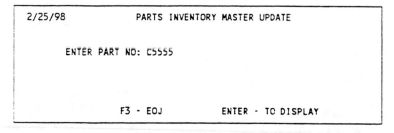

```
 ┌─────────────────────────────────────────────────────────────┐
 │ 2/25/98           PARTS INVENTORY MASTER UPDATE               │
 │                                                               │
 │                                                               │
 │      ENTER PART NO: C5555                                     │
 │                                                               │
 │                                                               │
 │                                                               │
 │                                                               │
 │           F3 - EOJ            ENTER - TO DISPLAY              │
 └─────────────────────────────────────────────────────────────┘
```

<u>Subfile display (before update)</u>:

```
 ┌───────────────────────────────────────────────────────────────────┐
 │ 13:10:51          PARTS INVENTORY MASTER UPDATE           2/25/98   │
 │                                                                     │
 │ PART#      PART NAME        ON HAND   ON ORDER  ALLOCATED  AVG COST │
 │                                                                     │
 │ C5555   POINT SETS            600                            850    │
 │ D9876   LOCKING GAS CAP        24        12        12        499    │
 │ E3459   LIQUID CAR WASH       360       120       480        179  - │
 │ E4555   TURTLE WAX           1200       480       900        236    │
 │ F6666   CHAMOIS (LARGE)       600       120       240        397  + │
 │                                                                     │
 │                                                                     │
 │                                                                     │
 │                                                                     │
 │        ENTER TO UPDATE              F5 - IGNORE UPDATE              │
 └───────────────────────────────────────────────────────────────────┘
```

Subfile display (after update):

```
| 13:10:51          PARTS INVENTORY MASTER UPDATE            1/25/96 |
|                                                                    |
|  PART#        PART NAME        ON HAND   ON ORDER ALLOCATED AVG COST|
|                                                                    |
|  C5555   MICROCOMPUTER           600       100              850    |
|  D9876   LOCKING GAS CAP          24        12        12    499    |
|  E3459   LIQUID CAR WASH         360       120       480    179    |
|  E4555   TURTLE WAX             1200       480       900    236    |
|  F6666   CHAMOIS (LARGE)         600       120       240    397  + |
|                                                                    |
|                                                                    |
|                                                                    |
|              ENTER TO UPDATE            F5 - IGNORE UPDATE          |
```

Programming Assignment 16-3: LOGICAL DELETION WITH A SUBFILE

Notes to the Instructor:

1. Display file includes four record formats: a prompt screen to enter the beginning part number, subfile record format, subfile control record format, and a command line record format.

2. In the subfile record format, note that the SPARTNO field is protected (**DSPART(PR)**) and is specified with a **B** (input/output) usage. The cursor is positioned at the PARTNAME field (**DSPATR(PC)**) which is also defined with a **B** usage.

3. In order for the select record(s) to be logically deleted, one character in the PARTNAME field value must be changed. When the program executes logical deletion processing, the **READC** operation will identify only those that has been changed by the operator. Otherwise, all of the records in the subfile would be deleted.

Display File Listing:

```
                              Data Description Source
SEQNBR *...+....1....+....2....+....3....+....4....+....5....+....6....+....7....+....8
  100   A                               REF(STAN/PA161P)
  200   A                               PRINT
  300   A                               CHGINPDFT(RI)
  400   A         R PROMPT
  500   A                               CA03(03 'EOJ')
  600   A                             1  2DATE EDTCDE(Y)
  700   A                             1 26'PARTS INVENTORY MASTER DELETION'
  800   A                               DSPATR(HI UL)
  900   A                             4 10'ENTER PART NO:' DSPATR(HI)
 1000   A           PART#      5   I  4 26
 1100   A                             8 20'F3-EOJ' DSPATR(HI)
 1200   A                             8 39'ENTER - TO DISPLAY' DSPATR(HI)
 1300
 1400     * Define subfile record....
 1500   A         R SFRECORD            SFL
 1600   A           SARTNO     R    B  6  3REFFLD(PARTNO) DSPATR(PR)
 1700   A           SARTNAME   R    B  6 12REFFLD(PARTNAME) DSPATR(PC)
 1800   A           SMTONHAND  R    B  6 39REFFLD(AMTONHAND)
 1900   A           SMTONORDERR     B  6 50REFFLD(AMTONORDER)
 2000   A           SMTALCATEDR     B  6 60REFFLD(AMTALCATED)
```

```
2100    A           SVGCOST    R     B  6 68REFFLD(AVGCOST)
2200
2300       * Define subfile control record....
2400    A           R CTRLRECORD           SFLCTL(SFRECORD)
2500    A                                  SFLSIZ(10)
2600    A                                  SFLPAG(5)
2700    A  80                              SFLCLR
2800    A  81                              SFLDSP
2900    A  81                              SFLDSPCTL
3000    A  81                              SFLEND
3100    A                                  OVERLAY
3200    A                                  CA05(05 'IGNORE DELETION')
3300    A                            1  2TIME DSPATR(HI)
3400    A                            1 26'PARTS INVENTORY MASTER DELETION'
3500    A                               DSPATR(HI UL)
3600    A                            1 73DATE EDTCDE(Y) DSPATR(HI)
3700    A                            4  3'PART#' DSPATR(HI)
3800    A                            4 17'PART NAME' DSPATR(HI)
3900    A                            4 38'ON HAND' DSPATR(HI)
4000    A                            4 49'ON ORDER' DSPATR(HI)
4100    A                            4 59'ALLOCATED' DSPATR(HI)
4200    A                            4 70'AVG COST' DSPATR(HI)
4300
4400       * Command record....
4500    A           R CMDRECORD
4600    A  70                        13  1'*NO RECORDS IN DATA FILE'
4700    A                               DSPATR(HI)
4800    A                            16 20'ENTER TO DELETE' DSPATR(  HI)
4900    A                            16 49'F5-IGNORE DELETE' DSPATR(HI)
              * * * * *  E N D   O F   S O U R C E   * * * * *
```

Compile Program Listing:

```
Line    <--------------------- Source Specifications ---------------------><---- Comments ----> Do
Number  ....1....+....2....+....3....+....4....+....5....+....6....+....7....+....8....+....9....+...10 Num
                    S o u r c e   L i s t i n g
    1 * Deletion processing with a subfile...
    2 FPa163sf   CF   E           WORKSTN SFILE(Sfrecord:Sfrrno)
      *--------------------------------------------------------------------------*
      *                           RPG name        External name                  *
      * File name. . . . . . . . : PA163SF        STAN/PA163SF                   *
      * Record format(s) . . . . : PROMPT         PROMPT                         *
      *                            SFRECORD        SFRECORD                       *
      *                            CTRLRECORD      CTRLRECORD                     *
      *                            CMDRECORD       CMDRECORD                      *
      *--------------------------------------------------------------------------*
    3 FPa161p    UF   E           K DISK
    4
      *--------------------------------------------------------------------------*
      *                           RPG name        External name                  *
      * File name. . . . . . . . : PA161P         STAN/PA161P                    *
      * Record format(s) . . . . : PA161PR        PA161PR                        *
      *--------------------------------------------------------------------------*
    5 DSfrrno         S         4  0                        subfile rcrd counter
    6
    7=IPROMPT
      *--------------------------------------------------------------------------*
      * RPG record format . . . . : PROMPT                                       *
      * External format  . . . . . : PROMPT : STAN/PA163SF                       *
      *--------------------------------------------------------------------------*
    8=I                           A   1   1 *IN03               EOJ
    9=I                           A   2   6 PART#
   10=ISFRECORD
      *--------------------------------------------------------------------------*
      * RPG record format . . . . : SFRECORD                                     *
      * External format  . . . . . : SFRECORD : STAN/PA163SF                     *
      *--------------------------------------------------------------------------*
   11=I                           A   1   5 SARTNO
   12=I                           A   6  25 SARTNAME
   13=I                           S  26  31 OSMTONHAND
   14=I                           S  32  37 OSMTONORDER
   15=I                           S  38  43 OSMTALCATED
   16=I                           S  44  50 2SVGCOST
```

```
17=ICTRLRECORD
    *------------------------------------------------------------------------*
    * RPG record format  . . . . :  CTRLRECORD                               *
    * External format  . . . . . :  CTRLRECORD : STAN/PA163SF                *
    *------------------------------------------------------------------------*
18=I                          A    1    1 *IN05                IGNORE DELETION
19=ICMDRECORD                                                  IGNORE DELETION
    *------------------------------------------------------------------------*
    * RPG record format  . . . . :  CMDRECORD                                *
    * External format  . . . . . :  CMDRECORD : STAN/PA163SF                 *
    *------------------------------------------------------------------------*
20=IPA161PR                                                    IGNORE DELETION
    *------------------------------------------------------------------------*
    * RPG record format  . . . . :  PA161PR                                  *
    * External format  . . . . . :  PA161PR : STAN/PA161P                    *
    *------------------------------------------------------------------------*
21=I                          A    1    5 PARTNO
22=I                          A    6   25 PARTNAME
23=I                          P   26   29 OAMTONHAND
24=I                          P   30   33 OAMTONORDER
25=I                          P   34   37 2AVGCOST
26=I                          P   38   41 OAMTALCATED
27=I                          P   42   45 OEOQ
28=I                          P   46   49 OSAFTYSTOCK
29=I                          P   50   51 OLEADTIME
30=I                          A   52   54 WARELOCATN
31 C             EXFMT     Prompt                        display prompt scrn
32 C             DOW       *IN03 = *OFF                  dow ind 30 is off    B01
33 C             EVAL      *IN80 = *ON                   sfl clear control    01
34 C             WRITE     CtrlRecord                    clear subfile        01
35 C             EVAL      *IN80 = *OFF                  turn off indicator   01
36 C             EVAL      Sfrrno = *ZERO                initialize counter   01
37 C             SETOFF                       707172     turn off program ind 01
38 C      Part#  SETLL     Pa161p                        positn to = or > key 01
39 C             READ      Pa161p              ----70    read a pf record     01
40
41  * If one or more records are stored in the physical file, load the
42  * subfile until end of the physical file is read or subfile is full..
43
44 C             IF        *IN70 = *OFF                  no pf record test    B02
45 C             DOW       *IN71 = *OFF                  sf load control      B03
46 C             EXSR      Pf2Sf                         branch to subroutine 03
47 C             EVAL      Sfrrno = Sfrrno + 1           increment counter    03
48 C             WRITE     SfRecord            ----71    write rcd to subfile 03
49 C             IF        *IN71 = *OFF                  subfile full?        B04
50 C             READ      Pa161p              ----71    read next pf record  04
51 C             ENDIF                                   end inner IF group   E04
52 C             ENDDO                                   end inner dow group  E03
53 C             ENDIF                                   end outer dow group  E02
54
55  * Display subfile or message if no records in the physical file...
56
57 C             WRITE     CmdRecord                     display constants    01
58 C             EVAL      *IN81 = *ON                   turn on display ind  01
59 C             EXFMT     CtrlRecord                    dsp sf & constants   01
60 C             EVAL      *IN81 = *OFF                  turn off display ind 01
61
62  * Delete physical file record(s) with modified subfile record(s).
63
64 C             DOW       *IN72 = *OFF AND *IN70 = *OFF end of sf and pf?    B02
65 C             READC     SfRecord            ----72    read changed sf recd 02
66 C             IF        *IN72 = *ON                   sf at end?           B03
67 C             LEAVE                                   exit dow group       03
68 C             ENDIF                                   end IF group         E03
69
70  * Delete physical file record with changed subfile record(s)...
71
72 C      SartNo CHAIN     Pa161p              99----    get pf record        02
73 C             IF        *IN99 = *ON                   pf record not found? B03
74 C             LEAVE                                   exit dow group       03
75 C             ENDIF                                   end IF group         E03
76 C             EXSR      Sf2Pf                         branch to subroutine 02
77 C             DELETE    Pa161pr                       delete pf record     02
78 C             ENDDO                                   end inner dow group  E02
```

```
79
80 C                   EXFMT     Prompt                              dsp prompt screen     01
81 C                   ENDDO                                         end outer dow group  E01
82
83 C                   EVAL      *INLR = *ON                         end program
84
85 * Move physical file field values to display file fields....
86
87 C     Pf2Sf         BEGSR                                         begin subroutine
88 C                   EVAL      Sartno = Partno                     from pf to df fields
89 C                   EVAL      SartName = PartName                 move pf to df fields
90 C                   EVAL      SmtOnHand = AmtOnHand               move pf to df fields
91 C                   EVAL      SmtOnOrder = AmtOnOrder             move df to pf field
92 C                   EVAL      SmtAlCated = AmtAlCated             move pf to df field
93 C                   EVAL      SvgCost = AvgCost                   move pf to df field
94 C                   ENDSR                                         end subroutine
95
96 * Move display file field values to physical file fields....
97
98 C     Sf2Pf         BEGSR                                         begin subroutine
99 C                   EVAL      Partno = Sartno                     from pf to df fields
100 C                  EVAL      PartName = SartName                 move pf to df fields
101 C                  EVAL      AmtOnHand = SmtOnHand               move pf to df fields
102 C                  EVAL      AmtOnOrder = SmtOnOrder             move df to pf field
103 C                  EVAL      AmtAlCated = SmtAlCated             move pf to df field
104 C                  EVAL      AvgCost = SvgCost                   move pf to df field
105 C                  ENDSR                                         end subroutine
106=OPROMPT
    *-----------------------------------------------------------------------------------*
    * RPG record format  . . . . : PROMPT                                               *
    * External format  . . . . . : PROMPT : STAN/PA163SF                                *
    *-----------------------------------------------------------------------------------*
107=OSFRECORD
    *-----------------------------------------------------------------------------------*
    * RPG record format  . . . . : SFRECORD                                             *
    * External format  . . . . . : SFRECORD : STAN/PA163SF                              *
    *-----------------------------------------------------------------------------------*
108=O                 SARTNO            5A CHAR       5
109=O                 SARTNAME         25A CHAR      20
110=O                 SMTONHAND        31S ZONE     6,0
111=O                 SMTONORDER       37S ZONE     6,0
112=O                 SMTALCATED       43S ZONE     6,0
113=O                 SVGCOST          50S ZONE     7,2
114=OCTRLRECORD
    *-----------------------------------------------------------------------------------*
    * RPG record format  . . . . : CTRLRECORD                                           *
    * External format  . . . . . : CTRLRECORD : STAN/PA163SF                            *
    *-----------------------------------------------------------------------------------*
115=O                 *IN80             1A CHAR       1
116=O                 *IN81             2A CHAR       1
117=OCMDRECORD
    *-----------------------------------------------------------------------------------*
    * RPG record format  . . . . : CMDRECORD                                            *
    * External format  . . . . . : CMDRECORD : STAN/PA163SF                             *
    *-----------------------------------------------------------------------------------*
118=O                 *IN70             1A CHAR       1
    * * * * *  E N D  O F  S O U R C E  * * * *
```

PROMPT record display (with response entered):

```
 2/28/98            PARTS INVENTORY MASTER DELETION

      ENTER PART NO: D9876




            F3 - EOJ          ENTER - TO DISPLAY
```

Subfile display (before deletion:

```
13:27:51              PARTS INVENTORY MASTER DELETION              2/28/98


  PART#        PART NAME        ON HAND   ON ORDER  ALLOCATED  AVG COST

  D9876    LOCKING GAS CAP      000024    000012    000012   0000499
  E3459    LIQUID CAR WASH      000360    000120    000480   0000179
  E4555    TURTLE WAX           001200    000480    000900   0000236
  F6666    CHAMOIS (LARGE)      000600    000120    000240   0000397
  G7800    ARMOR ALL            002800    000840    001400   0000219   +




            ENTER TO DELETE              F5 - IGNORE DELETE
```

Subfile display (after deletion):

```
13:28:11              PARTS INVENTORY MASTER DELETION              2/28/98


  PART#        PART NAME        ON HAND   ON ORDER  ALLOCATED  AVG COST

  E3459    LIQUID CAR WASH      000360    000120    000480   0000179
  E4555    TURTLE WAX           001200    000480    000900   0000236
  F6666    CHAMOIS (LARGE)      000600    000120    000240   0000397
  G7800    ARMOR ALL            002800    000840    001400   0000219
  H1000    NO TOUCH FOAM        001350    000360    000800   0000275   +




            ENTER TO DELETE              F5 - IGNORE DELETE
```

Note: Record with PART# D9876 was logically deleted.

Programming Assignment 16-4: ADDITION PROCESSING WITH A
                              SUBFILE
Notes to the Instructor:

1. Display file includes four record formats: an entry screen
   to enter adds data, subfile record format, subfile control
   record format, and a command line record format.

2. Subfile record fields are defined as B (input/output) usage.
   Subfile fields are loaded by input from the entry screen and
   then values after review of the subfile display are output
   to the physical file.

3. SFLDROP keyword is included in the subfile's control record
   to support the wrapping of field values. Pressing Command
   Key 8 after the subfile is displayed controls this function.

Display File Listing:

```
                            Data Description Source
SEQNBR   *...+....1....+....2....+....3....+....4....+....5....+....6....+....7....+....8
  100      A                              REF(STAN/PA161P)
  200      A                              PRINT
```

```
 300     A                                          CHGINPDFT(RI)
 400     A                       R ENTRY
 500     A                                          CA03(03 'EOJ')
 600     A                                          CA05(05 'REDISPLAY')
 700     A                                          CA07(07 'END OF SF LOAD')
 800     A                                        1  2DATE EDTCDE(Y) DSPATR(HI)
 900     A                                        1 26'PARTS INVENTORY MASTER ADDITION'
1000     A                                          DSPATR(HI UL)
1100     A                                        3 22'PART NUMBER:' DSPATR(HI)
1200     A          PARTNO     R    I  3 38
1300     A                                        5 22'PART NAME:' DSPATR(HI)
1400     A          PARTNAME   R    I  5 38
1500     A                                        7 22'AMT ON HAND:' DSPATR(HI)
1600     A          AMTONHAND  R    I  7 38
1700     A                                        9 22'AMT ON ORDER:' DSPATR(HI)
1800     A          AMTONORDERR     I  9 38
1900     A                                       11 22'AVG COST:' DSPATR(HI)
2000     A          AVGCOST    R    I 11 38
2100     A                                       13 22'AMT ALLOCATED:' DSPATR(HI)
2200     A          AMTALCATEDR     I 13 38
2300     A                                       15 22'EOQ:' DSPATR(HI)
2400     A          EOQ        R    I 15 38
2500     A                                       17 22'SAFETY STOCK:' DSPATR(HI)
2600     A          SAFTYSTOCKR     I 17 38
2700     A                                       19 22'LEAD TIME:' DSPATR(HI)
2800     A          LEADTIME   R    I 19 38
2900     A                                       19 44'WH LOCATION:' DSPATR(HI)
3000     A          WARELOCATNR     I 19 58
3100     A                                       21 17'F3-EOJ' DSPATR(HI)
3200     A                                       21 27'F5-REDISPLAY' DSPATR(HI)
3300     A                                       21 42'F7-END LOAD' DSPATR(HI)
3400     A                                       22 26'ENTER-LOAD TO SUBFILE' DSPATR(HI)
3500     A        * Define subfile record....
3600     A                       R SFRECORD            SFL
3700     A                                             SFLNXTCHG
3800     A          PARTNO     R    B  6  3
3900     A 99                                          DSPATR(BL)
4000     A          PARTNAME   R    B  6 12
4100     A          AMTONHAND  R    B  6 39
4200     A          AMTONORDERR     B  6 50
4300     A          AMTALCATEDR     B  6 60
4400     A          AVGCOST    R    B  6 70
4500     A          EOQ        R    B  7  2
4600     A          SAFTYSTOCKR     B  7 12
4700     A          LEADTIME   R    B  7 27
4800     A          WARELOCATNR     B  7 40
4900
5000     A        * Define subfile control record....
5100     A                       R CTRLRECORD          SFLCTL(SFRECORD)
5200     A                                             SFLRNA
5300     A                                             SFLSIZ(10)
5400     A                                             SFLPAG(5)
5500     A 80                                          SFLCLR
5600     A 80                                          SFLINZ
5700     A 81                                          SFLDSP
5800     A 81                                          SFLDSPCTL
5900     A 81                                          SFLEND
6000     A                                             SFLDROP(CF08)
6100     A 99                                          SFLMSG('DUPLICATE PART NO' 99)
6200     A                                             OVERLAY
6300     A                                        1  2TIME DSPATR(HI)
6400     A                                        1 26'PARTS INVENTORY MASTER ADDITION'
6500     A                                          DSPATR(HI UL)
6600     A                                        1 73DATE EDTCDE(Y) DSPATR(HI)
6700     A                                        4  3'PART#' DSPATR(HI)
6800     A                                        4 17'PART NAME' DSPATR(HI)
6900     A                                        4 38'ON HAND' DSPATR(HI)
7000     A                                        4 49'ON ORDER' DSPATR(HI)
7100     A                                        4 59'ALLOCATED' DSPATR(HI)
7200     A                                        4 70'AVG COST' DSPATR(HI)
7300     A                                        5  3'EOQ' DSPATR(HI)
7400     A                                        5  9'SAFETY STOCK' DSPATR(HI)
7500     A                                        5 24'LEAD TIME' DSPATR(HI)
7600     A                                        5 36'WH LOCATION' DSPATR(HI)
```

```
7700
7800        * Command record....
7900        A         R CMDRECORD
8000        A                              16 22'ENTER TO ADD RECORDS' DSPATR(HI)
8100        A                              16 45'F8 - TO FOLD' DSPATR(HI)
                 * * * * * E N D   O F   S O U R C E   * * * * *
```

Compiled Program Listing:

```
Line    <--------------------- Source Specifications --------------------------><---- Comments ----> Do
Number  ....1....+....2....+....3....+....4....+....5....+....6....+....7....+....8....+....9....+...10 Num
                        S o u r c e   L i s t i n g
   1  * Addition processing with a subfile...
   2  FPa164sf  CF   E           WORKSTN SFILE(Sfrecord:Sfrrno)
      *-----------------------------------------------------------------------------------------------*
      *                          RPG name              External name                                  *
      * File name. . . . . . . . : PA164SF             STAN/PA164SF                                    *
      * Record format(s) . . . . : ENTRY               ENTRY                                           *
      *                            SFRECORD            SFRECORD                                        *
      *                            CTRLRECORD          CTRLRECORD                                      *
      *                            CMDRECORD           CMDRECORD                                       *
      *-----------------------------------------------------------------------------------------------*
   3  FPa161p    O  A E          K DISK
   4
      *-----------------------------------------------------------------------------------------------*
      *                          RPG name              External name                                  *
      * File name. . . . . . . . : PA161P              STAN/PA161P                                     *
      * Record format(s) . . . . : PA161PR             PA161PR                                         *
      *-----------------------------------------------------------------------------------------------*
   5  DSfrrno         S          4 0                               subfile rcrd counter
   6
   7=IENTRY
      *-----------------------------------------------------------------------------------------------*
      * RPG record format . . . . : ENTRY                                                             *
      * External format . . . . . : ENTRY : STAN/PA164SF                                              *
      *-----------------------------------------------------------------------------------------------*
   8=I                           A    1    1 *IN03                   EOJ
   9=I                           A    2    2 *IN05                   REDISPLAY
  10=I                           A    3    3 *IN07                   END OF SF LOAD
  11=I                           A    4    8 PARTNO
  12=I                           A    9   28 PARTNAME
  13=I                           S   29   34 OAMTONHAND
  14=I                           S   35   40 OAMTONORDER
  15=I                           S   41   47 2AVGCOST
  16=I                           S   48   53 OAMTALCATED
  17=I                           S   54   59 OEOQ
  18=I                           S   60   65 OSAFTYSTOCK
  19=I                           S   66   68 OLEADTIME
  20=I                           A   69   71 WARELOCATN
  21=ISFRECORD
      *-----------------------------------------------------------------------------------------------*
      * RPG record format . . . . : SFRECORD                                                          *
      * External format . . . . . : SFRECORD : STAN/PA164SF                                           *
      *-----------------------------------------------------------------------------------------------*
  22=I                           A    1    5 PARTNO
  23=I                           A    6   25 PARTNAME
  24=I                           S   26   31 OAMTONHAND
  25=I                           S   32   37 OAMTONORDER
  26=I                           S   38   43 OAMTALCATED
  27=I                           S   44   50 2AVGCOST
  28=I                           S   51   56 OEOQ
  29=I                           S   57   62 OSAFTYSTOCK
  30=I                           S   63   65 OLEADTIME
  31=I                           A   66   68 WARELOCATN
  32=ICTRLRECORD
      *-----------------------------------------------------------------------------------------------*
      * RPG record format . . . . : CTRLRECORD                                                        *
      * External format . . . . . : CTRLRECORD : STAN/PA164SF                                         *
      *-----------------------------------------------------------------------------------------------*
  33=I                           A    1    1 *IN99                   DUPLICATE PART NO
  34=ICMDRECORD                                                      DUPLICATE PART NO
      *-----------------------------------------------------------------------------------------------*
      * RPG record format . . . . : CMDRECORD                                                         *
```

```
     * External format . . . . . : CMDRECORD : STAN/PA164SF                          *
     *--------------------------------------------------------------------------------*
 35 C                    DOU       *IN03 = *ON                        dou ind 71 is on    B01
 36
 37  * Load subfile with records entered in Entry display record....
 38 C                    DOW       *IN71 = *OFF                       dow sf is not full  B02
 39 C                    EXFMT     Entry                              display entry screen 02
 40
 41 C        *IN03       CABEQ     *ON          Eoj                   eoj test            02
 42 C        *IN05       CABEQ     *ON          Skip                  redisplay test      02
 43 C                    IF        *IN07 = *ON                        end of sf adds test B03
 44 C                    LEAVE                                        exit dow group      03
 45 C                    ENDIF                                        end if group        E03
 46
 47 C                    EVAL      Sfrrno = Sfrrno + 1                increment counter   02
 48 C                    WRITE     SfRecord                  ----71   load record to sf   02
 49 C        Skip        TAG                                          label for cab instr. 02
 50 C                    ENDDO                                        end dow group       E02
 51
 52  * Display subfile with add records...
 53
 54 C                    WRITE     CmdRecord                          clear subfile       01
 55 C                    EVAL      *IN81 = *ON                        turn on indicator   01
 56 C                    EXFMT     CtrlRecord                         sf clear control    01
 57 C                    EVAL      *IN81 = *OFF                       turn off indicator  01
 58
 59  * Add subfile records to the physical file....
 60
 61 C                    EVAL      Sfrrno = 1                         increment counter   01
 62 C                    READC     SfRecord                  ----72   read changed sf rcd 01
 63
 64 C                    DOW       *IN72 = *OFF                       sf load control     B02
 65 C                    WRITE     pA161PR                   --99--   add record to sf    02
 66 C                    IF        *IN99 = *ON                        duplicate record?   B03
 67  * Highlight duplicate record....
 68 C                    UPDATE    SfRecord                           highlight dup record 03
 69
 70  * Redisplay with error message....User must correct part
 71  * number to continue adds processing....
 72
 73 C                    EVAL      *IN81 = *ON                        turn on display ind 03
 74 C                    EVAL      *IN99 = *ON                        turn on display ind 03
 75 C                    EXFMT     CtrlRecord                         redisplay subfile   03
 76 C                    EVAL      *IN81 = *OFF                       turn on display ind 03
 77 C                    EVAL      *IN99 = *OFF                       turn on display ind 03
 78 C                    EVAL      Sfrrno = Sfrrno + 1                initialize sf countr 03
 79 C                    READC     SfRecord                  ----72   read next sf record 03
 80 C                    ITER                                         turn off error indtr 03
 81 C                    ELSE                                         dsp sf & constants  X03
 82 C                    EVAL      Sfrrno = Sfrrno + 1                initialize sf countr 03
 83 C                    READC     SfRecord                  ----72   read next sf record 03
 84 C                    ENDIF                                        dsp prompt screen   E03
 85
 86 C                    ENDDO                                        end outer dow group E02
 87
 88 C                    EXSR      ClearSR                            branch to subroutine 01
 89 C        Eoj         TAG                                          label to CAB instr. 01
 90 C                    ENDDO                                        end dow group       E01
 91
 92 C                    EVAL      *INLR = *ON                        end program
 93
 94  * Subroutine to clear subfile and initialize record counter....
 95
 96 C        ClearSR     BEGSR                                        begin subroutine
 97 C                    EVAL      *IN80 = *ON                        turn on clear indctr
 98 C                    WRITE     CtrlRecord                         clear subfile
 99 C                    EVAL      *IN80 = *OFF                       turn of indicator
100 C                    EVAL      Sfrrno = *ZERO                     initialize counter
101 C                    SETOFF                                7172-- turn off indicators
102 C                    ENDSR                                        end subroutine
103=OENTRY
     *--------------------------------------------------------------------------------*
     * RPG record format . . . . : ENTRY                                              *
     * External format . . . . . : ENTRY : STAN/PA164SF                              *
```

```
      *------------------------------------------------------------------------------*
   104=OSFRECORD
      *------------------------------------------------------------------------------*
      * RPG record format  . . . . :  SFRECORD                                       *
      * External format  . . . . . :  SFRECORD : STAN/PA164SF                        *
      *------------------------------------------------------------------------------*
   105=O                        *IN99           1A CHAR     1
   106=O                        PARTNO          6A CHAR     5
   107=O                        PARTNAME       26A CHAR    20
   108=O                        AMTONHAND      32S ZONE    6,0
   109=O                        AMTONORDER     38S ZONE    6,0
   110=O                        AMTALCATED     44S ZONE    6,0
   111=O                        AVGCOST        51S ZONE    7,2
   112=O                        EOQ            57S ZONE    6,0
   113=O                        SAFTYSTOCK     63S ZONE    6,0
   114=O                        LEADTIME       66S ZONE    3,0
   115=O                        WARELOCATN     69A CHAR     3
   116=OCTRLRECORD
      *------------------------------------------------------------------------------*
      * RPG record format  . . . . :  CTRLRECORD                                     *
      * External format  . . . . . :  CTRLRECORD : STAN/PA164SF                      *
      *------------------------------------------------------------------------------*
   117=O                        *IN80           1A CHAR     1
   118=O                        *IN81           2A CHAR     1
   119=O                        *IN99           3A CHAR     1           DUPLICATE PART NO
   120=OCMDRECORD
      *------------------------------------------------------------------------------*
      * RPG record format  . . . . :  CMDRECORD                                      *
      * External format  . . . . . :  CMDRECORD : STAN/PA164SF                       *
      *------------------------------------------------------------------------------*
   121=OPA161PR
      *------------------------------------------------------------------------------*
      * RPG record format  . . . . :  PA161PR                                        *
      * External format  . . . . . :  PA161PR : STAN/PA161P                          *
      *------------------------------------------------------------------------------*
   122=O                        PARTNO          5A CHAR     5
   123=O                        PARTNAME       25A CHAR    20
   124=O                        AMTONHAND      29P PACK    6,0
   125=O                        AMTONORDER     33P PACK    6,0
   126=O                        AVGCOST        37P PACK    7,2
   127=O                        AMTALCATED     41P PACK    6,0
   128=O                        EOQ            45P PACK    6,0
   129=O                        SAFTYSTOCK     49P PACK    6,0
   130=O                        LEADTIME       51P PACK    3,0
   131=O                        WARELOCATN     54A CHAR     3
      * * * *  E N D   O F   S O U R C E  * * * *
```

Entry display (with data entered:

```
 3/15/98                PARTS INVENTORY MASTER ADDITION

                PART NUMBER:    A100C

                PART NAME:      PRESTONE DE-ICER

                AMT ON HAND:        C

                AMT ON ORDER:     144

                AVG COST:         259

                AMT ALLOCATED:      O

                EOQ:              144

                SAFETY STOCK:     100

                LEAD TIME:      10   WH LOCATION:


        F3-EOJ    F5-REDISPLAY   F7-END LOAD
                  ENTER-LOAD TO SUBFILE
```

207

Subfile display before F8 is pressed (records folded):

```
16:21:04              PARTS INVENTORY MASTER ADDITION           3/15/98


PART#          PART NAME           ON HAND   ON ORDER  ALLOCATED  AVG COST
EOQ    SAFETY STOCK   LEAD TIME  WH LOCATION

A1000     PRESTONE DE-ICER                     144                  259

C5000     CHAMOIS (LARGE)                      120        12        675

D9876     LOCKING GAS CAP                      144                  115




              ENTER TO ADD RECORDS   F8 - TO FOLD
```

Subfile display after F8 is pressed (records folded):

```
16:21:04              PARTS INVENTORY MASTER ADDITION           3/15/98


PART#          PART NAME           ON HAND   ON ORDER  ALLOCATED  AVG COST
EOQ    SAFETY STOCK   LEAD TIME  WH LOCATION

A1000     PRESTONE DE-ICER                     144                  259
 144         100          10

C5000     CHAMOIS (LARGE)                      120        12        675
 120          24          15

D9876     LOCKING GAS CAP                      144                  115
  24          12          90


              ENTER TO ADD RECORDS   F8 - TO FOLD
```

Programming Assignment 16-5: WINDOWING WITH A SUBFILE

Notes to the Instructor:

1. A second physical file must be created and loaded with
    the given data before this assignment is started.

2. To save time, if assignment 16-1 was completed, a copy may
    be made and modified for this assignment.

3. Refer to the specifications for information about the window
    that must be included in the display file.

4. The RPG IV program is written so that only one record is
    displayed in the subfile. All of the records related to
    that part number are displayed in the window record with
    the roll up key.

Display File Listing:

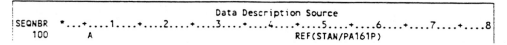

```
                                  Data Description Source
SEQNBR  *...+....1....+....2....+....3....+....4....+....5....+....6....+....7....+....8
  100       A                              REF(STAN/PA161P)
```

```
200      A                               PRINT
300      A                               CHGINPDFT(RI)
301       * Prompt record....
400      A          R PROMPT
500      A                               CA03(03 'EOJ')
600      A                             1  2DATE EDTCDE(Y)
700      A                             1 26'PARTS INVENTORY MASTER INQUIRY'
800      A                               DSPATR(HI UL)
900      A                             4 10'ENTER PART NO:' DSPATR(HI)
1000     A          PART#      5  I   4 26
1001     A 99                            ERRMSG('RECORD NOT FOUND' 99)
1100     A                             8 20'F3-EOJ' DSPATR(HI)
1200     A                             8 39'ENTER - TO DISPLAY' DSPATR(HI)
1300
1301      * Inquiry screen for Pa161p (master file)....
1302     A          R INQRECORD
1303     A                               CF04(04 'DISPLAY WINDOW')
1304     A                             1  2TIME
1305     A                             1 26'PARTS INVENTORY MASTER INQUIRY'
1306     A                               DSPATR(HI UL)
1307     A                             1 73DATE EDTCDE(Y)
1308     A                             4  3'PART#'
1309     A                             4 17'PART NAME'
1310     A                             4 38'ON HAND'
1311     A                             4 49'ON ORDER'
1312     A                             4 59'ALLOCATED'
1313     A                             4 70'AVG COST'
1600     A          PARTNO     R       O  6  3
1700     A          PARTNAME   R       O  6 12
1800     A          AMTONHAND  R       O  6 39EDTCDE(1)
1900     A          AMTONORDERR        O  6 50EDTCDE(1)
2000     A          AMTALCATEDR        O  6 60EDTCDE(1)
2100     A          AVGCOST    R       O  6 68EDTCDE(1)
2101     A                            20 20'ENTER TO CONTINUE' DSPATR(HI)
2102     A                            20 40'F4 - INVOICE WINDOW' DSPATR(HI)
2104     A          R ERRORDSP            OVERLAY
2105     A N98                         22  1'NO INVOICES FOR CUSTOMER'
2106     A                               DSPATR(HI)
2200
2201      * Subfile record for Pa165p (invoices) file....
2202     A          R SFWINDOW            SFL
2203     A          VNAME      15   O  3  3
2204     A          VTEL#      10  00  3 20
2205
2300      * Define subfile control record....
2400     A          R CTRLRECORD          SFLCTL(SFWINDOW)
2401     A                               WINDOW(11 22 6 35)
2402     A                               WDWBORDER((*CHAR '        ') -
2403     A                               (*DSPATR RI))
2500     A                               SFLSIZ(4)
2600     A                               SFLPAG(2)
2700     A 80                            SFLCLR
2800     A 81                            SFLDSP
2900     A 81                            SFLDSPCTL
3000     A 81                            SFLEND
3100     A                               OVERLAY
              * * * * *  E N D   O F   S O U R C E  * * * *
```

Compiled Program Listing:

```
Line     <------------------- Source Specifications ----------------------------><---- Comments ----> Do
Number   ....1....+....2....+....3....+....4....+....5....+....6....+....7....+....8....+....9....+...10 Num
                   S o u r c e    L i s t i n g
    1  * Inquiry processing with a subfile and windowing....
    2 FPa165sf  CF  E          WORKSTN SFILE(Sfwindow:Sfrrno)
    *--------------------------------------------------------------------------------------*
    *                        RPG name          External name                               *
    * File name. . . . . . . . :  PA165SF       STAN/PA165SF                                *
    * Record format(s) . . . . . :  PROMPT       PROMPT                                     *
    *                            INQRECORD     INQRECORD                                     *
    *                            ERRORDSP      ERRORDSP                                      *
    *                            SFWINDOW      SFWINDOW                                      *
```

209

```
     *                                    CTRLRECORD        CTRLRECORD                                *
     *-------------------------------------------------------------------------------------------------*
  3 FPa161p   IF  E       K DISK
     *-------------------------------------------------------------------------------------------------*
     *                                    RPG name           External name                             *
     * File name. . . . . . . . . :       PA161P             STAN/PA161P                                *
     * Record format(s) . . . . . :       PA161PR            PA161PR                                    *
     *-------------------------------------------------------------------------------------------------*
  4 FPa165p   IF  E       K DISK
  5
     *-------------------------------------------------------------------------------------------------*
     *                                    RPG name           External name                             *
     * File name. . . . . . . . . :       PA165P             STAN/PA165P                                *
     * Record format(s) . . . . . :       PA165PR            PA165PR                                    *
     *-------------------------------------------------------------------------------------------------*
  6 DSfrrno         S           4 0                                         subfile rcrd counter
  7
  8=IPROMPT
     *-------------------------------------------------------------------------------------------------*
     * RPG record format . . . . :        PROMPT                                                        *
     * External format . . . . . :        PROMPT : STAN/PA165SF                                         *
     *-------------------------------------------------------------------------------------------------*
  9=I                            A    1    1 *IN03                          EOJ
 10=I                            A    2    2 *IN99                          RECORD NOT FOUND
 11=I                            A    3    7 PART#
 12=IINQRECORD
     *-------------------------------------------------------------------------------------------------*
     * RPG record format . . . . :        INQRECORD                                                     *
     * External format . . . . . :        INQRECORD : STAN/PA165SF                                      *
     *-------------------------------------------------------------------------------------------------*
 13=I                            A    1    1 *IN04                          DISPLAY WINDOW
 14=IERRORDSP                                                               DISPLAY WINDOW
     *-------------------------------------------------------------------------------------------------*
     * RPG record format . . . . :        ERRORDSP                                                      *
     * External format . . . . . :        ERRORDSP : STAN/PA165SF                                       *
     *-------------------------------------------------------------------------------------------------*
 15=ISFWINDOW                                                               DISPLAY WINDOW
     *-------------------------------------------------------------------------------------------------*
     * RPG record format . . . . :        SFWINDOW                                                      *
     * External format . . . . . :        SFWINDOW : STAN/PA165SF                                       *
     *-------------------------------------------------------------------------------------------------*
 16=I                            A    1   15 VNAME
 17=I                            S   16   25 OVTEL#
 18=ICTRLRECORD
     *-------------------------------------------------------------------------------------------------*
     * RPG record format . . . . :        CTRLRECORD                                                    *
     * External format . . . . . :        CTRLRECORD : STAN/PA165SF                                     *
     *-------------------------------------------------------------------------------------------------*
 19=IPA161PR
     *-------------------------------------------------------------------------------------------------*
     * RPG record format . . . . :        PA161PR                                                       *
     * External format . . . . . :        PA161PR : STAN/PA161P                                         *
     *-------------------------------------------------------------------------------------------------*
 20=I                            A    1    5 PARTNO
 21=I                            A    6   25 PARTNAME
 22=I                            P   26   29 OAMTONHAND
 23=I                            P   30   33 OAMTONORDER
 24=I                            P   34   37 2AVGCOST
 25=I                            P   38   41 OAMTALCATED
 26=I                            P   42   45 OEOQ
 27=I                            P   46   49 OSAFTYSTOCK
 28=I                            P   50   51 OLEADTIME
 29=I                            A   52   54 WARELOCATN
 30=IPA165PR
     *-------------------------------------------------------------------------------------------------*
     * RPG record format . . . . :        PA165PR                                                       *
     * External format . . . . . :        PA165PR : STAN/PA165P                                         *
     *-------------------------------------------------------------------------------------------------*
 31=I                            A    1    5 PARTNO
 32=I                            A    6   20 VNAME
 33=I                            A   2*   35 VADDRS
 34=I                            A   36   50 VCITY
 35=I                            A   5*   52 VSTATE
 36=I                            P   53   55 OVZIP
```

```
37=I                           P  56   61 OVTEL#
38 C                 EXFMT     Prompt                                display prompt scrn
39 C                 DOW       *IN03 = *OFF                          dow ind 30 is off      B01
40 C       Part#     CHAIN     Pa161p                      99----    get record from pf     01
41 C                 IF        *IN99 = *OFF                          record found?          B02
42
43  * If record found, display inquiry screen with part information...
44 C                 EXFMT     InqRecord                             display inquiry scrn   02
45 C                 EVAL      *IN80 = *ON                           turn on clearing ind   02
46 C                 WRITE     CtrlRecord                            clear subfile          02
47 C                 EVAL      *IN80 = *OFF                          turn off clearing in   02
48 C                 SETOFF                                71----    turn off indicator     02
49
50  * If no records in Pa165p (Invoice file) and F4 is pressed (window
51  * requested), display error message at the bottom of the screen....
52
53 C       PartNo    SETLL     Pa165p                      ----98    find record            02
54 C                 IF        *IN98 = *OFF AND *IN04 = *ON          rcd fnd & F4 pressed B03
55 C                 EXFMT     ErrorDsp                              display eror msg       03
56 C                 ENDIF                                           end inner IF group     E03
57
58  * If records for customers in Pa165P (invoice file) and subfile not
59  * at End, load subfile with a record....
60 C                 EVAL      Sfrrno = *ZERO                        initialize counter     02
61 C                 DOW       *IN98 = *ON AND *IN71 = *OFF          rcd fnd & load ctrl  B03
62 C                 READE     pA165P                      ----71    read  the PF record    03
63 C                 EVAL      Sfrrno = Sfrrno + 1                   increment sf counter   03
64 C                 IF        *IN71 = *OFF                          subfile full test    B04
65 C                 WRITE     SfWindow                              write rcd to sf        04
66 C                 ENDIF                                           end if group           E04
67 C                 ENDDO                                           end dow group          E03
68
69  * If records are found in Pa165p (Invoices) file and F4 pressed,
70  * display subfile....
71
72 C                 IF        *IN98 = *ON AND *IN04 = *ON                                 B03
73 C                 EVAL      *IN81 = *ON                           turn on display ind    03
74 C                 EXFMT     CtrlRecord                            dsp sf & constants     03
75 C                 EVAL      *IN81 = *OFF                          turn off display ind   03
76 C                 ENDIF                                           end inner if group     E03
77 C                 ENDIF                                           end outer if group     E02
78
79  * Display Prompt screen to continue inquiry or end the job....
80 C                 EXFMT     Prompt                                dsp prompt screen      01
81 C                 ENDDO                                           end outer dow group  E01
82
83 C                 EVAL      *INLR = *ON                           end program
84=OPROMPT
    *------------------------------------------------------------------------*
    * RPG record format  . . . . : PROMPT                                    *
    * External format  . . . . . : PROMPT : STAN/PA165SF                     *
    *------------------------------------------------------------------------*
85=O                *IN99             1A CHAR       1            RECORD NOT FOUND
86=OINQRECORD
    *------------------------------------------------------------------------*
    * RPG record format  . . . . : INQRECORD                                 *
    * External format  . . . . . : INQRECORD : STAN/PA165SF                  *
    *------------------------------------------------------------------------*
87=O                PARTNO            5A CHAR       5
88=O                PARTNAME         25A CHAR      20
89=O                AMTONHAND        31S ZONE     6,0
90=O                AMTONORDER       37S ZONE     6,0
91=O                AMTALCATED       43S ZONE     6,0
92=O                AVGCOST          50S ZONE     7,2
93=OERRORDSP
    *------------------------------------------------------------------------*
    * RPG record format  . . . . : ERRORDSP                                  *
    * External format  . . . . . : ERRORDSP : STAN/PA165SF                   *
    *------------------------------------------------------------------------*
94=O                *IN98             1A CHAR       1
95=OSFWINDOW
    *------------------------------------------------------------------------*
    * RPG record format  . . . . : SFWINDOW                                  *
    * External format  . . . . . : SFWINDOW : STAN/PA165SF                   *
```

```
    *----------------------------------------------------------------------------*
    96=0                    VNAME              15A CHAR      15
    97=0                    VTEL#              25S ZONE      10,0
    98=0CTRLRECORD
    *----------------------------------------------------------------------------*
    * RPG record format  . . . . :  CTRLRECORD
    * External format  . . . . . :  CTRLRECORD : STAN/PA165SF
    *----------------------------------------------------------------------------*
    99=0                    *IN80              1A CHAR       1
   100=0                    *IN81              2A CHAR       1
    * * * *  E N D   O F   S O U R C E  * * * *
```

Prompt display:

```
3/20/98              PARTS INVENTORY MASTER INQUIRY


     ENTER PART NO: A2345



          F3 - EOJ          ENTER - TO DISPLAY
```

Subfile Display Before Windowing:

```
9:56:30              PARTS INVENTORY MASTER INQUIRY           3/20/98


PART#       PART NAME        ON HAND    ON ORDER  ALLOCATED  AVG COST

A2345    AC SPARK PLUGS          0      18,000     5,000       .75








          ENTER TO CONTINUE    F4 - INVOICE WINDOW
```

Subfile Display After Windowing (Invoices found):

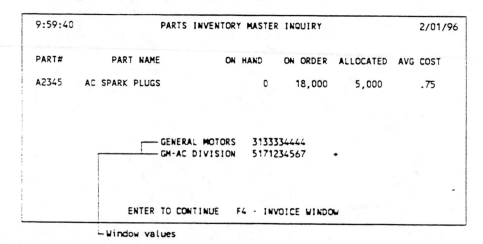

```
9:59:40              PARTS INVENTORY MASTER INQUIRY           2/01/96

PART#       PART NAME        ON HAND    ON ORDER  ALLOCATED  AVG COST

A2345    AC SPARK PLUGS          0      18,000     5,000       .75




          ┌── GENERAL MOTORS    3133334444
          └──── GM-AC DIVISION   5171234567      .




          ENTER TO CONTINUE    F4 - INVOICE WINDOW
```
└ Window values

Note: Reverse image was specified in the DDS for the window border.
      However, a print of the screen image will not show the reverse
      image border.

CHAPTER 17
QUESTION ANSWERS

1. a) Merging of two or more physical files for processing.
   b) Processing one or more physical files in an order different than the stored data (arrival sequence files) or base index (keyed sequence files).
   c) Selection or omission of records from one or more physical files during processing.

2. a) Records may be added without destroying the sorted integrity of one or more physical files.
   b) Records may be logically deleted without reorganizing the physical file to purge the records.
   c) Because logical files do not contain data, they require less storage than a file created by a Regular sort or Summary sort.
   d) Different logical files may access the same physical file(s) in any order or format.
   e) Logical files only have to be compiled to be ready for execution whereas files created by the Sort utility require that a sort program be executed.

3. **NO.** DDS (Data Description Specifications). **NO.**

4. *Nonjoin* and *join*. A *nonjoin* logical file processes two or more physical files by merging. A *join* logical file processes two or more physical file by creating one record in storage that is a composite of the selected fields from each of the physical files specified in the joining process.

5. An *access path*.

6. A *file* or *record level* keyword that specifies the physical file(s) accessed by the logical file.

7. **R** indicates following entry is a *record level* entry (physical file's record name).

8. Physical file's record name.

9. Physical file name.

10. A key level entry that creates an access path (index) for the physical file's BALANCE field.

11. In an ascending order by the BALANCE field values.

12. All of them.

13. Two.

14. Specifies the physical file record format to be accessed. Only has to be used when the logical file record name is from another physical file.

15. In the related physical file's record format.

16. Processes the data records in the physical files in a descending ACCT# and ACTNO (key fields) order.

17. TWO.

18. Specifies that there is no matching field in the GLEDGER file for the GLTRANS file's TDATE field.

19. The first (primary) file specified in the DDS coding. Subsequent processing will depend on the key field values.

20. **JFILE** - Identifies the physical files to be accessed by the *join* logical file.

    JOIN - Joins physical files for processing. Only two physical files may be specified in a **JOIN** statement. If <u>three</u> physical files are to be joined, <u>two</u> **JOIN** statements are required and so forth.

    JFLD - Identifies the <u>from-field</u> and the <u>to-field</u> that will join the physical files for processing.

    JREF - Identifies the physical file field to be accessed. Required when more than one physical file in the join process has the same **JFLD** name.

    JDUPSEQ - Specifies the order in which the records form physical files that have duplicate join fields (**JFLD**) will be processed.

    DYNSLT - Required when the **JDFTVAL** is specified. Causes record selection to occur when a record is read instead of after it is stored.

21. **JFILE** (*Record Level*); **JOIN** (*Join Level*); **JFLD** (*Join Level*); **JREF** (*Field Level*); **JDUPSEQ** (*Join Level*); **DYNSLT** (*File Level*)

22. TWO. SUMMARY.

23. INV#. Ascending INV# order.

24. Identifies from which file (1 or 2) the INV# values are accessed.

25. Would include the SUMMARY (primary) file's records that do not have a match to be processed in the join.

26. Based on some **RANGE**, **COMP**, or **VALUES** criteria, select control "selects" certain data records for processing. Using the same test criteria, omit control "omits" certain data records for processing.

27. **RANGE**, **COMP**, and **VALUES**.

28. <u>Keyword</u>   <u>Function</u>

     RANGE   Selects or omits records within the specified range of field values.

     COMP   Selects or omits records that have a field value based on the relational test value(s).

     VALUES   Selects or omits records that have a field value equal to the values included in the **VALUES** statement.

29. Select fields are identified by an **S** in column 17 of the related DDS statement. Omit fields are identified by an **O** in column 17. A blank in column 17 of a statement following a **S** or **O** statement, indicates that it is in an **AND** relationship with the previous **S** or **O** statement. A statement following with an **S** or **O** in column 17 indicates that it is in an **OR** relationship with the previous **S** or **O** statement.

30. The specified key field (CUSTNO) will process the CUSTMERS file in ascending customer number field order.

The select statement (STATE) is in an **AND** relationship with BALANCE. Records will be <u>selected</u> for processing that have a CT, NY, or NJ value for STATE "and" have a BALANCE value greater than 5000.00.

Records will be <u>omitted</u> from processing that have a RATING field value of A or C.

PROGRAMMING ASSIGNMENTS

Programming Assignment 17-1: STUDENT TRANSCRIPTS (USING A NON-JOIN LOGICAL FILE)

<u>Notes to the Instructor</u>:

1. Two physical files: a student master and course file must be created and loaded with data before this assignment is started.

2. A nonjoin logical file must be created and specified in the RPG IV program to process the two physical files in the required order to generate the transcripts.

<u>Logical File Listing</u>:

```
SEQNBR  *...+....1....+....2....+....3....+....4....+....5....+....6
  100    A         R PA171PR              PFILE(PA171P)
  200    A         K SS#
  300    A         K *NONE
  400    A         K *NONE
  500    A         R PA171P2R             PFILE(PA171P2)
  600    A         K CSS#
  700    A         K CDATE
  800    A         K CNO
```

215

Compiled Program Listing:

Syntax of the Program:

1. On line 10, the date keyword **DATFMT(*YMD)** defines the standalone YyMmDd field into a yymmdd format. It is used to
   convert the CDate field from the course file (Pa171p2) to a
   date format by the MOVE instruction on line 64. Note that
   the MOVE instruction on line 63 initially loads the value
   from the packed numeric field CDate (in an yymmdd format)
   to the date formatted field YyMmDd.

   On line 11, the date keyword **DATFMT(*MDY/)** will convert
   the format from YyMmDd to an edited MmDdYy format for the
   report. The MOVE instruction on line 65 performs the
   conversion process by moving the value in YYMmDd to MmDdYy.

2. Control break for a student's transcript is controlled by
   the IF instruction on line 47 which transfers control to the
   BreakSR where the student's CumQpa is computed

3. At end of file (last record processing), the BreakSR subroutine is accessed again (line 73) to compute the CumQpa
   and print the QpaLine for the last student.

```
Line    <---------------------- Source Specifications ----------------------------><---- Comments ----> Do
Number  ....1....+....2....+....3....+....4....+....5....+....6....+....7....+....8....+....9....+...10 Num
                         S o u r c e   L i s t i n g
   1 * PA 17-1: Student transcripts (non-join logical file)....
   2 FPa171lfn  IF   E           K DISK
     *------------------------------------------------------------------------------------------------*
     *                                RPG name           External name                                *
     * File name. . . . . . . . :     PA171LFN           STAN/PA171LFN                                 *
     * Record format(s) . . . . . :   PA171PR            PA171PR                                       *
     *                                PA171P2R           PA171P2R                                      *
     *------------------------------------------------------------------------------------------------*
   3 FQsysprt   O   F  132          PRINTER OFLIND(*INOF)
   4
   5 * Define work and CDate manipulation fields....
   6 DQPA             S           3  0
   7 DTotalQPA        S           5  0
   8 DTotCredits      S           3  0
   9 DCumQPA          S           3  2
  10 DYyMmDd          S            D  DATFMT(*YMD)                     format for CDate fld
  11 DMmDdYy          S            D  DATFMT(*MDY/)                    edited date format
  12
  13=IPA171PR
     *------------------------------------------------------------------------------------------------*
     * RPG record format . . . . :    PA171PR                                                          *
     * External format . . . . . :    PA171PR : STAN/PA171LFN                                          *
     *------------------------------------------------------------------------------------------------*
  14=I                              P   1    5 OSS#
  15=I                              A   6   25 SNAME
  16=I                              A  26   45 SADD1
  17=I                              A  46   60 SADD2
  18=I                              A  61   80 SCITY
  19=I                              A  81   82 SSTATE
  20=I                              P  83   85 OSZIP
  21=I                              A  86  105 SMAJOR
  22=IPA171P2R
     *------------------------------------------------------------------------------------------------*
     * RPG record format . . . . :    PA171P2R                                                         *
     * External format . . . . . :    PA171P2R : STAN/PA171LFN                                         *
     *------------------------------------------------------------------------------------------------*
  23=I                              P   1    5 OCSS#
```

216

```
24=I                            A   6  25 CNAME
25=I                            A  26  31 CNO
26=I                            P  32  35 OCDATE
27=I                            P  36  37 OCINST#
28=I                            A  38  38 CMARK
29=I                            P  39  39 OCREDIT
30 C              EVAL      *INOF = *ON              turn on OF indicator
31 C              READ      Pa171lfn          ----LR read first lf record
32 C
33 C              DOW       *INLR = *OFF            dow LR is off          B01
34
35  * Print headings for student transcript....
36 C              IF        *INOF = *ON             overflow ind. on?      B02
37 C              EXCEPT    HdgLine                 print heading lines    02
38 C              EVAL      *INOF = *OFF            turn off OF indicatr   02
39 C              ENDIF                             end IF group           E02
40
41 C              READ      Pa171lfn          ----LR read next record      01
42 C              IF        *INLR = *ON             end of logical file? B02
43 C              LEAVE                             yes-exit dow group     02
44 C              ELSE                              lf not at end          X02
45
46  * Test for control break (change in student's SS#)....
47 C              IF        SS# <> Css#             control break test     B03
48 C              EXSR      BreakSR                 ctrl brk-brnch to sr   03
49 C              ELSE                              no control break       X03
50
51 C              SELECT                            begin select group     B04
52 C              WHEN      CMark = 'A'             test for mark          X04
53 C              EVAL      Qpa = Credit * 4        computer qpa           04
54 C              WHEN      CMark = 'B'                                    X04
55 C              EVAL      Qpa = Credit * 3                               04
56 C              WHEN      CMark = 'C'             test for mark          X04
57 C              EVAL      Qpa = Credit * 2        compute qpa            04
58 C              WHEN      CMark = 'D'                                    X04
59 C              EVAL      Qpa = Credit * 1        compute qpa            04
60 C              OTHER                             instruction for F      X04
61 C              EVAL      Qpa = Credit * 0        compute qpa            04
62 C              ENDSL                             end select group       E04
63
64 C              MOVE      CDate       YyMmDd      move to date format    03
65 C              MOVE      YYMmDd      MmDdYy      to edit date format    03
66 C              EVAL      TotalQPA = TotalQPA + QPA   accumulate qpa     03
67 C              EVAL      TotCredits = TotCredits + Credit  accumulate credit 03
68 C              EXCEPT    Detailine               print detail line      03
69 C              ENDIF                             end IF group           E03
70 C              ENDIF                             end IF group           E02
71 C              ENDDO                             end dow group          E01
72
73 C              EXSR      BreakSR                 for last rcd process
74
75  * Compute cumulative qpa for the student....
76 C    BreakSR   BEGSR                             begin subroutine
77 C              IF        TotCredits > 0          greater than zero?     B01
78 C              EVAL      CumQpa = TotalQpa / TotCredits   compute cum qpa  01
79 C              EXCEPT    QpaLine                 print QpaLine          01
80 C              ELSE                              no courses action      X01
81 C              EXCEPT    NoneLine                print error msg        01
82 C              ENDIF                             end IF group           E01
83
84  * Initialize cumulative fields....
85 C              EVAL      TotalQpa = *ZERO        initialize field
86 C              EVAL      TotCredits = *ZERO      initialize field
87 C              EVAL      *INOF = *ON             turn on OF indicator
88 C              ENDSR                             end subroutine
89
90 OQsysprt    E            HdgLine        1 01
91 O                                    43 'ABC COMMUNITY/TECHNICAL'
92 O                                    51 'COLLEGE'
93 O           E            HdgLine        1
94 O                                    38 'TEMPORARY STUDENT'
95 O                                    49 'TRANSCRIPT'
96 O           E            HdgLine        3
97 O                                    34 'AS OF'
```

```
 98 O                          UDATE        Y    43
 99 O            E             HdgLine      1
100 O                          SName            20
101 O                          SS#              35 'O   -   -      '
102 O            E             HdgLine      1
103 O                          SAdd1            20
104 O            E             HdgLine      1
105 O                          SAdd2            15
106 O            E             HdgLine      3
107 O                          SCity            20
108 O                          SState           23
109 O                          SZip             30
110 O                                           49 'MAJOR:'
111 O                          SMajor           70
112 O            E             HdgLine      1
113 O                                           43 'SEMESTER'
114 O                                           52 'INSTR'
115 O            E             HdgLine      2
116 O                                            8 'COURSE #'
117 O                                           26 'COURSE NAME'
118 O                                           40 'DATE'
119 O                                           51 'CODE'
120 O                                           63 'CREDITS'
121 O                                           71 'MARK'
122 O            E             DetaiLine    1
123 O                          Cno               7
124 O                          CName            30
125 O                          MmDdYy           43
126 O                          CInst#           51
127 O                          Credit           60
128 O                          CMark            70
129 O            E             NoneLine     2
130 O                                           31 '**NO COURSE RECORDS'
131 O                                           39 'FOUND**'
132 O            E             QpaLine      3
133 O                                           16 'CUMULATIVE QPA:'
134 O                          CumQpa       1   21
     * * * * *  E N D   O F   S O U R C E  * * * * *
```

Printed transcripts:

```
------------------------------------------------------
                ABC COMMUNITY/TECHNICAL COLLEGE
                TEMPORARY STUDENT TRANSCRIPT
                     AS OF  1/16/98


    HENRY CHURCHILL        011-11-1111
    1640 PARK AVENUE
    APT 10
    NORWALK           CT  06854        MAJOR: DATA PROCESSING

                                 SEMESTER    INSTR
    COURSE #      COURSE NAME       DATE      CODE    CREDITS    MARK

    ACD101    ENGLISH COMPOSITION  12/15/96    300       3        C
    DPS100    INTRO TO PROGRAMMING 12/15/96    104       4        A
    DPS200    INTRO TO RPG/400     05/21/97    221       4        A
    DPS210    COBOL I              05/21/97    221       4        A
    MTH100    COLLEGE ALGEBRA I    12/15/97    161       3        C



    CUMULATIVE QPA: 3.33
------------------------------------------------------
                ABC COMMUNITY/TECHNICAL COLLEGE
                TEMPORARY STUDENT TRANSCRIPT
                     AS OF  1/16/98


    GEORGE ROOSEVELT       011-22-3333
    25 BURNT PLAINS
    DARIEN            CT  06853        MAJOR: COMPUTER SCIENCE
```

218

COURSE #	COURSE NAME	SEMESTER DATE	INSTR CODE	CREDITS	MARK
CSC101	COMPUTER SCIENCE I	12/15/96	190	4	B
CSC202	COMPUTER SCIENCE II	05/21/97	180	4	C
MTH201	CALCULUS I	05/21/97	167	3	B

CUMULATIVE QPA: 2.63

ABC COMMUNITY/TECHNICAL COLLEGE
TEMPORARY STUDENT TRANSCRIPT
AS OF   1/16/98

NELSON FORD   022-44-5555
26 PEARSALL PLACE
SUITE 30
STAMFORD   CT   06850   MAJOR: DATA PROCESSING

COURSE #	COURSE NAME	SEMESTER DATE	INSTR CODE	CREDITS	MARK
DPS100	INTRO TO PROGRAMMING	12/15/96	104	4	C
DPS110	MICROCOMPUTERS I	12/15/96	200	4	A

CUMULATIVE QPA: 3.00

ABC COMMUNITY/TECHNICAL COLLEGE
TEMPORARY STUDENT TRANSCRIPT
AS OF   1/16/98

WILLIAM CARTER   033-77-8999
853 WOOD AVENUE
APT 45
BRIDGEPORT   CT   06601   MAJOR: COMPUTER SCIENCE

COURSE #	COURSE NAME	SEMESTER DATE	INSTR CODE	CREDITS	MARK
CSC101	COMPUTER SCIENCE I	12/15/96	190	4	C
CSC120	PASCAL I	12/15/96	180	4	A

CUMULATIVE QPA: 3.00

ABC COMMUNITY/TECHNICAL COLLEGE
TEMPORARY STUDENT TRANSCRIPT
AS OF   1/16/98

PHILIP BUSH   041-66-8888
102 VIRGINIA AVENUE
GREENWICH   CT   06740   MAJOR: COMPUTER SCIENCE

COURSE #	COURSE NAME	SEMESTER DATE	INSTR CODE	CREDITS	MARK
ACD101	ENGLISH COMPOSITION	12/15/96	300	3	F
MTH201	CALCULUS I	12/15/96	167	3	D
SCS101	PHYSICS I	12/15/96	075	4	C
CSC202	COMPUTER SCIENCE II	05/21/97	180	4	C
CSC210	C PROGRAMMING I	05/21/97	182	4	B

CUMULATIVE QPA: 1.72

```
                    ABC COMMUNITY/TECHNICAL COLLEGE
                      TEMPORARY STUDENT TRANSCRIPT
                          AS OF  1/16/98


FRANK TRUMAN              055-11-9999
7 BOOT SHOP LANE
NEW HAVEN            CT   06554          MAJOR: DATA PROCESSING

                                  SEMESTER    INSTR
                                  DATE        CODE      CREDITS     MARK
COURSE #       COURSE NAME

ACD210    AMERICAN STUDIES        05/21/96     299         3         A
DPS110    MICROCOMPUTERS I        12/15/96     200         4         A
ACD211    ENGLISH LITERATURE      05/21/97     300         3         B



CUMULATIVE QPA: 3.70
-------------------------------------------------------------------
                    ABC COMMUNITY/TECHNICAL COLLEGE
                      TEMPORARY STUDENT TRANSCRIPT
                          AS OF  1/16/98


FREDERICK GRANT           066-22-7777
14 GETTYSBURG PLACE
BRISTOL             CT   06770          MAJOR: DATA PROCESSING

                                  SEMESTER    INSTR
COURSE #       COURSE NAME        DATE        CODE      CREDITS     MARK

          **NO COURSE RECORDS FOUND**
-------------------------------------------------------------------
```

Programming Assignment 17-2: STUDENT TRANSCRIPTS (USING A JOIN LOGICAL FILE)

Notes to the Instructor:

1. If assignment 17-1 was completed, have students modify it to process the two physical files with a join logical file and generate the required transcripts.

2. If assignment 17-1 was not completed, students must refer to the documentation for that assignment and create and load the physical files and reference the student transcript report format.

Join Logical File Listing:

```
 100      A       R LA171LFJR
 200      A                               JFILE(PA171P PA17IP2)
 300      A       J                       JOIN(1 2)
 400      A                               JFLD(SS# CSS#)
 500      A         SS#
 600      A         SNAME
 700      A         SADD1
 800      A         SADD2
 900      A         SCITY
1000      A         SSTATE
1100      A         SZIP
1200      A         SMAJOR
1300      A         CSS#
1400      A         CNAME
1500      A         CNO
```

```
     1600        A              CDATE
     1700        A              CINST#
     1800        A              CMARK
     1900        A              CREDIT
     2000        A          K   SS#
```

Compiled Program Listing:

```
Line    <-------------------- Source Specifications ---------------------------><---- Comments ----> Do
Number  ....1....+....2....+....3....+....4....+....5....+....6....+....7....+....8....+....9....+...10 Num
                          S o u r c e   L i s t i n g
    1  * PA 17-2: Student transcripts (join logical file)....
    2  FPa172lfj  IF   E          K DISK
       *------------------------------------------------------------------------------------------*
       *                                 RPG name        External name                            *
       * File name. . . . . . . . :      PA172LFJ        STAN/PA172LFJ                             *
       * Record format(s) . . . . :      LA171LFJR       LA171LFJR                                *
       *------------------------------------------------------------------------------------------*
    3  FQsysprt   O    F  132         PRINTER OFLIND(*INOF)
    4
    5  * Define work and CDate manipulation fields....
    6  DSS#Hold           S              9 0                        hold fld for ctr brk
    7  DQPA               S              3 0
    8  DTotalQPA          S              5 0
    9  DTotCredits        S              3 0
   10  DCumQPA            S              3 2
   11  DYyMmDd            S              D   DATFMT(*YMD)            format for CDate fld
   12  DMmDdYy            S              D   DATFMT(*MDY/)           edited date format
   13
   14=ILA171LFJR
       *------------------------------------------------------------------------------------------*
       * RPG record format  . . . . :   LA171LFJR                                                 *
       * External format  . . . . . :   LA171LFJR : STAN/PA172LFJ                                 *
       *------------------------------------------------------------------------------------------*
   15=I                          P   1    5 0SS#
   16=I                          A   6   25  SNAME
   17=I                          A  26   45  SADD1
   18=I                          A  46   60  SADD2
   19=I                          A  61   80  SCITY
   20=I                          A  81   82  SSTATE
   21=I                          P  83   85 0SZIP
   22=I                          A  86  105  SMAJOR
   23=I                          P 106  110 0CSS#
   24=I                          A 111  130  CNAME
   25=I                          A 131  136  CNO
   26=I                          P 137  140 0CDATE
   27=I                          P 141  142 0CINST#
   28=I                          A 143  143  CMARK
   29=I                          P 144  144 0CREDIT
   30 C                 EVAL      *INOF = *ON                       turn on OF indicator
   31 C                 READ      Pa172lfj              ----LR      read first lf record
   32 C                 EVAL      SS#Hold = SS#                     init. ctrl brk field
   33 C
   34 C                 DOW       *INLR = *OFF                      dow LR is off        B01
   35
   36  * Print headings for student transcript....
   37 C                 IF        *INOF = *ON                       overflow ind. on?    B02
   38 C                 EXCEPT    HdgLine                           print heading lines   02
   39 C                 EVAL      *INOF = *OFF                      turn off OF indicatr  02
   40 C                 ENDIF                                       end IF group         E02
   41
   42  * Test for control break (change in student's SS#)....
   43 C                 IF        SS# <> SS#Hold                    control break test   B02
   44 C                 EXSR      BreakSR                           ctrl brk-brnch to sr  02
   45 C                 ITER                                        perform dow iteraton  02
   46 C                 ENDIF                                       no control break     E02
   47
   48 C                 SELECT                                      begin select group   B02
   49 C                 WHEN      CMark = 'A'                       test for mark        X02
   50 C                 EVAL      Qpa = Credit * 4                  computer qpa          02
   51 C                 WHEN      CMark = 'B'                                            X02
```

221

```
 52 C                      EVAL      Qpa = Credit * 3                                         02
 53 C                      WHEN      CMark = 'C'                        test for mark        X02
 54 C                      EVAL      Qpa = Credit * 2                   compute qpa           02
 55 C                      WHEN      CMark = 'D'                                             X02
 56 C                      EVAL      Qpa = Credit * 1                   compute qpa           02
 57 C                      OTHER                                        instruction for F    X02
 58 C                      EVAL      Qpa = Credit * 0                   compute qpa           02
 59 C                      ENDSL                                        end select group     E02
 60
 61 C                      IF        CNo = *BLANK                       no value CDate?      B02
 62 C                      MOVE      990101         CDate               init. with dummy val  02
 63 C                      ENDIF                                        end IF group         E02
 64 C                      MOVE      CDate          YyMmDd              move to date format   01
 65 C                      MOVE      YYMmDd         MmDdYy              to edit date format   01
 66 C                      EVAL      TotalQPA = TotalQPA + QPA          accumulate qpa        01
 67 C                      EVAL      TotCredits = TotCredits + Credit   accumulate credit     01
 68 C                      EXCEPT    Detailine                          print detail line     01
 69 C                      READ      Pa172lfj               ----LR      read next record      01
 70 C                      ENDDO                                        end dow group        E01
 71
 72 C                      EXSR      BreakSR                            for last rcd process
 73
 74 * Compute cumulative qpa for the student....
 75 C      BreakSR         BEGSR                                        begin subroutine
 76 C                      IF        TotCredits > 0                     greater than zero?   B01
 77 C                      EVAL      CumQpa = TotalQpa / TotCredits      compute cum qpa       01
 78 C                      EXCEPT    QpaLine                            print QpaLine         01
 79 C                      ELSE                                         no courses action    X01
 80 C                      EXCEPT    NoneLine                           print error msg       01
 81 C                      ENDIF                                        end IF group         E01
 82
 83 * Initialize cumulative fields....
 84 C                      EVAL      TotalQpa = *ZERO                   initialize field
 85 C                      EVAL      TotCredits = *ZERO                 initialize field
 86 C                      EVAL      *INOF = *ON                        turn on OF indicator
 87 C                      EVAL      SS#Hold = SS#                      init. holding field
 88 C                      ENDSR                                        end subroutine
 89
 90 OQsysprt   E           HdgLine         1 01
 91 O                                          43 'ABC COMMUNITY/TECHNICAL'
 92 O                                          51 'COLLEGE'
 93 O          E           HdgLine         1
 94 O                                          38 'TEMPORARY STUDENT'
 95 O                                          49 'TRANSCRIPT'
 96 O          E           HdgLine         3
 97 O                                          34 'AS OF'
 98 O                      UDATE         Y     43
 99 O          E           HdgLine         1
100 O                      SName               20
101 O                      SS#                 35 'O  -  -    '
102 O          E           HdgLine         1
103 O                      SAdd1               20
104 O          E           HdgLine         1
105 O                      SAdd2               15
106 O          E           HdgLine         3
107 O                      SCity               20
108 O                      SState              23
109 O                      SZip                30
110 O                                          49 'MAJOR:'
111 O                      SMajor              70
112 O          E           HdgLine         1
113 O                                          43 'SEMESTER'
114 O                                          52 'INSTR'
115 O          E           HdgLine         2
116 O                                           8 'COURSE #'
117 O                                          26 'COURSE NAME'
118 O                                          40 'DATE'
119 O                                          51 'CODE'
120 O                                          63 'CREDITS'
121 O                                          71 'MARK'
122 O          E           DetaiLine       1
123 O                      Cno                  7
124 O                      CName               30
125 O                      MmDdYy              43
```

222

```
126 O              CInst#        51
127 O              Credit        60
128 O              CMark         70
129 O      E       NoneLine   2
130 O                           31 '**NO COURSE RECORDS'
131 O                           39 'FOUND**'
132 O      E       QpaLine    3
133 O                           16 'CUMULATIVE QPA:'
134 O              CumQpa     1  21
     * * * * *  E N D   O F   S O U R C E  * * * * *
```

Printed transcripts: (refer to the transcript listings for assignment 16-2)

Programming Assignment 17-3: MONTHLY SALES REPORT (USING A NON-JOIN LOGICAL FILE)

Notes to the Instructor:

1. Two physical files: a salesperson master and transaction file must be created and loaded with data before this assignment is started.

2. A nonjoin logical file must be created and specified in the RPG IV program to process the two physical files in the required order to generate each salespersons monthly and weekly sales report.

3. A data area must be created in which the report date is stored. Note that it is implicitly accessed in the program by a *data area data structure (lines 6 and 7)*.

4. Holding fields (Salp#Hold, Brnch#Hold, SpnameHold, MhtoDtHold are defined on lines 18-21. Salp#Hold and Brnch#Hold are used to test for their related control breaks. SpnameHold and MhtoDTHold fields store the related data from the primary file record so that it will not be lost when a secondary file record is processed.

Logical File Listing:

```
SEQNBR *...+....1....+....2....+....3....+....4....+....5....+....6
  100        * Non-join logical file
  200    A        R PA173PR              PFILE(PA173P)
  300    A        K BRNCH#
  400    A        K SALP#
  500    *
  600    A        R PA173P2R             PFILE(PA173P2)
  700    A        K BRNHNO
  800    A        K SALPNO
```

Compiled Program Listing:

```
Line   <------------------- Source Specifications -------------------------><---- Comments ----> Do
Number ....1....+....2....+....3....+....4....+....5....+....6....+....7....+....8....+....9....+...10 Num
                      S o u r c e   L i s t i n g
   1 * PA 17-3: Monthly sales report (non-join logical file)....
   2 FPa173lfn IF   E        K DISK
     *---------------------------------------------------------------------------------------------*
     *                         RPG name           External name                                   *
```

223

```
      * File name. . . . . . . . :  PA173LFN        STAN/PA173LFN                        *
      * Record format(s) . . . . :  PA173PR         PA173PR                              *
      *                             PA173P2R        PA173P2R                             *
      *---------------------------------------------------------------------------------*
    3 FQsysprt   O   F  132       PRINTER OFLIND(*INOF)
    4
    5 * Access data area data structure for report date....
    6 DPa173da       UDS
    7 D Date                1      6
    8
    9 * Define work fields....
   10 DReportDate     S           6  0
   11 DDailySales     S           7  2
   12 DWeeklyTotl     S           8  2
   13 DMthlyTotl      S           9  2
   14 DWeekBTotl      S           9  2
   15 DMthBTotl       S          10  2
   16 DWeekCTotl      S          10  2
   17 DMthCTotl       S          11  2
   18 DSalp#Hold      S           3  0                       Salp# holding field
   19 DBrnch#Hold     S           2  0                       Brnch# holding field
   20 DSpnameHold     S          20                          SpName holding field
   21 DMhtoDtHold     S           9  2                       MhtoDt holding field
   22
   23=IPA173PR
      *---------------------------------------------------------------------------------*
      * RPG record format . . . . :  PA173PR                                             *
      * External format . . . . . :  PA173PR : STAN/PA173LFN                             *
      *---------------------------------------------------------------------------------*
   24=I                     P    1    2 0SALP#
   25=I                     P    3    4 0BRNCH#
   26=I                     A    5   24  SPNAME
   27=I                     P   25   29 2MHTODT
   28=IPA173P2R
      *---------------------------------------------------------------------------------*
      * RPG record format . . . . :  PA173P2R                                            *
      * External format . . . . . :  PA173P2R : STAN/PA173LFN                            *
      *---------------------------------------------------------------------------------*
   29=I                     P    1    2 0SALPNO
   30=I                     P    3    4 0BRNHNO
   31=I                     P    5    7 2UNITSP
   32=I                     P    8    9 0QTYSLD
   33=I                     P   10   13 0SALDAT
   34 C             READ    Pa173lfn                    ----LR  read first lf record
   35 C             EXSR    HouseKSR                             branch to subroutine
   36
   37 C             DOW     *INLR = *OFF                         dow LR is off        B01
   38
   39 * Print headings for branch....
   40 C             IF      *INOF = *ON                          overflow ind. on?    B02
   41 C             EXCEPT  HdgLine                              print heading lines   02
   42 C             EVAL    *INOF = *OFF                         turn off OF indicatr  02
   43 C             ENDIF                                        end IF group         E02
   44
   45 C             READ    Pa173lfn                    ----LR  read next lf record   01
   46 C             IF      *INLR = *ON                          end of lf?           B02
   47 C             LEAVE                                        exit dow group        02
   48 C             ENDIF                                        end if group         E02
   49 * Test for branch and salesperson control breaks....
   50 C             SELECT                                       begin select group   B02
   51 C             WHEN    Brnch# <> Brnch#Hold                 control break?       X02
   52 C             EXSR    SalpSR                               branch to subroutine  02
   53 C             EXSR    BrnchSR                              branch to subroutine  02
   54 C             READ    Pa173lfn                    ----LR  read next record      02
   55 C             WHEN    Salp# <> Salp#Hold                   control break?       X02
   56 C             EXSR    SalpSR                               branch to subroutine  02
   57 C             READ    Pa173lfn                    ----LR  read next record      02
   58 C             ENDSL                                        end select group     E02
   59
   60 C             EVAL    DailySales = UnitSp * QtySld          compute DailySales   01
   61 C             EVAL    WeeklyTotl = WeeklyTotl + DailySales  accum WeeklyTotl     01
   62 C             ENDDO                                        end dow group        E01
   63
   64 C             EXSR    EofFSR                               sr for lr processing
```

```
 65
 66 C     HousekSR      BEGSR                                  begin subroutine
 67 C                   MOVE      Date        ReportDate       move to numeric fld
 68 C                   EVAL      Salp#Hold = Salp#            init. holding field
 69 C                   EVAL      Brnch#Hold = Brnch#          init. holding field
 70 C                   EVAL      SpnameHold = Spname          init. holding field
 71 C                   EVAL      MhtoDtHold = MhtoDt          init. holding field
 72 C                   EVAL      *INOF = *ON                  turn on OF indicator
 73 C                   ENDSR                                  end subroutine
 74
 75 C     SalpSR        BEGSR                                  begin subroutine
 76 C                   EVAL      MhtoDtHold = MhtoDtHold + WeeklyTotl   accum MhtoDtHold
 77 C                   EVAL      WeekBTotl = WeekBTotl + WeeklyTotl     accum WeekBTotl
 78 C                   EVAL      MthBTotl = MthBTotl + MhtoDtHold       accum MthBTotl
 79 C                   EXCEPT    DetaiLine                    print DetaiLine
 80 C                   EVAL      Salp#Hold = Salp#            init. Salp#Hold fld
 81 C                   EVAL      SpnameHold = SpName          init. SpnameHold fld
 82 C                   EVAL      MhtoDtHold = MhtoDt          init. MhtoDtHold fld
 83 C                   EVAL      WeeklyTotl = *ZERO           Init. WeeklyTotl fld
 84 C                   ENDSR                                  end subroutine
 85 C
 86 C     BrnchSR       BEGSR                                  begin subroutine
 87 C                   EVAL      WeekCTotl = WeekCTotl + WeekBTotl      accum WeekCTotl
 88 C                   EVAL      MthCTotl = MthCTotl + MthBTotl         accum MthCTotl
 89 C                   EXCEPT    BranchLine                   print record
 90 C                   EVAL      Brnch#Hold = Brnch#          init. Brnch#Hold
 91 C                   EVAL      WeekBTotl = *ZERO            init. WeekBTotl
 92 C                   EVAL      MthBTotl = *ZERO             init. MthBTotl
 93 C                   EVAL      *INOF = *ON                  turn on OF indicator
 94 C                   ENDSR                                  end subroutine
 95
 96 C     EofFSR        BEGSR                                  begin subroutine
 97 C                   EXSR      SalpSR                       branch to subroutine
 98 C                   EXSR      BrnchSR                      exit to subroutine
 99 C                   EXCEPT    CompnyLine                   print CompnyLine
100 C                   ENDSR                                  end subroutine
101
102 OQsysprt  E         HdgLine          1 01
103 O                                        56 'WEEKLY SALES REPORT BY'
104 O                                        74 'SALESMAN & BRANCH'
105 O                                        87 'PAGE'
106 O                   PAGE               95
107 O         E         HdgLine          3
108 O                                        58 'FOR THE WEEK ENDING'
109 O                   ReportDate      Y  67
110 O         E         HdgLine          2
111 O                                        25 'BRANCH'
112 O                   Brnch#          Z  28
113 O         E         HdgLine          2
114 O                                        32 'SALESMAN NO'
115 O                                        51 'SALESMAN NAME'
116 O                                        75 'WEEKLY SALES'
117 O                                        92 'MONTHLY SALES'
118 O         E         DetaiLine        1
119 O                   SalP#Hold          28
120 O                   SpNameHold         53
121 O                   WeeklyTotl       1 74
122 O                   MhtodtHold       1 91
123 O         E         BranchLine  1
124 O                                        57 'TOTAL BRANCH SALES'
125 O                   WeekBTotl        1 74
126 O                   MthBTotl         1 91
127 O         E         CompnyLine  1   01
128 O                                        58 'TOTAL COMPANY SALES'
129 O                   WeekCTotl        1 74
130 O                   MthCTotl         1 91
     * * * * *   E N D   O F   S O U R C E   * * * * *
```

<u>inted Report</u>:

```
-------------------------------------------------------------------
|        WEEKLY SALES REPORT BY SALESMAN & BRANCH      PAGE      1 |
|              FOR THE WEEK ENDING 11/06/97                        |
|                                                                 |
```

```
BRANCH 10

  SALESMAN NO       SALESMAN NAME           WEEKLY SALES      MONTHLY SALES

        123      RICHARD H MACY               4,200.00         16,524.15
        234      JOHN GIMBEL                  9,000.00         17,635.79
        345      JOHN WANAMAKER              11,000.00         21,000.00

                 TOTAL BRANCH SALES          24,200.00         55,159.94
----------------------------------------------------------------------------
                 WEEKLY SALES REPORT BY SALESMAN & BRANCH        PAGE     2
                     FOR THE WEEK ENDING 11/06/97



BRANCH 20

  SALESMAN NO       SALESMAN NAME           WEEKLY SALES      MONTHLY SALES

        456      BERT ALTMAN                  3,080.00          3,880.00
        567      ROGER PEET                   2,100.00         34,100.00

                 TOTAL BRANCH SALES           5,180.00         37,980.00

----------------------------------------------------------------------------
                 WEEKLY SALES REPORT BY SALESMAN & BRANCH        PAGE     3
                     FOR THE WEEK ENDING 11/06/97


BRANCH 30

  SALESMAN NO       SALESMAN NAME           WEEKLY SALES      MONTHLY SALES

        678      JOHN PENNY                  16,635.90        125,202.90

                 TOTAL BRANCH SALES          16,635.90        125,202.90



----------------------------------------------------------------------------

                 TOTAL COMPANY SALES         46,015.90        218,342.84

----------------------------------------------------------------------------
```

Programming Assignment 17-4: MONTHLY SALES REPORT (USING A JOIN LOGICAL FILE)

Notes to the Instructor:

1. If assignment 17-3 was completed, have students modify it to process the two physical files with a join logical file and generate the required sales report.

2. If assignment 17-3 was not completed, students must refer to the documentation for that assignment and create and load the physical files and reference the student transcript print format.

Join Logical File Listing:

```
SEQNBR    *...+....1....+....2....+....3....+....4....+....5....+....6....+....7....+....8
  100     A         R PA174LFJR
  200     A                                            JFILE(PA173P PA173P2)
  300     A         J                                  JOIN(1 2)
  400     A                                            JFLD(BRNCH# BRNHNO)
  500     A                                            JFLD(SALP# SALPNO)
  600     A           BRNCH#
  700     A           SALP#
  800     A           SPNAME
  900     A           MHTODT
 1000     A           UNITSP
 1100     A           QTYSLD
 1200     A           SALDAT
 1300     A         K BRNCH#
 1400     A         K SALP#
```

Compiled Program Listing:

```
Line    <--------------------- Source Specifications --------------------------><---- Comments ----> Do
Number  ....1....+....2....+....3....+....4....+....5....+....6....+....7....+....8....+....9....+...10 Num
                           S o u r c e   L i s t i n g
   1  * PA 17-3: Monthly sales report (join logical file)....
   2  FPa174lfj  IF   E          K DISK
      *-------------------------------------------------------------------------------------------*
      *                                                                                           *
      *                               RPG name          External name                            *
      * File name. . . . . . . . . :  PA174LFJ          STAN/PA174LFJ                             *
      * Record format(s) . . . . . :  PA174LFJR         PA174LFJR                                 *
      *-------------------------------------------------------------------------------------------*
   3  FQsysprt   O    F  132        PRINTER OFLIND(*INOF)
   4
   5  * Access data area data structure for report date....
   6  DPa173da        UDS
   7  D Date                    1      6
   8
   9  * Define work fields....
  10  DReportDate     S               6 0
  11  DDailySales     S               7 2
  12  DWeeklyTotl     S               8 2
  13  DMthlyTotl      S               9 2
  14  DWeekBTotl      S               9 2
  15  DMthBTotl       S              10 2
  16  DWeekCTotl      S              10 2
  17  DMthCTotl       S              11 2
  18  DSalp#Hold      S               3 0
  19  DBrnch#Hold     S               2 0
  20  DSpnameHold     S              20
  21  DMhtoDtHold     S               9 2
  22
  23 =IPA174LFJR
      *-------------------------------------------------------------------------------------------*
      * RPG record format  . . . . :  PA174LFJR                                                   *
      * External format  . . . . . :  PA174LFJR : STAN/PA174LFJ                                   *
      *-------------------------------------------------------------------------------------------*
  24 =I                      P    1    2 OBRNCH#
  25 =I                      P    3    4 OSALP#
  26 =I                      P    5    6 OSALPNO
  27 =I                      A    7   26  SPNAME
  28 =I                      P   27   31 2MHTODT
  29 =I                      P   32   34 2UNITSP
  30 =I                      P   35   36 OQTYSLD
  31 =I                      P   37   40 OSALDAT
  32 C            READ      Pa174lfj                            ----LR    read first lf record
  33 C            EXSR      HouseKSR                                      branch to subroutine
  34
  35 C            DOW       *INLR = *OFF                                  dow LR is off        B01
  36
  37  * Print headings for branch....
  38 C            IF        *INOF = *ON                                   overflow ind. on?    B02
  39 C            EXCEPT    HdgLine                                       print heading lines  02
  40 C            EVAL      *INOF = *OFF                                  turn off OF indicatr 02
  41 C            ENDIF                                                   end IF group         E02
  42
```

```
 43  * Test for branch and salesperson control breaks....
 44 C               SELECT                                           begin select group    B02
 45 C               WHEN      Brnch# <> Brnch#Hold                   control break?         X02
 46 C               EXSR      SalpSR                                 branch to subroutine  02
 47 C               EXSR      BrnchSR                                branch to subroutine  02
 48 C               WHEN      Salp# <> Salp#Hold                     control break?         X02
 49 C               EXSR      SalpSR                                 branch to subroutine  02
 50 C               ENDSL                                            end select group      E02
 51
 52 C               EVAL      DailySales = UnitSp * QtySld           compute DailySales    01
 53 C               EVAL      WeeklyTotl = WeeklyTotl + DailySales   accum DailySales      01
 54 C               READ      Pa174lfj                     ----LR    read next record      01
 55 C               ENDDO                                            end dow group         E01
 56
 57 C               EXSR      EofFSR                                 for last rcd process
 58
 59 C    HousekSR   BEGSR                                            begin subroutine
 60 C               MOVE      Date           ReportDate             move to numeric fld
 61 C               EVAL      SalP#Hold = Salp#
 62 C               EVAL      Brnch#Hold = Brnch#                    init. Brnch#Hold
 63 C               EVAL      SpnameHold = Spname
 64 C               EVAL      MhtoDtHold = MhtoDt
 65 C               EVAL      *INOF = *ON            .               turn on OF indicator
 66 C               ENDSR                                            end subroutine
 67
 68 C    SalpSR     BEGSR                                            begin subroutine
 69 C               EVAL      MhtoDtHold = MhtoDtHold + WeeklyTotl   accum WeeklyTotl
 70 C               EXCEPT    DetailLine                             print weekly total
 71 C               EVAL      WeekBTotl = WeekBTotl + WeeklyTotl     accum WeekBTotl
 72 C               EVAL      MthBTotl = MthBTotl + MhtodtHold       accum MthDTotl
 73 C               EVAL      Salp#Hold = Salp#
 74 C               EVAL      SpnameHold = Spname
 75 C               EVAL      MhtoDtHold = MhtoDt
 76 C               EVAL      WeeklyTotl = *ZERO                     init. MtoDTotl to 0
 77 C               ENDSR                                            end subroutine
 78 C
 79 C    BrnchSR    BEGSR                                            begin subroutine
 80 C               EXCEPT    BranchLine                             print record
 81 C               EVAL      WeekCTotl = WeekCTotl + WeekBTotl      accum WeekCTotl
 82 C               EVAL      MthCTotl = MthCTotl + MthBTotl         accum MthCTotl
 83 C               EVAL      Brnch#Hold = Brnch#
 84 C               EVAL      WeekBTotl = *ZERO                      init. WeekBTotl to 0
 85 C               EVAL      MthBTotl = *ZERO                       init. MthBTotl to 0
 86 C               EVAL      *INOF = *ON                            turn on OF indicator
 87 C               ENDSR                                            end subroutine
 88
 89 C    EofFSR     BEGSR                                            begin subroutine
 90 C               EXSR      SalpSR                                 branch to subroutine
 91 C               EXSR      BrnchSR                                exit to subroutine
 92 C               EXCEPT    CompnyLine                             print CompnyLine
 93 C               ENDSR                                            end subroutine
 94
 95 OQsysprt   E          HdgLine       1 01
 96 O                                          56 'WEEKLY SALES REPORT BY'
 97 O                                          74 'SALESMAN & BRANCH'
 98 O                                          87 'PAGE'
 99 O                          PAGE           95
100 O          E          HdgLine       3
101 O                                          58 'FOR THE WEEK ENDING'
102 O                          ReportDate   Y 67
103 O          E          HdgLine       2
104 O                                          25 'BRANCH'
105 O                          Brnch#       Z 28
106 O          E          HdgLine       2
107 O                                          32 'SALESMAN NO'
108 O                                          51 'SALESMAN NAME'
109 O                                          75 'WEEKLY SALES'
110 O                                          92 'MONTHLY SALES'
111 O          E          DetailLine    1
112 O                          Salp#Hold       28
113 O                          SpNameHold      53
114 O                          WeeklyTotl   1  74
115 O                          MhtodtHold   1  91
116 O          E          BranchLine  1
```

```
117 0                                   57 'TOTAL BRANCH SALES'
118 0                    WeekBTotl    1  74
119 0                    MthBTotl     1  91
120 0          E         CompnyLine 1
121 0                                   58 'TOTAL COMPANY SALES'
122 0                    WeekCTotl    1  74
123 0                    MthCTotl     1  91
     * * * *  E N D   O F   S O U R C E   * * * *
```

Printed Report: (refer to the report for assignment 17-3)

CHAPTER 18
QUESTION ANSWERS

1. Printer files (**PRTF**) are externally defined files created in the same manner as physical and display files. They format the design of a printed report.

2. Advantages:

   a. More than one program may access the same report format.
   b. Changes to an existing report format that is common to more than one program are made only to one source.
   c. Laser printer fonts, features, and controls may be accessed by printer files; not possible with traditional RPG coding for printed output.
   d. RPG IV programs that access printer files contain less coding and are therefore easier to maintain.
   e. Parallel the feature unique to the AS/400 where physical display, and logical files are externally defined.

   Disadvantages:

   a. Unfamiliar syntax.
   b. RPG logic cycle related to report generation cannot be specified in a program. Programmer-supplied coding to control headings, detail output, totals, and page overflow must be provided by the programmer.

3. Following DDS (*Data Description Specifications*) syntax and entering the coding with **SEU**. The Printer file source must be compiled in the same manner as physical, display, and logical files.

4. As a statement in the File Description Specifications. Page overflow indicators (OA-OG, OV) are not supported.

5. **DATE**   - Accesses the system date in an MMDDYY format.

   SPACEA - Advances the printer carriage the number of lines specified with this keyword (0, 1, 2, or 3) <u>after</u> the related line is printed.

   TIME   - Accesses the system time in an HH:MM:SS format. Note that the colons are included.

   EDTWRD - Provides for the editing of numeric field values. Follows RPG/400 syntax rules for **EDTWRD** formats.

   SKIPA - Advances the printer carriage to the line specified with this keyword <u>after</u> the related line is printed.

   PAGNBR - Provides for automatic page numbering beginning with 0001 to 9999.

>   **SPACEB** - Advances the printer carriage the number of lines
>   specified with this keyword (0, 1, 2, or 3) <u>before</u>
>   the related line is printed.
>
>   **SKIPB** - Advances the printer carriage to the line specified
>   with this keyword <u>before</u> the related line is printed.
>
>   **EDTCDE** - Any of the RPG IV edit codes (1, 2, 3, 4, A, B, C,
>   D, J, K, L, M) may be specified with this keyword to
>   generated the editing supported. New edit codes N, O
>   P, and Q provide for floating minus signs in addition
>   to the attributes common to edit codes 1, 2, 3, and 4.

6. In the *Functions* field (columns 45-80) of the *Data Description Specifications*.

7. MMDDYY.

8. HH:MM:SS

9. 3.

10. Printer carriage will advance to line 6 <u>before</u> printing.

11. a) **EDTCDE(1);** b) **EDTCDE(Y);** c) **EDTCDE(J);** d) **EDTCDE(2);**

12. a) **EDTWRD('$bb,bbb.bb');** b) **EDTWRD('bbb,b$0.bb')**
    c) **EDTWRD('0bbb-bb-bbbb');** d) **EDTWRD('0bbb&bb&bbbb')**
    e) **EDTWRD('0(bbb)-bbb-bbbb');** f) **EDTWRD('bbb,bb*.bb&CREDIT');**
    g) **EDTWRD('bb0b');** h) **EDTWRD('0b/bb/bb');**
    i) **EDTWRD('b,bb0.bb-')**

13. By calculation statements instead of unsupported page overflow indicators.

14. Coding sequence includes programmer-supplied values for a line counter and page length. The function of each statement is detailed below.

<u>Line#</u>	<u>Function</u>
1	Prevents the **IF** group from executing when indicator 10 is "on".
2	Initializes the line counter (LineCounter) to a value greater than the number of lines per page (55).
3	Defines the page length (Pagelength) as 54 lines.
4	Turns on indicator 10 so that the IF test on line 1 is never true again for subsequent processing.
5	The ENDIF operation ends the IF group.

15. The statements in this sequence control page overflow and

the printing of heading, detail, and total lines.

Line#   Functions

1   The value in LineCountr is compared to the value in
     PageLegth. When the value in LineCountr is greater
     than or equal to the value in PageLength, statement 2
     is executed, which causes the HeadngLine record in the
     printer file to be printed.

2   In the syntax of the **PRTF**, the HeadngLine record in-
     cludes a **SKIPB** keyword and one or more heading lines.
     This IF instruction controls page overflow and writes
     the output lines included in the HeadngLine record.

3   The line counter field (LineCountr) is initialized to 6,
     indicating the number of lines used when the HeadngLine
     record is printed.

4   The **ENDIF** operation ends the **IF** group.

5   The constants and variables included in the **PRTF**
     record DetailLine are printed by this **WRITE** instruction.

6   The line counter (LineCountr) is incremented by 2, indi-
     cating the number of lines used when the DetailLine
     record is printed.

Note: Remind students that page skipping and spacing con-
      trol is included in the syntax of the printer file
      and not in the related RPG IV program.

16. HeadngLine and DetailLine are record formats defined in
    the DDS coding unique to printer files. They are coded as
    any other DDS record formats (R in column 17, record name
    in columns 19-28, and so forth). Skipping and spacing con-
    trol, constants, variables, editing, and keywords unique to
    laser printers may be included in the syntax of a printer
    file's records.

17. Creates a printer file object. Defaults may be changed to
    create a printer file "shell" and/or access the fonts sup-
    ported by a laser printer.

18. When controls are required (specific font) that are not
    available in the RPG IV compiler.

PROGRAMMING ASSIGNMENTS

Notes to the Instructor:

1. Remind students that the assignments for, this chapter
   require that an assignment from another chapter be modi-

fied and/or referenced to support a printer file instead of traditional RPG controlled printed reports.

2. If the referenced assignments were not previously completed, you may want to assign a different one.

Programming Assignment 18-1: SALES JOURNAL

Compiled Printer File Listing:

```
                            Data Description Source
SEQNBR  *...+....1....+....2....+....3....+....4....+....5....+....6....+....7....+....8
  100   A                                    REF(P61PSM)
  200   A           R HDG                    SKIPB(1)
  300   A                                    2DATE EDTCDE(Y)
  400   A                                    44'SALES JOURNAL'
  500   A                                    91'PAGE' ·
  600   A                                    96PAGNBR EDTCDE(2) SPACEA(2)
  700   A                                    89'TOTAL AMOUNT' SPACEA(1)
  800   A                                    4'DATE'
  900   A                                    20'ACCOUNT DEBITED'
 1000   A                                    46'INVOICE NO'
 1100   A                                    59'AMOUNT OF SALE'
 1200   A                                    77'SALES TAX'
 1300   A                                    91'OF SALE' SPACEA(2)
 1400   A           R DETAIL                 SPACEA(2)
 1500   A             SALEDATE   R           2EDTCDE(Y)
 1600   A             CUSTNAME   R           14
 1700   A             INVOICE#   R           49
 1800   A             SALEAMOUNTR            61EDTCDE(1)
 1900   A             SALESTAX      6  2     77EDTCDE(1)
 2000   A             GROSSSALE     8  2     90EDTCDE(1)
 2100   A   *
 2200     *ERROR MESSAGE 1..........
 2300   A           R ERROR1                 SPACEA(2)
 2400   A             SALEDATE   R           2EDTCDE(Y)
 2500   A             CUSTNAME   R           14
 2600   A             INVOICE#   R           49
 2700   A                                    59'...SALE AMOUNT ZERO...'
 2800   A   *
 2900     *ERROR MESSAGE 2.........
 3000   A           R ERROR2                 SPACEA(2)
 3100   A             SALEDATE   R           2EDTCDE(Y)
 3200   A             CUSTNAME   R           14
 3300   A             INVOICE#   R           49
 3400   A                                    59'...SALE AMOUNT NEGATIVE...'
 3500   A   *
 3600     * TOTALS..........
 3700   A           R TOTALS                 SPACEB(1)
 3800   A             TOTALSALES    8  2     60EDTCDE(1)
 3900   A             TOTALTAX      7  2     76EDTCDE(1)
 4000   A             TOTALGROSS    9  2     88EDTCDE(1)
              * * * * *  E N D   O F   S O U R C E  * * * * *
```

Compiled Program Listing:

```
Line    <---------------------- Source Specifications ----------------------------><---- Comments ----> Do
Number  ....1....+....2....+....3....+....4....+....5....+....6....+....7....+....8....+....9....+...10 Num
                      S o u r c e   L i s t i n g
  1  * PA 18-1: Sales Journal....
  2 FP61psm    IF  E           DISK
     *-------------------------------------------------------------------------------------*
     *                        RPG name        External name                                *
     * File name. . . . . . . . . :  P61PSM   STAN/P61PSM                                   *
     * Record format(s) . . . . . :  P61PSMR  P61PSMR                                       *
```

```
      *-----------------------------------------------------------------------*
    3 FPa181prt  O    E              PRINTER
    4
      *-----------------------------------------------------------------------*
      *
      * File name. . . . . . . . :   RPG name        External name
      * Record format(s) . . . . :   PA181PRT        STAN/PA181PRT
      *                              HDG             HDG
      *                              DETAIL          DETAIL
      *                              ERROR1          ERROR1
      *                              ERROR2          ERROR2
      *                              TOTALS          TOTALS
      *-----------------------------------------------------------------------*
    5 DSalesTax        S              6 2
    6 DGrossSale       S              8 2
    7 DTotalSales      S              8 2
    8 DTotalTax        S              7 2
    9 DTotalGross      S              9 2
   10 DLinesUsed       S              2 0                        linecounter
   11 DLinesPage       S              2 0                        lines per page
   12
   13=IP61PSMR
      *-----------------------------------------------------------------------*
      * RPG record format  . . . . :  P61PSMR
      * External format  . . . . . :  P61PSMR : STAN/P61PSM
      *-----------------------------------------------------------------------*
   14=I                        P    1    4 0SALEDATE
   15=I                        A    5   33  CUSTNAME
   16=I                        P   34   37 0INVOICE#
   17=I                        P   38   41 2SALEAMOUNT
   18 C           EVAL      LinesUsed = 15                       init. line counter
   19 C           EVAL      LinesPage = 14                       init. lines per page
   20
   21 C           READ      P61psm                        ----LR read first record
   22 C           DOW       *INLR = *OFF                         dow LR is off        B01
   23
   24  * Test for new page, print headings, and initialize line counter
   25 C           IF        LinesUsed > LinesPage                test for next page   B02
   26 C           WRITE     Hdg                                  write heading lines  02
   27 C           EVAL      LinesUsed = 6                        init. LinesUsed      02
   28 C           ENDIF                                          end IF group         E02
   29
   30 C           SELECT                                         begin select group   B02
   31 C           WHEN      SaleAmount = *ZERO                   equal to zero?       X02
   32 C           WRITE     Error1                               print zero msg       02
   33 C           WHEN      SaleAmount < *ZERO                   less than zero?      X02
   34 C           WRITE     Error2                               print negative msg   02
   35 C           OTHER                                          positive SaleAmount  X02
   36 C           EVAL(H)   SalesTax = SaleAmount * .075         compute SalesTax     02
   37 C           EVAL      GrossSale = SaleAmount + SalesTax    compute GrossSales   02
   38 C           WRITE     Detail                               print good record    02
   39 C           EVAL      TotalSales = TotalSales + SaleAmount compute TotalSales   02
   40 C           EVAL      TotalTax = TotalTax + SalesTax       compute TotalTax     02
   41 C           EVAL      TotalGross = TotalGross + GrossSale  compute TotalGross   02
   42 C           ENDSL                                          end SELECT group     E02
   43 C                                                                               E02
   44 C           EVAL      LinesUsed = LinesUsed + 2            increment LinesUsed  01
   45 C           READ      P61psm                        ----LR read next record     01
   46 C           ENDDO                                          end dow group        E01
   47
   48 C           WRITE     Totals                               print total line
   49=OHDG
      *-----------------------------------------------------------------------*
      * RPG record format . . . . :  HDG
      * External format . . . . . :  HDG : STAN/PA181PRT
      *-----------------------------------------------------------------------*
   50=ODETAIL
      *-----------------------------------------------------------------------*
      * RPG record format . . . . :  DETAIL
      * External format . . . . . :  DETAIL : STAN/PA181PRT
      *-----------------------------------------------------------------------*
   51=O                      SALEDATE           6S ZONE      6,0
   52=O                      CUSTNAME          35A CHAR       29
```

```
53=0                        INVOICE#           41S ZONE    6,0
54=0                        SALEAMOUNT         48S ZONE    7,2
55=0                        SALESTAX           54S ZONE    6,2
56=0                        GROSSSALE          62S ZONE    8,2
57=0ERROR1
      *-------------------------------------------------------------------------*
      * RPG record format  . . . . :  ERROR1                                    *
      * External format  . . . . . :  ERROR1 : STAN/PA181PRT                    *
      *-------------------------------------------------------------------------*
58=0                        SALEDATE            6S ZONE    6,0
59=0                        CUSTNAME           35A CHAR     29
60=0                        INVOICE#           41S ZONE    6,0
61=0ERROR2
      *-------------------------------------------------------------------------*
      * RPG record format  . . . . :  ERROR2                                    *
      * External format  . . . . . :  ERROR2 : STAN/PA181PRT                    *
      *-------------------------------------------------------------------------*
62=0                        SALEDATE            6S ZONE    6,0
63=0                        CUSTNAME           35A CHAR     29
64=0                        INVOICE#           41S ZONE    6,0
65=0TOTALS
      *-------------------------------------------------------------------------*
      * RPG record format  . . . . :  TOTALS                                    *
      * External format  . . . . . :  TOTALS : STAN/PA181PRT                    *
      *-------------------------------------------------------------------------*
66=0                        TOTALSALES          8S ZONE    8,2
67=0                        TOTALTAX           15S ZONE    7,2
68=0                        TOTALGROSS         24S ZONE    9,2
       * * * *  E N D  O F  S O U R C E  * * * *
```

Printed Report:

8/3196		SALES JOURNAL				PAGE 1
DATE	ACCOUNT DEBITED	INVOICE NO	AMOUNT OF SALE	SALES TAX	TOTAL AMOUNT OF SALE
8/01/96	HUDSON MOTOR CAR COMPANY	040000	812.00	60.90	872.90
8/09/96	PACKARD COMPANY	040001	...SALE AMOUNT ZERO...		
8/11/96	THE HUPMOBILE COMPANY	040002	8,570.10	642.76	9,212.86
8/16/96	THE TUCKER CAR COMPANY	040003	...SALE AMOUNT NEGATIVE...		
8/21/96	AUBURN INCORPORATED	040004	45.00	3.38	48.38

8/31/96		SALES JOURNAL				PAGE 2
DATE	ACCOUNT DEBITED	INVOICE NO	AMOUNT OF SALE	SALES TAX	TOTAL AMOUNT OF SALE
8/27/96	BRICKLIN LIMITED	040005	1,068.91	80.17	1,149.08
8/30/96	THE LOCOMOBILE CAR COMPANY	040006	2,140.00	160.50	2,300.50
8/31/96	STUDEBAKER CARS INCORPORATED	040007	50.50	3.79	54.29
			12,686.51	951.50	13,638.01

Programming Assignment 18-2: SALESPERSON SALARY/COMMISSION REPORT

Notes to the Instructor:

1. Remind students that Printer Files (PRTFs) do not support page

overflow indicators. Consequently, this program includes prog-
grammer-supplied page overflow as controlled by the instructions on lines 24, 25, 31, 33, and 76.

Compiled Printer File Listing:

```
                              Data Description Source
SEQNBR    *...+....1....+....2....+....3....+....4....+....5....+....6....+....7....+....8
  100     A                                      REF(P62PSM)
  200     A          R HDG                       SKIPB(1)
  300     A                                      1DATE EDTCDE(Y)
  400     A                                      52'COMMISSION REPORT'
  500     A                                      103'PAGE'
  600     A                                      108PAGNBR EDTCDE(Z) SPACEA(3)
  700     A                                      101'SALARY/' SPACEA(1)
  800     A                                        1'SALESMAN #'
  900     A                                       18'SALESMAN NAME'
 1000     A                                       41'EMP YRS'
 1100     A                                       51'GROSS SALES'
 1200     A                                       67'RETURNS'
 1300     A                                       82'NET SALES'
 1400     A                                       99'COMMISSION' SPACEA(2)
 1500     A          R DETAIL                     SPACEA(2)
 1600     A            SALEPERSN#R                3
 1700     A            SALEPNAME R                13
 1800     A            YRSEMPLYEDR                43EDTCDE(Z)
 1900     A            SALEAMOUNTR                51EDTCDE(1)
 2000     A            SALERETURNR                65EDTCDE(1)
 2100     A            NETSALES       8  2        81EDTCDE(1)
 2200     A            COMMISSION     8  2        99EDTCDE(1)
 2300     *
 2400     * TOTAL LINE....
 2500     A          R TOTALS                     SPACEB(1)
 2600     A                                       33'TOTALS..........'
 2700     A            TOTALSALES     9  2        49EDTCDE(1)
 2800     A            TOTRETURNS     8  2        64EDTCDE(1)
 2900     A            TOTNETSALE     9  2        79EDTCDE(1)
 3000     A            TOTALCOMM      9  2        97EDTCDE(1)
                        * * * * *  E N D   O F   S O U R C E  * * * * *
```

Compiled Program Listing:

```
Line    <---------------------- Source Specifications ---------------------><---- Comments ----> Do
Number  ....1....+....2....+....3....+....4....+....5....+....6....+....7....+....8....+....9....+...10 Num
                        S o u r c e   L i s t i n g
  1  * PA 18-2: Salesman Salary/Commission Report....
  2 FP62psm   IF  E           DISK
     *-------------------------------------------------------------------*
     *                         RPG name           External name          *
     * File name. . . . . . . : P62PSM            STAN/P62PSM            *
     * Record format(s) . . . : P62PSMR           P62PSMR               *
     *-------------------------------------------------------------------*
  3 FPa182prt O   E           PRINTER
  4
     *-------------------------------------------------------------------*
     *                         RPG name           External name          *
     * File name. . . . . . . : PA182PRT          STAN/PA182PRT          *
     * Record format(s) . . . : HDG               HDG                   *
     *                         DETAIL            DETAIL                 *
     *                         TOTALS            TOTALS                 *
     *-------------------------------------------------------------------*
  5 DExtraSales     S           8 2
  6 DExtraComm      S           8 2
  7 DCommSales      S           8 2
  8 DNetSales       S           8 2
  9 DSalary         S           8 2
 10 DCommission     S           8 2
 11 DTotalSales     S           9 2
```

```
  12 DTotReturns          S              8 2
  13 DTotNetSale          S              9 2
  14 DTotalComm           S              9 2
  15 DLinesUsed           S              2 0                    line counter
  16 DLinesPage           S              2 0                    lines per page
  17
  18=IP62PSMR
     *-------------------------------------------------------------------*
     * RPG record format  . . . . :  P62PSMR                             *
     * External format  . . . . . :  P62PSMR : STAN/P62PSM              *
     *-------------------------------------------------------------------*
  19=I                           A     1    5 SALEPERSN#
  20=I                           A     6   30 SALEPNAME
  21=I                           P    31   32 0YRSEMPLYED
  22=I                           P    33   37 2SALEAMOUNT
  23=I                           P    38   41 2SALERETURN
  24 C              EVAL      LinesUsed = 15                   init. LinesUsed
  25 C              EVAL      LinesPage = 14                   init. LinesPage
  26 C              READ      P62psm                    ----LR read first record
  27
  28 C              DOW       *INLR = *OFF                     dow LR is off       B01
  29
  30 * Heading control....
  31 C              IF        LinesUsed > LinesPage            new page test       B02
  32 C              WRITE     Hdg                              print heading lines 02
  33 C              EVAL      LinesUsed = 8                    init. linesUsed     02
  34 C              ENDIF                                      end IF group        E02
  35
  36 * Housekeeping....
  37 C              EVAL      ExtraComm = *ZERO                initialize field    01
  38 C              EVAL      ExtraSales = *ZERO               initialize field    01
  39 C              EVAL      CommSales = *ZERO                initialize field    01
  40
  41 * Compute Commission Sales...
  42 C              EVAL      NetSales = SaleAmount - SaleReturn  compute net sales 01
  43 C              IF        NetSales > 2000                  > 2000?             B02
  44 C              EVAL      CommSales = NetSales - 2000      compute commsales   02
  45 C              ENDIF                                      end IF group        E02
  46
  47 * Calculations for employees with less than 2 years employment..
  48 C              SELECT                                     begin select group  B02
  49 C              WHEN      YrsEmplyed < 2                   equal to zero?      X02
  50 C              EVAL      Salary = 600                     initialize Salary   02
  51 C              EVAL      Commission = CommSales * .12     compute Commission  02
  52 C              IF        CommSales > 25000                > 25000?            B03
  53 C              EVAL      ExtraSales = CommSales - 25000   compute ExtraSales  03
  54 C              EVAL      ExtraComm = ExtraSales * .02     compute ExtraComm   03
  55 C              ENDIF                                      end IF group        E03
  56
  57 * Calculations for employees with 2 or more years employment..
  58 C              OTHER                                                          X02
  59 C              EVAL      Salary = 1000                    initialize Salary   02
  60 C              EVAL      Commission = CommSales * .20     compute Commission  02
  61 C              IF        CommSales > 30000                > 25000?            B03
  62 C              EVAL      ExtraSales = CommSales - 30000   compute ExtraSales  03
  63 C              EVAL      ExtraComm = ExtraSales * .05     compute ExtraComm   03
  64 C              ENDIF                                      end IF group        E03
  65 C              ENDSL                                      end SELECT group    E02
  66
  67 * Compute salary + commissions amount....
  68 C              EVAL      Commission = Commission + Salary + ExtraComm compute Commission 01
  69
  70 * Accumulate Totals....
  71 C              EVAL      TotalSales = TotalSales + SaleAmount   compute TotalSales 01
  72 C              EVAL      TotReturns = TotReturns + SaleReturn   compute TotReturns 01
  73 C              EVAL      TotNetSale = TotNetSale + NetSales     compute TotNetSale 01
  74 C              EVAL      TotalComm = TotalComm + Commission     compute TotalComm 01
  75 C              WRITE     Detail                           print DetailLine    01
  76 C              EVAL      LinesUsed = LinesUsed + 2        increment LinesUsed 01
  77 C                                                                             01
  78 C              READ      P62psm                    ----LR read next record    01
  79 C              ENDDO                                      end dow group       E01
```

237

```
80
81 C                     WRITE     Totals                              print total line
82=OHDG
    *-------------------------------------------------------------------------------*
    * RPG record format . . . . : HDG                                               *
    * External format . . . . . : HDG : STAN/PA182PRT                               *
    *-------------------------------------------------------------------------------*
83=ODETAIL
    *-------------------------------------------------------------------------------*
    * RPG record format . . . . : DETAIL                                            *
    * External format . . . . . : DETAIL : STAN/PA182PRT                            *
    *-------------------------------------------------------------------------------*
84=O                     SALEPERSN#        5A CHAR      5
85=O                     SALEPNAME        30A CHAR     25
86=O                     YRSEMPLYED       32S ZONE     2,0
87=O                     SALEAMOUNT       40S ZONE     8,2
88=O                     SALERETURN       47S ZONE     7,2
89=O                     NETSALES         55S ZONE     8,2
90=O                     COMMISSION       63S ZONE     8,2
91=OTOTALS
    *-------------------------------------------------------------------------------*
    * RPG record format . . . . : TOTALS                                            *
    * External format . . . . . : TOTALS : STAN/PA182PRT                            *
    *-------------------------------------------------------------------------------*
92=O                     TOTALSALES        9S ZONE     9,2
93=O                     TOTRETURNS       17S ZONE     8,2
94=O                     TOTNETSALE       26S ZONE     9,2
95=O                     TOTALCOMM        35S ZONE     9,2
    * * * * *  E N D   O F   S O U R C E  * * * * *
```

Printed Report:

1/22/98		COMMISSION REPORT				PAGE 1
SALESMAN #	SALESMAN NAME	EMP YRS	GROSS SALES	RETURNS	NET SALES	SALARY/ COMMISSION
11111	SIEGFRIED HOUNDSTOOTH	4	11,250.50	1,000.00	10,250.50	2,650.10
11112	FELIX GOODGUY	1	28,000.00	.00	28,000.00	3,740.00
22222	OTTO MUTTENJAMMER	6	100,000.00	.00	100,000.00	24,000.00
33333	HANS OFFENHAUSER	1	2,500.00	700.00	1,800.00	600.00

1/22/98		COMMISSION REPORT				PAGE 2
SALESMAN #	SALESMAN NAME	EMP YRS	GROSS SALES	RETURNS	NET SALES	SALARY/ COMMISSION
44444	BARNEY OLDFIELD	3	1,900.00	.00	1,900.00	1,000.00
55555	WILLIAM PETTY	2	22,000.00	.00	22,000.00	5,000.00
	TOTALS.........		165,650.50	1,700.00	163,950.50	36,990.10

Programming Assignment 18-3: VOTER REPORT BY TOWN, COUNTY, AND STATE TOTALS

Compiled Printer File Listing:

```
                              Data Description Source
SEQNBR  *...+....1....+....2....+....3....+....4....+....5....+....6....+....7....+....8
  100    A                                        REF(P71PSM)
  200    A              R HDG1                     SPACEB(1)
  300    A                                        1DATE EDTCDE(Y)
  400    A                                        35'STATE OF CONFUSION'
  500    A                                        77'PAGE'
  600    A                                        82PAGNBR EDTCDE(Z) SPACEA(1)
  700    A                                        24'VOTERS REPORT BY DISTRICT, TOWN, -
  800    A                                          & COUNTY' SPACEA(3)
  900    A              R HDG2                     SPACEA(1)
 1000    A                                        20'DISTRICT'
 1100    A                                        34'TOWN'
 1200    A                                        44'COUNTY'
 1300    A                                        63'VOTERS'
 1400    * DETAIL RECORD........
 1500    A              R DETAIL                   SPACEB(1)
 1600    A                 DISTRICTNOR             22
 1700    A                 TOWNNO    R             34
 1800    A                 COUNTYNO  R             45
 1900    A                 VOTERS    R             63EDTCDE(1)
 2000    * TOWN TOTAL LINE RECORD.......
 2100
 2200    A              R TOWNRCD                  SPACEB(2)
 2300    A                                        23'TOTAL VOTERS FOR TOWN'
 2400  . A                 TOWN#HOLD      3        45
 2500    A                 TOWNTOTAL      7   0    61EDTCDE(1)
 2600    A                                        71'*' SPACEA(1)
 2700    * COUNTY TOTAL LINE RECORD.......
 2800    A              R COUNTYRCD                SPACEB(1)
 2900    A                                        23'TOTAL VOTERS FOR COUNTY'
 3000    A                 CONTY#HOLD     2        47
 3100    A                 CONTYTOTAL     8   0    60EDTCDE(1)
 3200    A                                        71'**'
 3300    * STATE TOTAL LINE RECORD.......
 3400    A              R STATERCD                 SPACEB(3)
 3500    A                                        23'TOTAL VOTERS FOR STATE'
 3600    A                 STATETOTAL     9   0    59EDTCDE(1)
                         * * * * *  E N D  O F  S O U R C E  * * * * *
```

Compiled Program Listing:

```
Line  <--------------------- Source Specifications --------------------><---- Comments ----> Do
Number ....1....+....2....+....3....+....4....+....5....+....6....+....7....+....8....+....9....+...10 Num
                        S o u r c e   L i s t i n g
  1  * PA 18-3: Voter report by town and state totals....
  2  FP71psm   IF  E        K DISK
     *--------------------------------------------------------------------------------*
     *                                                                                *
     *                             RPG name         External name                     *
     * File name. . . . . . . . . : P71PSM          STAN/P71PSM                        *
     * Record format(s) . . . . . : P71PSMR         P71PSMR                            *
     *--------------------------------------------------------------------------------*
  3  FPa183prt  O  E           PRINTER
  4
     *--------------------------------------------------------------------------------*
     *                             RPG name         External name                     *
     * File name. . . . . . . . . : PA183PRT        STAN/PA183PRT                      *
     * Record format(s) . . . . . : HDG1            HDG1                               *
     *                              HDG2            HDG2                               *
     *                              DETAIL          DETAIL                             *
     *                              TOWNRCD         TOWNRCD                            *
     *                              COUNTYRCD       COUNTYRCD                          *
     *                              STATERCD        STATERCD                           *
     *--------------------------------------------------------------------------------*
  5  DTownTotal       S         7  0
  6  DContyTotal      S         8  0
  7  DStateTotal      S         9  0
  8  DTime            S         6  0
```

```
    9
   10=IP71PSMR
      *------------------------------------------------------------------------------------*
      * RPG record format  . . . . :  P71PSMR                                               *
      * External format  . . . . . :  P71PSMR : STAN/P71PSM                                 *
      *------------------------------------------------------------------------------------*
   11=I                                 A    1    4  DISTRICTNO
   12=I                                 A    5    7  TOWNNO
   13=I                                 A    8    9  COUNTYNO
   14=I                                 P   10   13  0VOTERS
   15 C                   READ      P71psm                          ----LR    read first record
   16 C                   EXSR      HousekepSR                                exit to subroutine
   17 C                   EXSR      HeadingSR                                 branch to subroutine
   18 C                   DOW       *INLR = *OFF                              dow LR is off      B01
   19
   20  * Test for control breaks....
   21 C                   SELECT                                             begin SELECT group B02
   22 C                   WHEN      Conty#Hold <> CountyNo                    county control break X02
   23 C                   EXSR      TownSR                                    branch to subroutine  02
   24 C                   EXSR      CountySR                                  branch to subroutine  02
   25 C                   EXSR      HeadingSR                                 branch to subroutine  02
   26 C                   WHEN      Town#Hold <> TownNo                       town control break? X02
   27 C                   EXSR      TownSR                                    branch to subroutine  02
   28 C                   ENDSL                                              end SELECT group   E02
   29
   30 C                   EVAL      TownTotal = TownTotal + Voters            accum TownTotal    01
   31 C                   WRITE     Detail                                    print detail record 01
   32
   33 C                   READ      P71psm                          ----LR    read next record   01
   34 C                   ENDDO                                              end dow group      E01
   35
   36  * Branch to end of file subroutine....
   37 C                   EXSR      EofSR                                     branch to subroutine
   38
   39  * Begin subroutines....
   40 C     HouseKepSR    BEGSR                                              begin subroutine
   41 C                   EVAL      Conty#Hold = CountyNo                     init. holding field
   42 C                   EVAL      Town#Hold = TownNo                        init. holding field
   43 C                   TIME                      Time                      access system time
   44 C                   ENDSR                                              end subroutine
   45
   46  * Heading control....
   47 C     HeadingSR     BEGSR
   48 C                   WRITE     Hdg1                                      print heading lines
   49 C                   WRITE     Hdg2
   50 C                   ENDSR                                              end subroutine
   51
   52 C     TownSR        BEGSR                                              begin subroutine
   53 C                   EVAL      ContyTotal = ContyTotal + TownTotal       accum contytotAl
   54 C                   WRITE     TownRcd                                   print town total
   55 C                   EVAL      Town#Hold = TownNo                        init. holding field
   56 C                   EVAL      TownTotal = *ZERO                         init. towntotal to 0
   57 C                   ENDSR                                              end subroutine
   58
   59 C     CountySR      BEGSR                                              begin subroutine
   60 C                   EVAL      StateTotal = StateTotal + ContyTotal      accum statetotal
   61 C                   WRITE     CountyRcd                                 print county total
   62 C                   EVAL      Conty#Hold = CountyNo                     init. holding field
   63 C                   EVAL      ContyTotal = *ZERO                        init contytotal to 0
   64 C                   ENDSR                                              end subroutine
   65
   66 C     EofSR         BEGSR                                              begin subroutine
   67 C                   EXSR      TownSR                                    branch to subroutine
   68 C                   EXSR      CountySR                                  branch to SR
   69 C                   WRITE     StateRcd                                  print state total
   70 C                   ENDSR                                              end subroutine
   71=OHDG1
      *------------------------------------------------------------------------------------*
      * RPG record format  . . . . :  HDG1                                                  *
      * External format  . . . . . :  HDG1 : STAN/PA183PRT                                  *
      *------------------------------------------------------------------------------------*
   72=OHDG2
```

```
*-------------------------------------------------------------------------------*
* RPG record format  . . . . :  HDG2                                            *
* External format  . . . . . :  HDG2 : STAN/PA183PRT                            *
*-------------------------------------------------------------------------------*
73=ODETAIL
   *----------------------------------------------------------------------------*
   * RPG record format  . . . . :  DETAIL                                       *
   * External format  . . . . . :  DETAIL : STAN/PA183PRT                       *
   *----------------------------------------------------------------------------*
74=0                        DISTRICTNO        4A CHAR        4
75=0                        TOWNNO            7A CHAR        3
76=0                        COUNTYNO          9A CHAR        2
77=0                        VOTERS           15S ZONE        6,0
78=OTOWNRCD
   *----------------------------------------------------------------------------*
   * RPG record format  . . . . :  TOWNRCD                                      *
   * External format  . . . . . :  TOWNRCD : STAN/PA183PRT                      *
   *----------------------------------------------------------------------------*
79=0                        TOWN#HOLD         3A CHAR        3
80=0                        TOWNTOTAL        10S ZONE        7,0
81=OCOUNTYRCD
   *----------------------------------------------------------------------------*
   * RPG record format  . . . . :  COUNTYRCD                                    *
   * External format  . . . . . :  COUNTYRCD : STAN/PA183PRT                    *
   *----------------------------------------------------------------------------*
82=0                        CONTY#HOLD        2A CHAR        2
83=0                        CONTYTOTAL       10S ZONE        8,0
84=OSTATERCD
   *----------------------------------------------------------------------------*
   * RPG record format  . . . . :  STATERCD                                     *
   * External format  . . . . . :  STATERCD : STAN/PA183PRT                     *
   *----------------------------------------------------------------------------*
85=0                        STATETOTAL        9S ZONE        9,0
  * * * * *  E N D   O F   S O U R C E  * * * * *
```

Printed Report:

```
-----------------------------------------------------------------------------
2/01/98                         STATE OF CONFUSION              PAGE    1
                      VOTERS REPORT BY DISTRICT, TOWN, & COUNTY


           DISTRICT      TOWN      COUNTY           VOTERS

               1000       100        10            215,625
               1010       100        10             82,784
               1020       100        10            104,716
               1030       100        10             12,899
               1040       100        10            267,004

               TOTAL VOTERS FOR TOWN 100           683,028 *

               2000       200        10             57,800
               2010       200        10             14,111
               2020       200        10            118,923
               2030       200        10             73,807

               TOTAL VOTERS FOR TOWN 200           264,641 *

               TOTAL VOTERS FOR COUNTY 10          947,669 **
-----------------------------------------------------------------------------
2/01/98                         STATE OF CONFUSION              PAGE    2
                      VOTERS REPORT BY DISTRICT, TOWN, & COUNTY


           DISTRICT      TOWN      COUNTY           VOTERS

               3000       300        30            200,749
               3010       300        30            111,111
```

```
|        TOTAL VOTERS FOR TOWN 300           311,860 *         |
|                                                              |
|        TOTAL VOTERS FOR COUNTY 30          311,860 **        |
|--------------------------------------------------------------|
| 2/01/98                 STATE OF CONFUSION         PAGE   3  |
|             VOTERS REPORT BY DISTRICT, TOWN, & COUNTY        |
|                                                              |
|         DISTRICT    TOWN     COUNTY          VOTERS          |
|           4000      400        40            67,242         |
|           4010      400        40           104,338         |
|           4020      400        40            99,917         |
|           4030      400        40           178,615         |
|           4040      400        40           222,234         |
|           4050      400        40            33,845         |
|           4060      400        40           117,871         |
|           4070      400        40            64,899         |
|           4080      400        40            45,348         |
|           4090      400        40           888,888         |
|                                                              |
|        TOTAL VOTERS FOR TOWN 400         1,823,197 *        |
|                                                              |
|        TOTAL VOTERS FOR COUNTY 40        1,823,197 **       |
|                                                              |
|        TOTAL VOTERS FOR STATE            3,082,726          |
|--------------------------------------------------------------|
```

Programming Assignment 18-4: INCOME STATEMENT BY QUARTERS

<u>Notes to the Instructor</u>:

1. This is an example of where a printer file may be more complicated to program than traditional RPG output coding for a report.

2. Because the assignment includes arrays, individual elements cannot be accessed by indexing in the printer file. Considerably more coding (EVAL instructions) is required in the RPG IV program and the DDS for the printer file (individual fields).

3. Remind students that the runtime array (DataAry) is loaded with data by the input instructions on lines 25 through 28.

<u>Compiled Printer File Listing</u>:

```
SEQNBR  *...+....1....+....2....+....3....+....4....+....5....+....6....+....7....+....8
  100   A        R HDGS                   SKIPB(1)
  200   A                                 34'DAGWOOD COMPANY' SPACEA(1)
  300   A                                 33'INCOME STATEMENT'
  400   A                                 SPACEA(1)
  500   A                                 30'FOR YEAR ENDING'
  600   A                                 46'12/31/'
  700   A          YEAR       2  0        52SPACEA(2)
  800   A                                 32'1Q'
  900   A                                 43'2Q'
 1000   A                                 54'3Q'
 1100   A                                 65'4Q'
 1200   A                                 76'TOTAL' SPACEA(2)
 1300   *
 1400   A        R SALR                   SPACEA(1)
 1500   A                                 2'SALES'
 1600   A          SAL1       6  0        28EDTWRD('$&    , 0')
 1700   A          SAL2       6  0        39EDTWRD('$&    , 0')
```

```
1800    A           SAL3        6  0    50EDTWRD('$&   ,   0')
1900    A           SAL4        6  0    61EDTWRD('$&   ,   0')
2000    A           TSALES      7  0    72EDTWRD('$& ,   ,   0')
2100       *
2200    A    R CGSR                     SPACEA(1)
2300    A                               2'LESS COST OF SALES'
2400    A           CGS1        6  0    30EDTWRD('    ,   0')
2500    A           CGS2        6  0    41EDTWRD('    ,   0')
2600    A           CGS3        6  0    52EDTWRD('    ,   0')
2700    A           CGS4        6  0    63EDTWRD('    ,   0')
2800    A           TCOST       7  0    74EDTWRD(' ,   ,   0')
2900       *
3000    A    R GPR                      SPACEA(1)
3100    A                               3'GROSS PROFIT'
3200    A           GP1         6  0    28EDTWRD('$&   ,   0')
3300    A           GP2         6  0    39EDTWRD('$&   ,   0')
3400    A           GP3         6  0    50EDTWRD('$&   ,   0')
3500    A           GP4         6  0    61EDTWRD('$&   ,   0')
3600    A           TGROSS      7  0    72EDTWRD('$& ,   ,   0')
3700       *
3800    A    R OER                      SPACEA(1)
3900    A                               2'LESS OPERATING EXPENSES'
4000    A           OE1         6  0    30EDTWRD('    ,   0')
4100    A           OE2         6  0    41EDTWRD('    ,   0')
4200    A           OE3         6  0    52EDTWRD('    ,   0')
4300    A           OE4         6  0    63EDTWRD('    ,   0')
4400    A           TEXP        7  0    74EDTWRD(' ,   ,   0')
4500       *
4600    A    R NIR                      SPACEA(2)
4700    A                               3'NET INCOME(LOSS-)'
4800    A           NI1         6  0    28EDTWRD('$&   ,   0-')
4900    A           NI2         6  0    39EDTWRD('$&   ,   0-')
5000    A           NI3         6  0    50EDTWRD('$&   ,   0-')
5100    A           NI4         6  0    61EDTWRD('$&   ,   0-')
5200    A           TNET        7  0    72EDTWRD('$& ,   ,   0-')
5300       *
5400    A    R PCTR
5500    A                               2'PCT OF NET INCOME TO SALES'
5600    A           PT1         4  2    31EDTCDE(J)
5700    A           PT2         4  2    42EDTCDE(J)
5800    A           PT3         4  2    53EDTCDE(J)
5900    A           PT4         4  2    63EDTCDE(J)
6000    A           TPCT        4  2    77EDTCDE(J)
```

Compiled Program Listing:

```
Line  <-------------------- Source Specifications -------------------------><---- Comments ----> Do
Number ....1....+....2....+....3....+....4....+....5....+....6....+....7....+....8....+....9....+...10 Num
                          S o u r c e   L i s t i n g
  1 * PA 18-4 Income Statement by Quarters....
  2 FP102psm  IF  E           DISK
    *-------------------------------------------------------------------------------------------*
    *                         RPG name            External name                                 *
    * File name. . . . . . . . . : P102PSM         STAN/P102PSM                                  *
    * Record format(s) . . . . . : P102PSMR        P102PSMR                                      *
    *-------------------------------------------------------------------------------------------*
  3 FPA184prt  O  E           PRINTER
  4
  5 * Define arrays....
    *-------------------------------------------------------------------------------------------*
    *                         RPG name            External name                                 *
    * File name. . . . . . . . . : PA184PRT        STAN/PA184PRT                                 *
    * Record format(s) . . . . . : HDGS            HDGS                                          *
    *                             SALR            SALR                                          *
    *                             CGSR            CGSR                                          *
    *                             GPR             GPR                                           *
    *                             OER             OER                                           *
    *                             NIR             NIR                                           *
    *                             PCTR            PCTR                                          *
```

```
              *-------------------------------------------------------------------------*
     6 DDataAry        S              6  0 DIM(4)                                         *
     7 DSalesAry       S              6  0 DIM(4)
     8 DCostAry        S              6  0 DIM(4)
     9 DGProfitAry     S              6  0 DIM(4)
    10 DExpenseAry     S              6  0 DIM(4)
    11 DNProfitAry     S              6  0 DIM(4)
    12 DDecPctAry      S              4  4 DIM(4)
    13 DPercentAry     S              4  2 DIM(4)
    14
    15 DTotDecPct      S              4  4
    16
    17 * Load runtime array (DataAry)....
    18 IP102psmr
    19 I               Qtr1Amt                     DataAry(1)
    20 I               Qtr2Amt                     DataAry(2)
    21 I               Qtr3Amt                     DataAry(3)
    22 I               Qtr4Amt                     DataAry(4)
    23
              *-------------------------------------------------------------------------*
              * RPG record format  . . . . :  P102PSMR                                   *
              * External format  . . . . . :  P102PSMR : STAN/P102PSM                    *
              *-------------------------------------------------------------------------*
    24=I                      A    1    1 ACTCODE
    25=I                      P    2    3 OYEAR
    26=I                      P    4    7 ODATAARY(1)
    27=I                      P    8   11 ODATAARY(2)
    28=I                      P   12   15 ODATAARY(3)
    29=I                      P   16   19 ODATAARY(4)
    30 C           READ      P102Psm                        ----LR   read first record
    31 C           WRITE     Hdgs                                    print heading lines
    32 C           DOW       *INLR = *OFF                            dow LR is off          B01
    33
    34 C           SELECT                                            begin select group     B02
    35 C           WHEN      ActCode = 'S'                           ActCode = S?           X02
    36 C           MOVEA     DataAry       SalesAry                  load salesary           02
    37 C           XFOOT     SalesAry      TSales                    crossfoot for total     02
    38 C           EVAL      Sal1 = DataAry(1)                       load PRTF field         02
    39 C           EVAL      Sal2 = DataAry(2)                       load PRTF field         02
    40 C           EVAL      Sal3 = DataAry(3)                       load PRTF field         02
    41 C           EVAL      Sal4 = DataAry(4)                       load PRTF field         02
    42 C           WRITE     Salr                                    print PRTF record       02
    43
    44 C           WHEN      ActCode = 'C'                           ActCode = C?           X02
    45 C           MOVEA     DataAry       CostAry                   load costary            02
    46 C           XFOOT     DataAry       TCost                     crossfoot for total     02
    47 C           EVAL      Cgs1 = DataAry(1)                       load PRTF field         02
    48 C           EVAL      Cgs2 = DataAry(2)                       load PRTF field         02
    49 C           EVAL      Cgs3 = DataAry(3)                       load PRTF field         02
    50 C           EVAL      Cgs4 = DataAry(4)                       load PRTF field         02
    51 C           WRITE     Cgsr                                    print PRTF record       02
    52
    53 C           EVAL      GProfitAry = SalesAry - CostAry         computeTgross|profit    02
    54 C           EVAL      Gp1 = GProfitAry(1)                     load PRTF field         02
    55 C           EVAL      Gp2 = GProfitAry(2)                     load PRTF field         02
    56 C           EVAL      Gp3 = GProfitAry(3)                     load PRTF field         02
    57 C           EVAL      Gp4 = GProfitAry(4)                     load PRTF field         02
    58 C           XFOOT     GProfitAry    TGross                    cross foot array        02
    59 C           WRITE     Gpr                                     print PRTF record       02
    60
    61 C           WHEN      ActCode = 'E'                           ActCode = E?           X02
    62 C           MOVEA     DataAry       ExpenseAry                load expenseary         02
    63 C           XFOOT     ExpenseAry    Texp                      crossfoot for total     02
    64 C           EVAL      Oe1 = DataAry(1)                        load PRTF field         02
    65 C           EVAL      Oe2 = DataAry(2)                        load PRTF field         02
    66 C           EVAL      Oe3 = DataAry(3)                        load PRTF field         02
    67 C           EVAL      Oe4 = DataAry(4)                        load PRTF field         02
    68 C           WRITE     Oer                                     print PRTF record       02
    69 C           ENDSL                                             end select group       E02
    70
    71 C           READ      P102Psm                        ----LR   read next record        01
    72 C           ENDDO                                             end dow group          E01
```

```
73
74 C              EVAL      NProfitAry = GProfitAry - ExpenseAry    compute net profit
75 C              EVAL      Ni1 = NProfitAry(1)                     load PRTF field
76 C              EVAL      Ni2 = NProfitAry(2)                     load PRTF field
77 C              EVAL      Ni3 = NProfitAry(3)                     load PRTF field
78 C              EVAL      Ni4 = NProfitAry(4)                     load PRTF field
79 C              XFOOT     NProfitAry    TNet                      cross foot array
80 C              WRITE     Nir                                     print PRTF record
81
82 C              EVAL      TotDecPct = TNet / TSales               compute totpercent
83 C              EVAL      Tpct = TotDecPct * 100                  compute totpercent
84 C              EVAL(H)   DecPctAry = NProfitAry / SalesAry       compute decimal pct
85 C              EVAL      PercentAry = DecPctAry * 100            compute percents
86 C              EVAL      Pt1 = PercentAry(1)                     load PRTF field
87 C              EVAL      Pt2 = PercentAry(2)                     load PRTF field
88 C              EVAL      Pt3 = PercentAry(3)                     load PRTF field
89 C              EVAL      Pt4 = PercentAry(4)                     load PRTF field
90 C              WRITE     Pctr                                    print PRTF record
91=OHDGS
     *-------------------------------------------------------------------*
     * RPG record format  . . . . :  HDGS                                *
     * External format  . . . . . :  HDGS : STAN/PA184PRT               *
     *-------------------------------------------------------------------*
92=O                      YEAR                 2S ZONE      2,0
93=OSALR
     *-------------------------------------------------------------------*
     * RPG record format  . . . . :  SALR                                *
     * External format  . . . . . :  SALR : STAN/PA184PRT               *
     *-------------------------------------------------------------------*
94=O                      SAL1                 6S ZONE      6,0
95=O                      SAL2                12S ZONE      6,0
96=O                      SAL3                18S ZONE      6,0
97=O                      SAL4                24S ZONE      6,0
98=O                      TSALES              31S ZONE      7,0
99=OCGSR
     *-------------------------------------------------------------------*
     * RPG record format  . . . . :  CGSR                                *
     * External format  . . . . . :  CGSR : STAN/PA184PRT               *
     *-------------------------------------------------------------------*
100=O                     CGS1                 6S ZONE      6,0
101=O                     CGS2                12S ZONE      6,0
102=O                     CGS3                18S ZONE      6,0
103=O                     CGS4                24S ZONE      6,0
104=O                     TCOST               31S ZONE      7,0
105=OGPR
     *-------------------------------------------------------------------*
     * RPG record format  . . . . :  GPR                                 *
     * External format  . . . . . :  GPR : STAN/PA184PRT                *
     *-------------------------------------------------------------------*
106=O                     GP1                  6S ZONE      6,0
107=O                     GP2                 12S ZONE      6,0
108=O                     GP3                 18S ZONE      6,0
109=O                     GP4                 24S ZONE      6,0
110=O                     TGROSS              31S ZONE      7,0
111=OOER
     *-------------------------------------------------------------------*
     * RPG record format  . . . . :  OER                                 *
     * External format  . . . . . :  OER : STAN/PA184PRT                *
     *-------------------------------------------------------------------*
112=O                     OE1                  6S ZONE      6,0
113=O                     OE2                 12S ZONE      6,0
114=O                     OE3                 18S ZONE      6,0
115=O                     OE4                 24S ZONE      6,0
116=O                     TEXP                31S ZONE      7,0
117=ONIR
     *-------------------------------------------------------------------*
     * RPG record format  . . . . :  NIR                                 *
     * External format  . . . . . :  NIR : STAN/PA184PRT                *
     *-------------------------------------------------------------------*
118=O                     NI1                  6S ZONE      6,0
119=O                     NI2                 12S ZONE      6,0
120=O                     NI3                 18S ZONE      6,0
```

```
121=0                    NI4              24S ZONE      6,0
122=0                    TNET             31S ZONE      7,0
123=0PCTR
     *----------------------------------------------------------------*
     * RPG record format  . . . . :  PCTR                             *
     * External format  . . . . . :  PCTR : STAN/PA184PRT             *
     *----------------------------------------------------------------*
124=0                    PT1               4S ZONE      4,2
125=0                    PT2               8S ZONE      4,2
126=0                    PT3              12S ZONE      4,2
127=0                    PT4              16S ZONE      4,2
128=0                    TPCT             20S ZONE      4,2
     * * * * *  E N D   O F   S O U R C E  * * * * *
```

Printed Report:

```
                        DAGWOOD COMPANY
                        INCOME STATEMENT
                     FOR YEAR ENDING 12/31/98

                         1Q        2Q        3Q        4Q        TOTAL

SALES                 $ 200,000 $ 175,000 $ 210,000 $ 309,000 $  894,000
LESS COST OF SALES      100,000    92,000   120,000   209,000    521,000
 GROSS PROFIT         $ 100,000 $  83,000 $  90,000 $ 100,000 $  373,000
LESS OPERATING EXPENSES  70,000    52,000    89,000   105,000    316,000
 NET INCOME(LOSS-)    $  30,000 $  31,000 $   1,000 $   5,000-$   57,000

PCT OF NET INCOME TO SALES 15.00   17.71      .47     1.61-       6.38
```

CHAPTER 19
CHAPTER ANSWERS

1. The inclusion of RPG IV programs into a modular program and/or procedures. Field addresses in storage are passed to and received from standalone modules as required.

2. *Dynamic binding and Static binding.*

3. For *Dynamic binding*, the **CRTBNDRPG** command must be used to compile the RPG IV program. With **Static binding**, the **CRTRPGMOD** command must be used.

4. The *"calling"* RPG IV program is the one that initially passes values to another program. A *"called"* program is one that receives the values from the *"calling"* program.

5. The **CALL** operation is used with *Dynamic binding* and the **CALLB** operation with *Static binding*.

6. To receive parameter values from the *"calling"* program, the *"called"* program must include an instruction with ***ENTRY** in *Factor 1* and the **PLIST** operation name in the *OpCode&Ext* field. The required number of **PARM** instructions must follow and be in the same order as the fields in the "calling" program. The field names include in the **PARM** instructions do not have to be the same as those in the *"calling"* program, but must have the same field attributes.

7. Control is returned back to the "calling" program when a **RETURN** instruction is encountered or when an instruction that turns on indicator **LR** is executed.

8. No. However, they must be in the same order as in the *"calling"* program and have the same field attributes.

9. The parameter addresses of the fields or literals in the **PARM** instructions in the *"calling"* program and <u>not</u> actual field values.

10. With Dynamic binding, a *"called"* program is bound to the *"calling"* program by a **CALL** instruction in the *"calling"* program.

11. A field name, named constant, array, or literal. Any of these items must contain the name of the program to be called.

12. If a **PARM** instruction immediately follows a **CALL** instruction or if the "called" program does not access parameters, an entry in the *Result* field may be omitted.

13. A **PLIST** instruction begins a parameter list that includes one or more **PARM** instructions in both the "calling" and "called" program.

14. A **PARM** instruction passes the addresses of fields or literals to the "called" program. The "called" program accesses the addresses by related **PARM** instructions an ***ENTRY** instruction.

15. The value in Charge is moved to the Amount field before passing the address of the parameter. When the "*called*" program returns control back to the "*calling*" program, the value in Amount is moved to the Rating item.

16. The **PLIST** instruction identifies the entry point in the "*called*" program for the **PARM** instructions that follow.

17. Receives the address of the first value sent from the "*calling*" *program.*

18. *Amt1 (Result* field item) recieves the address of the second item passed from the "calling" program and the value is automatically moved to Rating (*Factor 1* item).

    When control is returned back to the "calling" program, the value in Charge (*Factor 2* item) is moved to Amt1 (*Result* field Item).

19. Returns control back to the "calling program".

20. Turning on the **LR** indicator will provide the same control.

21. A collection of commonly used procedures from one or more module objects.

22. By a special *Binder Language* accessed in SEU by the source type **END**.

23. The **CRTSRVPGM** command.

24. Create a program with the **CRTPGM** command to bind the service program to the calling program into a run-time unit.

25. Identifies the beginning of the list of exports from the service program.

26. Identifies the symbol (module, procedure, data item) name to be exported (controlled) by the service program. Any number may be included in a service program.

27. Identifies the end of the list of exports from the service program.

28. *Binder* language with the source type **END**.

PROGRAMMING ASSIGNMENTS

Programming Assignment 19-1: CREDIT SALES REPORT

1. Inform students that this assignment requires the completion of

1.   Inform students that this assignment requires the completion of two RPG IV programs; a "calling" and a "called" program.

2.   *Dynamic binding* was used for this assignment which required that:

   a. A **CALL** instruction be included in the "calling" program (a **CALLB** instruction is required for *static binding*).

   b. Both the "calling" and "called" programs must be compiled with the **CRTBNDRPG** (*Create Bound RPG*) command when *dynamic binding* is selected.

Calling program listing:

```
Line     <------------------ Source Specifications ------------------------><---- Comments ----> Do
Number   ....1....+....2....+....3....+....4....+....5....+....6....+....7....+....8....+....9....+...10 Num
                            S o u r c e   L i s t i n g
    1  * PA 19-1: Credit sales report - calling program....
    2
    3 FPa191p   IF  E        K DISK
       *-----------------------------------------------------------------------------------------*
       *                                RPG name         External name                           *
       * File name. . . . . . . . . :   PA191P           STAN/PA191P                             *
       * Record format(s) . . . . . :   PA191PR          PA191PR                                 *
       *-----------------------------------------------------------------------------------------*
    4 FQsysprt   O   F  132          PRINTER OFLIND(*INOF)
    5
    6  * Define work fields....
    7 DMthNo          S             2                                    field for parm
    8 DYear           S             2                                    field for parm
    9 DCatDate        S            14                                    field for parm
   10 DNetAmount      S             8 2                                  field for parm
   11 DHhMmSs         S             6 0
   12 DTotalSales     S             9 2
   13
   14=IPA191PR
       *-----------------------------------------------------------------------------------------*
       * RPG record format  . . . . :   PA191PR                                                  *
       * External format  . . . . . :   PA191PR : STAN/PA191P                                    *
       *-----------------------------------------------------------------------------------------*
   15=I                        A     1    4  ACTNUMBER
   16=I                        A     5   29  ACTNAME
   17=I                        P    30   33 OSALESDATE
   18=I                        P    34   36 OINVOICENO
   19=I                        P    37   41 2SALE_AMT
   20 C               EVAL      *INOF = *ON                      turn on OF indicator
   21 C               MOVE      UMONTH         MthNo             initialize MthNo
   22 C               MOVE      UYEAR          Year              initialize Year
   23 C               READ      Pa191p                   ----LR  read first record
   24 C               DOW       *INLR = *OFF                     dow lr is off          B01
   25
   26  * Pass parameters to and receive from the called program....
   27 C               CALL      'PA191R2'                        call the rpg program   01
   28 C               PARM                     MthNo             send address to prg    01
   29 C               PARM                     Year              send address to prg    01
   30 C               PARM                     Sale_Amt          send address to prg    01
   31 C               PARM                     CatDate           send address to prg    01
   32 C               PARM                     NetAmount         send address to rpg    01
   33
   34  * Access system time and print headings....
   35 C               IF        *INOF = *ON                      indicator of on?       B02
   36 C               TIME                     HhMmSs            access system time     02
   37 C               EXCEPT    HdgLine                          print heading lines    02
   38 C               EVAL      *INOF = *OFF                     turn off of indicatr   02
   39 C               ENDIF                                      end IF group           E02
   40
   41 C               EXCEPT    Detailine                        print detailine        01
   42
```

```
43 C                    EVAL      TotalSales = TotalSales + NetAmount      accum TotalSales amt  01
44 C                    READ      Pa191p                           ----LR  read next record      01
45 C                    ENDDO                                              end dow group        E01
46
47 C                    EXCEPT    Totaline                                 print totaline
48
49 OQsysprt    E        HdgLine        1 01
50 O                    HhMmSs             8 '  :  :  '
51 O                                      45 'CREDIT SALES REPORT'
52 O                                      70 'PAGE'
53 O                    PAGE              75
54 O           E        HdgLine        3
55 O                                      30 'FOR'
56 O                    CatDate           45
57 O           E        HdgLine        1
58 O                                      22 'ACCOUNT'
59 O                                      58 'INVOICE'
60 O           E        HdgLine        2
61 O                                      11 'SALE DATE'
62 O                                      21 'NUMBER'
63 O                                      42 'ACCOUNT NAME'
64 O                                      57 'NUMBER'
65 O                                      73 'SALE AMOUNT'
66 O           E        DetailIne      2
67 O                    SalesDate    Y    10
68 O                    ActNumber         20
69 O                    ActName           49
70 O                    InvoiceNo         57
71 O                    NetAmount    1    73
72 O           E        TotalIne       1
73 O                                      60 'TOTAL CREDIT SALES....'
74 O                    TotalSales   1    73
     * * * * *  E N D   O F   S O U R C E  * * * * *
```

Called program listing:

```
Line    <--------------------- Source Specifications ---------------------------><---- Comments ----> Do
Number  ....1....+....2....+....3....+....4....+....5....+....6....+....7....+....8....+....9....+...10 Num
                        S o u r c e   L i s t i n g
    1  * PA 19-1: called program that looks up a table of month numbers and
    2  * a table of month names, concatenate the report date, determines the
    3  * the net amount of the sale after the applicate sales discount....
    4
    5  * Define compile time tables....
    6 DTabMthno       S             2    DIM(12) ASCEND CTDATA
    7 DTabName        S             9    DIM(12) ALT(TabMthno)
    8
    9  * Define workfield....
   10 DDiscount       S             7 2
   11 DMthNo          S             2
   12 DYear           S             2
   13 DCatDate        S            14
   14 DSale_Amt       S             8 2
   15 DNetAmount      S             8 2
   16
   17  * Parameters received from the "calling" program....
   18 C     *ENTRY      PLIST                                              begin plist
   19 C                 PARM                    MthNo
   20 C                 PARM                    Year
   21 C                 PARM                    Sale_Amt
   22 C                 PARM                    CatDate
   23 C                 PARM                    NetAmount
   24
   25  * Look up the month name from a compile time table * concatenate parts
   26 C     MthNo       LOOKUP    TabMthNo      TabName           ----90   lookup table
   27 C                 IF        *IN90 = *ON                              table entry found?   B01
   28 C*                MOVEL     TabName       CatDate                    move left to field
   29 C                 EVAL      CatDate = %TRIMR(TabName) + ' ' + '19' + Yearconcatenate elements  01
   30 C                 ENDIF                                              end if group         E01
   31
   32  * Determine applicable sales discount....
   33 C                 SELECT                                             begin select group   B01
   34 C                 WHEN      Sale_Amt > 50000                         sale_amt > 50000?     X01
```

```
35 C                    EVAL      Discount = Sale_Amt * .05      compute discount      01
36 C                    WHEN      Sale_Amt >= 30001              sale_amt > 50000?     X01
37 C                    EVAL      Discount = Sale_Amt * .04      compute discount      01
38 C                    WHEN      Sale_Amt >= 10001              sale_amt > 50000?     X01
39 C                    EVAL      Discount = Sale_Amt * .025     compute discount      01
40 C                    WHEN      Sale_Amt >= 5000               sale_amt > 50000?     X01
41 C                    EVAL      Discount = Sale_Amt * .015     compute discount      01
42 C                    ENDSL                                    end select group      E01
43
44 C                    EVAL      NetAmount = Sale_Amt - Discount   compute Netamount
45 C                    EVAL      Discount = *ZERO               initialize discount
46 C                    RETURN                                   return to calling pg
     * * * * *   E N D   O F   S O U R C E   * * * * *
                  C o m p i l e   T i m e   D a t a
47 **CTDATA TabMthNo
   *------------------------------------------------------------*
   * Table . . . : TABMTHNO    Alternating Table . . . . : TABNAME    *
   *------------------------------------------------------------*
48 01JANUARY
49 02FEBRUARY
50 03MARCH
51 04APRIL
52 05MAY
53 06JUNE
54 07JULY
55 08AUGUST
56 09SEPTEMBER
57 10OCTOBER
58 11NOVEMBER
59 12DECEMBER
* * * * *   E N D   O F   C O M P I L E   T I M E   D A T A   * * * * *
```

Printed Report:

```
15:19:01                CREDIT SALES REPORT                PAGE    1
                         FOR JANUARY 1998

                ACCOUNT                        INVOICE
    SALE DATE   NUMBER    ACCOUNT NAME          NUMBER    SALE AMOUNT

     1/03/98    1000    IVAN SNODSMITH          13568      6,107.98
     1/05/98    1200    THERESA PIRES           13569     67,431.14
     1/08/98    1300    RALPH SCADDED           13570     43,910.65
     1/15/98    1400    HENRY CARLSON           13571     29,153.37
     1/22/98    1500    JUAN HERNANDEZ          13572     95,307.95
     1/28/98    1600    IRA FINKELSTEIN         13573      4,620.18

                              TOTAL CREDIT SALES....     246,531.27
```

Programming Assignment 19-2: MORTGAGE PAYMENT SCHEDULE

Notes to the Instructor:

1. Inform students that this assignment requires the completion of two RPG IV programs; a "calling" and a "called" program.

2. *Dynamic binding* was used for this assignment which required that:

    a. A **CALL** instruction be included in the "calling" program

251

(a **CALLB** instruction is required for *static binding*).

b. Both the "calling" and "called" programs must be compiled with the **CRTBNDRPG** (*Create Bound RPG*) command when *dynamic binding* is selected.

Calling program listing:

```
Line    <-------------------- Source Specifications -------------------------><---- Comments ----> Do
Number  ....1....+....2....+....3....+....4....+....5....+....6....+....7....+....8....+....9....+...10 Num
                        S o u r c e   L i s t i n g
   1  * Chapter 19 - Lab 2 - Calling program (using dynamic binding)....
   2 FC192pf     IF   E        K DISK
     *--------------------------------------------------------------------------------*
     *                              RPG name        External name                     *
     * File name. . . . . . . . :  C192PF           STAN/C192PF                        *
     * Record format(s) . . . . . :  C192PFR          C192PFR                         *
     *--------------------------------------------------------------------------------*
   3 FQsysprt    O    F  132        PRINTER OFLIND(*INOF)
   4
   5 DMthpaymt        S             7  2                              monthly payment
   6 DTotInt          S            11  2                              total int on loan
   7 DLoan#_Hold      S             5
   8 DRateperyr       S             5  3
   9
  10=IC192PFR

     *--------------------------------------------------------------------------------*
     * RPG record format  . . . . :  C192PFR                                          *
     * External format  . . . . . :  C192PFR : STAN/C192PF                            *
     *--------------------------------------------------------------------------------*
  11=I                        A    1    5 LOAN_NO
  12=I                        A    6   25 MORTGAGOR
  13=I                        P   26   27 OTIMEINYRS
  14=I                        P   28   30 5INT_RATE
  15=I                        P   31   34 OPRINCIPAL
  16=I                        P   35   36 OPAYTPERYR
  17 C              EVAL      *INOF = *ON                    turn on OF indicator
  18
  19 C              READ      C192pf                  ----LR read first record
  20 C
  21 C              DOW       *INLR = *OFF                   do while LR is off     B01
  22
  23 C              IF        *INOF = *ON                    overflow ind on?       B02
  24 C              EXCEPT    HdgLine1                       print first heading     02
  25 C              ENDIF                                    end IF group           E02
  26
  27 C              IF        Loan#_Hold <> Loan_No          test for loan break    B02
  28 C              EVAL      Rateperyr = Int_Rate * 100     convert dec to pct      02
  29 C              EXCEPT    HdgLine2                        print other hdgs        02
  30 C              EVAL      Loan#_Hold = Loan_No            init hold field         02
  31 C              ENDIF                                    end IF group           E02
  32 C                                                                              E02
  33 C              CALL      'C192R2'                        call program            01
  34 C              PARM                TimeInYrs                                     01
  35 C              PARM                Int_Rate                                      01
  36 C              PARM                Principal                                     01
  37 C              PARM                PaytPerYr                                     01
  38 C              PARM                MthPaymt                                      01
  39 C              PARM                Totint                                        01
  40 C              EXCEPT    DetaiLine                      print detail line       01
  41 C              READ      C192pf                  ----LR read next record        01
  42 C              ENDDO                                    end dow group          E01
  43
  44 OQsysprt    E            HdgLine1      2 01
  45 O                        Udate        Y    10
  46 O                                          51 'MORTGAGE PAYMENT SCHEDULE'
  47 O                                          70 'PAGE'
  48 O                        PAGE             75
  49 O           E            HdgLine2      2
  50 O                                          12 'LOAN NUMBER:'
  51 O                        Loan_No          18
  52 O                                          33 'MORTGAGOR:'
```

```
53 O                         Mortgagor           54
54 O                                             67 'RATE/YR:'
55 O                         Rateperyr    1
56 O
57 O                                             75 '%'
58 O          E              Hdgline2     2
59 O                                             16 'LOAN AMOUNT'
60 O                                             39 'MONTHLY PAYMENT'
61 O                                             69 'TOTAL INTEREST FOR LOAN'
62 O          E              DetaiLine    4
63 O                         Principal    3   14
64 O                         MthPaymt     1   36
65 O                         TotInt       1   60
   * * * * *  E N D   O F   S O U R C E  * * * * *
```

Called Program Listing:

```
Line   <-------------------- Source Specifications ----------------------><---- Comments ----> Do
Number ....1...+....2....+....3....+....4....+....5....+....6....+....7....+....8....+....9....+...10 Num
                        S o u r c e   L i s t i n g
   1 * Ch19 - Lab 2 - Called Program....
   2
   3 * Define parameters passed from calling program....
   4 DTimeInYrs      S            2 0
   5 DInt_Rate       S            5 5
   6 DPrincipal      S            6 0
   7 DPaytPerYr      S            2 0
   8 DMthPaymt       S            7 2
   9 DTotInt         S           11 2
  10
  11 * Define work field....
  12
  13 DPerdRate       S           11 9
  14 DTotPaymts      S            9 2
  15 DPayPer         S            4 0
  16
  17 * Receive parameter values from calling program....
  18 C     *ENTRY     PLIST
  19 C                PARM                TimeInYrs     2 0
  20 C                PARM                Int_Rate      5 5
  21 C                PARM                Principal     6 0
  22 C                PARM                PaytPerYr     2 0
  23 C                PARM                MthPaymt      7 2
  24 C                PARM                TotInt       11 2
  25
  26 C                EVAL     PerdRate = Int_Rate/PaytPerYr
  27 C                EVAL     PayPer= TimeInYrs*PaytPerYr
  28 C                EVAL     MthPaymt =(Principal/((1-(1/(((1+PerdRate)
  29 C                         **PayPer)))/PerdRate))
  30
  31 * Compute total interest to be paid on loan...
  32 C                EVAL     TotPaymts = MthPaymt * TimeInYrs * PaytPerYr
  33 C                EVAL     TotInt = TotPaymts - Principal
  34 C                EVAL     *INLR = *ON
  35 C                RETURN                                return control
   * * * * *  E N D   O F   S O U R C E  * * * * *
```

Printed Report:

```
 1/08/99              MORTGAGE PAYMENT SCHEDULE              PAGE    1

LOAN NUMBER: 12345    MORTGAGOR: HENRY W. LONGFELLOW    RATE/YR: 6.450 %

      LOAN AMOUNT         MONTHLY PAYMENT       TOTAL INTEREST FOR LOAN

        20000               390.85                 3,451.00



LOAN NUMBER: 13333    MORTGAGOR: EDGAR A. POE           RATE/YR: 8.000 %
```

253

```
        LOAN AMOUNT          MONTHLY PAYMENT        TOTAL INTEREST FOR LOAN

           56000                410.90                   91,924.00


LOAN NUMBER: 22222    MORTGAGOR: GEOFFREY CHAUCER        RATE/YR: 9.000 %

        LOAN AMOUNT          MONTHLY PAYMENT        TOTAL INTEREST FOR LOAN

           60000                760.05                   31,206.00


LOAN NUMBER: 22333    MORTGAGOR: JOHN MILTON            RATE/YR: 7.250 %

        LOAN AMOUNT          MONTHLY PAYMENT        TOTAL INTEREST FOR LOAN

          200000                912.10                  128,356.00
```

Programming Assignment 19-3: MORTGAGE PAYMENT SCHEDULE (USING STATIC BINDING)

Notes to the Instructor:

1. Inform students that this assignment requires the completion of RPG IV programs; a "calling" and a "called" program.

2. *Static binding* was used for this assignment which required that:

    a. A **CALLB** instruction be included in the "calling" program (a **CALL** instruction is required for dynamic *binding*).

    b. Both the "calling" and "called" programs must be compiled with the **CRTRPGMOD** (*Create RPG Module*) command when *dynamic binding* is selected.

    c. After the RPG IV program are compiled, a *Service Program* must be created to link the "calling" and "called" programs togethe

Calling program listing:

                    (Same as PA19-1 (calling program)

Called Program listing:

                    (Same as PA19-1 (called program)

Service Program listing:

1. The source code for a *Service Program* is created using a special bin language with **SEU** by the source type **END**.

```
FMT **    ...+... 1 ...+... 2 ...+... 3 ...+... 4
          *************** Beginning of data ******
0001.00            STRPGMEXP  SIGNATURE(*GEN)
0002.00            EXPORT     SYMBOL('PA193R2')
0003.00            ENDPGMEXP
          **************** End of data *********
```

254

CRTSRVPGM command display:

2. After the source code is saved, the *Service Program* is compiled with
    CRTSRVPGM (*Create Service Program*) command.

    Except for the Service program name (**PA193SRVP**) and the Module name
    (**PA191R2**), which is the called program, all other entries are
    defaults.

```
              Create Service Program (CRTSRVPGM)

  Type choices, press Enter.

  Service program . . . . . . . .   PA193SRVP    Name
    Library . . . . . . . . . .      *CURLIB     Name, *CURLIB
  Module . . . . . . . . . . . .    PA191R2      Name, generic*, *SRVPGM, *ALL
    Library . . . . . . . . . .      STAN        Name, *LIBL, *CURLIB...
              + for more values
  Export . . . . . . . . . . . .    *SRCFILE     *SRCFILE, *ALL
  Export source file . . . . . .    QSRVSRC      Name, QSRVSRC
    Library . . . . . . . . . .      *LIBL       Name, *LIBL, *CURLIB
  Export source member . . . . .    *SRVPGM      Name, *SRVPGM
  Text 'description' . . . . . .    create service program for PA19-1
                                                              Bottom
```

Then, a program that links everything together is created with the
CRTPGM (*Create Program*) command. Note that the Program entry in
the first display (**PA193R1**) is the "calling" program and the
binding service program (**PA193SRVP**) in the second display is the
service program created previously by the **CRTSRVPGM** command (see
above figure). All other entries are defaults.

```
                 Create Program (CRTPGM)

  Type choices, press Enter.

  Program . . . . . . . . . . . . > PA193R1     Name
    Library . . . . . . . . . . .    *CURLIB    Name, *CURLIB
  Module . . . . . . . . . . . .    *PGM        Name, generic*, *PGM, *ALL
    Library . . . . . . . . . . .               Name, *LIBL, *CURLIB...
              + for more values
  Text 'description' . . . . . .    *ENTMODTXT

                 Additional Parameters
  Program entry procedure module   *FIRST       Name, *FIRST, *ONLY, *PGM
    Library . . . . . . . . . .                 Name, *LIBL, *CURLIB...
                                                              More...


  F3=Exit  F4=Prompt  F5=Refresh  F12=Cancel  F13=How to use this display
  F24=More keys

- - - - - - - - - - - - - - - - - - - - - - - - - - - - - - - - - - - -

                 Create Program (CRTPGM)

  Type choices, press Enter.

  Bind service program . . . . .   PA193SRVP    Name, generic*, *NONE, *ALL
    Library . . . . . . . . . .                 Name, *LIBL
              + for more values
  Binding directory . . . . . .    *NONE        Name, *NONE
    Library . . . . . . . . . .                 Name, *LIBL, *CURLIB...
              + for more values
  Activation group . . . . . . .   *NEW         Name, *NEW, *CALLER
  Creation options . . . . . . .                *GEN, *NOGEN, *NODUPPROC...
              + for more values
  Listing detail . . . . . . . .   *NONE        *NONE, *BASIC, *EXTENDED...
```

```
Allow Update . . . . . . . . . .   *YES         *YES, *NO
User profile . . . . . . . . . .   *USER        *USER, *OWNER
Replace program  . . . . . . . .   *YES         *YES, *NO
Authority  . . . . . . . . . . .   *LIBCRTAUT   Name, *LIBCRTAUT, *CHANGE...

                                                                More...


F3=Exit   F4=Prompt   F5=Refresh   F12=Cancel   F13=How to use this display
F24=More keys
```

<u>Printed Report</u>:

(Same as that generated by PA19-1)

CHAPTER 20
QUESTION ANSWERS

1. All commands begin with a three-letter verb indicating the type of action to be taken, followed by a subject (one to four letters). In addition, a subject may have a modifier. For example, in the command **CRTCLPGM** the verb is CRT (create), the subject is PGM (program) and the modifier is CL (command language).

2. A value <u>must</u> be entered for a command's required parameters. Optional parameters contain default values which the programmer may choose to accept or may override with another entry.

3. **Positional format** and **keyword format**.

4. **PGM**

5. **DCL   VAR(&DATE)   TYPE(*DEC)   LEN(6 0)   VALUE(063095)**

6. **A plus sign (+).**

7. **ENDPGM**

8. **CHGVAR VAR(&SIX)   VALUE(%SST(&TEN 6 1))**

9. **SNDRCVF**

10. **IF   COND(&COST *GT 100.00) THEN(CALL TOOMUCH)**

11. **RCVF**

12. By using the **MONMSG** command to monitor for the system message **CPF0864** (end-of-file).

13. **CHGVAR VAR(&TODAY)   VALUE('Today is' *BCAT &DAY)**

14. **CHGVAR VAR(&TODAY)   VALUE('Today is ' *CAT &DAY)**

15. **CLOF**

16. **CHGVAR VAR(&TOTAL)   VALUE(&SUM)**

17. The Command Processing Program (CPP) is specified in the **Program to Process Command** parameter.

PROGRAMMING ASSIGNMENTS

Notes to the Instructor:

The following programming assignments require the use of three programs which the programmer has already written. We used the

Chapter 20 - Control Language Programming

Sales Journal from Programming Assignment 18-1, the Sales Person Salary/Commission Report from Programming Assignment 18-2, and the Income Statement from Programming Assignment 18-4. However, any RPG IV programs which the programmer has already created may be used.

Programming Assignment 20-1: CONSECUTIVE PROGRAM PROCESSING

Compiled CLP Listing:

```
                             Control Language Source
SEQNBR *...+... 1 ...+... 2 ...+... 3 ...+... 4 ...+... 5 ...+... 6 ...+... 7 ...+... 8
  100- /*-------------------------------------------------------------------*/
  200- /*  CHAPTER 20 - PROGRAMMING ASSIGNMENT 1                             */
  300- /*              EXECUTE THREE PROGRAMS CONSECUTIVELY                  */
  400- /*-------------------------------------------------------------------*/
  500-          PGM
  600-          CALL     PGM(P181RSM) /* SALES JOURNAL */
  700-          CALL     PGM(P182RSM) /* SALARY/COMMISSION RPT */
  800-          CALL     PGM(P184RSM) /* INCOME STATEMENT */
  900-          ENDPGM
                    * * * * *  E N D   O F   S O U R C E  * * * * *
```

Programming Assignment 20-2: THE SALES DEPARTMENT REPORT MENU

Compiled DDS for Display File Listing:

```
                             Data Description Source
SEQNBR *...+....1....+....2....+....3....+....4....+....5....+....6....+....7....+....8
  100     A*-------------------------------------------------------------------
  200     A*  CHAPTER 20 PROGRAMMING ASSIGNMENT 2 - SALES DEPT RPT MENU
  300     A*-------------------------------------------------------------------
  400     A                                    DSPSIZ(24 80 *DS3)
  500     A          R MENU
  600     A                                    CF03(03 'Exit')
  700     A                                    PRINT
  800     A                              3  2USER
  900     A                              3 65DATE
 1000     A                                    EDTCDE(Y)
 1100     A                              4 65TIME
 1200     A                              6 23'WORLD-WIDE COCONUTS, INC'
 1300     A                              7 23'SALES DEPARTMENT REPORTS'
 1400     A                             10 17'1.  Sales Journal'
 1500     A                             11 17'2.  Sales Person Salary/Commission-
 1600     A                                    Report'
 1700     A                             12 17'3.  Income Satatement'
 1800     A                             19  9'Selection:'
 1900     A          OPTION         1  I 19 20VALUES('1' '2' '3' ' ')
 2000     A                             23  9'F3 - Exit'
                    * * * * *  E N D   O F   S O U R C E  * * * * *
```

Compiled CLP Listing:

```
                             Control Language Source
SEQNBR *...+... 1 ...+... 2 ...+... 3 ...+... 4 ...+... 5 ...+... 6 ...+... 7 ...+... 8
  100- /*-------------------------------------------------------------------*/
  200- /*  CHAPTER 20 - PROGRAMMING ASSIGNMENT 2                             */
  300- /*              THE SALES DEPARTMENT REPORT MENU                      */
  400- /*              Introduces:                                          */
  500- /*              1. Processing a display file in a CLP                */
  600- /*              2. Using the IF command to test a program variable  */
  700- /*-------------------------------------------------------------------*/
  800-          PGM
  900-          DCLF     FILE(P192DSM) RCDFMT(MENU)
        QUALIFIED FILE NAME - SMYERS/P192DSM
```

258

```
               RECORD FORMAT NAME - MENU
                 CL VARIABLE    TYPE    LENGTH    PRECISION    TEXT
                 &IN03          *LGL     1                     Exit
                 &OPTION        *CHAR    1
1000-   SHOWME:   SNDRCVF   RCDFMT(MENU)
1100-             IF        COND(&IN03 *EQ '1') THEN(GOTO ENDIT)
1200-             IF        COND(&OPTION *EQ '1') THEN(CALL PGM(P181RSM))
1300-             IF        COND(&OPTION *EQ '2') THEN(CALL PGM(P182RSM))
1400-             IF        COND(&OPTION *EQ '3') THEN(CALL PGM(P184RSM))
1500-             GOTO      CMDLBL(SHOWME)
1600-   ENDIT:    ENDPGM
                  * * * * *  E N D   O F   S O U R C E  * * * * *
```

Programming Assignment 20-3: THE PROGRAM FILE

Compiled DDS for Physical File Listing:

```
                                  Data Description Source
SEQNBR  *...+....1....+....2....+....3....+....4....+....5....+....6....+....7....+....8
  100         A*--------------------------------------------------------------------
  200         A*   PGMS - REPORT PROGRAMS FILE
  300         A*        CHAPTER 20 PROGRAMMING ASSIGNMENT 3
  400         A*--------------------------------------------------------------------
  500         A       R PGMREC
  600         A         ZPGM        10         COLHDG('PROGRAM NAME')
  700         A         ZDESC       25         COLHDG('PROGRAM TITLE')
  800         A       K ZPGM
                  * * * * *  E N D   O F   S O U R C E  * * * * *
```

Physical File Data:

```
                         Display Physical File Member
File . . . . . . :  PGMS          Library . . . . :  SMYERS
Member . . . . . :  PGMS          Record . . . . . :  1
Control . . . . .                 Column . . . . . :  1
Find . . . . . . .
*...+....1....+....2....+....3....+
P181RSM    SALES JOURNAL
P182RSM    SALARY/COMMISSION REPORT
P184RSM    INCOME STATEMENT
                  ****** END OF DATA ******
```

Compiled CLP Listing:

```
                                  Control Language Source
SEQNBR  *...+... 1 ...+... 2 ...+... 3 ...+... 4 ...+... 5 ...+... 6 ...+... 7 ...+... 8
  100-  /*-----------------------------------------------------------------*/
  200-  /*   CHAPTER 20 - PROGRAMMING ASSIGNMENT 3                         */
  300-  /*            THE PROGRAM FILE                                     */
  400-  /*            Introduces:                                          */
  500-  /*            1. Processing a database file in a CLP               */
  600-  /*            2. The MONMSG command                                */
  700-  /*-----------------------------------------------------------------*/
  800-            PGM
  900-            DCLF      FILE(PGMS)  RCDFMT(PGMREC)
          QUALIFIED FILE NAME - SMYERS/PGMS
            RECORD FORMAT NAME - PGMREC
               CL VARIABLE    TYPE    LENGTH    PRECISION    TEXT
               &ZPGM          *CHAR    10                    PROGRAM NAME
               &ZDESC         *CHAR    25                    PROGRAM TITLE
 1000-            OVRDBF    FILE(PGMS) TOFILE(*FILE) NBRRCDS(1) +
 1100                         SEQONLY(*YES 1)
 1200-  READIT:   RCVF      RCDFMT(*FILE)
 1300-            MONMSG    MSGID(CPF0864) EXEC(GOTO ALLDONE)
 1400-            CALL      PGM(&ZPGM)
```

259

```
1500-            GOTO      CMDLBL(READIT)
1600-  ALLDONE:  ENDPGM
                      * * * * *  E N D   O F   S O U R C E  * * * * *
```

Programming Assignment 20-4: THE RUNPGMS COMMAND

CRTCMD Prompts to create RUNPGMS Command:

```
                        Create Command (CRTCMD)
Type choices, press Enter.
Command  . . . . . . . . . . . > RUNPGMS        Name
   Library . . . . . . . . . . >   SMYERS       Name, *CURLIB
Program to process command . . > p193csm        Name, *REXX
   Library . . . . . . . . . . >   smyers       Name, *LIBL, *CURLIB
Source file . . . . . . . . . > QCMDSRC        Name
   Library . . . . . . . . . . >   SMYERS       Name, *LIBL, *CURLIB
Source member . . . . . . . . > RUNPGMS        Name, *CMD
Text 'description' . . . . . .   *SRCMBRTXT

                        Additional Parameters

Replace command . . . . . . . > *YES           *YES, *NO
```

Compiled Command Listing:

```
                        Command Definition Source
SEQNBR  *...+... 1 ...+... 2 ...+... 3 ...+... 4 ...+... 5 ...+... 6 ...+... 7 ...+... 8
 100-    CMD              PROMPT('RUN PROGRAMS')
                      * * * * *  E N D   O F   S O U R C E  * * * * *
```